"The authors provide a comprehensive guide to the assessment of municipal fiscal health and stress that will be essential for local and state officials, analysts, and students and researchers. The data and measures available to public finance analysts has proliferated, but, until now, there was no clear guide on how to use it. This book teaches the reader the science and the art of municipal financial analysis and will be used for years."

John R. Bartle, *University of Nebraska at Omaha, United States*

"Despite local government's indispensable contributions to our communities and the many billions of dollars that flow into local government budgets, there is no obvious way to judge the financial condition of these institutions. *Understanding Municipal Fiscal Health* provides a much-needed explanation of the inescapable complexities of measuring the financial condition of local governments. It covers the spectrum of issues that must be considered when attempting to measure the financial performance of organizations that don't exist for a financial purpose! It also offers practical examples and insights that can help scholars and practitioners better apply the discipline of financial condition analysis to local governments and, thereby, support their continued viability."

Shayne Kavanagh, *Government Finance Officers Association, United States*

Understanding Municipal Fiscal Health

Understanding Municipal Fiscal Health provides an in-depth assessment of the fiscal health of cities throughout the United States.

The book examines the tools currently available to cities for designing a revenue structure, measuring fiscal conditions and measuring fiscal health. It explains how artificial policies such as tax and expenditure limitations influence fiscal policies, and how communities can overcome socioeconomic and state-policy barriers to produce strong fiscal conditions. The authors go beyond simple theory to analyze patterns of fiscal health using actual financial, demographic, and TEL data from an accurate data source, the Government Financial Officers Association survey. The book offers a solid basis of empirical evidence including quantitative case studies—complete with discussion questions—to help practitioners better understand the environment in which they are functioning and the policy tools they need to help advocate for change.

This book teaches the reader the science and art of municipal financial analysis, and will be invaluable for local and state officials, analysts, and students and researchers.

Craig S. Maher is a full professor and current director of the School of Public Administration at the University of Nebraska at Omaha, United States.

Sungho Park is an assistant professor of public policy and administration in the Department of Political Science at the University of Alabama, United States.

Bruce D. McDonald III is an associate professor of public budgeting and finance at North Carolina State University, United States.

Steven C. Deller is a professor of agricultural and applied economics at the University of Wisconsin–Madison, United States, and a community economic development specialist with its Division of Extension.

Understanding Municipal Fiscal Health

A Model for Local Governments in the USA

Craig S. Maher,
Sungho Park,
Bruce D. McDonald III
and Steven C. Deller

Routledge
Taylor & Francis Group
NEW YORK AND LONDON

Designed cover image: © Getty Images

First published 2023
by Routledge
605 Third Avenue, New York, NY 10158

and by Routledge
4 Park Square, Milton Park, Abingdon, Oxon OX14 4RN

Routledge is an imprint of the Taylor & Francis Group, an informa business

ISBN: 978-1-4398-5471-6 (hbk)
ISBN: 978-1-032-05542-8 (pbk)
ISBN: 978-0-429-27076-5 (ebk)

DOI: 10.4324/9780429270765

Typeset in Adobe Garamond Pro
by Apex CoVantage, LLC

I dedicate this book to my family: my wife Kerry, my three children, Aidan, Liam and Callan, and our cats. Without their love and encouragement, this project would not have come to fruition. I also want to thank my students and colleagues, in particular Drs. John Bartle and Carol Ebdon, from whom I have learned so much. Finally, I wish to acknowledge the academy and local government professionals who manage financial challenges on a daily basis. I hope that this project reflects that which I have learned from you over the years.

—CSM

To my mentors, Drs. Craig Maher and Carol Ebdon. I could not have successfully contributed to this book without what I have learned from them. I also dedicate this book to my best friends, Heide Yang and Jihyun Park, who have helped me keep smiling and laughing while I have gone through this long process. The belief that this book will be read by students, researchers, colleagues, and practitioners has consistently motivated me in this challenging project. I also dedicate this book to them.

—SP

3: 4641 1921 18238 1275 (1–145) 29047

—BDM

My contribution to this study would not have been possible without David Chicoine and Norman Walzer, who exposed me to the importance of local governments in community economic development.

—SCD

Contents

Figures

Tables

Author Biographies

Steven C. Deller is a professor of agricultural and applied economics at the University of Wisconsin–Madison, United States, and a community economic development specialist with its Division of Extension. His work generally concerns community economic development, with a focus on smaller communities and rural areas. He co-authored the textbook *Community Economics: Linking Theory and Practices* and has co-edited five books, each focusing on community, rural and regional economic development, including most recently *Local Food Systems and Community Economic Development*. He has served as the president of the North American Regional Science Council, the Mid-Continent Regional Science Association and the Southern Regional Science Association. He is the recipient of the North American Regional Science Council's Walter Isard Award for Distinguished Scholarly Achievement in the Field of Regional Science. He is a Fellow of both the Southern and the Mid-Continent Regional Science Associations.

Craig S. Maher is a full professor and current director of the School of Public Administration at the University of Nebraska at Omaha, United States. He earned his M.A. and Ph.D. in political science from the University of Wisconsin–Milwaukee, United States. His primary research interest is public finance, with emphases on financial condition analysis, fiscal federalism, and revenue policy. In 2013 and 2017, he received awards from the Association of Government Accountants and the *Journal of Public and Nonprofit Affairs*, respectively. In 2011, he received the Alberta S. Kimball Endowed Professor award from the University of Wisconsin–Oshkosh, United States, for his research on municipal finance. He is a research fellow at the Center for Great Plains Studies, United States, and has been asked to speak at a number of events, including presentations at Zhengzhou University (ZZU), China, in 2018, and Siauliai University, Lithuania, in 2019. He has served on the board of directors for the American Society of Public Administration's (ASPA) Section on Public Performance and Management, the National League of Cities and Urban Institute's Advisory Legislating-for-Results Advisory Committee, and the Government Accounting Standards Board's (GASB) Service

Efforts and Accomplishments (SEA) Task Force. He was appointed to Wisconsin Governor Doyle's Task Force on Milwaukee County Finances. He was also elected and subsequently reelected to the Wauwatosa, Wisconsin City Council in 2004 and 2008.

Bruce D. McDonald III is an associate professor of public budgeting and finance at North Carolina State University, United States. He also serves as the editor-in-chief of *Public Administration*, co-editor-in-chief of the *Journal of Public Affairs Education*, and editor of Routledge's Public Affairs Education Book Series. He received a B.A. in communications from Mercer University, United States, an M.A. in international peace and conflict resolution from American Military University, United States, an M.Sc. in economic history from the London School of Economics, United Kingdom, an M.Ed. in training and instructional design from North Carolina State University, United States, and a Ph.D. in public administration and policy from Florida State University, United States. His research focuses on public budgeting and finance in the context of the fiscal health of local governments. His extensive publications have appeared in such journals as the *Journal of Public Administration Research and Theory*, *Public Administration Review*, and the *American Review of Public Administration*.

Sungho Park is an assistant professor of public policy and administration in the Department of Political Science at the University of Alabama, United States. He received a B.A. in public administration and economics and an M.P.A. from Sungkyunkwan University, South Korea, followed by a Ph.D. in public administration from the University of Nebraska at Omaha, United States. His research interests include state and local budgeting and finance, with emphases on fiscal federalism, fiscal rules and institutions, and fiscal condition. He has published in *The American Review of Public Administration*, *Public Budgeting and Finance*, *Local Government Studies* and other journals.

Acknowledgments

This labor of love started out as a concept following the Great Recession of 2007–2009. We are grateful that it took more than a decade to come together, because we have been able to apply an additional decade's worth of research and knowledge to the project. The years following the Great Recession have been full of struggles and hardships for municipal governments. Municipal officials have toiled diligently to help their communities recover, even while encountering another set of struggles related to the COVID-19 pandemic. This book builds on the invaluable experiences of these officials. Many of them, especially those whom we interviewed for this book, have generously shared their time with us. This book could not exist without their input.

As we discuss throughout the book, an extensive body of research on fiscal health and fiscal condition analysis has informed our approach to this project. Those who have influenced this project most heavily include both scholars—notably, Robert Berne, Rebecca Hendrick, Beth Honadle, Jonathan Justice, Eric Scorsone, and Richard Schramm—and professional organizations such as the International City/County Managers Association, Government Accounting Standards Board, and Government Finance Officers Association (GFOA). We are sincerely grateful for their help and guidance, particularly the assistance received from Shayne Kavanagh of the GFOA. We hope our book will advance the field and build on the excellent work of these scholars and practitioners.

We also appreciate the help received from our respective institutions and the editorial team at Routledge. Finally, we acknowledge a debt to the students in our budgeting and financial management courses. They taught us as much as we tried to help them advance their professional careers.

Chapter 1

Introduction

The nation's nearly 20,000 municipal governments are an indispensable part of the American government system.[1] As a crucial wheel of American democracy, municipal governments are responsive to their citizens' political and policy preferences (Tausanovitch & Warshaw, 2014). They also play a vital role in delivering core public services such as public safety, public works, housing, and community economic development (Shafritz et al., 2015). In fulfilling these functions, municipal officials make decisions on organizational structures, staffing, planning, and programs, just to name a few areas. They also make municipal fiscal decisions, determining how to secure and allocate the resources needed to operate their governmental functions.

The past two decades have brought significant changes to municipal government finances. These include fiscal shocks caused by the Great Recession of 2007–2009, the COVID-19 pandemic, management challenges caused by state rules that creating tax and expenditure limits (TELs), balanced-budget requirements, debt limits, and state fiscal monitoring systems. Municipal revenues have also been impacted by inflows of federal funds associated with COVID-19, anti–property tax sentiments, and the expansion of online sales tax collections following the 2017 U.S. Supreme Court's decision in *South Dakota v. Wayfair Inc.* This breadth of changes and challenges offers an opportunity to revisit approaches to assessing municipal governments' fiscal health. Building on previous studies including Maher (2022) and Maher, Ebdon et al. (2020), we present a framework for examining the fiscal condition of municipal governments.

DOI: 10.4324/9780429270765-1

Our Approach to Financial Condition Analysis

Both scholars and practitioners of public finance have sought to understand more fully the causal mechanisms in municipal government fiscal systems, with the aim of promoting policies and strategies to enhance fiscal health. These studies have typically focused on the influence of a government's policies or socioeconomic conditions (see, e.g., Clark, 1994; Honadle et al., 2004; Ladd & Yinger, 1989). They have shown that municipal governments are open systems. That is, they both influence and are influenced by their environment (Justice & Scorsone, 2013; Tang et al., 2014).

According to Maser (1985, 1998) and McDonald and Gabrini (2014), the environmental characteristics that drive a municipal government's actions are the political, governmental, economic, and sociodemographic conditions of a community (Gabrini, 2010; Wang et al., 2007). The political and governmental conditions establish the rules that guide the government and the direction in which it is headed. Economic conditions, or the wealth and income capacity of the population, provide the tax base and allow for the expansion of the types of services provided beyond basic protective services and into areas such as economic development. As for sociodemographic conditions, different communities and households have their own priorities, resulting in various expectations regarding the types and quantities of services provided. To fully grasp why financial conditions can vary so wildly between municipalities, we need to better understand these environmental characteristics and how they influence a municipality's fiscal health.

Political and Governmental Influences

A government's fiscal health is determined largely by the circumstances in which the government finds itself. The conditions under which the government operates may be legal and institutional in nature, but they may also be political, as the partisan composition of a governing body establishes the political equilibrium within which all policies are adopted and implemented. Since local governments are creations of the state, subject to rules and regulations that guide their structure and behavior (Goodman et al., 2021; McDonald & Gabrini, 2014), this equilibrium must be maintained at both the state and local levels.

In most states, municipal governments are established by state statute, and in some instances, they are codified in the state constitution. This means that state governments, broadly speaking, establish the roles, responsibilities, and authority of municipal governments. State statutes largely determine how municipal governments can and cannot function. Although municipal officials have some ability to influence these rules through the political process, the decisions are substantially outside their control. This fact has been widely acknowledged in the literature, but we have recently noticed growing interest in state oversight of municipal government finances (Pew Charitable Trusts, 2016b). Somewhat ironically, this renewed interest is occurring during an era of intergovernmental fiscal retrenchment; that is, state statutes increasingly dictate which municipal services must be provided even while state governments reduce the intergovernmental aid required to provide those services.

According to Maser (1985, 1998), the rules and regulations imposed by a state create a form of contractual relationship between the state and the citizens of the municipal government. This relationship influences the parameters of internal arrangements within which government officials establish, expand, and implement policies, including those related to the government's finances. Although municipal governments have some flexibility to establish their own service programs and revenue policies, state governments often constrain local governments' ability to make changes. Thus, a municipal government's political and governmental conditions include the range of options available to it to address financial problems (Hendrick & Crawford, 2014). Heller (2005, p. 3) characterized this relationship as "the availability of budgetary room that allows a government to provide resources for a desired purpose without any prejudice to the sustainability of government's financial position."

Understanding a municipality's organizational design is critical to understanding its fiscal health. Once established, the structure of a government's policy space becomes relatively fixed; however, as the constraints on a municipal government change, so does the environment in which it makes policy decisions. Similarly, a policy change can alter the municipality's capacity to address financial issues. If the conditions provide greater space or opportunity for policy action, a municipality becomes more able to implement the set of services and tax preferences desired by its population. As the municipality's financial environment changes, broader decision-making space allows the municipality to adjust its policies accordingly. Such a situation should enable the government to maximize its fiscal health.

A number of studies have shown the influence of a municipality's political and governmental conditions on its fiscal health (Clark, 1994; Honadle et al., 2004; Ladd & Yinger, 1989). Hendrick (2004) adopted a systems approach to understanding fiscal health, proposing that as an open system, a government is influenced by its institutions and by the municipal and regional environment. Using a series of indicators (e.g., the characteristics and fiscal structure of a government's environment) to capture various dimensions of fiscal health, she tested the approach using a sample of 264 municipal governments in the Chicago metropolitan area. Hendrick's results showed that fiscal health can be a function of several factors, including governmental and community characteristics.

Although states have always established the fiscal options of municipalities—for example, their taxing authority—they have also recently been active in controlling or further limiting municipal governments' fiscal options, particularly on the revenue side through TELs (Decker, 2021). TELs have several implications within the context of this discussion. First, they have shifted municipal reliance away from property taxes. The revenue gap has been largely filled by greater reliance on sales taxes, fees, and other charges, and to a lesser extent on individual income taxes. From a financial management perspective, municipal officials need to recognize that revenues are less predictable or stable than previously, because sales tax collections are more susceptible to economic fluctuations than property taxes. This change means in turn that municipalities must prepare better for future fiscal shocks, such as by building up reserves during periods of economic growth. Such a reserves policy becomes even more acute for municipalities functioning under balanced-budget requirements, which prevent them from incurring deficits.

Knowing a municipality's political and governmental conditions provides an understanding not only of its institutional structure but also of its capacity to address challenges to its fiscal health. Central to this capacity is the municipal government's relationship with the state. Of particular significance in this regard are the restrictions placed on revenue sources and mandates regarding program and service provision. Restrictive state control can leave little room for municipal autonomy. Evidence of such control can be seen in state policies that limit changes in tax sources, such as increasing the property tax rate. Ultimately, state-imposed limitations restrict a municipal government's ability to increase revenues to cover budgetary shortfalls (Maher et al., 2011), limiting the space in which they can maneuver to address fiscal issues. In contrast, governments with broader flexibility enjoy more freedom to adopt new revenue streams or adjust existing ones according to the budgetary needs of their community.

Economic Influences

The influence of economic conditions on fiscal health has been an area of study in the public administration and public finance literature for decades. From an economic perspective, the fiscal health of a government reflects not just the government's internal financial capacity, but also the resources of the entire community (Oi, 1995). The expectation underlying this approach is that governments have the capacity to commandeer community resources should the need arise. This can be accomplished through policy tools, such as an increase in tax rates or the imposition of new taxes, as well as through legal tools such as eminent domain.

When economic conditions are strong, they provide a growing tax base that helps to keep a municipality fiscally healthy. Beyond providing a robust tax base and higher levels of economic wealth, economic strength allows for expansions of services into sectors such as economic development, parks and recreation, and libraries. The economic development literature (e.g., Henry et al., 1997; Shaffer et al., 2004, 2006) has found that investments in "quality of life" services create a self-reinforcing, or endogenous, economic growth and development cycle. Such an upward spiral can enhance the fiscal health of the municipality, better positioning it for future economic shocks.

On the other hand, communities with relatively low levels of economic wealth and income often face greater difficulty in sustaining their fiscal health. The ability to generate revenues is limited and demands on the government for core protective and social services are greater. If the economic growth and development of communities depends increasingly on quality-of-life factors, then less wealthy municipalities are disadvantaged by their lesser capacity to make such investments, causing patterns of divergence and inequity to be reinforced. Most relevant to this study, municipalities servicing lower-income communities tend to face higher levels of fiscal distress and are seldom in good position to withstand shocks to the economy.

Although conceptually, the linkages between economic well-being and municipal fiscal health are straightforward and intuitive, the empirical literature studying these linkages has faced significant challenges. The economic side of this work tends to be plagued by measurement issues, even though the challenges here are much more contained than those on the accounting or budgetary side. Measurement approaches on the economic side typically turn to the economic growth and development literature for guidance. As fiscal health generally reflects the capacity of a community's economy, the fiscal health indicators are often the same as those that drive economic growth: the community's gross domestic product, physical capital, private investments, and the size and skill of its labor force, among others. On occasion, researchers might take a step further and focus less on the overall size of the economy, choosing instead to examine how the government draws on those resources. One example of this method in practice is Ladd and Yinger (1989; see also Chernick & Reschovsky, 2017). As better fiscal and budgetary metrics have become available, scholars and practitioners have tended to rely on these financial metrics. However, from our perspective, the substantial relationship between economic well-being and fiscal health cannot be overlooked.

Sociodemographic Influences

When municipal government decision makers are crafting fiscal policies, they are implicitly attempting to match government services with the preferences of municipal residents. Although these decisions are made within the context of institutional requirements (mostly those imposed by the state government, as discussed above), the preferences of residents must also be considered. We have seen how economic well-being, generally understood in terms of income and/or poverty, influences fiscal policies and thus fiscal health, but communities are heterogenous in their expectations of their municipal government. For example, an older community will demand a different mix of services when compared to one with many younger families and school-age children. Within the public administration literature, the ability of municipal officials to match policies and spending to residents' preferences is commonly referred to as municipal government effectiveness (Deller & Maher, 2009).

Much of the empirical literature that has sought to better understand how sociodemographic differences affect fiscal policies has been built on the median voter framework (e.g., Chicoine et al., 1989; Holcombe, 1980, 1989). Whereas the theoretical framework has been widely challenged (Gouveia & Masia, 1998; Turnbull & Mitias, 1999), the empirical results of this large literature are consistent: sociodemographic factors are important in understanding differences in the preferences of residents, and hence fiscal policies. While this literature remains dominated by economic factors (income, poverty, growth), the role of sociodemographic heterogeneity across municipalities must also be taken into account.

Existing Frameworks for Fiscal Condition Analysis

The preceding discussion sets the stage for our approach to financial condition analysis. Of course, considering the environment in which a municipality operates, as we have emphasized above, is not new. Four approaches to municipal fiscal health have influenced our approach to this project: Berne and Schramm (1986), Hendrick (2011), Honadle et al. (2004), and the International City/County Management Association's (ICMA) Financial Trend Monitoring System (FTMS; Nollenberger et al., 2003). Berne and Schramm (1986) wrote during an era when the fiscal challenges facing many U.S. municipal governments were related to the Reagan administration's policy of "devolution" or fiscal decentralization. During the Reagan years, fiscal responsibility for many programs formerly funded at the federal level was transferred to states, and in turn to local governments. Berne and Schramm's seminal work emphasized a model that is temporal in nature and requires an appreciation of the dynamics that exist between government finances and the environment. They tended to focus more on external influences such as regional and national economies as well as community factors that play an important role in understanding fiscal condition, including sociodemographic characteristics such as the makeup of the population and how that makeup is changing over time. Economic factors can include general economic wealth and income or changes in the economy, such as recessionary pressures. Another category of external factors is the statutory or constitutional rules that dictate how municipalities function. Internal effects include policies that have an impact on short and longer-term fiscal condition, such as long-term liabilities.

The simplified framework shown in Figure 1.1 summarizes Berne and Schramm's model of fiscal condition analysis, whereby available resources are affected by both external and internal factors, which are mainly economic and

Figure 1.1 Berne and Schramm's Framework of Government Fiscal Condition

demographic in nature. Expenditure pressure is also influenced by current and past policies. Interestingly, government structure and political considerations do not appear in their framework. Techniques for analysis offered by Berne and Schramm include cross-sectional analysis (to assess the municipal government's fiscal position relative to comparable communities), time series, and ratio analysis.

Hendrick (2011) offered an expansion of Berne and Schramm's model by explicitly considering how a municipal government's own structure and behavior can affect its fiscal condition. She defined a fiscal crisis as "entrenched economic deficits that make it very difficult to collect enough revenue to cover spending demands" (p. 1). A crisis is exacerbated by employment decline and population outmigration. According to Hendrick (2011), recent municipal government crises were a combination of political fragmentation, lack of fiscal discipline, incompetence, and bad fiscal decisions. Thus, while Hendrick acknowledged economic and demographic factors, she presumed that municipal governments have effective ways of responding to the fiscal environment. This is a significant departure from Berne and Schramm.

According to Hendrick, financial condition is a state of equilibrium between different dimensions of government's fiscal sphere (Figure 1.2). Fiscal health is both a state of being and an ongoing process that reflects the extent to which a government's fiscal structure is adapted to the environment and whether the government can maintain or improve this balance in the future. As already noted, she assumes that governments have the capacity to manage that balance. Here, capacity can range from administrative and/or financial skills to the political capital to effectively work across differences.

The third significant influence on this project is Honadle et al. (2004), who designed their framework in the spirit of both Hendrick (2011) and Berne and Schramm (1986), with a focus on an open-systems model, but with important differences. Honadle et al. paid particular attention to distinguishing factors that affect fiscal health based on what the local government can and cannot control. Thus, factors influencing a municipal government's fiscal condition that are outside its control include natural disasters, the economy (regional and national), and demographic characteristics such as birth rates, aging, and migration patterns. Governments must find ways to adapt to all these factors. Furthermore, they have little control over state policies and aid payments, economic conditions, and the demand for municipal services. On the other hand, municipal governments do

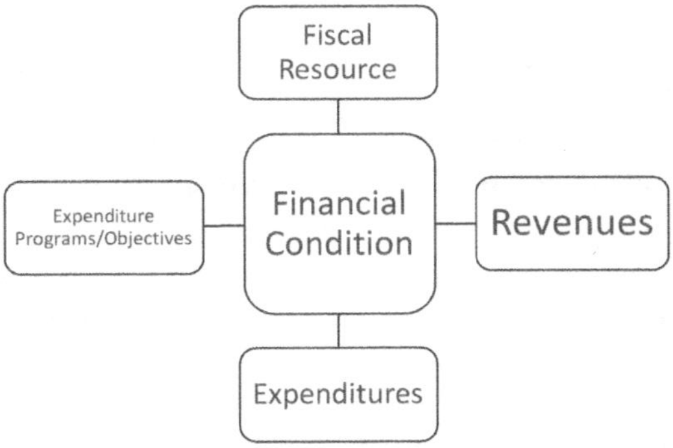

Figure 1.2 Hendrick's Framework of Government Fiscal Condition

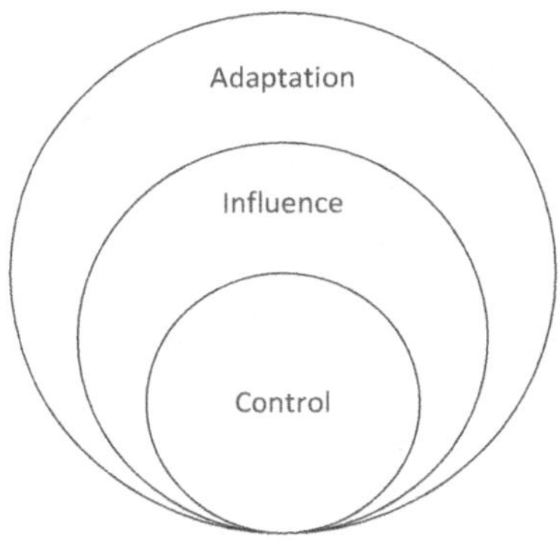

Figure 1.3 Honadle, Costa, and Cigler's Framework of Government Fiscal Condition

have control over the means by which to finance services as well as over managerial decisions and policies.

Thus, the framework of Honadle et al. contains three nested factors: control, influence, and adaptation (Figure 1.3). What does the municipal government have control over, and what is beyond its control? Are municipal leaders, both staff and elected officials, worrying about issues that are beyond their control, or do they focus their attention on matters that are within their control? Although it may sometimes be politically convenient to draw attention to issues beyond one's control, doing so can misuse valuable and limited resources. What factors do municipal government officials have some capacity to influence, and to what extent? For example, is the municipal government actively involved in shaping regional economic growth and development policies? Obviously, municipal efforts will not counter macroeconomic trends such as those that drove the Great Recession, but they can help to mitigate some economic threats. Most importantly, can the municipal government adapt to changing sociodemographic and economic conditions? The ability to learn and adapt can place the municipal government on a more solid financial footing.

The ICMA's FTMS exhibits significant consistency with these previous frameworks and is probably the approach best known and most widely used by practitioners (e.g., Town of Carrboro, North Carolina, 2013; Town of Northborough, Massachusetts, 2015). In essence, the FTMS advises practitioners to examine trends in their community's environment, including economic and demographic trends, risks present in the natural environment, and the political culture, in arriving at policy decisions that affect the community's fiscal condition. In many respects, academics have sought to replicate the FTMS with a series of models aimed at measuring aspects of fiscal health and stress, incorporating a set of variables that assess the socioeconomic, political, and fiscal culture (Gorina et al., 2019; Jacob & Hendrick, 2013; Kloha et al., 2005; Maher et al., 2016; McDonald, 2018; McDonald & Maher, 2020; Park, 2018b; Wang et al., 2007).

What have we learned? The Great Recession received heightened attention from academics and practitioners due to its severity and longevity. Much of the subsequent literature focused on measuring and predicting fiscal distress, along with continuing the 40-year tradition—dating back to New York City's near-bankruptcy in the 1970s—of measuring and assessing the broader concept of fiscal condition. Overall, these studies fostered a greater understanding and appreciation of influencing factors and operational issues. The empirical evidence has been overwhelmingly consistent that aggregate measures of fiscal health offered by scholars such as Brown (1993), Kloha et al. (2005), Wang et al. (2007), and others are ineffective and mask variations in aspects of fiscal condition (Clark, 2015; Crosby & Robbins, 2013; McDonald & Maher, 2020; Stone et al., 2015).

We also have a better sense of what fiscal health indicators can predict fiscal stress (Clark, 2015; Gorina et al., 2018; Stone et al., 2015). Recent literature has remained remarkably consistent in terms of the measures associated with fiscal stress, which is typically operationalized in terms of bankruptcy filings (however, see Gorina et al., 2018). Whether through analysis of case studies (Stone et al., 2015) or panel dataset analyses, fiscal slack, typically measured by the variables of reserves and debt accumulation, is closely associated with fiscal distress (McDonald & Maher, 2020; Stone et al., 2015). These academic findings are also consistent with the emphases of ratings agencies (such as Moody's or Standard and Poor's) and professional organizations. The National League of Cities' (NLC) annual survey of city finance officials also tends to monitor trends in reserves.

Where Are the Gaps?

What remains to be studied or better understood? A good number of studies and models have examined measures of fiscal condition as predictors of fiscal health or distress. We also have many studies of institutional designs and their effects on fiscal outcomes. Existing studies and frameworks have helped us understand the importance of the difference between factors over which municipal governments have significant, minimal, or no control. However, we still lack a comprehensive understanding of the determinants of a municipality's fiscal condition and the strategies that could prevent future fiscal distress.

The challenges involved in modeling fiscal health and stress tend to fall into three categories: (1) access to data, (2) operational definitions, and (3) determining appropriate time lags. Regarding the first point, the most respected data source, at least from the perspective of academics, is audited comprehensive financial reports (ACFRs). ACFRs offer consistency in cross-sectional measurement and provide the breadth of fiscal data needed for analysis. The challenges with relying on ACFRs is that key variables have changed over time, including fund balances, making it difficult to develop appropriate data analyses over long time periods. Another challenge is that only a small fraction of communities (mostly large cities) produce ACFRs. Thus, small and medium-sized municipalities are ignored. Some states, such as New York and Wisconsin, provide detailed annual audited data for all municipal governments over a number of years. But is the institutional structure of those states sufficiently generalizable to make these case studies applicable to, for example, Texas or Florida? Unfortunately, the Annual Survey of State and Local Government Finances, conducted every five years by the U.S. Census Bureau, has several well-documented flaws, making it largely unsuitable for many studies of municipal governments' fiscal health and/or stress.

Operational issues are rampant in this area of research. It can be argued that we have been studying the same concepts for more than 40 years and yet each study measures fiscal health and fiscal stress differently. The lack of consistent measurements makes it harder to generalize across studies. Many of these measures are driven by the availability of data, which, as we just noted, is often problematic. The same problem applies to the third challenge, identifying appropriate time lags when connecting economic and demographic trends to fiscal health. In some instances, decades of economic and demographic change led to fiscal distress (e.g., Flint and Detroit, Michigan). In other instances, more immediate shocks led to distress (San Bernardino and Stockton, California). Kloha et al. (2005) and Maher, Oh et al. (2020) used two-year changes in economic variables but offered little justification for choosing that time frame. Again, municipal context matters: the drivers of fiscal health in areas that once depended heavily on manufacturing are fundamentally different from the drivers in places experiencing wild economic swings (e.g., associated with the energy industry) or sustained, long-term economic growth.

Prior to the pandemic, there was evidence that despite one of the longest periods of economic growth, recovery was not uniform across municipalities. As noted above, the recovery from the Great Recession has been inconsistent across municipalities, states, and regions, with some coping better and recovering much more quickly than others. For instance, in one recent study of the fiscal health of large U.S. cities, researchers found that most cities were still losing intergovernmental aid, growth in property tax collections varied greatly across the United States, and neither spending nor reserves had achieved pre-recession levels (Pew Charitable Trusts, 2016a). The variability in city recovery offers the opportunity to explore the extent to which city policy actions and regional and/or national economic conditions affect recovery.

Recent headlines, for good reason, have focused on the health aspects of the COVID-19 pandemic, but municipal fiscal health has also been affected despite the significant financial resources provided by the federal government, especially the Coronavirus Aid, Relief, and Economic Security Act or CARES Act (Maher, Hoang et al., 2020; McDonald & Larson, 2020). As in the Great Recession, analyzing the variability in municipal fiscal health has been quite complex. For instance, Chicago had serious fiscal woes, particularly excessive debt, well before the pandemic. Other municipalities have fared relatively well. Maher, Hoang et al. (2020) found that most cities in Nebraska and the Great Plains area were largely unaffected and that municipal officials still believed they were in good fiscal health. The CARES Act has helped municipalities cover costs but has also sometimes given a false impression that the nation has fully recovered from the Great Recession.

Although COVID-19 has been rightfully viewed as a crucial key turning point in state and local economies, there was growing angst about an oncoming recession prior to the pandemic. For instance, in its 2019 survey of city finance officials, the NLC (2019) found that many city officials anticipated a recession as early as 2020. These officials based their assessment on declining revenue growth and increasing expenditures, particularly personnel-related expenditures. Little did the NLC know how insightful this statement would be in 2020:

> Looking beyond 2019, the resilience of city fiscal conditions will be tested by looming economic headwinds, largely driven by trade. Meanwhile, the cost of healthcare and pensions is rising faster than inflation and placing pressure on spending. Combined with state policies that impede local fiscal autonomy, these factors all have the potential to further constrain city budgets.
>
> (NLC, 2019, p. 8)

The extant frameworks give us a structure that can inform how we think about fiscal health, what to measure, and the degree to which a set of factors can impact fiscal health. An underexplored area of fiscal health research, however, is how officials think through the decision-making process. An array of metrics has been suggested for monitoring fiscal condition, but there is limited empirical evidence that the prescribed metrics actually affect policy. For instance, Maher and Deller (2011, 2013a) examined the extent to which objective metrics used to assess financial conditions (e.g., fund balances and debt levels) were associated with municipal decision makers' view of the situation. Surprisingly, the authors found no association between officials' perceptions of fiscal condition and commonly identified metrics. Similarly, in a more recent study, Kim, Maher et al. (2018) found that *perceptions* of fiscal condition were much better predictors of actions taken than objective measures. According to Maher and Deller (2011, p. 445), "If local officials' perceptions do not match objective measures, then attempts to better understand policy responses to fiscal stress become extremely difficult." One important goal of our research project was to better understand the decision-making "black box" during periods of fiscal distress.

An Alternative Framework for Financial Condition Analysis

The main intent of this study is to provide a tool that enables assessment of the fiscal health of U.S. municipal governments and captures the roles of socioeconomic conditions, institutional settings, external pressures, and internal structures (see Figure 1.4). Using a logic model framework, we attempt to demonstrate how these inputs are converted into outputs (fiscal structures and decisions), thereby allowing for the measurement and assessment of fiscal health (outcomes). This framework will be explained through discussions of various environmental factors, macro-trends in municipal finance, research on key concepts such as fiscal condition and fiscal stress, and a series of case studies highlighting small and midsize municipalities throughout the United States. The target audience is managers, administrators, finance officers and others interested in understanding the dynamics associated with municipal budgetary decisions, fiscal condition, and policy actions (including both municipal and state-level responses to municipal fiscal condition). The study includes detailed descriptive analyses of revenues, expenditures, and fiscal health along with in-depth discussion of measurement techniques.

Chapter 2 discusses the inputs that feed into the fiscal decision-making process through which all municipal governments go when setting fiscal policies. What are the institutional settings that establish the rules of the game by which municipal governments much operate? Has the state imposed restrictive TELs that limit municipalities' flexibility? What external pressures—for example, rules

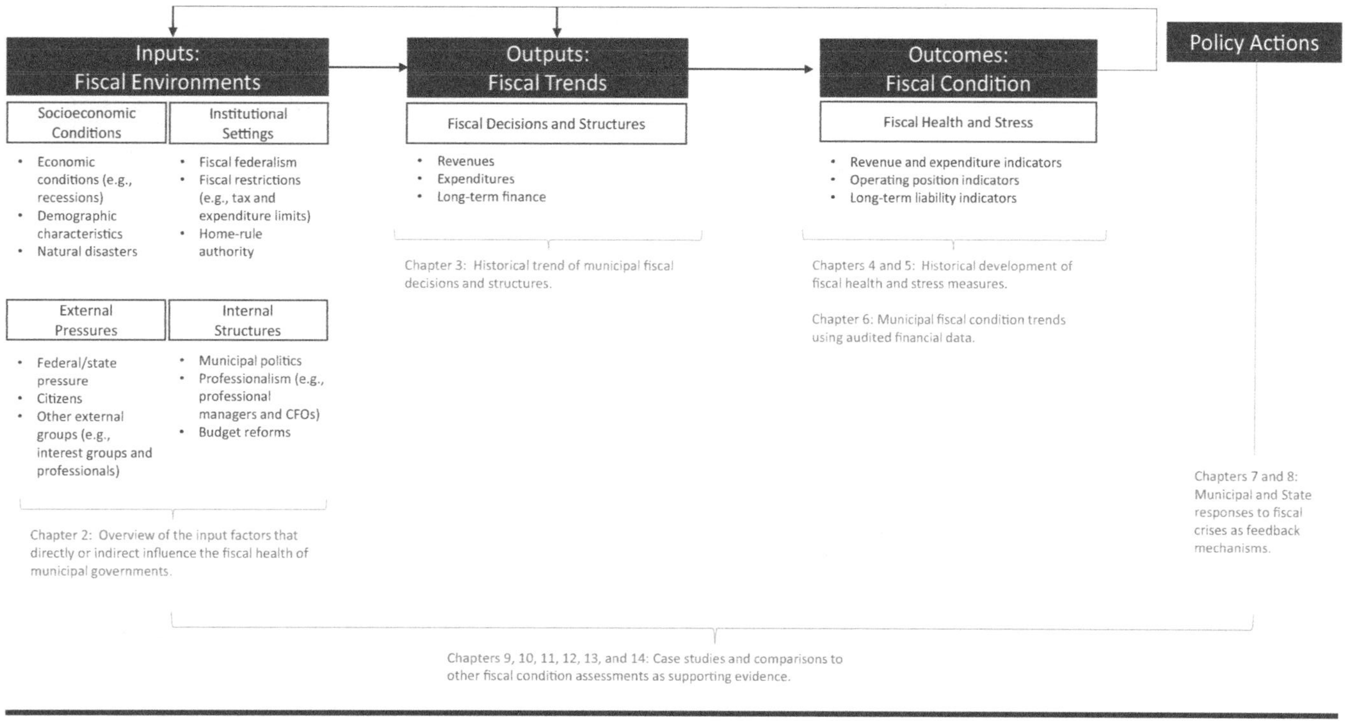

Figure 1.4 An Open-Systems Model and Book Outline

and regulations on the use of grants-in-aid from higher units of government, or the presence of active citizen or business interest groups—come into play in the establishment of fiscal policies? What socioeconomic factors are present in the community? Is the community gaining or losing jobs, people, and businesses? What is happening to the housing market and family incomes? How is the municipal government structured? Does the staff report to the mayor or council? Is there a strong central administrative executive? What is the process for making budget requests? All these considerations can shape fiscal decisions and ultimately the municipal government's fiscal health.

In Chapter 3, we rely on the Census Bureau's Survey of State and Local Finance, after discussing the well-known limitations of these data, to provide a historical overview of fiscal trends of municipal governments. Where does the money tend to come from (revenues), and where does it tend to go (expenditures)? Given the degree of variation in municipal fiscal patterns, we explore fiscal trends over time, by population groupings and across geographic regions. Basic questions addressed include (a) whether expenditure and revenue shares have changed over the study period and (b) whether those shares vary by state population and/or by geographic region. This analysis provides a context for the fiscal health analysis.

In Chapters 4 and 5, we discuss in detail the history of alternative measures of fiscal health and review the range of alternative set of measures suggested, such as the ICMA's FTMS, Brown's (1993) 10-point test, and the approaches of Wang et al. (2007). We describe each alternative's strengths and weaknesses in depth. Chapter 5 pays particular attention to differences between the notions of fiscal health and fiscal stress. Although these two terms are often used interchangeably, there are important conceptual and practical differences between them. We summarize the research on that issue and provide a framework for thinking about the assessment and prediction of fiscally distressed municipalities. This chapter carries particular practical relevance because practitioners and academics need to understand the key distinctions between municipal fiscal health and fiscal stress and their implications.

In Chapter 6, we draw on the Government Finance Officers Association's financial indicators database and present 29 fiscal condition measures that help us interpret trends. Many of these measures, such as expenditures (per capita governmental and general funds) and revenues (general and governmental, taxes and intergovernmental aid), are consistent with the indicators reviewed in Chapter 4, but we also discuss a range of other measures or indicators such as operating position (reserves, cash, and investments), enterprise funds, and long-term debt (governmental and enterprise). Relying on 2016 fiscal data, we focus on ten key indices and break them down by region and population size. In essence, these breakdowns offer updated metrics consistent with Ken Brown's popular 10-point test.

Chapters 7 and 8 review municipal and state government responses, respectively, to fiscal stress. During periods of fiscal stress, municipalities are forced to behave differently than would be expected under normal circumstances. In

Chapter 7, we offer three theoretical descriptions of municipal responses to fiscal stress as well as survey data collected during the COVID-19 pandemic. We conclude the chapter with practical tips for municipal officials recovering from a period of fiscal stress. Chapter 8 looks at how states respond when confronted with fiscally stressed municipalities, with a particular focus on state bankruptcy laws and monitoring systems. Detroit, Michigan is the best-known example of a municipal bankruptcy, but since 1938, there have been about 700 such filings in the United States. Central to this discussion is the breadth of variation across states in terms of monitoring and responding to municipal fiscal distress. The chapter concludes with a review of studies that have tried to empirically assess the effectiveness of state interventions and oversight of municipal fiscal condition.

Chapters 9 to 13 present five detailed, original case studies: Flint, Michigan; Wichita, Kansas; North Lauderdale, Florida; Havelock, North Carolina; and Commerce, California. In each case study, we explore the institutional structures within which the municipality operates and provide a descriptive analysis of their respective fiscal situations. We highlight the unique underlying factors that affected each municipality's fiscal situation and how each municipality responded, or failed to respond, to that situation. We derive important lessons that other municipal governments can apply. We know that many of the fiscal indicators discussed in Chapters 4, 5, and 6 can come across as sterile and difficult to understand or appreciate; these case studies are intended to bring those indicators to life and show how municipalities can find themselves in intolerable fiscal situations, how they typically react to such crises, and how to avoid falling into such situations.

Chapter 14 offers a summary of the case studies, which is followed by an examination of commonly used fiscal condition analysis tools, including Kloha et al. (2005), Wang et al. (2007), and Moody's (2009). We discuss how each of these tools calculates financial condition measures and how each one could be used to evaluate fiscal condition in our five case studies. We then describe challenges associated with each approach in comparison with our open-systems approach. The final chapter summarizes key takeaways from the book, major lessons and implications for municipal fiscal practice and policy, and fruitful questions and agendas for future research.

Note

1. We use the definition of municipal governments suggested by the U.S. Census Bureau (2020), as "organized local governments authorized in state constitutions and statutes and established to provide government for a specific concentration of population in a defined area; includes those governments designated as cities, villages, boroughs (except in Alaska), and towns (except in the six New England states, Minnesota, New York, and Wisconsin)."

Chapter 2

Inputs

Municipal Fiscal Environments

Municipal government officials do not make fiscal decisions about taxation and expenditures in a vacuum. Rather, an array of factors shapes municipalities' fiscal decisions and, in turn, their fiscal health. This chapter focuses on the municipal fiscal environment, in which such factors generate institutional, political, and administrative dynamics. Municipal fiscal environments correspond to what are commonly described as *system inputs* in the open-systems literature.

As outlined in our open-systems model (see Figure 1.4), the open-systems literature has identified four core dimensions of system inputs in a broader context of public administration and policy: socioeconomic conditions, institutional settings, external pressures, and internal structures (Almond & Powell, 1978; Meier & Bohte, 2007; Ripley & Franklin, 1975; Stazyk & Goerdel, 2011; Wang et al., 2012). These four core dimensions are also applicable to municipal fiscal environments; municipal fiscal decisions and fiscal health as system outputs and outcomes, respectively, are a function of those four sets of inputs (see also ICMA, 2016). The goal of this chapter is to understand how each environmental dimension shapes municipal fiscal decisions and structures. We also call attention to some selected factors in each dimension to depict the actual context of U.S. municipal finance.

Socioeconomic Conditions

As discussed in Chapter 1, socioeconomic conditions, which encompass both economic and sociodemographic influences reflect a combination of multiple

DOI: 10.4324/9780429270765-2

social and economic factors such as population, income, educational attainment, ethnicity, and unemployment. Public administration researchers often identify socioeconomic conditions as shaping the market for public services (Almond & Powell, 1978; Meier & Bohte, 2007; Selden, 1997). In other words, they affect the demand and supply sides of municipal government operations, thereby determining the equilibrium price and quantity of municipal services.

From the municipal finance standpoint, socioeconomic conditions decide the amount of municipal spending needed to produce a necessary level of various services (Chapman & Gorina, 2012; Deno & Mehay, 1987). As noted by Deller and Maher (2009), the ability of municipal officials to match policies and spending to the demands of residents is often described in terms of *effectiveness*, while the ability to produce public services at the lowest cost to the taxpayer centers around notions of *efficiency*. Socioeconomic conditions also define municipal resource capacities such as tax bases and revenue income, which play a vital role in shaping each municipality's supply curve (Hendrick, 2002; Sun, 2014). In practical terms, socioeconomic conditions portray what municipal officials are expected to do and identify the fiscal options available for them, thereby helping to shape their actual choices and actions (Hendrick, 2004).

Obvious examples of municipal socioeconomic factors include economic conditions. Researchers generally agree with the following observations regarding the fiscal impacts of economic conditions (see Arapis & Reitano, 2018; Christian & Bush, 2018; Maher & Deller, 2007). First, throughout history, American municipalities have experienced numerous economic upturns and downturns. Second, economic upturns tend to help municipal governments sustain or improve their service capacity, because they reduce the demand for social-service spending while revenues increase, thus allowing municipal governments to accumulate fiscal slack resources. Third, economic downturns place a heavy burden on municipal resources in the short or long run as they erode municipal tax and revenue bases. In bad economic times, resources are scarce but municipal spending needs rise significantly because people are in great need of public services.

The impact of economic downturns is particularly critical to municipal governments. Since the late 1990s, the United States has experienced three recessions: the 2001 recession, the Great Recession of 2007–2009, and the ongoing (as of this writing) recession induced by COVID-19 (National Bureau of Economic Research, 2021). Going farther back, one finds cycles of economic downturns including the oil shock recessions of the 1970s and early 1980s. The most common measures used to track economic conditions include gross domestic product (GDP) (Figure 2.1), the unemployment rate (Figure 2.2), and income levels (Figure 2.3). Each one has its strengths and weaknesses, but for our purposes, clear patterns emerge with each measure. We will consider each one in turn.

For GDP, which is largely considered the primary measure of economic activity, evidence of downturns in the late 1970s and early 1980s is clear, as are the

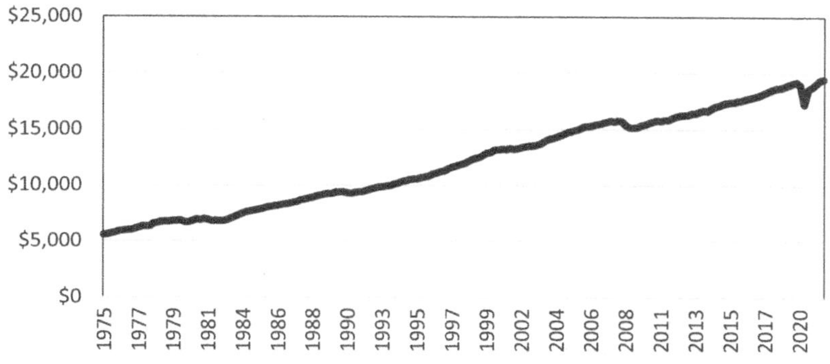

Figure 2.1 Real Gross Domestic Product for the United States (Billions of Dollars)

Source: U.S. Bureau of Labor Statistics

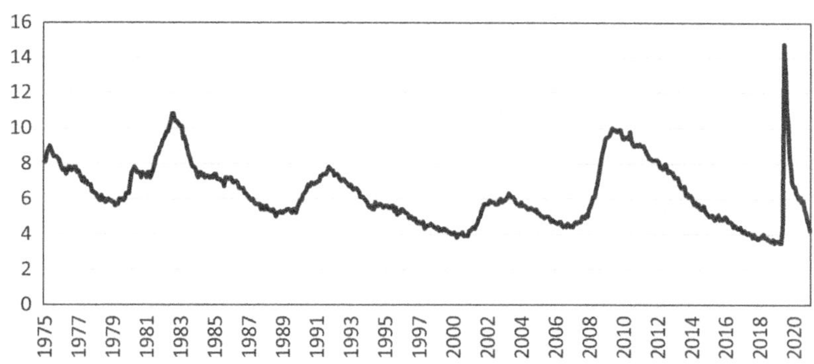

Figure 2.2 Unemployment Rate for the United States (Percentage)

Source: U.S. Bureau of Labor Statistics

slowdown in 1990 and the downturn in the early 2000s. But compared to the Great Recession, these prior events were relatively modest. The impact of the COVID-19 recession is also clearly evident in the GDP data.

The second most frequently used measure of the overall economy is the unemployment rate, because the data are produced each month with a fairly rapid turnaround time, thereby providing a picture of the current situation. Here, the

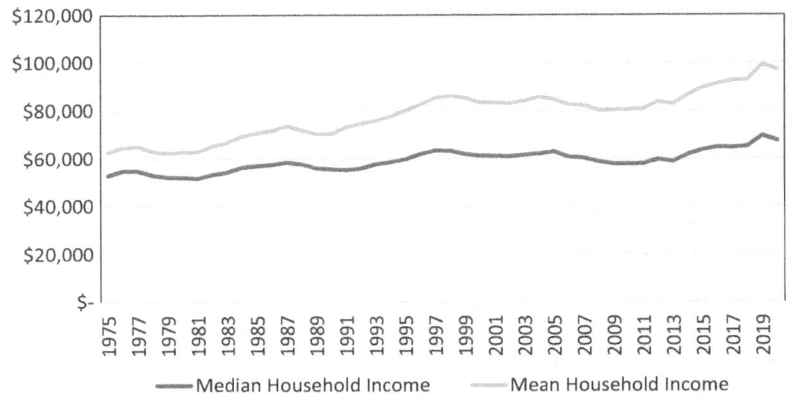

Figure 2.3 Average Real Household Income
Source: U.S. Census Bureau

patterns of economic downturns are much more pronounced than with the GDP data. Although the unemployment rate peaked at a higher level in 1983 than during the Great Recession, the relatively low levels of unemployment for almost two decades prior to the Great Recession tended to amplify the severity of that economic shock.

The unemployment data also show a relatively longer lag period during the recovery from the Great Recession, lasting almost ten years in many parts of the United States. The clear spike in unemployment during the COVID pandemic, meanwhile, does not follow historical patterns of a buildup to a peak and then a steady decline. Indeed, by the beginning of spring 2022, the national unemployment rate had returned to the rates immediately prior to the COVID-19 recession. This rapid spike and then an equally rapid drop are quite unusual, almost as though the labor markets were turned off and then back on again. The labor markets in the COVID-19 recession have actually been very tight, with growing labor shortages that have affected not only businesses but also municipal governments in their ability to hire and retain employees.

The third measure, household income, also shows periods of economic recession, but the patterns appear to fall in between the more stable GDP measure and the greater volatility of unemployment rates. Two patterns in the household income data warrant mention. First, after adjusting for inflation growth, median household income is relatively modest and appears flat for long periods of time, whereas mean household income is growing at a more reasonable pace. Second, the gap between mean and median household income, a common measure of income inequality, appears to be widening.

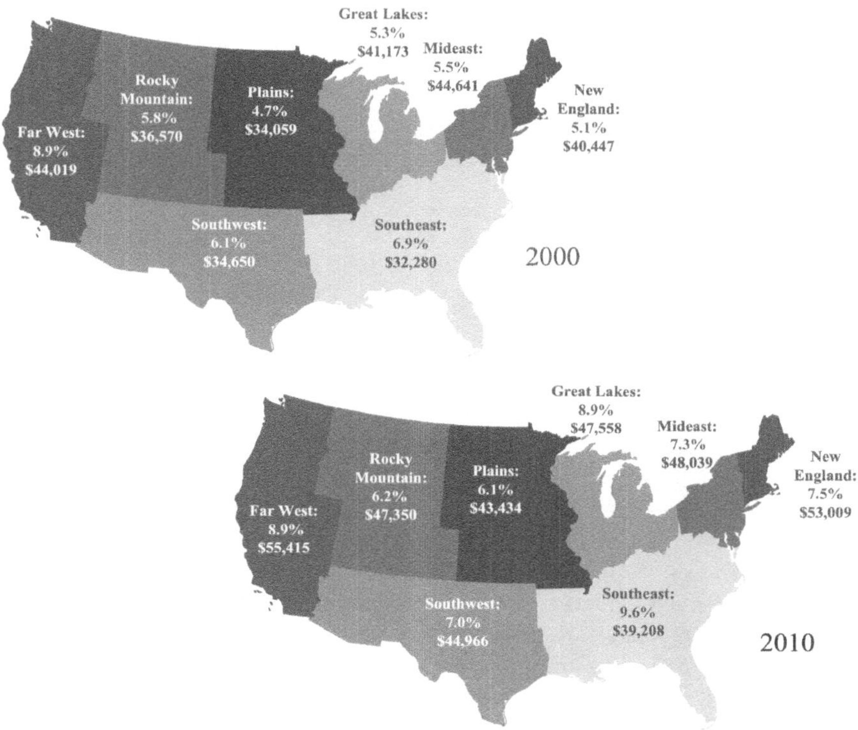

Figure 2.4 Municipal Unemployment Rate and Median Household Income by Region, 2000 and 2010

Source: U.S. Census Bureau; map created with MapChart.net (CC BY-SA 4.0)

Not all municipal governments are equally well positioned to handle economic busts. In the years before and after the Great Recession, there were clear regional variations in the average municipal unemployment rate and median household income (Figure 2.4). Municipalities in the Rocky Mountain region, for example, saw their average unemployment rate rise by only 0.4 percentage points; for Great Lakes municipalities, the average rise was 3.6 percentage points. Municipal governments in the two regions thus had to respond differently. According to Porter (2017), such divergences can exist for several reasons, including municipal differences in employment structure, income sustainability, labor participation, investment, and innovation capacity.

The Great Recession was different from the prior economic downturns in one large regard, which can best be seen by tracking housing prices (Figure 2.5). Here,

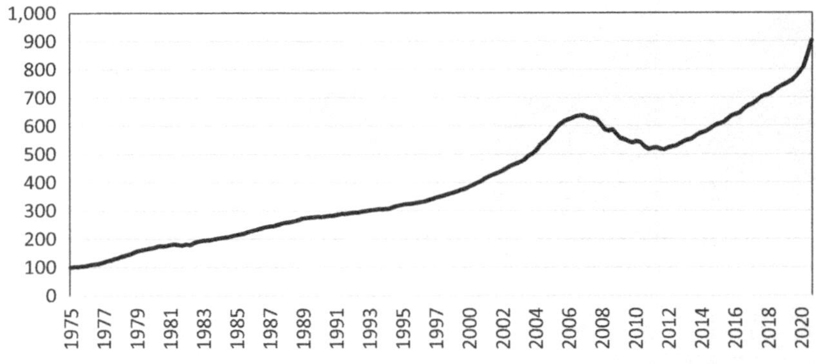

Figure 2.5 All-Transactions House Price Index for the United States
Source: U.S. Federal Housing Finance Agency

we track an index of all housing transaction prices over the same time period. Housing prices were remarkably stable throughout all prior recessions since the mid-1970s. There was some evidence of a slowdown in housing prices in the early 1980s, primarily as a result of very high interest rates, but even during that difficult period, the housing market was relatively stable. This stability has been a benefit to the many municipal governments that depend on the property tax as a primary source of revenue. But in the early to mid-2000s, the price of housing started to accelerate. In hindsight, a housing bubble was clearly forming as prices increased to an unsustainable level. In the middle of 2007, the bubble burst, the housing market collapsed, and the stability and predictability of property tax revenues were severely undermined.

What made the Great Recession different was not only the collapse of the housing market—and a home is often a household's largest financial asset—but the ramifications for the financial markets. Specifically, many mortgages backed by the value of a house are actively traded in the secondary financial markets, where mortgages can be bundled and sold as investment instruments. Because of the rapid acceleration of housing prices and the value of those mortgages, the secondary financial market became overheated. When the housing bubble burst, that secondary market collapsed, forcing well-known banks and financial institutions such as Bear Stearns and Lehman Brothers, along with nearly 500 smaller institutions, to close. This collapse of the secondary markets and of many banks and other financial institutions drove the severity of the Great Recession. The most recent data on housing prices suggest that we may be entering another housing bubble, but fundamental changes in the rules and regulations governing the

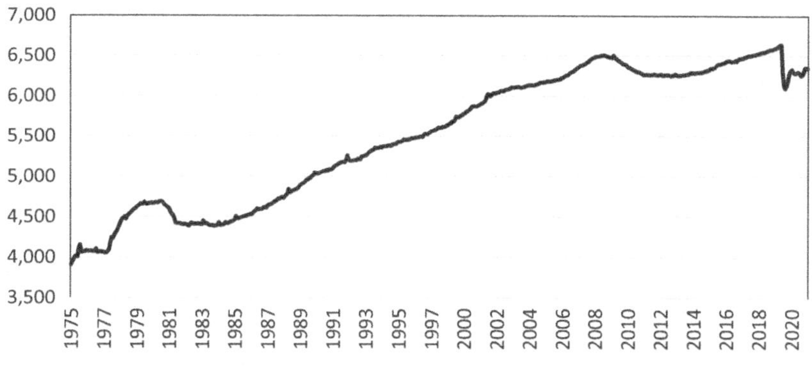

Figure 2.6 Non-Education Local Government Employment for the United States (Thousands)

Source: U.S. Bureau of Labor Statistics

secondary financial markets have greatly reduced the risk of repeating the financial crisis of the Great Recession.

Local government employment, which tends to be stable throughout swings in the economy, has been negatively impacted by three recessions over the previous several decades (Figure 2.6). The first noticeable impact on local government employment (excluding the education sector) was the recession of the early 1980s. This noticeable drop, however, was more a reflection of the Reagan administration's reversal of the policies of the Carter administration, which included an unusually large jump in local government employment. Not until the Great Recession almost 34 years later was there a noticeable drop in non-education local government employment. This 34-year pattern speaks to the overall stability of public-sector employment. Like much of the rest of the U.S. economy, however, local government employment did not return to its pre–Great Recession level for almost ten years.

The Great Recession dramatically affected local governments far beyond reduced personnel. A study by *Governing* magazine in 2015 identified 51 bankruptcy filings between 2000 and 2015, many of which were attributed directly to the Great Recession (Maciag, 2012). The highest-profile bankruptcy filers at the municipal level were Detroit, Michigan; San Bernardino, California; and Stockton, California. Other municipalities filing for bankruptcy between 2008 and 2015 included:

- The City of Hillview, Kentucky
- The Town of Mammoth Lakes, California

- The City of Harrisburg, Pennsylvania
- The City of Central Fall, Rhode Island
- The City of Vallejo, California
- The City of Gould, Alaska
- The Township of Westfall, Pennsylvania
- The Village of Washington Park, Illinois

The Pew Charitable Trusts (2010) studied the plight of U.S. cities and found that even in 2010, many large cities were facing fiscal pressures. In their study of 13 cities, all but one reported general fund shortfalls. Chicago, Illinois was most stressed, reporting a revenue shortfall for FY2010 in excess of $500 million, or 16.3% of its general fund. Kansas City, Missouri and Phoenix, Arizona followed with a FY2011 shortfall equal to 12.5% of their general fund. Pittsburgh, Pennsylvania was the only city in the study to report a FY2010 surplus, equal to 1.9% of the general fund.

These shortfalls posed short-run challenges, but for these cities and many others, municipal pensions present a major long-run threat. Pew Charitable Trusts (2010) found that three of the 13 cities studied had a pension funding ratio of 45% or less: Pittsburgh (34.3%), Chicago (42.7%), and Philadelphia (45%). The best-funded pension of the group was in Los Angeles (89.7%). We know that the Great Recession exacerbated fiscal challenges facing cities and that those effects lingered well beyond the recession's end.

The COVID-19 recession is far from comparable to the prior economic downturns. Indeed, we need to go back over 100 years to the 1918 Spanish flu pandemic to have any reasonable point of reference, and the structure of the economy is so fundamentally different, besides which World War I was in process, that attempts to make meaningful comparisons are fraught with potential errors. In addition, the U.S. federal government responded forcefully to the COVID-19 pandemic through the CARES Act of 2020, which injected $2 trillion into the economy, and the Consolidated Appropriations Act of 2020, which injected another $900 billion, followed by the American Rescue Plan Act of 2021 and its injection of another $1.9 trillion. Significant portions of these COVID-related stimulus packages have sought to help municipal governments weather the disruptions caused by COVID-19. It is too soon to tell if these aggressive federal policies cushioned municipal government from the economic stresses caused by COVID-19. The Great Recession, while severe and even alarmingly close to an economic depression, is more in line with other economic downturns, producing a more limited federal response. In addition, sufficient time has passed to review the lessons learned from that experience.

When we think about drivers of municipal service demand, the one that often rises to the top as a primary determinant, along with economic conditions, is population size. The demand for such services as police protection is largely driven

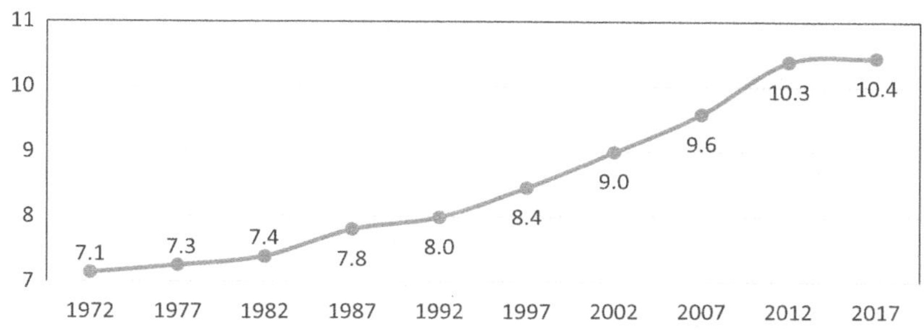

Figure 2.7 Average Municipal Population (Thousands)
Source: U.S. Census Bureau

by population, much like the demand for grocery stores. The trend in average municipal population has been a steady increase from 7,142 in 1972 to 10,449 in 2017 (Figure 2.7), indicating that the average municipal government in the United States has been consistently adding more service recipients. The average municipal population has increased by 31.6% from 1972 to 2017, paralleling the national population increase of 35.4% for the same period (U.S. Census Bureau, 1972–2017).

Population growth has sparked major increases in municipal service demand and resource needs (Das & Skidmore, 2017). Whether population growth has altered the unit cost of municipal service delivery, which is often measured as per-capita expenditures and/or revenues, remains unclear. Studies have reported mixed findings, primarily due to disagreements over economies of scale at the municipal level. Thus, we still do not know whether municipal governments realize cost advantages as their size of service production grows (in favor, see Bunch & Strauss, 1992; against, see Holcombe & Williams, 2009). One main reason for these mixed findings is that the underlying production structure and technology vary across different municipal services—for instance, police protection, fire protection, library services, or parks and recreation. The optimal size of government relative to population also varies across different services, thus introducing a certain degree of economic inefficiency into any municipal government.

More detailed demographic information for the average municipality over the last 50 years is presented in Table 2.1. Females have represented slightly more than half of the total municipal population. The average proportions of youth (25.3% in 2017) and older persons (18.3% in 2017) rates have consistently decreased and increased over time, respectively. The average educational attainment rate has increased from 53.8% to 86.7%, meaning that more municipal populations have completed high-school education. Municipalities have observed increased racial and ethnic diversity; the average nonwhite proportion was 6.9% in 1970 but

Table 2.1 Municipal Demographic Structure

Year	*Average female popula-tion (%)*	*Average youth population (0-19; %)*	*Average aging population (65+; %)*	*Average educational attainment (High school graduate or over/population +25; %)*	*Average nonwhite popula-tion (%)*
1970	51.9	36.3	14.7	53.8	6.9
1980	52.0	31.7	14.9	61.1	7.8
1990	52.1	28.9	17.1	69.9	10.2
2000	51.6	28.3	16.2	77.9	13.3
2010	50.9	26.6	16.4	83.7	14.5
2012	50.9	26.3	16.6	84.6	14.6
2014	50.9	25.9	17.0	85.4	14.8
2016	50.8	25.6	17.7	86.3	15.2
2017	50.8	25.3	18.3	86.7	15.6

Source: U.S. Census Bureau

15.6% in 2017. What are the implications for municipal finances and fiscal health as the population becomes older, more educated, and more racially and ethnically diverse?

Of course, not all municipalities mimic the average. Rather, there exist great variations in municipal demographic characteristics. Table 2.2 shows an increasing degree of population concentration in larger municipalities since 1972. For example, about 2% of all municipalities had a population over 50,000 in 1972; in 2017, the number increased by 1.8 percentage points (about 370 municipalities). Historically, U.S. population growth has tended to favor larger municipalities. Also, as of 2017, larger municipalities had more heavily female, young, educated, and nonwhite populations than their counterparts with smaller populations; in contrast, smaller municipalities had a larger share of the aging population. Again, what are the implications of these trends for fiscal policies and health?

Regional affiliation also matters to municipal demographic structures. For example, the Southeast, Plains, and Great Lakes regions have consistently had a higher concentration of municipalities for the last four decades (23.5%, 23.5%, and 20.3% of total municipalities, respectively, in 2017). As of 2017, the Far West (36,877.6) and New England (37,710.9) were home to municipalities with a larger average population. The nonwhite share of the total municipal population was significantly higher in municipalities in the Far West (29.2%) and Southeast (26.9%) while Plains municipalities had the highest percentage of older residents (19.5%).

How these variations actually shape municipal governments' fiscal decisions is still not fully known and is the focus of a large and growing literature. For

Table 2.2 Distribution and Demographic Structure of Municipalities by Size and Region

	Municipalities with population			
	less than or equal to 499	*between 500 and 4,999*	*between 5,000 and 49,999*	*more than or equal to 50,000*
1972 (%)	34.4	47.4	16.1	2.1
1997 (%)	32.4	46.2	18.5	2.9
2017 (%)	31.4	44.4	20.3	3.9
2017 only Average population (persons)	235.9	1,775.6	15,660.4	164,736.7
Female population (%)	49.9	51.2	51.2	51.1
Youth population (%)	23.5	26.2	26.4	26.3
Aging population (%)	20.2	18.0	15.6	13.2
Educational attainment (%)	86.1	86.6	88.1	86.6
Nonwhite population (%)	11.2	14.3	20.9	32.5

	Municipalities in							
	Far West	*Rocky Mountain*	*South west*	*South east*	*Plains*	*Great Lakes*	*Mideast*	*New England*
1972 (%)	5.6	4.3	9.1	22.7	24.6	20.9	11.8	1.0
1997 (%)	6.0	4.3	10.2	23.2	23.8	20.3	11.3	0.9
2017 (%)	6.1	4.4	10.3	23.5	23.5	20.3	11.1	0.8
2017 only Average population (persons)	36,877.6	9,412.5	15,143.3	9,031.6	3,541.8	8,246.6	11,317.8	37,710.9
Female population (%)	50.0	49.3	50.6	51.8	50.0	50.8	51.5	51.6
Youth population (%)	26.4	27.1	27.3	25.1	24.8	25.7	24.0	22.5
Aging population (%)	16.0	17.6	17.1	18.5	19.5	17.1	18.0	17.4
Educational attainment (%)	85.1	89.8	82.6	82.3	88.9	89.1	90.0	88.9
Nonwhite population (%)	29.2	7.9	19.5	26.9	7.2	8.6	12.9	15.0

Source: U.S. Census Bureau

example, Park (2018b) reported that an aging population is an important driver of municipal revenue and spending increases, whereas Chapman and Gorina (2012) found no relationship. One reason for this divergence is that there is no evident link between taxpayers' demographic status and their tax and service preferences. One clear implication of these findings, however, is that two municipal governments may confront widely differing spending needs and/or resource capacity due to their demographic differences. Even the preferences (demand for services) of older populations may vary in different parts of the United States.

In recent years, the impact of natural disasters has garnered significant attention from researchers and practitioners. While we have always been exposed to natural disasters, concern over their increased frequency and severity due to climate change is a major reason for this growing interest. According to Boustan et al. (2020), there have been 10,158 disasters, including 3,927 floods, 2,845 tornados, 1,667 winter storms, 910 forest fires, 742 hurricanes, and 67 of other types, in the United States from 1920 to 2010. Of this number, 292 were severe disasters, causing ten deaths or more. The ICMA (2015) reported that 76% of the 1,899 local governments responding to its survey had to respond to a major disaster over the past 15 years. Almost half said that their sustainability plans include a focus on disaster management. Alleviating the impact of disasters, therefore, is an important part of municipal operations. Recent disasters such as West Coast wildfires and the unprecedented COVID-19 pandemic have placed greater emphasis on such functions.

Mitigating disasters requires massive municipal fiscal efforts because of their unexpected and large-scale impacts. Hildreth (2009) examined the fiscal consequences of Hurricane Katrina for New Orleans, Louisiana, which experienced a 16% decrease in actual general fund revenues compared to the original budgeted amount. The city could achieve only a 5% decrease in actual general fund expenditures from the budgeted amount, generating a 212% increase in its deficit, or far more than the city's deficit growth of 61% during the Great Recession. Clearly, disasters can overwhelm municipal finance plans by suddenly extending the need–capacity gap. Although the federal government often steps in with assistance to help in offsetting the impacts of natural disasters, some of which goes to municipal governments, how much aid a local government will actually receive remains uncertain, because much of the funding is aimed at individuals, families, and businesses.

Institutional Settings

As introduced in Chapter 1, institutional settings can be viewed as a realm where certain "regularities in the patterns of human behavior" and "interaction" exist and can be observed (Crawford & Ostrom, 1995, p. 582). Institutional settings and such regularities are shaped by institutions that refer to "the rules of the game in a society or, more formally, are the humanly devised constraints that shape human interaction" (North, 1990, p. 6). Institutions, which can take different forms such as formal laws and rules or informal norms and understandings, are expected to "reduce uncertainty by providing a structure to everyday life" (North, 1990, p. 3) and, by doing so, to solve collective action problems in society.

Municipal fiscal decisions constitute social, political, and collective actions (von Hagen, 2002). Each municipality makes its decisions in settings established by various fiscal institutions or rules. More specifically, fiscal institutions determine what fiscal actions municipal officials can pursue in meeting service demand and in managing resources; they also create incentives for municipal officials to behave and make decisions in certain ways, or disincentives to prevent them from misbehaving (Brennan & Buchanan, 1979). Fiscal institutions, just like other institutions, are expected to play a role in controlling uncertainty and to contribute to mitigating collective action problems such as conflicting budget preferences, thereby maximizing each municipality's net budgetary gains.

A variety of fiscal rules or institutions have been implemented at the municipal level with the expectation that they can govern municipal financial decisions and fiscal outcomes. Fiscal federalism deserves our attention as it influences each municipality's initial fiscal landscape. American fiscal federalism involves three important characteristics. First, there are explicit and implicit relationships of interdependence between federal, state, and local governments. The second characteristic, decentralization, means that municipal (and more broadly local) service responsibilities and spending power are separated from the federal and state governments. Especially under the Reagan administration, fiscal decentralization shifted funding responsibilities for many government services to local units of government. Third, municipal governments have a level of fiscal independence because revenue-raising powers are divided among governments at different levels. As shown in Table 2.3, property taxes in the United States are used exclusively for local purposes while sales and income taxes are used mostly by the state and federal governments, respectively. This division contributes to municipal revenue-raising capacity, which has historically accounted for more than 70% of all municipal revenues (U.S. Census Bureau, 1972–2017).

The divisions among governments, however, are not always clear-cut because of the functional and fiscal interdependence among different levels of government. As shown in Figure 2.8, although each level of government consistently manages certain service responsibilities (such as public works at the local level), all three levels of government operate in some shared service areas such as public welfare, public safety, and community development. This commonality, coupled with some revenue sharing between governments as described in Table 2.3, allows decisions and actions at the federal and state levels to have institutional effects on municipal level by defining what municipal governments should and can do.

Table 2.3 Tax Revenue Composition by Government Level

	Federal	*State*	*Local (Municipal)*
Individual income taxes (%)	51.8	37.2	4.7 (10.0)
Corporate income taxes (%)	6.9	4.7	1.1 (3.3)
Other taxes (%)	41.2	58.1	94.2 (86.7)
Sales taxes (%)	0	48.3	17.5 (28.5)
Property taxes (%)	0	1.7	72.0 (49.8)
Others (%)	41.2	8.1	4.7 (8.4)
Total	100	100	100 (100)

Source: Office of Management and Budget and U.S. Census Bureau

Figure 2.8 Federal, State, and Local Major Functions
Source: Office of Management and Budget and U.S. Census Bureau

One example is the Community Development Block Grant (CDBG) program. Since its creation in 1974, this program has provided vital federal support for municipal community development projects. Despite its importance, CDBG has frequently been a political battleground, especially when the federal government has tried to cut funding levels (Patton, 2011). Municipalities object to such federal cuts because they reduce local governments' available resources and limit their options to achieve policy and service goals. The cuts also force municipalities to take greater responsibility for community development. This pattern can be observed not only with CDBG, but also with many other municipal services such as public safety and public welfare (Chernick & Reschovsky, 2001; Jordan, 2003).

Whereas fiscal federalism draws the general contours of municipal finance, other institutions such as state laws govern municipal fiscal decisions and outcomes (Advisory Commission on Intergovernmental Relations [ACIR], 1993). Over the last several decades, an increasing number of states have imposed municipal TELs, or constitutional and/or statutory restrictions on municipal taxing and spending authority (Mullins & Wallin, 2004), a step first taken by Alabama and Missouri in 1875. During the 1970s and 1980s, as a strong anti-tax mood moved across the country, many more states implemented municipal TELs, sometimes by popular referendum. Well-known examples include California's Proposition 13 and Massachusetts Proposition $2^1/_2$. According to Brown (2000), municipal TELs were "very much a part of [municipal] government fiscal reality" (p. 29) in the 1990s. As of 2017, 44 out of 50 states had some form of municipal TELs (Park, 2018a; see Table 2.4).

Table 2.4 State-Imposed Municipal TELs Across States, 2017

State	*Property tax rate lid*	*Property assessment lid*	*Property tax levy cap*	*General revenue limit*	*General expenditure limit*	*Full disclosure requirement*
Alabama	√					
Alaska	√		√			
Arizona	√	√	√		√	
Arkansas	√	√	√			
California	√	√			√	
Colorado	√		√	√	√	√
Connecticut						
Delaware						
Florida	√	√				√
Georgia						√
Hawaii						
Idaho	√		√			
Illinois	√		√			√
Indiana	√		√			
Iowa	√	√				
Kansas						√
Kentucky	√		√			√
Louisiana	√		√			
Maine			√			
Maryland		√				√
Massachusetts	√		√			

(*Continued*)

Table 2.4 (Continued)

State	*Property tax rate lid*	*Property assess-ment lid*	*Property tax levy cap*	*General revenue limit*	*General expen-diture limit*	*Full disclo-sure require-ment*
Michigan	√	√	√			√
Minnesota						√
Mississippi			√			
Missouri	√		√			
Montana			√			√
Nebraska	√			√		
Nevada	√		√			√
New Hampshire						
New Jersey					√	
New Mexico	√	√	√			
New York	√	√	√			
North Carolina	√					
North Dakota	√		√			
Ohio	√		√			
Oklahoma	√	√				
Oregon	√	√				
Pennsylvania	√					
Rhode Island			√			√
South Carolina						
South Dakota	√					
Tennessee						√
Texas	√		√			√
Utah						√
Vermont						
Virginia						√
Washington	√		√			√
West Virginia	√		√			√
Wisconsin			√			
Wyoming	√					

Source: Park (2018a, 2018b)

Though municipal TELs are now common across the United States, no two municipal TELs are exactly alike, for two broad reasons (Stallmann et al., 2017). First, states have developed their municipal TELs based on the following six basic types. How these six types are mixed in each state's legislation generates significant variations.

- *Rate lids applied specifically to property taxes* set a maximum amount by which municipal governments can increase property tax rates without legislative and/or voter approval. Thirty-one states had lids on municipal property tax rates as of 2017.
- *Limits on property assessment increases*: These limits circumscribe municipal governments' ability to generate greater revenues by raising assessed property values. These types of TELs are generally a response to rapid growth in property values due to strong real-estate markets. They were in effect in 11 states have as of 2017.
- *Property tax levy caps*: These are a relatively more stringent type of municipal TELs than the prior two, as the caps target the total amount of property taxes collected. Allowing only a certain percentage increase in municipal levies relative to the preceding year is a common form. Twenty-five states had levy caps as of 2017.
- *General revenue limits*: These limits are more comprehensive and stricter than the preceding types, as they go beyond property taxes to include all sources of revenue. Annual increases in municipal general revenues are subject to limits. As of 2017, only two states had such limits.
- *General expenditure limits*: These are a similar mechanism to general revenue limits in terms of their constraining mechanisms and binding nature. General expenditure limits are directed at total proposed budget amounts, appropriations for expenditures, or actual year-end spending. As of 2017, only four states had these limits.
- *Full disclosure requirements*: These are the least restrictive type of municipal TEL, generally requiring public advertisement, public discussion, or adoption of a resolution or ordinance before an increase in tax rates or levies. These requirements were stipulated in 18 states as of 2017.

Second, in each basic type, states can also choose different restrictions and exemptions. For example, Arkansas prevents municipalities from collecting property taxes greater than 5 mills of the assessed value, while Nevada limits municipal property tax rates to $3.64 per $100 of assessed value. Also, Colorado and Nebraska both have general revenue limits. However, Colorado's constitutional limit sets an allowable growth rate for general revenues except for some voter-approved taxes, which is equal to inflation plus annual net municipal growth, whereas Nebraska's statutory restriction allows 2.5% annual growth in municipal general revenues with several exemptions such as revenues for capital improvements, debt services, jointly financed services, natural disaster repairs, and judgments. These institutional variations, therefore, may generate different inputs into municipal fiscal decisions.

Many researchers have sought to measure the institutional heterogeneity of municipal TELs across states and understand their fiscal impacts. Springer et al. (2009) and Stallmann et al. (2017) have offered extensive summaries of those findings, indicating that municipal TELs have successfully restricted the size and growth of property taxes. As for whether municipal TELs affect overall municipal budgets, the academic evidence is inconclusive, primarily because municipal governments subject to TELs tend to turn instead to other funding sources such as income and sales taxes, user charges and fees, debt financing, and fiscal reserves. For example, in California under Proposition 13, many municipalities have aggressively pursued sales tax revenues to the extent of fostering retail sprawl, an unintended consequence.

Although municipal TELs are a significant part of municipal finance, states have also developed other fiscal institutions to govern how municipalities function. One significant example is balanced-budget requirements, which aim to prevent municipal governments from having negative budget balances in a fiscal year. As shown in Table 2.5, 25 states had imposed balanced-budget requirements on municipal governments as of 2017. Most of those states require municipal governments to have a balanced proposed and/or adopted budget rather than prohibiting actual year-end deficits. Lewis (1994) contended that even under these weaker forms of balanced-budget requirements, municipal governments still have a strong motivation to balance their actual budgets, either because of similar self-imposed requirements or because they strictly follow "the norm of balance" (p. 515) for political and administrative reasons.

Another important example is state-imposed debt limitations, which control either the process of debt issuance (e.g., by referendum requirements) and/or the amount of debt (e.g., by limiting it to a certain percentage of government income) (Yusuf et al., 2013). All 50 states have placed some form of debt limitations on municipal governments (ACIR, 1993; Park, 2018b). There is more variation with regard to the existence of bond referendum requirements, which were present in 39 states as of 2017 (see Table 2.5). Municipalities in those states must obtain voter approval to issue general obligation bonds or (in some cases) any bonds, thus creating a significant constraint on municipal funding options.

One rationale for such state-imposed fiscal rules and institutions is that municipal governments are legal creatures of the state. Hence, the argument runs, the state government should intervene responsibly to ensure that municipalities are efficient and accountable in their fiscal actions. However, statewide controls may not be appropriate for some municipalities because they operate in a unique environment. For instance, many states have one or two urban centers, and the

Table 2.5 Other State-Imposed Fiscal Rules on Municipal Governments, 2017

State	*Balanced budget requirements*	*Bond referendum requirements*	*State*	*Balanced budget requirements*	*Bond referendum requirements*
Alabama	√	√	Montana	√	√
Alaska		√	Nebraska	√	√
Arizona	√	√	Nevada	√	√
Arkansas		√	New Hampshire		√
California		√	New Jersey		
Colorado	√	√	New Mexico		√
Connecticut			New York		√
Delaware			North Carolina	√	√
Florida	√	√	North Dakota		√
Georgia	√	√	Ohio		√
Hawaii			Oklahoma	√	
Idaho	√	√	Oregon	√	√
Illinois	√	√	Pennsylvania		√
Indiana			Rhode Island	√	
Iowa			South Carolina		√
Kansas	√	√	South Dakota		√
Kentucky	√		Tennessee		√
Louisiana	√	√	Texas		√
Maine		√	Utah	√	√
Maryland			Vermont		
Massachusetts	√	√	Virginia		√
Michigan	√	√	Washington	√	√
Minnesota		√	West Virginia		√
Mississippi		√	Wisconsin	√	√
Missouri	√	√	Wyoming	√	√

Source: Park (2018a, 2018b)

rest of the state is largely rural. Nebraska is a good example—Omaha's population is 479,529 (in 2021), representing 25% of the state population. The median-sized Nebraska city has about 225 residents. In this context, a one-size fits all state policy makes little sense when the differences in service demands and revenue capacity are so vastly different across these communities.

Another important characteristic of municipal control is the status of home-rule statutes. As noted above, state government sets the rules of the game under which municipalities can function, by applying the principle known as Dillon's Rule, from a U.S. Supreme Court ruling in 1868 that established the theory of state preeminence over local governments. Some states, however, permit home rule, which gives municipalities (usually larger cities) greater flexibility to conduct business. Under home-rule charters, municipal governments can generally exercise more decision-making and managerial autonomy and avoid forms of state interference such as municipal TELs.

As detailed in Table 2.6, there is large variation across states, ranging from no home-rule municipalities in Alabama to more than 600 in Kansas. Another source of variation concerning home-rule charters is that specific municipal home-rule structures and laws vary by state. For example, all municipalities in Kansas have home-rule status, but they are still bound by state laws that are uniformly applicable to municipalities, such as a cap on property tax increases. All municipalities in North Carolina also have separate charters, but they are all granted by the state and do not provide full home-rule authority. Thus, the impact of such charters on municipal fiscal decisions can vary widely within and between states.

In the end, the level of heterogeneity across the states in terms of how municipalities are structured and concerning intergovernmental relations (which affects the flow of funds as well as the rules under which municipalities must function) makes the study of municipal fiscal health and strategies to promote it quite complicated. A strategy that may work for one set of municipalities within in a given state may not be appropriate for another set of municipalities elsewhere. Although this heterogeneity creates challenges for scholars of local government finance, policymakers and practitioners can still learn from models, case studies, and best practices. Our aim is to help municipal policymakers and practitioners make the most informed decisions possible. The specific municipal context matters, but applying lessons learned from other municipalities can contribute to a community's fiscal health.

External Pressures

External pressures (often referred to external expectations and weights) are intentional and purposive forces exerted by actors and groups outside an organization (Stazyk & Goerdel, 2011). In the case of municipal government operations, those

Table 2.6 Number of Municipalities with Home-Rule Charters by State, 2012

State	*Number of municipalities with home-rule charters (total number of municipalities)*	*State*	*Number of municipalities with home-rule charters (total number of municipalities)*
Alabama	0 (460)	Nebraska	2 (530)
Alaska	11 (149)	Nevada	12 (19)
Arizona	16 (91)	New Hampshire	13 (13)
Arkansas	0 (502)	New Jersey	6 (324)
California	121 (482)	New Mexico	12 (103)
Colorado	99 (271)	New York	62 (617)
Connecticut	26 (30)	North Carolina	553 (553)
Delaware	55 (57)	North Dakota	130 (357)
Florida	410 (410)	Ohio	234 (937)
Georgia	535 (535)	Oklahoma	86 (590)
Hawaii	0 (1)	Oregon	111 (241)
Idaho	1 (199)	Pennsylvania	38 (1,015)
Illinois	209 (1,298)	Rhode Island	7 (8)
Indiana	0 (569)	South Carolina	0 (269)
Iowa	5 (947)	South Dakota	10 (311)
Kansas	626 (626)	Tennessee	229 (345)
Kentucky	0 (418)	Texas	352 (1,213)
Louisiana	31 (304)	Utah	1 (245)
Maine	22 (22)	Vermont	34 (43)
Maryland	157 (157)	Virginia	229 (229)
Massachusetts	20 (53)	Washington	11 (281)
Michigan	323 (533)	West Virginia	108 (232)
Minnesota	107 (853)	Wisconsin	1 (596)
Mississippi	20 (298)	Wyoming	7 (99)
Missouri	44 (950)	Total	5,118 (19,514)
Montana	32 (129)		

Source: Lucy Burns Institute (2012) and Park (2018a)

Note: Total excludes the District of Columbia

actors and groups include, but are not limited to, general citizens, interest groups, professionals, and federal and state officials (Wang et al., 2012). External pressures deliver specific social and political preferences to municipal governments, thereby offering support for or opposition to their decisions and actions. By doing so, external pressures can incentivize municipal officials to allocate resources and make fiscal decisions in a certain direction.

For the federal and state governments as important external groups, one way to engage in municipal fiscal decisions is to rely on fiscal federalism; their decisions and actions in one policy area can directly define what they expect municipal governments to do in the same or even another area. Federal and state governments can also express policy preferences and shape municipal fiscal decisions in other ways, such as privatization. Barnekov and Rich (1989) identified several presidential initiatives on urban and local development during the 1970s and the 1980s as a strong force behind the increased use of privatization at the local level. Warner and Hebdon (2001), in their examination of municipalities in New York, also found that the election of a governor with a strong commitment to privatization pushed municipalities to move in this policy direction.

Federal and state governments not only apply policy channels to influence municipal fiscal decisions but can also express their preferences on municipal finance itself. The U.S. Government Accountability Office (GAO), for example, looks annually at local finance as part of its effort to understand the future fiscal conditions of policy partners and to ensure national fiscal sustainability (e.g., GAO, 2019). The GAO's reports have consistently suggested that local governments need to make substantial efforts to improve fiscal balance. By continuously drawing attention to this particular issue, it implicitly creates external pressures that may influence the decisions of municipal officials.

State governments have similar mechanisms by which to express their preferences on municipal finance. In fact, 47 of 50 states (all but Iowa, Maryland, and South Carolina) annually collect financial information from municipal governments, review their fiscal performance, and/or provide data to the public online (Chapman & Ascanio, 2020). For example, Massachusetts collects and publicly reports a municipal finance trend dashboard (see Table 2.7). Wisconsin annually audits municipal fiscal reports and publicly reports the data in a format that allows citizens, as well as municipal officials, to make comparisons to other municipalities. The Office of the New York State Comptroller (2021) uses such mechanism to enable municipal officials and taxpayers to respond more proactively to financial problems, help to sustain services, and improve transparency and accountability, all of which may reflect the state's interests and preferences on municipal finance. Some states, such as Maine, only collect and file municipal annual reports, without auditing or publicly releasing them.

Along with higher levels of government, citizens matter too. Citizens exert significant external pressure on municipal governments by expressing their policy

Table 2.7 Massachusetts' Municipal Finance Trend Dashboard

Category	*Detail*
Operating position	Certified free cash, stabilization fund balances, overlay reserves, general fund unassigned fund balances, self-insured health insurance trust fund balances, and uncollected real estate taxes
Unfunded liabilities	Pension and OPEB liabilities
Property taxes	Average single-family tax bills, new growth, levies, tax rates, assessed values, excess and override capacity and Proposition 2½ ballot questions
General fund revenues and expenditures	General fund revenues and expenditures
Demographics	Labor, income, population, and equalized property valuations
Debt	Outstanding debt, debt service, bond ratings, and authorized but unissued debt

Source: Massachusetts Division of Local Services (2020)

and fiscal preferences through several different channels. Traditional methods include voting in elections, responding to citizen surveys, and participation in public hearings; as methods of more direct engagement, citizens participate in neighborhood or district meetings and budget referenda (Ebdon, 2002; Ebdon & Franklin, 2004). In more recent years, participatory budgeting, which engages citizens in the budget process to deliberate on and substantively affect resource allocations, has spread rapidly across the country, especially among larger municipalities such as New York, Boston, and San Francisco (Gilman & Wampler, 2019).

The notion of government effectiveness comes into play here: how well do municipal officials match policies to the preferences of residents? Another important question is whether citizen pressures coming through different mechanisms actually affect municipal fiscal decisions. According to Matsusaka (2014), the answer is yes, for two reasons. First, citizen pressures can sometimes make municipal government decisions obvious; for example, if citizens approve a municipal bond issuance in a budget referendum, the municipality should issue the bond. Second, citizen participation can give municipal officials meaningful information on citizens' actual preferences, and failing to satisfy those preferences (i.e., poor effectiveness) could pose a political threat to municipal officials. Exactly how citizen pressures affect municipal fiscal decisions will vary by context and issue, as discussed by, for example, Ebdon (2002) and Farnham (1985).

Another set of external pressures on municipal governments comes from interest groups, which are composed of people and/or organizations who share the same concerns and interests and want to shape public policies in ways aligned with those concerns. Municipal fiscal decisions can vary depending on the behavior of interest groups and how municipal officials react to them. Literature on interest groups has focused almost exclusively on the national and state levels (Nownes, 2014), paying less attention to their influence at the local level, but local governments are subject to pressure from numerous such groups, including labor unions (Inman, 1982), rating agencies on the bond market (Omstedt, 2020), and business, and minority groups (Hajnal & Clark, 1998).

Nonprofit organizations also affect municipal fiscal decisions. Although traditionally, most research in this area has considered how governments impact nonprofits through grants and subsidies, some recent studies have examined the opposite relationship, or nonprofit organizations' effects on public expenditures through policy advocacy (Cheng, 2019) and their revenue effects such as through payments in lieu of taxes (Maher et al., 2018). Nonprofit organizations also offer support for municipal governments as policy implementers or agents. According to the ICMA's surveys on local service delivery methods (see Table 2.8), local governments rely on nonprofit organizations in different areas, especially for homeless, cultural, health, food, elderly, youth, and workforce services. Municipal reliance on nonprofit organizations instead of direct service provision or contracting with for-profit businesses may lead to different cost structures, resulting in different municipal fiscal decisions.

The last but not least set of external pressures comes from professional associations such as the ICMA, the Government Finance Officers Association (GFOA), the Governmental Accounting Standards Board (GASB), and many others. While representing the interest of their professional members or specific public interests, they also shape municipal finance by offering professional knowledge and skills. For example, the GFOA (2021) assists municipal finance by describing best practices in 11 areas, including accounting and financial reporting, capital planning, debt management, and pension and benefit administration. Recent evidence such as Park et al. (2021) confirms significant and positive changes in municipal fiscal practices due to these professional inputs.

Internal Structures

In a study of Jefferson County, Alabama, Yang (2019) found that fiscal mismanagement was a fundamental driver of the bankruptcy filing that occurred there in 2011. It is thus essential, as part of the overall fiscal environment, to consider what is happening with the government itself (McCabe et al., 2017; Nalbandian, 1990). Whereas the prior three dimensions—socioeconomic conditions, institutional settings, and external pressures—operate outside the government, the study of internal structures captures what is shaping municipal decisions and

Table 2.8 Local Governments Relying on Nonprofits for Service Delivery in Ten Major Areas

	2007 (total respondents vary as shown in parentheses)	*2012 (total respondents vary as shown in parentheses)*	*2017 (2,204 total respondents)*
Operation of homeless shelters (%)	56 (288)	52 (1,926)	50
Operation of museums (%)	38 (433)	40 (1,924)	48
Operation of cultural and arts programs (%)	35 (657)	38 (1,938)	41
Programs to address hunger (%)	Not included	48 (1,945)	40
Addiction treatment programs (%)	36 (395)	34 (1,962)	37
Mental health programs and facilities (%)	32 (369)	30 (1,773)	36
Elder nutrition programs (%)	Not included	41 (1,973)	35
In-home safety improvements for seniors (%)	Not included	25 (1,931)	33
Workforce development/job training programs (%)	25 (409)	23 (1,939)	30
Youth employment programs (%)	Not included	24 (1,930)	30

Source: ICMA (2007, 2012, 2019)

Note: In 2017, more than 80% of total 2,204 respondents were municipalities. The same information is not available for 2007 and 2012

actions from inside. The literature defines internal structures as "subject supports or compliance" from the inside (Almond & Powell, 1978, p. 11), "internal sources of power" (Meier & Bohte, 2007, p. 44), and "structural and process features of the agencies themselves" (Ripley & Franklin, 1975, p. 6). Internal structures encompass various factors such as political and management structures, knowledge and expertise, resource and capacity, and organizational culture. Internal factors not only play an important role as system inputs but also decide how other external inputs are related to certain outputs. Hence, they are often described as operating in a conversion process or in "the black box" (Andrews & Boyne, 2010, p. 443).

Municipal politics, as a political process and mechanism to define needs and allocate resources (Stoker, 1991), is an important internal factor. Despite the old claim that there was no clear meaning and impact of local-level politics (Adrian, 1952), municipal politics not only defines the overall political direction of municipal policy and fiscal decisions but also decides what external inputs municipal governments will be responsive to. Obviously, the elected chief executive (usually a mayor), if any, and the legislative body such as a council are key political players. Evidence indicates that elected mayors, especially based on their partisan affiliation, can generate substantial variations in municipal policy choices (Gerber & Hopkins, 2011) and fiscal decisions (de Benedictis-Kessner & Warshaw, 2016). De Benedictis-Kessner and Warshaw (2016) reported that Democratic mayors tend to spend more than Republican mayors, relying on debt rather than on tax increases. Due to the generally nonpartisan nature of municipal councils, evidence on the impact of council politics on municipal fiscal decisions is sparse. A cause-effect relationship is, however, anecdotally supported (Svara, 2003), so this could be a fruitful area for future empirical research.

There has also been a wave of increased professionalism within municipal governments. The development and widespread implementation of the council-manager form of government, which is seen as producing better operational performance than the mayor-council form due to the greater reliance on professional skills and expertise, since the early 1900s provides a good example. As shown in Table 2.9, the mayor-council form was dominant at the municipal level until the 1990s. We have observed a different trend since the 2000s; more than half of all municipalities now appear to operate under the council-manager form (see also Nelson & Svara, 2012).

Carr (2015) systematically reviewed the differences in performance between the two forms of municipal governance, suggesting that although we need more research to confirm which form yields better results, it is clear that the form of government affects municipal policy and fiscal decisions. Carr concluded that the precise fiscal impact of the council-manager form is contingent on other factors such as socioeconomic conditions and institutional settings. This conclusion is also supported by other studies, such as Park and Park (2018).

Table 2.9 Municipal Forms of Government by Share

Form	*1987*	*1992*	*2001*	*2006*	*2011*	*2018*
Mayor-council	65.5	67.9	38.5	35.4	33.0	38.2
Council-manager	12.9	15.1	53.7	57.3	59.0	48.2
Others	21.6	17.0	7.8	7.3	8.0	13.6

Source: U.S. Census Bureau (1987, 1992, 2017), ICMA (2001, 2006, 2011, 2018)

Note: We report percentage numbers because each year has a difference in a total number of survey respondents

The increasing role of professional chief financial officers, especially since the early 2000s, represents another example of efforts to enhance professionalism in municipal finance. According to Farmer's (2016) interviews with several municipal chief financial officers, their day-to-day jobs were formerly limited to handling "numbers—making sure the books were balanced, bills paid and audits clean." But now they are involved in many different aspects of municipal operations. Their expertise plays a larger role in shaping municipal financial decisions through varying channels, such as negotiating contracts and long-term planning. Moreover, they can be an invaluable source of information for elected officials, offering insights on everything from best practices to the institutional rules and regulations under which the municipal government functions.

According to the ICMA (2021), there are at least 3,684 municipal chief financial officers in the United States. Municipal governments with chief financial officers vary in size from smaller municipalities such as Bardstown, Kentucky (total population 13,094 in 2019) to large cities such as Dallas, Texas (1.3 million). Along this line, one recent study identified the advanced training that public officials obtained from educational institutions as a significant reason for changes in fiscal outcomes (Spreen et al., 2020).

It is widely believed that instilling greater professionalism in municipal finance and operations can improve fiscal stability and sustainability (Marlowe, 2005). This concern has been heightened amidst municipal experiences with economic fluctuations such as the Great Recession and disasters such as the recent health pandemic. As a result, accumulating fiscal slack for future use has become an important and widely adopted municipal fiscal practice. Although some municipal governments have a separate formal budget stabilization fund to hoard fiscal reserves (Snow et al., 2015), leaving unused balances in operating funds is a more commonly used method of municipal saving.

Professional associations support this practice by setting up a certain benchmark for municipal reserves. The GFOA benchmark for general fund balances, for example, is no less than two months of regular general fund operating revenues or expenditures (GFOA, 2021). Gorina et al. (2019), in their recent examination of 145 municipalities with a population over 25,000 from 2007 to 2012, found that almost all of them have engaged in saving practices to some degree. They also pointed out that variations in municipal saving practices are attributable to differences in need and capacity.

Municipal government finance and operations, therefore, can be characterized as a hybrid of professionalism and political accountability. This combination is present in the last internal factor we will discuss: budget reforms, or approaches to changing the government budgeting process by integrating information and/or advanced techniques into a political decision-making process (Rubin, 1990). At the municipal level, we have seen a remarkable spread of alternative budgeting systems as replacements for or supplements to conventional budgeting mechanisms, such as line-item budgeting (Rubin, 1992). Other examples include program budgeting, zero-based budgeting, and performance-based budgeting.

Performance-based budgeting, which aims to incorporate performance information into the government budgeting process, has become a widely accepted budgeting practice in recent decades. According to Poister and Streib's (1999) survey of 674 municipal governments in 1997, approximately 24% agreed on the importance of performance information for the budgeting process. According to a more recent survey report from the ICMA (2009), about 37% of the 2,214 local governments (including 1,661 municipal governments) that responded indicated using performance information in the budget process. More evidence is needed to ascertain whether budget reforms such as performance-based budgeting make significant changes in municipal fiscal decisions. It is, generally agreed, however, that such reform efforts alter the way in which municipal officials deliberate, communicate, and work (Rivenbark & Kelly, 2006).

Concluding Thoughts

In this chapter, we have explored the complex environment of municipal finance—specifically, the range of inputs that directly impact municipal governments' fiscal decisions and structures. To that end, we took the open-systems approach to municipal finance, which allowed us to explain municipal fiscal decisions as a function of the four core dimensions of system inputs: socioeconomic conditions, institutional settings, external pressures, and internal structures. We reviewed the factors within each dimension, such as economic conditions, demographic structures, state-imposed fiscal rules, interest groups, and different forms of government.

Of those four dimensions, what is the role of institutional settings on municipal financial decision-making—do fiscal institutions help or hinder? This question deserves particularly serious attention. There is a sizable body of work on the impacts of state restrictions related to TELs, debt limits, and balanced-budget requirements. The evidence is clear that these restrictions have affected revenue structures; in particular, municipal reliance on property taxes has diminished. The evidence is much more mixed about the impact on overall revenues and expenditures. Surprisingly, there has been less focus on the extent to which different forms of government and degrees of professionalism impact municipal fiscal decisions and fiscal health. This question definitely calls for further research.

Clearly, a wide variety of factors shape municipal fiscal decisions (and subsequently, municipal fiscal health) directly or indirectly, simultaneously or separately, and collectively or individually. This conclusion may not satisfy those who desire a parsimonious model of municipal fiscal decisions or who are looking for new, groundbreaking information about municipal finance. However, it will help us understand, describe, and explain municipal fiscal decisions in a precise and comprehensive manner, which is our goal in the next chapter.

Chapter 3

Outputs

Municipal Fiscal Trends

The New York State Comptroller announced in September 2019 that the City of Amsterdam was the most fiscally stressed local government in the state. Reasons for the city's dire fiscal stress included an erosion of the city's tax base due to a steady decline in manufacturing, the city's failure to foreclose on properties (particularly in recent years), and improper bookkeeping practices (Subik, 2019). A few months later, with the state's approval, the city decided to incur $7.7 million in debt to close its deficits, which had accumulated over the last ten years without being adequately addressed. In June 2020, a few months after the city's debt issuance and amidst the COVID-19 pandemic, the city adopted its 2020–2021 budget, which included a 4.18% increase in the property tax rate and a 1.38% increase in user fees (Becker, 2020). Can such decisions help the city recover from fiscal stress?

All municipalities make their fiscal decisions—such as developing new revenues, changing tax rates, shifting from reliance on one source to others, increasing or decreasing in expenditures, changing spending priorities, and debt financing—in specific circumstances or environments, as Amsterdam did. In this chapter, we seek to better understand such decisions as the outputs of the municipal fiscal system. We approach these decisions as municipal efforts to convert the environmental inputs discussed in the previous chapter into desired fiscal results. Those fiscal results, in turn, lead to municipal fiscal conditions, or system outcomes, which will be discussed in subsequent chapters. In this chapter, we also examine similarities and differences in the decisions made by U.S. municipal governments

DOI: 10.4324/9780429270765-3

in the complex environment of municipal finance. To do so, we first lay a foundation by identifying broad historical trends in municipal revenues, expenditures, and debt financing and considering why they are occurring.

We use data from the U.S. Census Bureau's Annual Survey of State and Local Government Finances (hereafter, the Census Finance Survey), which covers a more comprehensive range of municipalities and years than other existing budget data sources. The Census Bureau has performed this nationwide voluntary survey every year since the 1960s. It collects information on selected municipalities (in general, larger municipalities) in most years, a complete census is conducted in years ending in 2 and 7. Thus, we focus mainly on those years when fiscal information for all municipalities is available. A few municipalities are excluded from analysis because they did not participate in the survey or reported unreliable information, such as excessively large or small numbers. The Census Finance Survey does have some limitations, which are explained in Appendix A.

Municipal Expenditures

Spending patterns and structures vary across municipalities in response to a complicated set of input factors, as suggested by our framework. Nevertheless, we can identify overall trends, such as the historical trend of real (i.e., adjusted for inflation) municipal total general expenditures, shown in Figure 3.1. We adjust expenditures to population so that we can compare municipalities of different sizes. Total municipal general expenditures include operating expenditures and capital outlays but exclude expenditures for utility, liquor store, or social insurance trust purposes. Figure 3.1 also displays trends in real per-capita municipal total general *operating* expenditures. The difference between the two graph lines indicates the size of municipal capital spending.

Average per-capita total expenditures have grown consistently over the last four decades. Municipal governments, on average, spent $16.9 per capita in 1972, and their average total general spending was almost 83 times greater in 2017, at $1,401.3 per capita. Average per-capita total operating expenditures have shown a similar pattern of increase, from $14.0 per capita in 1972 to $1,170 per capita in 2017. This increase in average municipal total spending is partly attributable to growth in demand for government services. Generally, the demand for municipal services increases as a municipality grows in population. Municipal governments with political motivation to offer the desired level of public goods and services have to increase their spending (Bergstrom & Goodman, 1973; Borcherding & Deacon, 1972; Holcombe & Williams, 2008; Temple, 1996; Turnbull & Djoundourian, 1994)

Not all studies, however, have supported this demand-side argument (Bhattacharyya & Wassmer, 1995; Ott, 1980). According to the Buchanan-Niskanen-Tullock

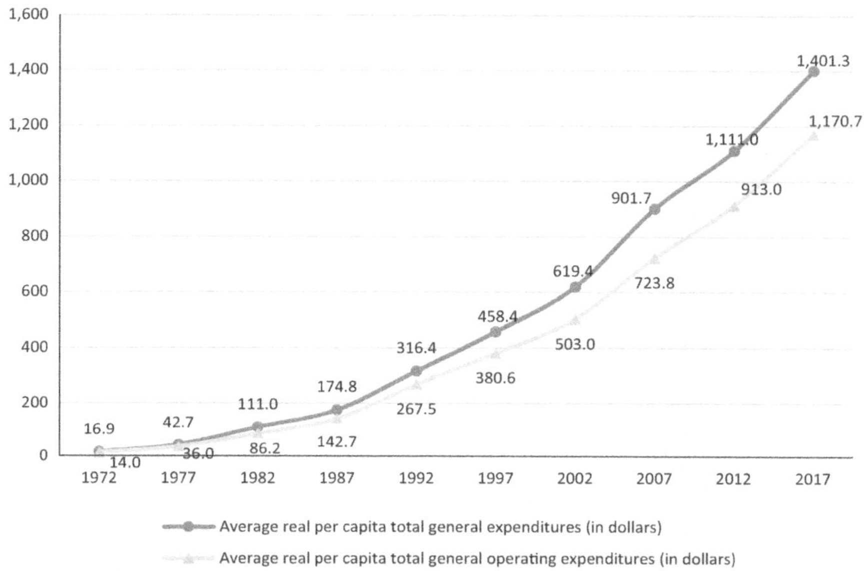

Figure 3.1 Municipal General Expenditures: Total and Operating Spending (Real per Capita)

Source: U.S. Census Bureau

Note: All fiscal information is adjusted for inflation (base year: 2017)

framework (Buchanan, 1967; Buchanan & Tullock, 1962; Niskanen, 1971, 1975, 1991), suppliers of municipal goods and services, such as political decision makers and administrators (or bureaucrats within the public-choice literature), drive increases in government expenditures. Acting with bounded rationality (as opposed to comprehensive rationality), they may fail to pursue socially optimal outcomes due to pursuing their own personal objectives or observing more mundane budgeting practices. Decision makers, for example, may be motivated to employ strategies that are more likely to be successful in the political budget process. They may prefer incremental rather than dramatic or varying budget increases because they are simpler, easier to calculate, and more acceptable by a broader range of budget stakeholders (Wildavsky, 1979). The historical growth of general expenditures in Figure 3.1, from this perspective, can result from such incremental yearly increases.

Care must be taken, however, to distinguish between elected officials who set budgets and administrators who inform the budgeting process. Bureaucrats may aim to enhance their own utility, and their utility-seeking behavior can lead to increased government spending. More specifically, a bureaucrat may take the department's or agency's budget as a source of funds to be used at the individual's discretion. The larger its budget, the more substantial power the department or agency can enjoy. Hence, bureaucrats, who know what they do better than their principals, tend to have a strong motivation to maximize their budgets by drawing on their information superiority (Bendor et al., 1987; Holcombe, 2005). As a result of bureaucrats' desire for budget maximization, government spending can be expected to grow consistently over time. Government spending, from this standpoint, may be higher than the socially optimal level without proper controls (Toma & Toma, 1980).

Institutional rules around budgeting processes can also influence growth patterns in expenditures. Consider the TEL imposed on Kansas local governments, which was lifted and then reimposed, providing a unique opportunity to study its impact on budgets. Springer et al. (2009) found that local officials generally used the upper limit for growth as the benchmark when setting the budget. For example, if the limit allowed a 2% increase, budgets increased by 2% regardless of needs. During the period when the TEL was relaxed, the average rate of increase actually declined. Springer et al. argued that local officials tended to use the maximum allowable increase under the TEL to reduce potential exposure to risks associated with more stringent TELs in the future. In the case of Kansas, the data suggests that expenditures actually increased more with TELs in place than without them.

Some other approaches also exist. For example, special interests can affect the amount of municipal spending. Interest groups can often exercise their influence on municipal governments through voting and lobbying. Studies have found that they not only affect municipal resource allocation (Liu et al., 2010), but also drive budget increases (Booms, 1966; Booth, 1978). For some policy-oriented researchers, a consistent increase in municipal spending is sustained by government decisions not to go back to the previous level of expenditures after certain punctuations and/or changes in policy agendas (Jordan, 2003). According to Rubin (1992), whose approach to municipal budgeting is described as synthetic, municipal spending increases can be fully understood only by considering several different factors such as politics, government structures, and environmental settings concurrently.

Although an overview of total expenditures provides useful insight, understanding what categories of expenditures contribute to the total is fundamental to understanding fiscal health. Are the increases observed in Figure 3.1 driven by core municipal services such as police and fire protection, or by services associated with higher incomes and quality of life such as parks and recreation, libraries, or educational programs (other than K-12 public education)? As shown in Table 3.1, we focus on nine major areas of municipal spending: police, fire, parks and recreation, public works, housing and community development, health and social services, other public security services, general government, and others. These

Table 3.1 Categories of Municipal Spending

Spending object	*Expenditure category in the Census Finance Survey*
Police	Police protection
Fire	Fire protection
Parks and recreation	Parks and recreation, and Libraries
Public works	Highways, Sewerage, Solid waste management, and Parking Facilities
Housing and community development	Housing and community development
Health and social services	Hospitals, Public welfare, and Health services
Other public security services	Protective inspection, and Correctional activities
General government administration	Financial administration, Staff management, and Judicial and legal
Miscellaneous	All others not included in the above categories

spending objects are consistent with the set of major local functions defined in the context of fiscal federalism in the previous chapter. Each object consists of one or more expenditure categories contained in the Census Finance Survey. For example, the police protection object corresponds to the expenditure category of police protection in the Census Finance Survey, while spending on public works is measured as a sum of highway, sewerage, solid waste management, and parking facility expenditures.

Though each municipality is likely to have its unique spending pattern, Table 3.2 shows that the core functions of public works, police, and general government administration have been occupying a larger part of municipal budgets in recent years. The average municipal government spent $2.9 per capita for public works purposes in 1972, corresponding to 17.2% of total general expenditures. It spent $313.1 per capita for the same purposes in 2017, or 22.3% of total general expenditures. This upward pressure on spending has been a driving force behind innovative alternative methods of municipal service delivery, such as contracting out (ICMA, 2019) and intermunicipal collaboration (Park et al., 2021).

Municipal police spending has grown from $2.0 per capita in 1972 to $194.4 per capita in 2017. It has accounted for 11% to 14% of municipal total general expenditures. Zhao et al. (2010), who examined 118 U.S. municipal governments, contended that the incrementalism idea is more dominant than other factors such as socioeconomic conditions and institutional settings in explaining this steady growth in police spending. In contrast, Jung (2006) reported evidence consistent

Table 3.2 Municipal General Expenditures by Object (Real per Capita)

	1972	*1977*	*1982*	*1987*	*1992*	*1997*	*2002*	*2007*	*2012*	*2017*
Total general expenditures	16.9	42.7	111.0	174.8	316.4	458.4	619.4	901.7	1,111.0	1,401.3
Total capital expenditures*	2.9 (17.2)	6.7 (15.7)	24.8 (22.3)	32.1 (18.4)	48.9 (15.5)	77.8 (17.0)	116.4 (18.8)	177.9 (19.7)	198.0 (17.8)	230.6 (16.5)
Total operating expenditure	14.0 (82.8)	36.0 (84.3)	86.2 (77.7)	142.7 (81.6)	267.5 (84.5)	380.6 (83.0)	503.0 (81.2)	723.8 (80.3)	913.0 (82.2)	1,170.7 (83.5)
Police	2.0 (11.8)	5.5 (12.9)	13.4 (12.1)	20.9 (12.0)	40.4 (12.8)	67.7 (14.8)	78.9 (12.7)	119.7 (13.3)	148.2 (13.3)	194.4 (13.9)
Fire	0.5 (3.0)	1.9 (4.4)	4.5 (4.1)	6.9 (3.9)	12.8 (4.0)	18.4 (4.0)	26.3 (4.2)	40.2 (4.5)	51.2 (4.6)	65.1 (4.6)
Parks and recreation	0.4 (2.4)	1.0 (2.3)	3.4 (3.1)	6.3 (3.6)	12.7 (4.0)	23.3 (5.1)	28.0 (4.5)	41.7 (4.6)	52.0 (4.7)	65.8 (4.7)
Public works	2.9 (17.2)	7.0 (16.4)	21.3 (19.2)	37.1 (21.2)	72.9 (23.0)	103.8 (22.6)	138.6 (22.4)	191.2 (21.2)	245.4 (22.1)	313.1 (22.3)
Housing and community development	0.03 (0.2)	0.09 (0.2)	0.7 (0.6)	1.8 (1.0)	3.7 (1.2)	6.3 (1.4)	8.8 (1.4)	14.6 (1.6)	15.9 (1.4)	13.9 (1.0)
Health and social services	0.4 (2.4)	1.1 (2.6)	4.8 (4.3)	6.8 (3.9)	15.0 (4.7)	17.3 (3.8)	22.2 (3.6)	32.8 (3.6)	45.0 (4.1)	55.4 (4.0)
Other public security services	0.001 (0.01)	0.08 (0.2)	0.3 (0.3)	0.8 (0.5)	1.5 (0.5)	2.4 (0.5)	3.5 (0.6)	6.9 (0.8)	6.7 (0.6)	31.1 (2.2)
General government administration	1.4 (8.3)	3.0 (7.0)	12.4 (11.2)	21.6 (12.4)	39.8 (12.6)	55.8 (12.2)	76.2 (12.3)	114.7 (12.7)	139.7 (12.6)	184.4 (13.2)
Miscellaneous	6.3 (37.3)	16.3 (38.2)	25.4 (22.6)	40.6 (23.2)	68.8 (21.7)	85.7 (18.7)	120.6 (19.5)	162.1 (18.0)	208.9 (18.8)	247.5 (17.7)

	1972	*1977*	*1982*	*1987*	*1992*	*1997*	*2002*	*2007*	*2012*	*2017*
Education	0.8 (4.7)	1.5 (3.5)	3.6 (3.2)	4.5 (2.6)	7.4 (2.3)	9.9 (2.2)	15.9 (2.6)	21.6 (2.4)	29.5 (2.7)	38.6 (2.8)
Debt interest	1.0 (5.9)	0.9 (2.1)	5.5 (5.0)	12.4 (7.1)	20.6 (6.5)	20.8 (4.5)	26.6 (4.3)	33.0 (3.7)	36.4 (3.3)	41.6 (3.0)
Others	4.5 (26.6)	13.9 (32.6)	16.3 (14.7)	23.7 (13.6)	40.8 (12.9)	55.0 (12.0)	78.1 (12.6)	107.5 (11.9)	143.0 (12.9)	167.3 (11.9)

* From 1972 to 2017, the public work object's average share of capital expenditures has been 49.8%. The housing and community development and parks and recreation objects together have shared 12.4% on average. The remaining 37.8% have been shared by the other objects.

Source: U.S. Census Bureau

Note: All fiscal information is adjusted for inflation (base year: 2017); each category's percentage share of total general expenditures in parenthesis

with the opposite view. A similar pattern exists for the general government administration object, where spending was $1.4 per capita in 1972 and $184.4 per capita in 2017 (8.3% and 13.2% of total general expenditures, respectively).

Expenditures for parks and recreation, fire, and health and social services have also exhibited consistent growth over the last four decades. The average municipal government spent $0.4 or $0.5 per capita on each of these three functions in 1972; it spent $55 to $66 per capita for the same service purposes in 2017. Each object represented approximately 4% of total general expenditures. Particularly for municipal health and social services, which are not a typical municipal function in the United States, the spending growth has been attributable to increasing delegation of service responsibility to municipalities and/or increasing municipal interest in these services (Committee for the Study of the Future of Public Health, 1988).

Housing and other public security services have been the two objects where municipal governments have spent the least. As of 2017, each accounted for only 1% to 2% of total general expenditures. The miscellaneous category has been large, but its proportion of total general expenditures has consistently decreased, from 37.3% in 1972 to 17.7% in 2017. This category not only includes government-wide administrative costs, such as debt interest payments, insurance premiums, and election spending, but also encompasses unique spending objects that exist only in selected municipalities. Good examples are municipalities in New York and some New England states where public schools operate as agencies of municipal governments. Although education is not a typical municipal function, these municipalities have sizable education spending.

In general, there have been no significant shifts in focus across categories of services in a relative sense. That is, the growth in expenditures was relatively consistent across each category. This is somewhat surprising because we would expect relative shifts as income and wealth have increased across the country. Specifically, we would expect expenditures on essential services, such as police and fire departments, to increase at a slower rate than quality-of-life services such as parks and recreation. This expectation, however, assumes that income or wealth growth is evenly distributed across municipalities. This is likely an unreasonable assumption, as some locations are growing rapidly while others are stagnant and even declining. Hence, the national average will mask these differences. To gain a better understanding, we need to group municipalities into categories and reexamine these patterns across the different groupings.

We explore two specific groupings, by population size and region. For this analysis, we limit our discussions to the most current data available (2017). In Table 3.3, we break out per-capita expenditures by service category across six different population-based groups. Municipal governments with a larger population size had higher per-capita general spending in 2017; the average spending of municipalities with population of 500,000 or more was 2.6 times higher than

Table 3.3 Municipal General Expenditures by Population (Per Capita)

	Police	*Fire*	*Parks and recreation*	*Public works*	*Housing and community development*	*Health and social services*	*Other public security services*	*General government admini-stration*	*Miscell-aneous*	*Capital expen-ditures*	*Total*
1–4,999	175.1 (13.1)	48.7 (3.6)	54.6 (4.1)	320.7 (23.9)	10.4 (0.8)	48.6 (3.6)	34.4 (2.6)	197.9 (14.8)	225.4 (16.8)	223.8 (16.7)	1,339.6 (100.0)
5,000–9,999	245.6 (16.4)	81.9 (5.5)	95.8 (6.4)	316.6 (21.1)	17.4 (1.2)	71.6 (4.8)	17.8 (1.2)	147.9 (9.9)	256.2 (17.1)	248.2 (16.6)	1,499.0 (100.0)
10,000–49,999	249.3 (16.0)	126.1 (8.1)	98.2 (6.3)	276.0 (17.8)	20.7 (1.3)	75.6 (4.9)	19.4 (1.2)	140.8 (9.1)	306.0 (19.7)	242.2 (15.6)	1,554.3 (100.0)
50,000–99,999	274.5 (15.5)	155.4 (8.8)	115.7 (6.5)	262.6 (14.8)	43.3 (2.4)	61.8 (3.5)	26.4 (1.5)	130.2 (7.4)	429.3 (24.3)	270.1 (15.3)	1,769.3 (100.0)
100,000–499,999	309.1 (15.6)	174.6 (8.8)	120.1 (6.1)	273.2 (13.8)	63.5 (3.2)	72.6 (3.7)	32.4 (1.6)	136.8 (6.9)	500.1 (25.3)	295.5 (14.9)	1,977.9 (100.0)
500,000 or over	380.3 (10.8)	195.4 (5.6)	149.0 (4.2)	318.5 (9.1)	132.8 (3.8)	582.9 (16.6)	76.2 (2.2)	180.1 (5.1)	1,019.5 (29.0)	476.6 (13.6)	3,511.3 (100.0)

Source: U.S. Census Bureau

Note: 2017 only; each category's percentage share of total general expenditures in parenthesis

their counterparts with population less than 5,000. The larger the municipality, the more it spent on functions such as police, fire, parks and recreation, housing and community development, health and social service, and miscellaneous purposes.

Two factors are in play when we consider the relationship between the size of the municipality (in terms of population) and expenditure patterns: market demand and costs of production (Shaffer et al., 2004). These factors influence what kinds of businesses the community can support. Although many factors influence market demand, at the community level population is a primary determinant. Communities with larger populations can sustain a larger number and wider variety of businesses. The same applies to municipal services. For example, a public library requires a minimum population size (demand threshold) before it makes sense economically. Thus, smaller municipalities frequently do not have a public library system at all. This pattern plays out across a wide range of municipal services, with larger municipalities offering a greater variety of services. Studies by Holcombe and Williams (2008) and Lee et al. (2016) found that higher population density, as well as racial heterogeneity, appeared to result in higher per-capita spending on some services, such as police and fire, though not on public works.

The second key factor underlying demand thresholds is the cost structure associated with the production of a given public service.[1] It is well understood within the public finance literature (Deller & Rudnicki, 1992) that municipalities face a U-shape cost curve regarding each of the services that they produce. At the smallest scale of operation (i.e., small populations), municipalities cannot capture cost savings through economies of size. As the size of the municipality increases, the per-unit cost production declines. There is, however, a tipping point where per-unit cost actually increases. This can be due to the nature of the production technology underlying the cost structure or higher factor input prices, such as the higher wages that prevail in larger municipalities. Thus, some of the differences in municipal expenditures across population categories can be explained by differences in service production costs.

One can conceptualize these two elements (demand and costs) through the notion of fixed costs associated with many public services. Many services require high levels of initial investment, such as a fire station and associated equipment for fire services, sewer systems and/or water treatment facilities, or physical facilities for libraries. These initial investments can be thought of as fixed costs that must be paid for by taxes. The key question is how to distribute these initial fixed costs over the taxpayer base. For many smaller communities, these fixed costs are substantial and cannot or will not be justified by the taxpayers (through their willingness and ability to pay). As the population (taxpayer) base increases, the fixed costs can be spread over a greater number of people, reducing the burden on any individual taxpayer. Larger municipalities are better positioned to absorb such fixed costs and hence to provide certain services that smaller municipalities cannot justify. For this reason, larger municipalities usually have higher levels of per-capita expenditures than smaller municipalities.

Other factors, such as political representation as an external pressure, also matter. Generally, municipal governments with political mechanisms designed to represent more diverse preferences (e.g., ward elections), which are often observed in larger municipalities, tend to spend more (Hajnal & Trounstine, 2010; Southwick, 1997). As our framework suggests, additional factors such as economic resilience (Chernick et al., 2011) and institutional settings (Shi et al., 2018) should be considered to fully explain between- and within-group variations in municipal spending.

Differences in municipal spending for 2017 by region and service object are shown in Table 3.4. At face value, regional differences in expenditures could be explained because of differences in resident tastes and preferences for services, or even by something as simple as differences in climate. For example, road maintenance costs are higher in northern regions of the United States because of the freeze-and-thaw cycle associated with the changing seasons. There are also historical institutional differences across the states. For example, New England's tradition of relying on town governments diverges from the widespread practice of relying on county governments in the southern and western states. The region from New York to Minnesota has a strong tradition of a tiered system of county and municipal governments. Even within a state, there can be historical institutional differences. For instance, northern Illinois is heavily influenced by the New York and Pennsylvania tradition of tiered governments, whereas the far southern part of Illinois is influenced by French traditions coming from Louisiana.

Municipal governments in New England spent $3,037.3 per capita, the highest amount of any region. However, this is due to the institutional tradition of making public education a municipal government responsibility. After excluding education spending ($1,285.8 per capita on average), New England municipalities had $1,751.5 per capita in total general spending, similar to municipal governments in the Rocky Mountain region. Far West governments had the second-highest level of total general spending, at $2,047.3 per capita. Their spending on police, public works, general government administration, and miscellaneous purposes corresponded to almost 68% of their total general expenditures. Municipal governments in the Rocky Mountain and Mideast regions had $1,775.5 and $1,560.3 of total per-capita general spending, respectively, in 2017. While Rocky Mountain municipalities had the highest capital spending ($382.3 per capita), municipal governments in the Mideast were the highest in public works spending ($440.7 per capita). Another noticeable difference between the two regions is that municipal governments in the Rocky Mountains spent significantly more on health and social services ($51.8 per capita) and general government administration ($280.5 per capita) than those in the Mideast ($15.3 and $166.9 per capita, respectively).

Table 3.4 Municipal General Expenditures by Region (Per Capita)

	Police	*Fire*	*Parks and recreation*	*Public works*	*Housing and community development*	*Health and social services*	*Other public security services*	*General government admini-stration*	*Miscell-aneous*	*Capital expendi-tures*	*Total*
Far West	268.9 (13.1)	93.1 (4.5)	109.5 (5.3)	338.6 (16.5)	24.7 (1.2)	51.8 (2.5)	35.1 (1.7)	280.5 (13.7)	503.8 (24.6)	341.3 (16.7)	2,047.3 (100.0)
Rocky Mountain	195.7 (11.0)	64.9 (3.7)	128.4 (7.2)	326.6 (18.4)	17.4 (1.0)	114.8 (6.5)	7.8 (0.4)	275.9 (15.5)	261.7 (14.7)	382.3 (21.5)	1,775.5 (100.0)
Southwest	225.0 (16.3)	75.7 (5.5)	47.5 (3.4)	237.9 (17.2)	7.1 (0.5)	41.0 (3.0)	21.9 (1.6)	296.0 (21.4)	209.8 (15.2)	222.1 (16.0)	1,384.0 (100.0)
Southeast	295.4 (23.0)	69.7 (5.4)	53.2 (4.1)	257.9 (20.0)	15.5 (1.2)	52.0 (4.0)	10.4 (0.8)	183.8 (14.3)	173.2 (13.5)	175.3 (13.6)	1,286.4 (100.0)
Plains	87.4 (7.0)	46.8 (3.7)	74.1 (5.9)	315.1 (25.1)	15.4 (1.2)	100.0 (8.0)	5.1 (0.4)	131.5 (10.5)	185.8 (14.8)	295.3 (23.5)	1,256.5 (100.0)
Great Lakes	152.4 (13.0)	68.7 (5.9)	53.3 (4.6)	330.5 (28.2)	7.5 (0.6)	21.0 (1.8)	4.4 (0.4)	152.2 (13.0)	217.8 (18.6)	163.1 (13.9)	1,170.9 (100.0)
Mideast	212.8 (13.6)	55.5 (3.6)	63.2 (4.1)	440.7 (28.2)	17.7 (1.1)	15.3 (1.0)	14.0 (0.9)	166.9 (10.7)	363.4 (23.3)	210.8 (13.5)	1,560.3 (100.0)
New England	214.5 (7.1)	160.2 (5.3)	67.6 (2.2)	341.7 (11.3)	21.8 (0.7)	118.9 (3.9)	13.7 (0.5)	111.0 (3.7)	1,707.5 (56.2)	280.4 (9.2)	3,037.3 (100.0)

Source: U.S. Census Bureau

Note: 2017 only; each category's percentage share of total general expenditures in parenthesis

Municipal governments in the remaining four regions spent less than their counterparts in the other regions above. Among these four regions, municipal governments in the Southwest spent the most per capita ($1,384.0), whereas Great Lakes municipal governments spent the least ($1,170.9). Municipal governments in the Southwest, on average, spent the least on parks and recreation ($47.5 per capita), public works ($237.9 per capita), and housing and community development ($7.1 per capita) of any region. Municipal governments in the Plains spent less on police ($87.4 per capita) and fire ($46.8 per capita) purposes than municipalities in the other regions. Miscellaneous spending and other public security services were the two areas where municipal governments in the Southeast ($173.2 per capita) and Great Lakes ($4.4 per capita) regions spent less than other municipalities, respectively. The average size of capital spending for Great Lakes municipalities was also smaller than that of municipalities in the other regions ($163.1 per capita).

Beyond the simple factors outlined above (e.g., climate and historical institutional differences) that could help to explain these spending patterns, the role of political ideology seems clear. Specifically, political ideology is a major determinant of residents' tastes and preferences, as well as their willingness to pay for services. In Figure 3.2, we compare average municipal per-capita total expenditures

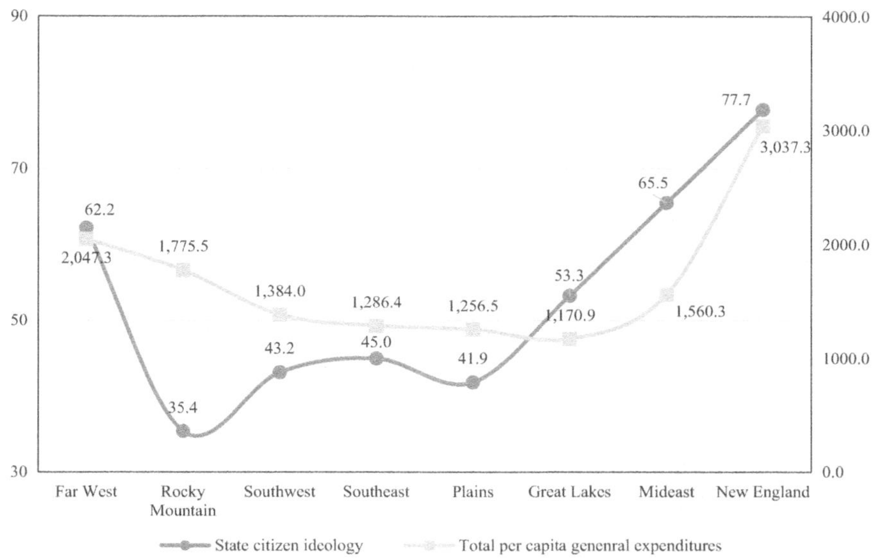

Figure 3.2 State Citizen Ideology and Total Municipal Expenditures

Source: U.S. Census Bureau and Fording (2021)

Note: State citizen ideology is more liberal when closer to 100

in 2017 with the average citizen's political ideology in 2016 (more liberal if closer to 100) for each region. The figure clearly shows that municipal per-capita total general spending is correlated with citizens' political ideology. More liberal regions such as the Far West (62.2) and New England (77.7) had relatively higher municipal expenditures. In contrast, relatively conservative regions such as the Plains (41.9) and Southeast (45.0) had lower per-capita spending. As discussed in the previous chapter, studies such as de Benedictis-Kessner and Warshaw (2016) reported evidence supporting this relationship between politics and spending at the municipal level.

While important, politics does not explain everything. The Rocky Mountain region is an example. Although citizens' political ideology was conservative, municipal per-capita spending in this region was higher than in some other less conservative regions. Zooming in to look at individual states, we find high municipal per-capita spending in Wyoming ($2,416.8), particularly due to their economic growth coupled with a moderate change in population since 2000 (Wyoming Economic Analysis Division, 2021). Municipal governments in the Great Lakes are another example. Their lower average per-capita spending, even though these states are less conservative than some other regions such as the Plains, could be attributable to their economic fluctuations before, during, and after the Great Recession (Anderson, 2010). Yet this generalization may not apply to Great Lakes cities such as Madison, Wisconsin, and Grand Rapids, Michigan, which have experienced a relatively robust recovery since 2010. These exceptional cases remind us again that although we can identify overall average trends, each municipal government operates in a complicated environment.

Municipal Revenues

The historical trend of average real per-capita municipal total general revenues (which include several different sources of revenue such as taxes, charges, and intergovernmental aid but exclude any portion of revenues transferred or contributed to or from utilities, liquor stores, or the insurance trust sector), is shown in Figure 3.3. In general, average per-capita municipal total general revenues have risen steadily since the 1970s. The average municipality received $1,509.4 of revenues per capita in 2017, which was almost 90 times greater than the $16.6 received in 1972. We observe a similar trend for per-capita own-source general revenues, which were $12.7 in 1972 and have grown consistently to reach $1,170.6 in 2017. Because most municipalities operate under balanced-budget requirements or (more precisely) cannot operate in deficit situations, the general pattern in revenues over time closely follows the trends in expenditures presented in Figure 3.1.

For some researchers, the need-capacity approach is an appropriate way to explain these trends. Simply put, municipal spending needs have increased over time, as described above, thereby inducing municipal governments to seek revenue

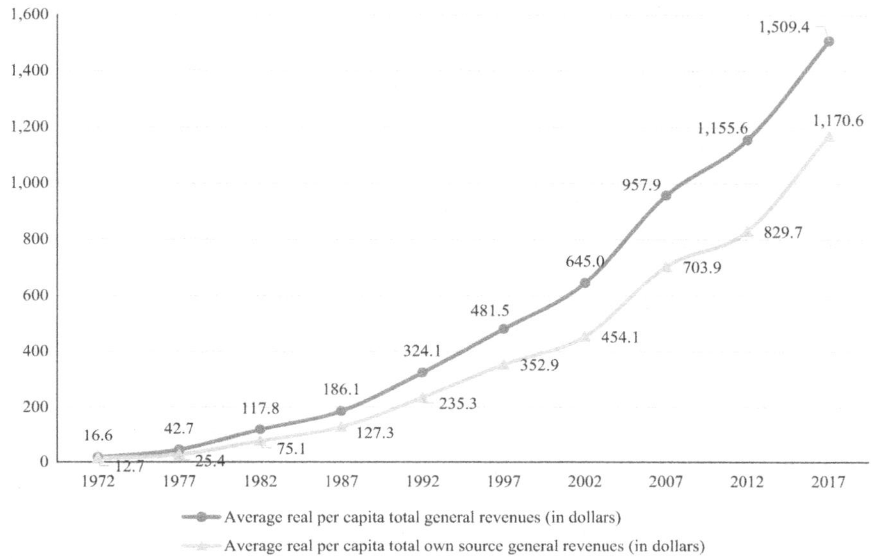

Figure 3.3 Municipal General Revenues: Total and Own Sources (Real per Capita)

Source: U.S. Census Bureau

Note: All fiscal information is adjusted for inflation (base year: 2017)

growth (Chapman & Gorina, 2012). On the capacity side, the growth of the economic base in which municipal governments operate is essential. Municipal governments rely on certain parts of the economic base or activities, such as individual transactions and personal assets, to generate revenues. Naturally, municipal governments are likely to experience stronger and sounder revenue bases as the economy grows. As noted in the introduction, although there have been some noticeable economic downturns (recessions), the United States has experienced consistent increases in domestic production, property values, and personal income over the last several decades (Bureau of Economic Analysis, 2021), contributing to the steady increase in municipal revenues (Wong, 2004).

Scholars in the public-choice strain, however, may raise a caveat regarding this constant revenue increase. Their fundamental idea is that municipal decision makers act as if they are rational, so they are motivated to maximize their utility on the revenue side. It is quite natural, therefore, that governments as leviathans "maximize revenues from whatever sources of taxation are made available to them constitutionally" (Brennan & Buchanan, 1980, p. 26). Such maximization could result in securing revenues that exceed actual spending needs or the socially optimal level, if there exist no proper mechanisms to hold governments accountable. From this standpoint, the consistent growth of municipal revenues reported in

Figure 3.3 may result from municipal decision makers' interest-seeking behavior or the absence of proper controls on municipal governments.

To better understand municipal revenue patterns, average trends of municipal taxes from 1972 to 2017 are provided in Table 3.5. While total per-capita general revenues have increased steadily, municipal per-capita taxes have also grown consistently. Taxes (property, sales, and in some cases income taxes) as a proportion in total revenues dropped between 1972 (45.8%) and 1982 (31.6%) but then rose again, reaching 46.0% in 2017. Property taxes have continuously been the leading tax source at the municipal level. The proportion of total general revenues from property taxes decreased in the 1970s and 1980s but took a slight upward turn between 1992 and 2017.

Per-capita sales taxes have increased consistently over time, from $0.8 per capita in 1972 to $193.3 per capita in 2017. Sales taxes' proportion of general revenues has also grown significantly, from 4.8% to 12.8%. A similar increasing pattern was observed for municipal income taxes, from $0.1 per capita (0.6%) in 1972 to $38.8 per capita (2.6%) in 2017. These figures indicate that sales and income taxes have supplanted a portion of property taxes in municipal taxes and general revenues. Other tax revenues (including, for example, license and gift taxes) have also increased per capita (from $1.0 to $44.2). But the proportion of this category in general revenues has been somewhat consistent since 1977.

These patterns in municipal taxes reflect an intense anti-tax mood in the 1970s and 1980s, which was attributable to three particular fiscal contexts. First, the size of government relative to income had been growing steadily since the 1950s; this led to sharp criticism of unresponsive governments, which were perceived as budget-maximizing units (Shadbegian, 1998; Toma & Toma, 1980). Second, the cost of public services had increased consistently since World War II. The efficiency of governments became subject to growing public backlash (ACIR, 1974; Dye & McGuire, 1997). Lastly, dissatisfaction with property tax administration and constant increases in land values also motivated a strong anti-property tax mood (Hill et al., 2006). This was often described as "the unpopularity of the property tax" (Cabral & Hoxby, 2012, p. 24). As a result, many states adopted stringent forms of restrictions on municipal property taxation and budgets, which, as discussed in the previous chapter, have successfully restricted municipal property taxes and motivated municipal governments to pursue alternative forms of unconstrained resources such as sales and income taxes along with other minor taxes.

Municipal governments have also turned to greater dependence on different service charges and/or fees, as shown in Table 3.6. Total service charges collected by the average municipal government in 1972 were $1.1 per capita. This figure has consistently grown since then, reaching $340.8 per capita in 2017. The proportion of general revenues from charges has increased rapidly, from 6.6% in 1972 to 22.6% in 2017. Sewerage charges have been the largest among the different municipal charges, followed by solid waste charges and hospital charges as of

Table 3.5 Municipal General Revenue Sources: Taxes (Real per Capita)

	1972	1977	1982	1987	1992	1997	2002	2007	2012	2017
Total general revenues	16.6	42.7	117.8	186.1	324.1	481.5	645.0	957.9	1,155.6	1,509.4
Total taxes	7.6 (45.8)	15.7 (36.8)	37.2 (31.6)	63.2 (34.0)	123.9 (38.2)	188.7 (39.2)	238.0 (36.9)	393.6 (41.1)	463.8 (40.9)	694.9 (46.0)
Property taxes	5.7 (34.3)	10.3 (24.1)	23.1 (19.6)	38.6 (20.7)	78.4 (24.2)	110.7 (23.0)	134.3 (20.8)	223.1 (23.3)	275.9 (23.9)	419.1 (27.8)
Sales taxes	0.8 (4.8)	3.6 (8.4)	9.4 (8.0)	16.2 (8.7)	30.5 (9.4)	53.7 (11.2)	65.3 (10.1)	105.3 (11.0)	126.7 (11.0)	193.3 (12.8)
Income taxes	0.1 (0.6)	0.6 (1.4)	1.8 (1.5)	3.1 (1.7)	5.9 (1.8)	9.8 (2.0)	12.4 (1.9)	30.3 (3.2)	27.4 (2.4)	38.8 (2.6)
Other taxes	1.0 (6.0)	1.2 (2.8)	2.9 (2.5)	5.3 (2.8)	9.1 (2.8)	14.5 (3.0)	26.0 (4.0)	34.9 (3.6)	33.8 (2.9)	44.2 (2.9)

Source: U.S. Census Bureau

Note: All fiscal information is adjusted for inflation (base year: 2017); each source's percentage share of total general revenues in parenthesis

Table 3.6 Municipal General Revenue Sources: Charges and Others (Real per Capita)

	1972	*1977*	*1982*	*1987*	*1992*	*1997*	*2002*	*2007*	*2012*	*2017*
Total general revenues	16.6	42.7	117.8	186.1	324.1	481.5	645.0	957.9	1,155.6	1,509.4
Total charges	1.1 (6.6)	3.8 (8.9)	17.5 (14.9)	29.6 (15.9)	62.8 (19.4)	97.9 (20.3)	133.9 (20.8)	197.1 (20.6)	264.9 (22.9)	340.8 (22.6)
Sewerage	0.4 (2.4)	1.0 (2.3)	4.1 (3.5)	11.5 (6.2)	27.0 (8.3)	41.4 (8.6)	61.6 (9.6)	92.1 (9.6)	126.3 (10.9)	155.8 (10.3)
Solid waste	0.1 (0.6)	0.3 (0.7)	1.3 (1.1)	3.2 (1.7)	7.7 (2.4)	13.9 (2.9)	20.3 (3.1)	28.1 (2.9)	38.1 (3.3)	43.1 (2.9)
Hospitals	0.3 (1.8)	0.7 (1.6)	4.4 (3.7)	4.4 (2.4)	8.5 (2.6)	10.3 (2.1)	12.0 (1.9)	19.6 (2.0)	28.1 (2.4)	38.9 (2.6)
Parks and recreation	0.06 (0.4)	0.1 (0.2)	0.5 (0.4)	1.3 (0.7)	2.3 (0.7)	4.0 (0.8)	6.3 (1.0)	9.8 (1.0)	15.5 (1.3)	19.4 (1.3)
Air transport	0.02 (0.1)	0.04 (0.1)	0.2 (0.2)	0.3 (0.2)	0.5 (0.2)	0.7 (0.1)	0.9 (0.1)	1.6 (0.2)	2.3 (0.2)	2.4 (0.2)
Housing and community	0.009 (0.1)	0.02 (0.0)	0.06 (0.1)	0.2 (0.1)	0.4 (0.1)	1.1 (0.2)	1.0 (0.2)	1.9 (0.2)	3.2 (0.3)	3.6 (0.2)
Others	0.2 (1.2)	1.6 (3.7)	6.9 (5.9)	8.7 (4.7)	16.4 (5.1)	26.5 (5.5)	31.8 (4.9)	44.0 (4.6)	51.4 (4.4)	77.6 (5.1)
Other own source revenues	4.0 (24.1)	5.9 (13.8)	20.4 (17.3)	34.5 (18.5)	48.6 (15.0)	66.3 (13.8)	82.2 (12.7)	113.2 (11.8)	101.0 (8.7)	134.9 (8.9)

Source: U.S. Census Bureau

Note: All fiscal information is adjusted for inflation (base year: 2017); each source's percentage share of total general revenues in parenthesis

2017. Other charges (for example, education, highway, parking, court, and public library fees) have also been significant revenue generators for municipal governments. Other own-source revenues, including payments in lieu of taxes from private sources, voluntary contributions, sponsorships, and sale of investments, have steadily declined as a proportion of total revenues since 1972, but have still been significant municipal revenue sources.

This trend is often described as revenue diversification, which primarily means that government revenue structures have shifted away from the traditional and most salient tax sources toward non-traditional revenue sources (Oates, 1991; Wagner, 1976). Historically, the tax revolt movement in the 1970s and 1980s and economic recessions, during which municipal governments experienced severe revenue constraints and hence were motivated to find new revenue sources, have been crucial moments for revenue diversification (Carroll, 2009; Hendrick, 2002).

The outcomes of revenue diversification remain unclear (Park & Park, 2018). Proponents argue that revenue diversification can help municipal fiscal sustainability, as it can make municipal revenue bases sound and robust. In essence, the logic behind portfolio theory in finance applies to municipal government fiscal policy: much as a diversified investment portfolio introduces lower risk and enhanced stability, a diversified stream of government revenues also contributes to stability and a certain degree of predictability. Opponents, however, insist that revenue diversification often leads to fiscal illusion, thereby resulting in unnecessary increases in municipal spending.

Our focus thus far has been on municipal own-source revenues, but increasingly municipalities are receiving larger absolute levels of intergovernmental aid from both federal and state governments, as shown in Table 3.7. Total per-capita intergovernmental aid to municipal governments has increased consistently since 1972. Its proportion of general revenues, however, has been waning except for a few years in the early 1970s (e.g., the Nixon administration policy of unrestricted general revenue sharing) and later around economic recessions. In the late 1970s and the 1980s, federal and state aid was generally high for countercyclical purposes, or to mitigate the impacts of municipal revenue restrictions. In many cases, as a growing number of states imposed limits on municipalities' ability to raise revenues (e.g., property tax limits), they also increased grants and aid to offset lost locally generated revenues. However, these funding increases in response to TELs were short-lived. Later, such aid programs were criticized for their inefficiency (Randall et al., 2016). Municipal governments, on the other hand, succeeded in increasing their own-source revenues sufficiently through diversification (Sun, 2014).

The growth in intergovernmental aid often took the form of contracts for services. Increasingly, municipalities, particularly smaller ones, have contracted with their larger neighbors for service, thus transferring funds from one municipality to

Table 3.7 Municipal General Revenue Sources: Intergovernmental Aid (Real per Capita)

	1972	*1977*	*1982*	*1987*	*1992*	*1997*	*2002*	*2007*	*2012*	*2017*
Total general revenues	16.6	42.7	117.8	186.1	324.1	481.5	645.0	957.9	1,155.6	1,509.4
Total IG aid	4.0 (24.1)	17.3 (40.5)	42.7 (36.2)	58.8 (31.6)	88.8 (27.4)	128.7 (26.7)	190.8 (29.6)	254.0 (26.5)	325.9 (28.2)	338.7 (22.5)
Federal IG aid	0.4 (2.4)	6.9 (16.2)	14.3 (12.1)	13.0 (7.0)	13.3 (4.1)	19.5 (4.0)	26.6 (4.1)	39.9 (4.2)	58.8 (5.1)	52.1 (3.5)
State IG aid	3.4 (20.5)	9.1 (21.3)	24.6 (20.9)	38.2 (20.5)	62.3 (19.2)	89.1 (18.5)	136.0 (21.1)	179.1 (18.7)	220.1 (19.0)	231.5 (15.3)
Local IG aid	0.2 (1.2)	1.3 (3.0)	3.7 (3.1)	7.7 (4.1)	13.2 (4.1)	20.1 (4.2)	28.3 (4.4)	35.1 (3.7)	46.9 (4.1)	55.1 (3.7)

Source: U.S. Census Bureau

Note: All fiscal information is adjusted for inflation (base year: 2017); each source's percentage share of total general revenues in parenthesis

another. This arrangement could be a direct contract between two parties, or many smaller municipalities may enter a cooperative agreement with a larger neighboring municipal government for police and fire protection, among other services. The pattern shown in Table 3.5 may reflect these intergovernmental relationships.

Now, let us turn to municipal general revenues by population size for the year 2017. When looking at expenditures, we saw notable differences by municipal size and geographic location; we would reasonably expect similar differences in revenues. As shown in Table 3.8, the average size of municipal per-capita total general revenues goes up with rising population size. For example, municipal governments with populations of less than 5,000 averaged $1,466.2 of per-capita total general revenues in 2017, whereas their counterparts with populations over 500,000 had $3,722.7 of per-capita total general revenues. A similar pattern exists for each revenue category. Per-capita property taxes and per-capita charges, for example, were 1.9 and 2.5 times greater, respectively, in municipalities with population over 500,000 than in those with fewer than 5,000 residents. Their proportions of overall general revenues, however, were relatively smaller in larger municipalities, where other revenue sources such as sales taxes, income taxes, and intergovernmental transfers were proportionally larger.

From the need-capacity standpoint introduced above, higher municipal revenues in larger municipalities make sense because these communities have to deal with a higher level of spending needs than their counterparts with smaller populations, as shown by the expenditure analysis results (see also Kioko & Martell, 2012). Their capacity to meet such higher spending needs while addressing resource constraints such as TELs is often supported by their strong revenue bases (Ladd & Bradbury, 1988) and greater diversification (Hendrick, 2002; Krane et al., 2004) compared to smaller communities. In addition, municipal governments' internal capacity may also matter. Using nontraditional revenue sources is an innovative step for municipalities (Afonso, 2018), and prior evidence suggests that larger population size is often correlated with greater capacity to seek and adopt innovations (Ahn, 2011; Berry & Berry, 2018). From the perspective of public administration capacity, larger municipalities have the professional staff to explore and use a wider range of revenue sources than smaller municipalities.

Similar to the results of our expenditure analysis, there are noticeable geographic differences in revenues (see Table 3.9). Municipal governments in New England ($3,097.1 per capita) and the Far West ($2,143.8 per capita) collected more revenues than municipal governments in the other regions. Municipal governments in the Rocky Mountain ($2,007.2 per capita), Southwest ($1,779.2 per capita), and Mideast ($1,584.9 per capita) regions had mid-size average revenues. Notably, in Southwest municipalities general revenues were significantly larger than general expenditures ($1,286.4 per capita). This result may be in line with Su (2019), who found that Southwest municipalities had the highest average level of accumulated fiscal slack. Municipal governments in the Southeast ($1,377.2

Table 3.8 Municipal General Revenues by Population (Per Capita)

	Property taxes	*Sales taxes*	*Income taxes*	*Other taxes*	*Charges*	*Other own source revenues*	*Intergovern-mental aid*	*Total*
1–4,999	413.0	176.8	30.3	40.3	320.8	137.2	347.8	1,466.20
	(28.2)	(12.1)	(2.1)	(2.7)	(21.9)	(9.4)	(23.7)	(100.0)
5,000–9,999	411.6	232	59.1	48.7	390.1	118.7	274.3	1,534.50
	(26.8)	(15.1)	(3.9)	(3.2)	(25.4)	(7.7)	(17.9)	(100.0)
10,000–49,999	431	234.1	69	58.7	400.6	124	293.7	1,611.10
	(26.8)	(14.5)	(4.3)	(3.6)	(24.9)	(7.7)	(18.2)	(100.0)
50,000–99,999	512.1	165.5	37.8	63.1	402.3	147	387.5	1,715.30
	(29.9)	(9.6)	(2.2)	(3.7)	(23.5)	(8.6)	(22.6)	(100.0)
100,000–499,999	493	349.4	47.7	71.3	459.2	165.8	469.3	2,055.70
	(24.0)	(17.0)	(2.3)	(3.5)	(22.3)	(8.1)	(22.8)	(100.0)
500,000 or more	799.1	501.9	353.7	101	804.2	257.2	905.6	3,722.70
	(21.5)	(13.5)	(9.5)	(2.7)	(21.6)	(6.9)	(24.3)	(100.0)

Source: U.S. Census Bureau

Note: 2017 only; each source's percentage share of total general revenues in parenthesis

Table 3.9 Municipal General Revenues by Region (Per Capita)

	Property taxes	*Sales taxes*	*Income taxes*	*Other taxes*	*Charges*	*Other own source revenues*	*Intergovern-mental aid*	*Total*
Far West	290.6	401.6	34.3	65.0	515.2	182.2	654.9	2,143.8
	(13.6)	(18.7)	(1.6)	(3.0)	(24.0)	(8.5)	(30.5)	(100.0)
Rocky Mountain	242.7	436.4	30.9	101.8	437.2	191.5	566.7	2,007.2
	(12.1)	(21.7)	(1.5)	(5.1)	(21.8)	(9.5)	(28.2)	(100.0)
Southwest	555.0	464.3	6.4	37.4	323.7	165.2	227.2	1,779.2
	(31.2)	(26.1)	(0.4)	(2.1)	(18.2)	(9.3)	(12.8)	(100.0)
Southeast	333.0	234.6	16.7	66.3	294.5	120.2	311.8	1,377.1
	(24.2)	(17.0)	(1.2)	(4.8)	(21.4)	(8.7)	(22.6)	(100.0)
Plains	376.5	143.5	2.9	23.8	400.2	119.9	297.4	1,364.2
	(27.6)	(10.5)	(0.2)	(1.7)	(29.3)	(8.8)	(21.8)	(100.0)
Great Lakes	336.9	43.6	100.0	23.0	318.6	136.0	317.4	1,275.5
	(26.4)	(3.4)	(7.8)	(1.8)	(25.0)	(10.7)	(24.9)	(100.0)
Mideast	774.8	28.3	83.6	51.0	228.2	118.9	300.1	1,584.9
	(48.9)	(1.8)	(5.3)	(3.2)	(14.4)	(7.5)	(18.9)	(100.0)
New England	1,520.6	20.6	1.5	26.6	400.1	112.6	1,015.1	3,097.1
	(49.1)	(0.7)	(0.0)	(0.9)	(12.9)	(3.6)	(32.8)	(100.0)

Source: U.S. Census Bureau

Note: 2017 only; each source's percentage share of total general revenues in parenthesis

per capita), Plains ($1,364.2 per capita), and Great Lakes ($1,275.5 per capita) regions had the lowest average per-capita total general revenues, parallel to the findings of our expenditure analysis.

Municipal governments in New England relied heavily on property taxes and intergovernmental transfers in 2017: $1,520.6 per capita (49.1% of total general revenues) and $1,015.1 per capita (32.8%), respectively. As discussed, the municipal education function, primarily funded by property taxes (e.g., in Connecticut and Rhode Island) and/or intergovernmental aid (e.g., Delaware and Vermont), was the main reason. In contrast, Far West and Rocky Mountain municipal governments collected significantly lower average property taxes in 2017. Instead, they relied more on sales taxes, income taxes, and intergovernmental transfers. From a fiscal restriction standpoint, this may be the result of historical tax revolt movements and subsequent state controls over municipal property taxes, which have occurred in, for example, California, Colorado, Idaho, Oregon, and Washington (Sigelman et al., 1983).

Whereas municipal governments in the Southeast, Plains, and Great Lakes regions relied quite evenly on property taxes, charges, and intergovernmental transfers, the analysis indicates that property taxes were the most salient revenue source for municipal governments in the Mideast and Southwest ($774.8 and $555.0 per capita, respectively). This may be attributable to certain states such as New Jersey ($2,557.3 per-capita property taxes) and Texas ($891.6 per-capita property taxes) where municipal governments have historically relied on property taxes more than any other revenue source (Gordon et al., 2016). Particularly in New Jersey, municipal governments have had fewer options for additional tax and revenue sources under state law; they may not collect sales (with few exceptions) or income taxes and can collect fees and charges only for certain specified purposes.

Municipal Debt

Municipal governments rely on debt financing when their resource capacity is insufficient to address short- and long-term service obligations; government debt "has to be paid off in the future to maintain a balance over time" (Rubin, 2019, p. 4). The historical trend of average real per-capita municipal total debt outstanding from 1972 to 2017 appears in Figure 3.4. The typical U.S. municipal government has consistently accumulated outstanding debt since the 1970s. The average municipality had $29.7 per capita of outstanding debt in 1972 but 50 times as much in 2017 ($1,499.4 per capita).

We disentangle total per-capita outstanding debt into three different categories: long-term debt outstanding for private purposes, long-term debt outstanding for other public purposes, and short-term debt. We report the findings

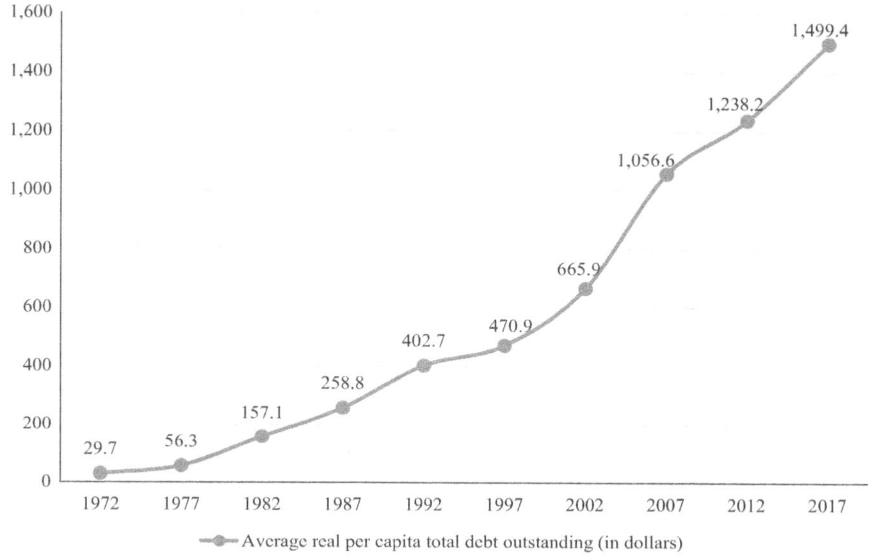

Figure 3.4 Municipal Debt Outstanding (Real per Capita)
Source: U.S. Census Bureau
Note: All fiscal information is adjusted for inflation (base year: 2017)

in Table 3.10. In comparison with long-term debt carried for a more extended period, short-term debt is typically payable within less than one year from its issuance and is generally incurred to address cash flow within a fiscal year or to balance the accounts at the end of the fiscal year. Long-term debt outstanding for private purposes means credit obligations of a municipal government to support private-sector activities such as industrial development or private ventures (e.g., stadiums and convention centers); otherwise, long-term debt outstanding is classified as for public purposes, such as infrastructure investments and other general operations (U.S. Census Bureau, 2006).

The average municipal government had $28.3 per capita of total long-term outstanding debt in 1972. Over the next 45 years, this figure rose to $1,458.4 per capita in 2017. The proportion of total debt that is long-term in nature has consistently exceeded 95%, increasing from 95.3% in 1972 to 97.9% in 2017. Most of the long-term outstanding debt that the average municipal government held was for other public purposes (65.8% to 97.5%). Per-capita municipal debt for other public purposes has increased significantly since 2002 due to economic recessions (Hildreth & Zorn, 2005). Average per-capita long-term outstanding debt for private purposes grew rapidly in the 1980s and 1990s especially. Studies offered some reasons for this phenomenon, including (1) competition among

Table 3.10 Municipal Outstanding Long-Term and Short-Term Debt (Real per Capita)

	1972	*1977*	*1982*	*1987*	*1992*	*1997*	*2002*	*2007*	*2012*	*2017*
Total debt outstanding	29.7	56.3	157.1	258.8	402.7	470.9	665.9	1,056.6	1,238.2	1,499.4
Total long-term debt outstanding	28.3 (95.3)	55.0 (97.5)	151.2 (96.3)	253.0 (98.3)	391.7 (97.5)	462.3 (98.3)	650.4 (97.8)	1,032.8 (98.4)	1,209.4 (98.3)	1,458.4 (97.9)
Private purposes	0.0 (0.0)	0.0 (0.0)	28.0 (17.5)	66.9 (20.0)	137.9 (31.7)	108.3 (21.4)	109.8 (15.6)	101.8 (6.9)	105.4 (6.2)	107.1 (5.5)
Other public purposes	28.3 (95.3)	55.0 (97.5)	123.2 (78.8)	186.1 (78.3)	253.8 (65.8)	354.0 (76.9)	540.6 (82.2)	931.0 (91.5)	1,104.0 (92.1)	1,351.3 (92.4)
Total short-term debt outstanding	1.3 (4.7)	1.4 (2.5)	5.9 (3.7)	5.8 (1.7)	11.0 (2.5)	8.6 (1.7)	15.5 (2.2)	23.7 (1.6)	28.8 (1.7)	41.0 (2.1)

Source: U.S. Census Bureau

Note: All fiscal information is adjusted for inflation (base year: 2017); each type's percentage share of total debt outstanding in parenthesis

jurisdictions to attract industrial firms and (2) changes in federal aid and tax policy such as the Tax Reform Act of 1986 (Bahl & Duncombe, 1993). Furthermore, with the historically low interest rates since the end of the Great Recession, the costs of incurring debt have been modest. Indeed, the very low interest rates make incurring debt to finance capital improvement plans or infrastructure projects seem economically prudent.

Total per-capita short-term outstanding debt has increased over time from $1.3 in 1972 to $41.0 in 2017. However, its proportion of total outstanding debt has dropped from 4.7% to 2.1%. Since the Census Finance Survey covers only debt outstanding and not debt issuance, this fact does not mean that the average municipal government has relied less on short-term debt. On the contrary, increasing municipal reliance on short-term debt such as bank loans and notes has been well documented by prior studies (Hildreth & Zorn, 2005; Ivanov & Zimmermann, 2018). In response, the General Accounting Standards Board issued a new accounting standard (GASB Statement 88) in 2018 that requires municipal governments to disclose information on their short-term debt in their annual financial reports (Farmer, 2018).

The constant increase in municipal debt can be attributed to increasing demands for public services and subsequent expansion of government activities at the municipal level. Farnham (1985) and Sharp (1986) focused on socioeconomic conditions as significant determinants of municipal debt use. Farnham (1985), in his examination of 2,087 municipalities, found that when a municipality had a larger total and youth population, it incurred more long-term and total debt. Socioeconomic factors can directly affect municipal debt levels through higher service demands; they can also indirectly impact municipal debt through lower borrowing costs (Palumbo & Zaporowski, 2012) or changes in municipal fiscal structures (Shon & Kim, 2019).

Economic growth patterns directly influence the need for capital (infrastructure) investments. Municipalities that are growing in terms of income, population, and/or employment find that the existing infrastructure becomes insufficient and that new investments to alleviate inadequate capacity are required. This requires incurring additional debt burdens. On the other hand, municipalities that are shrinking, or losing population and employment, may also need to make significant infrastructure reinvestments. When declining municipalities face revenue shortfalls, a common response is to defer infrastructure maintenance. While this strategy may address short-term revenue shortages, the deferred maintenance eventually results in an accelerating deterioration of essential infrastructure. In time, the costs of bringing required infrastructure back to acceptable standards requires major investments which in turn necessitate high levels of debt. The Flint, Michigan, water infrastructure disaster is one well-known example.

Alternatively, growth in municipal debt could result from government responses to fiscal constraints. Several prior studies have offered evidence that state-imposed TELs have led to increased municipal debt levels (Bennett & DiLorenzo, 1982;

Cope & Grubb, 1982; Sharp & Elkins, 1987). When state budgetary restrictions limit municipal revenue capacity and fiscal flexibility, municipal governments may incur more debt to address these constraints. However, more recent studies have found opposite evidence, suggesting that TELs are associated with a decrease in municipal debt levels (Kioko & Zhang, 2019; Maher & Deller, 2013b). This makes sense from a creditworthiness standpoint. Credit rating agencies often view the implementation of TELs as reducing municipal governments' capacity to pay their liabilities (Maher et al., 2016). Hence, when TELs appear, municipal governments may encounter higher borrowing costs, which can motivate decision makers to rely less on debt financing.

This increase in municipal debt levels is particularly interesting since, as discussed in the previous chapter, nearly all states have imposed limitations on municipal debt issuance and most of them also have bond referendum requirements at the municipal level. Theoretically, those rules are expected to reduce municipal debt. Our findings, however, may raise questions about the actual outcomes of these measures. It is, in fact, largely unclear whether the restrictiveness and scope of state-imposed debt limitations are effective in curbing municipal debt (Kiewiet & Szakaty, 1996; Yusuf et al., 2013). Kelly and Massey (1996), in their study of bond referendum requirements in the U.S. context, also asserted that municipal officials have been able to easily persuade voters to vote favorably on debt issues through voter education or public advertisements. Overall, the institutional design of state-imposed controls may make a difference in their results.

In Table 3.11, we analyze municipal debt levels in 2017 by population size. One noticeable observation is that per-capita total municipal debt outstanding was greater in larger municipalities. Governments with population of 500,000 or more had a significantly larger amount of per-capita total debt outstanding ($6,463.5) than the other population groups—4.7 times greater than municipalities of fewer than 5,000 people ($1,383.6 per capita). This is consistent with Farnham (1985) and Sharp (1986), who found that larger municipal population size is one of the most significant determinants of increased municipal debt use.

Another interesting observation is that larger municipalities have relied on debt for private purposes more than their counterparts with smaller populations. This may reflect the idea that municipal governments serving larger populations are more likely to adopt or attract large-scale investment projects for economic or industrial development (Man & Rosentraub, 1998). Smaller municipalities, on the other hand, have had proportionally greater amounts of per-capita short-term debt. As noted previously, these data do not fully capture the actual municipal use of short-term debt, because they report outstanding debt, not all issued debt. But they may reflect Lofton and Kioko's (2021) findings that smaller municipalities may have limited revenue capacity to pay back or avoid short-term debt.

Table 3.11 Municipal Outstanding Debt by Population (Per Capita)

	Long-term debt outstanding—Private purposes	*Long-term debt outstanding—Other public purposes*	*Short-term debt outstanding*	*Total*
1–4,999	81.0 (5.9)	1,258.8 (91.0)	43.8 (3.2)	1,383.6 (100.0)
5,000–9,999	117.1 (7.1)	1,505.4 (90.9)	33.3 (2.0)	1,655.8 (100.0)
10,000–49,999	209.7 (11.6)	1,564.9 (86.6)	32.7 (1.8)	1,807.3 (100.0)
50,000–99,999	199.8 (10.1)	1,748.2 (88.2)	33.2 (1.7)	1,981.2 (100.0)
100,000–499,999	357.0 (12.7)	2,432.4 (86.6)	18.2 (0.6)	2,807.6 (100.0)
500,000 or more	828.2 (12.8)	5,576.6 (86.3)	58.7 (0.9)	6,463.5 (100.0)

Source: U.S. Census Bureau

Note: 2017 only; each type's percentage share of total debt outstanding in parenthesis

Municipal per-capita outstanding debt by region in 2017 is presented in Table 3.12. Consistent with our revenue and expenditure analysis results, municipal governments in New England had the highest per-capita total outstanding debt in 2017 ($2,276.7). More than 95% of this amount ($2,165.4 per capita) was for other public purposes, including support for public schools. New England municipal governments also had $105.3 per capita in short-term outstanding debt (4.6% of the total). This relatively high number was caused primarily by municipalities in Massachusetts ($188.4 per capita), where public officials' fiscal flexibility is limited by a state-imposed binding cap on property taxes resulting from Proposition $2^1/_2$ (Rothenberg & Smoke, 1982).

Municipal governments in the Far West had the second-highest level of per-capita total outstanding debt ($1,655.7 per capita), exclusively for other public purposes. Within-group analysis shows that this result was heavily impacted by an excessive level of municipal debt outstanding in Honolulu, Hawaii ($5,227.6 per capita). The city has been cited by various sources (e.g., Truth in Accounting, 2021) as one of the nation's most fiscally stressed municipalities. The major reasons behind Honolulu's impoverished fiscal landscape include some recent

Table 3.12 Municipal Outstanding Debt by Region (Per Capita)

	Long-term debt outstanding—Private purposes	*Long-term debt outstanding—Other public purposes*	*Short-term debt outstanding*	*Total*
Far West	44.6 (2.7)	1,606.8 (97.0)	4.3 (0.3)	1,655.7 (100.0)
Rocky Mountain	140.6 (9.4)	1,341.9 (89.6)	15.3 (1.0)	1,497.8 (100.0)
Southwest	262.2 (18.0)	1,188.8 (81.5)	7.9 (0.5)	1,458.9 (100.0)
Southeast	133.8 (9.0)	1,347.1 (90.4)	8.8 (0.6)	1,489.7 (100.0)
Plains	109.5 (7.4)	1,355.3 (91.0)	24.6 (1.7)	1,489.4 (100.0)
Great Lakes	57.2 (3.7)	1,447.5 (94.2)	32.3 (2.1)	1,537.0 (100.0)
Mideast	21.1 (1.5)	1,128.0 (82.7)	215.5 (15.8)	1,364.6 (100.0)
New England	6.0 (0.3)	2,165.4 (95.1)	105.3 (4.6)	2,276.7 (100.0)

Source: U.S. Census Bureau

Note: 2017 only; each type's percentage share of total debt outstanding in parenthesis

political decisions that failed to address budget shortfalls, along with ongoing large-scale infrastructure projects.

Municipal governments in the Mideast had the lowest level of per-capita outstanding debt in 2017 ($1,364.6). However, there was considerable within-group variation here as well. Municipal governments in New Jersey and New York, on one hand, had sizable debt on average ($2,064.1 and $2,191.1 per capita, respectively). In particular, municipal governments in the two states had relatively higher average short-term outstanding debt ($390.3 and $556.7 per capita, respectively) than other municipalities in the region (see also Lofton & Kioko, 2021). On the other hand, municipal governments in Pennsylvania and Delaware had a relatively lower level of outstanding debt ($641.4 and $897.0 per capita, respectively).

Municipal governments in the remaining five regions—Rocky Mountain, Southwest, Southeast, Plains and Great Lakes—had similar levels and patterns of outstanding debt in 2017. Municipal debt for private purposes was relatively high in the Southwest, however. This was probably due to heavy use of debt for industrial development in Texas and New Mexico. Particularly in New Mexico, government debt such as industrial revenue bonds "has played the most significant role in defining a cost advantage on investment decisions," because there have been "limited incentives available in New Mexico" (Prager Company, 2002, p. 3).

Concluding Thoughts

To better understand notions of municipal fiscal health and craft strategies or best practices to enhance fiscal health, we need a solid understanding of where the money is coming from (revenues) and going (expenditures). In this chapter, we have laid a foundation to help us better understand those municipal fiscal trends. We first defined municipal fiscal decisions as responses to a variety of input factors suggested by our framework. To understand these varying decisions, we analyzed municipal fiscal trends in expenditures, revenues, and debt financing, using Census Finance Survey data from 1972 to 2017. We not only described average trends across municipalities but also illuminated significant variations among municipalities with different population sizes and by region. Several theoretical ideas such as incrementalism, budget-maximizing bureaucracy, punctuated equilibrium, the leviathan model of government, and revenue constraints and diversification were discussed to explain those trends. A multitude of input factors such as politics, service responsibilities, socioeconomic conditions, and fiscal rules and institutions were considered to understand fiscal variations among municipal governments.

Our findings in this chapter suggest several important policy questions. First, U.S. municipal governments have experienced consistent growth in spending, even relative to inflation. This raises an old but still unresolved question: what is the optimal level of government size and growth? Some might argue that municipal governments are inefficient with an excessive level of spending, while others might advocate that municipal spending is justifiable to secure an adequate or improved quantity and quality of services. If so, are current fiscal restrictions on municipal governments effective? Should they be sustained, revised, or removed? Second, is the current American municipal revenue system appropriate to meet increasing service needs and spending? Service needs increase when economic recessions and disasters hit communities, as the COVID-19 pandemic illustrated vividly. Do municipal governments have revenue structures that are resilient enough to address such needs? Third, what might be the long-term outcomes of increasing municipal reliance on debt financing? Debt financing could be readily justified during the recent period of historically low interest rates. But as interest rates return to levels more consistent with historical averages, will the high levels of debt, particularly long-term debt, create difficulties? Can municipal governments afford high debt levels as economic conditions improve? If not, should they be subject to stricter controls in addition to the recent GASB requirements? All these questions deserve further attention from scholars and practitioners.

We are now ready to move to a discussion of fiscal condition, which is treated as a system outcome in this book. First, we will consider measurement issues in the next two chapters. Our particular focus will be on understanding the historical development of the concept of fiscal condition, measuring fiscal health and stress, and systematic comparisons of different measures. Our approach to fiscal condition will resemble how we proceeded in this chapter: analyzing trends in municipal fiscal condition, followed by a robust discussion of the antecedents and consequences of municipal fiscal health and stress. Our synthetic framework will continue to guide our endeavor to understand the nature and dynamics of municipal fiscal conditions.

Note

1. This literature often refers to both scale and size efficiencies. From a purely technical perspective, scale economies refer to the underlying production technology, or production function, whereas size economics refer to the underlying cost function. Size economies introduce prices associated with inputs (e.g., labor wage rates), whereas scale economies do not consider differences in prices.

Chapter 4

Outcomes

Measuring Fiscal Health

A good deal of research has been produced seeking to operationalize fiscal health. Today, we understand fiscal health as a government's ability to balance its financial obligations with its available revenue streams (Maher, Ebdon et al., 2020; Maher & Nollenberger, 2009). How a government measures its fiscal health, however, has changed significantly over the years, largely due to lack of agreement on what constitutes fiscal health. Without a consistent definition, consensus on a consistent measurement approach has been absent.

To understand how fiscal health is measured and how that measurement has changed over time, we must first understand how the meaning of fiscal health has changed over time. Historically, the concept of a government's fiscal health has been defined in a number of ways, or through different lenses, both in the literature and in practice (Justice & Scorsone, 2013; McDonald, 2018). These lenses can be categorized as either accounting and budgetary or economic in nature. Although each lens attempts to determine similar aspects of the fiscal condition of a government, they do so do in the context of the fields that drive the lens.

From the accounting and public budgeting literature comes a view of fiscal health centered on a government's capacity to provide or expand a program or service. Historically, the budgeting side of the literature has pointed toward an understanding of fiscal health as simply "the extent to which [a government's] financial resources exceed its spending obligations" (Berry, 1994, p. 323). Although this was a simple view of fiscal health, it had the advantage of clarity

DOI: 10.4324/9780429270765-4

and comprehensibility (Honadle et al., 2004). As long as revenue was available to cover the cost of a program or service, the government was considered fiscally healthy.

The second lens by which to assess fiscal health is economic in nature. Whereas the accounting and budgetary lens focused on the financial capacity of a government, the economic lens focuses on the capacity of the community in which the government is situated. Municipal governments are established as a reflection of the community they serve, but they control only a small portion of the community's resources (Chernick & Reschovsky, 2017). From an economic perspective, a government's fiscal health is not just a reflection of its internal financial capacity, but also of the resources of the entire community (Oi, 1995). The assumption underlying this approach is that governments have the capacity to commandeer additional community resources should the need arise. This could be accomplished through policy tools, such as increasing tax rates or imposing new taxes, as well as through legal tools such as eminent domain.

The challenge to public administration is that although the lens has shifted, a clear, consistent, agreed-upon definition of fiscal health through the economic lens has not emerged. Without such an agreed-upon definition, how municipalities have viewed and measured their fiscal position has changed and diverged dramatically throughout the course of U.S. history. In some cases, this shift has even left some governments unaware of their perilous state until it was too late. However, the near-bankruptcy of New York City in the 1970s brought a much-needed focus to the issue of how fiscal health is defined, providing an opportunity for advances in how it is measured. Recent studies have further advanced this work by empirically testing the utility of fiscal health measures and measurement systems.

Historical Measurement Approaches

Historically, as noted above, the consideration of a government's financial position was based on cash sufficiency. Until the Middle Ages, European governments were typically considered private entities overseen by a king in a decentralized feudal system (Jang, 2012; Webber & Wildavsky, 1986). The activities and services provided by these governments belonged to the feudal king. If a king wished to engage in an activity or provide a service, there was little to stop him from doing so except availability of resources. If funding was not available from the king's coffers, the monarch could impose a tax or customs duty upon his subjects to cover the needed expense. From a financial perspective, as long as the cash revenue was available, the king was financially viable. Since the availability of revenue was a reflection of a king's capacity, wars might be fought or treaties brokered to improve a king's financial position or exhaust an enemy's resources. When cash was not available, kings looked for other resources that might be used in its place, often using marriages to shore up financial shortcomings and prevent potential adversaries from taking actions that would require considerable expense.

Beginning in the early modern era, from the 15th to the 18th century, the concept of a public government expanded, and along with this change came new financial tools (Latouche, 1961; Levy, 1988; Webber & Wildavsky, 1986). Governments were still somewhat private in nature, in that they focused primarily on providing services to the monarchy, but they also exhibited increasing concern for providing services to their constituents. The expanded role of services brought with it an expanded need for resources. To accommodate that need, the advent of the banking system facilitated the marketing of state debt. The considerations of creditworthiness provided by these banks represent the first tangible development in how fiscal health was interpreted. In the Middle Ages, governments were constrained by how much resources they had on hand, but the opportunity to incur debt led banks to consider the likelihood of repayment as a determining factor in the issuance of credit. Among the factors that influenced their determination included whether kings could acquire additional resources through war and the capital resources governments had at their disposal that could be used as collateral, such as ships and castles. In modern terms, these factors reflect the idea of treating current or prospective assets as contributors to a government's financial condition.

Despite societal progress, this early modern understanding of fiscal health remained in place through much of the 20th century in the United States. The U.S. Constitution made Congress responsible for establishing a federal budget but did not establish any process by which the allocation should be made (Mikesell, 2016). The absence of a budgeting process caused Congress to view the government's financial position through the lens of financial efficiency (Hanna, 1907). That is, fiscal health was based on the availability of revenue to meet the government's expenses. If the government had the resources to fund a service or project, and if Congress was willing to allocate that funding, then funding was provided. As long as money was available, the government was viewed as financially viable. Debt was a concern, but it was a tool of last resort, and the capacity to make payments on the debt was more important than the overall size of the debt or any other long-term implications resulting from the debt (Bogart, 1912). According to Foote (1911), providing oversight and a check on the use of taxing power and budgeting allocations was the only way to ensure that a government followed appropriate financial policies and stayed within its available funds. Although occasionally a state or local government adopted an audit function to ensure the accuracy of its financial records, the financial efficiency perspective was not only passed down to states and local governments but was actively encouraged as a means to effectively manage the government (Upson, 1935).

Not until the Progressive movement and the formation of the New York Bureau of Municipal Research did perceptions of governments' financial condition began to expand. The premise of the New York Bureau and the bureau movement generally was that effectiveness should be considered alongside efficiency (Dahlberg, 1966; Hatcher et al., 2021). Using the principles of scientific management to improve the governmental process, the Bureau believed that a government could improve its effectiveness while maintaining its position of financial efficiency (Jin, 2020). Although this conviction was not a measurement system of fiscal health per se, it was an approach to understanding a government's financial position so as to maximize the services it provided while minimizing the cost involved (McDonald, 2010).

The Bureau's approach to understanding governmental finance was met with positive reviews (Dahlberg, 1966). During the 1910s and 1920s, the bureau movement spread nationwide, with municipal governments across the country establishing their own municipal bureaus, many of which had a hand in establishing the budget processes and finance management practices of their respective governments, with the perspective of financial effectiveness and efficiency at the forefront of their work.

The progress made during the bureau movement was challenged by the onset of the Great Depression, which saw significant declines in the revenue received by municipal governments at a time when community needs for public services were at their highest (Upson, 1935). As communities became fiscally constrained due to their limited resources, the federal government stepped in to provide what it could through the New Deal (Smith, 2014). Although the federal government funded a variety of programs, those most closely linked to municipal governments were typically infrastructure-related, such as the building of roads, bridges, and other capital projects. Ultimately, the financial pressure faced by municipalities became too much, forcing 4,770 municipal units to default in the 1930s, nearly all of which were smaller governments (Hempel, 1973).

As Hempel (1973) notes, the rise in defaults and bankruptcies in the 1930s caused the federal government to reconsider the laws that permitted municipal bankruptcy. Although the Municipal Bankruptcy Act of 1934 and its amendments attempted to address how financially stressed governments responded to their poor fiscal health, it did little to constrain the behavior that led to this condition and did nothing to measure the risk of fiscal distress or predict its onset.

After the initial wave of municipal collapses in the 1930s, further progress in understanding and measuring the fiscal health of municipal governments came from a renewed interest in budgetary processes and financial management control (Bland & Overton, 2019). Efforts such as the creation of the National Committee on Municipal Accounting, the emergence of fund accounting, the planning, programming, budgeting system, and encouragement to incorporate performance measurement into the budgeting process followed, in line with the New York Bureau's recommendations for effective and efficient management. These efforts, however, did little to move the concept of fiscal health and its measurement for municipalities beyond the availability of cash on hand. Meanwhile, 362 municipalities declared bankruptcy between 1938 and 1972, and in nearly all cases, the government's true financial position did not become apparent until after the filing (Hempel, 1973).

While governments struggled to understand and measure fiscal health, the private sector took a more proactive role in its assessment. Financial ratios emerged in the 1890s as a result of the introduction of single-name paper loans (Horrigan, 1968). In the 1870s, commercial banks began requesting financial statements from companies for use in making lending decisions, but the volume of information presented in the statements became a hindrance to meaningful analysis. As commercial banks looked for ways to improve their work, they experimented with different approaches. The incorporation of scientific ideas into the private sector during the Industrial Revolution led to applications of Euclidean geometry, including the use of ratios to understand how complex data interact. As Foulke (1961) noted, this trend resulted in the development of the current ratio, which compares a company's current assets to its current liabilities, as a quick tool for understanding and comparing the fiscal health of private companies.

In the years after the development of the current ratio, dozens of other ratios were created to provide a more in-depth understanding of a business's financial condition and to reflect activities with which the business is involved. By 1919, more than 200 ratios had been established to reflect the unique intricacies of organizations (McDonald, 2019; Wall, 1919), leading researchers to look for ways to mitigate the proliferation of ratios by clarifying which ones should be utilized to measure a corporation's fiscal health (Horrigan, 1968; Wall, 1919). Financial ratios may provide a picture of an organization's fiscal health, but utilizing too many ratios or the wrong ones can produce misleading results (Altman, 1968). Ultimately, Altman's (1968) work on corporate bankruptcy clarified which ratios should be used in assessing a firm's financial position. Altman's work may have resolved the debate on how to measure the fiscal health of businesses, but the translation of those ratios to the government context came much later.

The Rise of Measurement Systems: 1970s-1990s

From the perspective of measuring fiscal health as the availability of cash on hand and adopting policies and practices to ensure that this balance was successfully maintained, the traditional approaches to understanding, measuring, and controlling the fiscal health of municipal governments appeared to be generally successful. Despite the rapid rise in defaults in the 1930s and the subsequent onset of municipal bankruptcy filings (Hempel, 1973), by the 1970s municipal governments appeared fairly stable. Only eight U.S. municipal organizations filed for bankruptcy in the 1960s, and only two filed in the early 1970s. When concerns regarding the solvency of a municipality emerged, they usually involved small municipalities such as Saluda, North Carolina (population about 550), and Ranger, Texas, (population about 3,100), both of which filed for bankruptcy in 1971. Given the rarity of financial hardship and the size of the communities experiencing the difficulty when it did arise, it was believed that governments did not need to adopt a complex system to measure fiscal health like those that had emerged for businesses in the private sector.

The assumption that tracking a municipality's fiscal health was important only for small communities was shattered in February 1975 with New York City's dramatic default (Gramlich, 1976). The economic stagnation of the 1970s, coupled with middle-class flight to the suburbs, had hit New York City particularly hard, draining the city of substantial tax revenue. As a result, the city could not pay its operating expenses with the tax revenue it received, nor could it borrow additional funds due to its inability to make payments on the debt. Although New York City had been able to make its payments up to February 1975—making it a fiscally healthy city based on the prevailing understanding of government fiscal health at the time—its dire problems highlighted a fault in the measurement system, showing that the fiscal health of a government could not be ensured by a single measurement. The city had been borrowing heavily since FY1961 to cover its budget deficits, thus incurring rising debt payments.

Several solutions were proposed to correct the city's problems, including establishment of a Municipal Assistance Corporation (MAC) by the city and an Emergency Financial Control Board (EFCB) by the state. Both the MAC and EFCB took broad outlooks on what was causing the financial hardships and what would be needed to address them. The solutions included drastic budget cuts, budgetary reforms, and adherence to generally accepted accounting practices, but they also highlighted the need for a broader understanding of fiscal health and how to measure it.

Some efforts to reconsider measurement of a municipality's fiscal health had already begun (Bank Management Committee, 1963; Carelton & Lerner, 1969; Hastie, 1972), but only after that the New York City crisis did they gain momentum. Measuring fiscal health as the excess of revenue over expenditures might be sufficient for smaller communities with simpler finances and easier transparency, but the size of the bureaucracy and the complexity of existing financial arrangements typical of larger governments could conceal their true financial position. Much of the work on the fiscal health of municipal governments during the 1970s was based on the assumption that the cycle of poverty was inevitable (Stonecash & McAfee, 1981), and that if large municipalities were to survive, a better understanding of their financial status was needed to ensure their sustained operation.

The success of Altman's (1968) work in predicting corporate bankruptcy offered a natural model for scholars seeking improved systems to measure municipal fiscal health. In its report on city financial emergencies, the Advisory

Commission on Intergovernmental Relations (ACIR, 1973) concluded that a system should include attention to several factors, including federal and state aid, welfare payments, pension obligations, and short-term debt. Using Altman's work as a framework and the ACIR's approach for what should be important, Michel (1977) built one of the first models to help clarify what is and is not important to municipal fiscal health. To determine what to include in the model, Michel used the bond ratings of the 50 largest municipalities in the country. Although not a direct measurement of fiscal health per se, bond ratings do reflect the bond industry's perception of a government's capacity to pay off its debt. Ultimately, Michel's model found that per-capita debt and revenue were the greatest contributors to a municipality's rating, though other factors such as intergovernmental aid also played a role.

Michel's work was valuable in helping to clarify what determines a municipality's fiscal health, but the utility of his findings was minimal. It was not practical at that time for municipalities to apply his methodological approach, and Michel did not provide an objective measure of fiscal health by which municipalities could judge their position and react accordingly. The U.S. Department of the Treasury (1978) attempted to understand the fiscal strain placed on municipal governments by creating an index that relied on population change, income per capita, own-source revenue, long-term debt per capita, and change in the market value of property. This index could then be combined with other similar indices to create a composite index of fiscal strain, with municipalities being categorized as having low, moderate, or high strain.

The Municipal Finance Officers Association (1978) also attempted to interpret the financial position of municipalities, examining 29 financial indicators across five dimensions of a municipal government: economic vitality, financial independence and flexibility, municipal productivity, financial management practices, and the treatment of current costs. Rather than creating a single measure or indicator of a government's fiscal health, this study argued for an individualistic approach to measuring health. That is, to understand the true position of a government, the variables known to indicate stress should be viewed individually rather than collectively. Only then could one see trends across the various indicators and understand the importance of those trends.

Despite these valiant efforts, the contributions of the U.S. Department of the Treasury and the Municipal Finance Officers Association never caught on as effective tools for measuring a municipality's fiscal health. The first widely received effort to overcome this persistent problem came in 1981 with the development of the Financial Trend Monitoring System (FTMS), created by the International City/County Management Association (ICMA). The measurement systems created and adopted within the private sector had prioritized simplicity and utility over complexity, but without a sense of which financial ratios best indicated a municipal government's financial position, the creation of a simple measurement system was unlikely. The FTMS, however, took a more fluid approach. Its incorporation of a large number of variables enabled administrators to choose among the ratios based on their needs and what they felt best reflected the communities they represented (Justice & Scorsone, 2013). The resulting measurement system was a combination of 36 different financial indicators across seven areas of local government finance plus an additional four areas that could influence the behavior and institutions of local governments (Groves et al., 1981). The structure of the areas and their respective indicators are shown in Table 4.1.

Table 4.1 FTMS Indicators

Financial factor	*Indicator*
Revenues	Revenue per capita
	Restricted revenues
	Intergovernmental revenues
	Elastic tax revenues
	One-time revenues
	Property tax revenues
	Uncollected property taxes
	User charge coverage
	Revenue shortfalls
Expenditures	Expenditures per capita
	Employees per capita
	Fixed costs
	Fringe benefits
Operating position	Operating deficits
	Enterprise losses
	General fund balances
	Liquidity
Debt structure	Current liabilities
	Long-term debt
	Debt service
	Overlapping debt
Unfunded liabilities	Unfunded pension liability
	Pension assets
	Accumulated employee leave liability
Condition of capital plant	Maintenance effort

Financial factor	*Indicator*
	Level of capital outlet
	Depreciation
Community needs and resources	Population
	Median age
	Personal income
	Poverty households or public assistance recipients
	Property value
	Residential development
	Vacancy rates
	Employment base
	Business activity
External economic conditions	
Intergovernmental constraints	
Natural disasters and emergencies	
Political culture	

Source: Groves et al. (1981)

In practice, the FTMS provided a broad means of diagnosing the stability or direction of a municipal government's financial condition. The government's budget and finance staff would graph the variables of interest to the government over time and combine the individual graphs to form a broad picture or profile of the government's financial trend. The resulting approach allowed a full understanding of fiscal health to emerge by considering what was occurring in different areas of the government's operations. The system did provide a framework for understanding a municipality's fiscal health that could be adapted to each community, but it still had significant shortcomings. Groves et al. (1981) noted, for instance, that the breadth of data needed for the system was not always available to all governments, meaning that many of them could not implement the system as designed. And McDonald (2018) and McDonald and Maher (2020) pointed out that the high degree of flexibility inherent in systems such as the FTMS could be abused. Since governments and their staff were judged by how well they managed the government's financial resources, there was a natural incentive to select for inclusion in the profiles whichever variables provided the most positive reflection of the government's condition, regardless of what its true condition was.

Other efforts to address the shortcomings of the FTMS were developed during the 1980s and early 1990s, among which the most prominent was the 10-point test developed by Brown (1993). Working with the GFOA, Brown sought to establish an approach to measuring fiscal health that was both easy to understand and easy to use. To overcome the challenge of data availability and the burdensome nature of including too many variables, Brown focused only on the most commonly used financial ratios, choosing ten to reflect the five dimensions of financial condition. For an overview of the ratios and the dimensions of condition used in this test, see Table 4.2.

Brown's 10-point test operated by peer comparison. Municipal governments would calculate their own ratios and the ratios of other peer governments. The ratios were then placed into quartiles to determine which quartile the government's ratio fell into, relative to the comparable sample. Next, scores would be

Table 4.2 Brown's 10-Point Test

Indicator	*Dimension*	*Measurement*
Total revenues per capita	Revenue	Total revenues for all governmental funds (excluding capital project funds) divided by population
Intergovernmental revenues/Total revenues percentage	Revenue	Intergovernmental revenues for the general fund divided by total general fund revenues
Property tax or own source tax revenues/Total revenues percentage	Revenue	Total tax revenues levied locally for the general fund divided by total general fund revenues
Total expenditures per capita	Expenditure	Total expenditures for all governmental funds (excluding capital project funds) divided by population
Operating surplus or deficit/Operating revenues percentage	Operating position	General fund operating surplus or deficit divided by total general fund revenues
General fund balance/ General fund revenues percentage	Operating position	General fund unreserved fund balance divided by total general fund revenues
Enterprise funds working capital coverage percentage	Operating position	Current assets of enterprise funds divided by current liabilities of enterprise funds

Indicator	*Dimension*	*Measurement*
Long-term debt/Assess value percentage	Debt	Long term general obligation debt divided by total general fund revenues
Debt service/Operating revenues percentage	Debt	General obligation debt service divided by total general fund revenues
Postemployment benefit assets/Liabilities percentage	Unfunded liability	Funded ratio (i.e., actuarial value of plan assets/actuarial accrued liability)

Source: Maher and Nollenberger (2009)

assigned (from −1 for the lowest quartile to 2 for the highest quartile). Adding the scores for each ratio produced a fiscal health score that could range from −10 to 20. The result was not an independent measure of fiscal health, but rather a measure of health relative to the comparable sample of governments used. If it a government received a score of − 5 or less, it was classified among the most fiscally unhealthy governments; those with scores of 10 or higher were considered among the most fiscally healthy.

The simplicity of Brown's test caused it to quickly become one of the most commonly used measurement systems (Honadle et al., 2004; Mead, 2006, 2013). The fixed nature of the test limited governments' ability to choose what measures to include, and the fiscal health score produced by the test provided a consistent measure that was easy to understand and could be observed over time. Furthermore, implementation was simple and straightforward. The ratios used in the test were both easy to calculate and, because the information could be found in a municipal government's financial reports, easily accessible. Ultimately, it allows municipal government administrators to retrieve the necessary data from the statements of comparable governments, determine where their government falls in comparison to the other governments, and render an interpretation of that position as an indication of fiscal health.

Modernizing Systems: 1990s-2000s

After the creation of the ICMA's FTMS and Brown's 10-point test, the measurement of fiscal health balanced out. Municipalities could choose between two widely accepted systems to measure and understand their financial condition, and academics had two systems that were relatively easy to manage and implement in their research. However, as the 1990s progressed and throughout the 2000s, considerable change occurred in how fiscal health is viewed and measured.

A series of events in the early to mid-1990s raised new concerns about the financial position of municipalities around the country. After several years of a weakening economy, the United States experienced an economic recession from 1990 to 1991. The Tax Reform Act of 1986 led to the end of the real-estate boom that municipalities had enjoyed in the early to mid-1980s (Auerbach & Slemrod, 1997). The results included a noticeable decline in property values and significant job losses, both of which strained municipalities' fiscal health. Anticipating a rise in problems with its municipal governments, in 1990 Michigan became one of the first states to create a formal program to monitor municipal fiscal health and intervene as needed (Huh et al., 2015). The township of Royal Oak was the first to fall into state concern and was quickly placed under the charge of an emergency financial manager (Stanton, 2016).

In fall 1990, Philadelphia, Pennsylvania entered into a period of extreme fiscal stress (Camp-Landis, 2020). After years of trying to balance the budget through cuts and tax increases, Philadelphia ended FY1990 with a general fund deficit of $73 million, plus an additional anticipated deficit of $136 million for FY1991. Its financial problems worsened further when its access to the bond market for working capital and long-term borrowing was cut off. By January 1991, the city was forced to resort to borrowing from banks and the city's pension funds, at interest rates that exceeded 24%. In spring 1991, the state legislature responded by creating the Pennsylvania Intergovernmental Corporation Authority (PICA), a state agency charged with overseeing the city's financial behavior and issuing bonds to help fund the city's operating deficit.

The experiences of Royal Oak and Philadelphia were part of a growing trend that involved broader consideration of the fiscal health of municipal governments. Historically, municipal governments were given considerable freedom to manage their own affairs (Kim, McDonald et al., 2018), but the continued reemergence of financial problems and the rise of program shifting from state to municipal governments (Goodman et al., 2021) fostered a desire for greater awareness of what was going on within the municipalities. This attention was matched by the release of a series of new statements by the GASB. Established in 1984, the GASB is the leading standard-setting body for state and local governments in the United States. In its early years, the GASB focused on developing the generally accepted accounting principles that apply in a governmental context (Roybank et al., 2012), but the 1990s became a decade of sweeping reform with the issuance of 25 standards, each of which impacted how a municipal government's fiscal health was understood. At the root of these statements were fundamental changes in how basic financial statements should be formatted and what information they should include, but they also adjusted the accounting interpretation of liabilities, specifically by requiring the inclusion of pension liabilities on the financial statements of public organizations (Kim, Maher et al., 2018).

As the GASB issued an increasing number of standards to guide the financial behavior and reporting of municipal governments, a growing number of states required their municipal governments to adhere to GASB standards (Kim, McDonald et al., 2018). From a practitioner's perspective, this trend brought new concerns to light on issues of fiscal health that should be monitored, such as pension liabilities, but it also provided an opportunity to improve the associated measurement systems. As more governments adhered to GASB standards, the comparability of data over time and across governments improved. Ultimately, this led to the updating of both the FTMS and the 10-point test.

In 2003, the FTMS underwent revision at the hands of Nollenberger et al. (2003). In this process, consideration was given to the broad spectrum of fiscal health indicators reflected in the original 1981 version. When first created, the system identified 11 dimensions of influence on fiscal health, although the 36 variables to be collected covered only seven of these dimensions. At the time, it was believed that a system based on a large number of variables would allow municipalities to choose the picture of fiscal health that best suited their community, given the availability of data. The consistency of financial data produced as a result of GASB standards addressed the earlier concerns about data availability and consistency of measurement, allowing the updated FTMS to focus on a more encompassing picture rather than just on one that could be easily produced.

The expansion of the FTMS reconsidered not only what dimensions should be covered and measured, but *how* they should be measured. Among the updates was the incorporation of measures of environmental and organizational factors. The new FTMS includes 42 different indicators in its assessment of fiscal health (Nollenberger et al. 2003). The capacity for consistent measurement provided by the GASB standards removed the opportunity for municipal officials to pick and choose which variables they wished to include, but it also expanded a system that was already cumbersome to use. The FTMS still did not deliver a clear picture of fiscal health; rather, it relied on the artful interpretation of more than three dozen time graphs to give a sense of a municipality's condition.

Efforts were also made to improve Brown's 10-point test (Maher & Nollenberger, 2009). One of the ongoing concerns regarding the test was its relative nature (Kleine et al., 2003). Rather than measuring the fiscal health of a municipality, the test provided only a comparative perspective that rated the financial position of one municipality in comparison to its peers. Although Brown's test had accomplished what the previous measurement systems could not—namely, awarding a single composite score to describe a municipality's fiscal health—the outcome could be skewed by a careful selection of allegedly comparable governments. Alternatively, if a sufficient number of the comparable governments are facing fiscal challenges themselves, the municipal government of interest may appear artificially to be in solid fiscal health.

To address the shortcomings of this test, Kleine et al. (2003) took advantage of the move to standardize financial data and proposed a variant that scores a municipality independent of peer comparisons (see also Kloha et al., 2005). In the revised test, municipal governments are given a score based on where they fall in relation to an established standard on each of the nine measures now included in the test. For example, if the real taxable value growth over two years is greater than 1, the municipality would be given one point. The evaluation criteria for each measure are determined by a study of municipal governments within the state. In the case of Kleine et al. (2003), municipal governments from Michigan were used.

Mead (2006) also attempted to update Brown's 10-point test, arguing that Brown's version was insufficient due to its failure to include long-term financial data as a factor in fiscal health. Prior to the issuance of GASB Statement 34 in 1999, long-term financial information was not available in statements related to governmental funds, but the GASB's efforts to improve reporting for municipal governments allowed for the introduction of long-term data alongside the short-term perspective that the test was already presenting. The result was a new test that still incorporated ten ratios, but over more dimensions of a government's finances. The initial test covered five domains within its measures; Mead's covered eight. Despite the better coverage, however, Mead did little to overcome the earlier criticisms of peer comparison, and his revised test has rarely been used in practice.

Mead's approach to updating Brown's 10-point test does point to an emerging trend. Although the FTMS and 10-point test emerged as the dominant systems for measuring a municipality's fiscal health, satisfaction with the processes of measuring and the utility of the results was low. During the 1990s and 2000s, there emerged a tendency to treat the measurement of fiscal health on an ad hoc or boutique basis that suited the needs of the creator of the analysis. Neither of the updates by Kleine et al. (2003) or Mead (2006) did much to influence how fiscal health was being measured, but they did effectively meet the authors' own needs. Kleine et al. (2003), for example, created their test for the state of Michigan, where all three authors were employed at the time. Similarly, Mead's test was devised to serve the GASB, where he was employed, and its efforts to demonstrate the benefits of new government-wide financial statements.

The ad hoc or boutique approach was not limited to employers; it also spilled over into academia. For example, in his textbook on financial management, which has become standard reading in most MPA programs, Finkler (2001) argued for an approach to measuring the fiscal health of public organizations that involved picking and choosing among dozens of financial ratios based on the story one wishes to tell. Academic researchers developed their own tools or combinations of ratios to measure fiscal health, with nearly every study reinventing the measurement based on the availability of data or what suited the needs of the researcher (e.g., Hendrick, 2004; Honadle et al., 2004).

The most notable of such efforts came from Wang et al. (2007). The authors wanted to address the shortcomings of the existing measurement systems; they also wanted to move away from measuring where a government's fiscal health was headed and instead focus on its condition at a particular point in time. To accomplish this, they selected 11 indicators that captured what they viewed as the four dimensions of fiscal health: cash solvency, budget solvency, long-run solvency, and service solvency. Following the premise of a score-based test, the indicators were put into their absolute value and then averaged across dimensions. The resulting scores on each dimension could be added together to provide a single measure of fiscal health, referred as the Financial Condition Index (FCI). See Table 4.3 for an overview of the dimensions and their respective indicators.

Although ad hoc and boutique measurement approaches to financial condition measurement may have dominated this time period, none of them managed to

Table 4.3 Wang, Dennis, and Tu's Solvency Test

Indicator	*Dimension*	*Measurement*
Cash ratio	Cash solvency	(Cash + cash equivalents + investments)/Current liabilities
Quick ratio	Cash solvency	(Cash + cash equivalents + investments + receivables)/ Current liabilities
Current ratio	Cash solvency	Current assets/Current liabilities
Operating ratio	Budget solvency	Total revenues/Total expenses
Surplus (deficit) per capita	Budget solvency	Total surplus (deficit)/Population
Net asset ratio	Long-run solvency	Restricted and unrestricted net assets/Total assets
Long-term liability ratio	Long-run solvency	Long-term (non-current) liabilities/Total assets
Long-term liability per capita	Long-run solvency	Long-term (non-current) liabilities/population
Tax per capita	Service solvency	Total taxes/Population
Revenue per capita	Service solvency	Total revenues/Population
Expenses per capita	Service solvency	Total expenses/Population

Source: Wang et al. (2007)

achieve widespread adoption. Only the 2003 update to the FTMS demonstrated staying power, and even it was only a minor update of an already widely accepted measurement system. However, the onset of the Great Recession presented new, severe challenges to municipal governments, and its impact on municipal government solvency highlighted a flaw in the measurement systems used up to that time. For many municipalities, the dire financial position they were in became clear only when it was too late.

Post-Great Recession Realizations: 2010s to the Present

The Great Recession, in addition to posing a significant fiscal threat to municipal governments, showed that the systems developed to measure the financial condition of municipalities did not always reflect their true position. Though municipal bankruptcies are rare, 69 such filings occurred in the aftermath of the recession (Maciag, 2014). When Detroit, Michigan, filed for bankruptcy in 2013, for example, many of the leading measurement systems suggested that the city was financially stable (McDonald, 2018). Brown's 10-point test even rated Detroit as one of the healthiest large municipalities in the country. The need to declare bankruptcy obviously suggested otherwise.

This failure to predict the true financial position of municipalities prior to the recession was a failure in the measurement of fiscal health. The peer comparison nature of the 10-point test created problems because it assumed that the peers were fiscally sound. If they were not, the test's indications that a municipality was doing fairly well relative to its comparison group would be of little value. The FTMS provided a strong perspective, but interpreting its findings was as much art as science.

Furthermore, the ad hoc and boutique measurements relied upon ratio analysis. The problem with this approach is that without any clarification of which ratios matter, the measurement of fiscal health could be produce only an image of fiscal health from the analyst's particular vantage point. The type of financial obligation an analyst is interested in determines how the measurement of a government's condition is carried out. An analyst concerned about the government's immediate capacity to provide services may focus on measuring its efficiency ratio (the ratio of total expenditures to total revenue). Alternatively, someone concerned about the government's ability to pay for its pension programs may examine coverage ratios (which reflect an organization's capacity to meet its short-term and long-term liabilities). Such approaches provide interesting insight into the organization's financial health, but each one focuses narrowly on a single aspect of the broader fiscal condition. The result of the pick-and-choose method of measurement is that analysts can pick only the measures that give the perspective they want to produce.

In response to the failures of the measurement systems from previous periods, research into the measurement of fiscal health during the post-recession years focused on determining how fiscal health is measured. Rather than devising new tests, however, most of the work centered on clarifying what among the existing processes matters in the determination of a municipality's financial position. The start of this effort came with the publication of the *Handbook of Local Government Fiscal Health* by Levine et al. (2013). Each of the book's 20 chapters discussed matters related to the fiscal health of local governments; however, the chapters by Jacob and Hendrick (2013) and Justice and Scorsone (2013) focused specifically on the measurement of fiscal health and fiscal stress, respectively.

Jacob and Hendrick (2013) reviewed the previous approaches to measuring fiscal health in search of a methodological recommendation. They concluded that fiscal health is less an issue of position or condition and more of a "dynamic and fluid process" (p. 35). Because of this fluidity, no single measurement system is likely to provide an appropriate or complete understanding of a municipality's condition. Rather, they argued that the battery of existing measures should be maintained, but that the choice of which measurement system to use should depend upon the situation of the government. Given the role of the political/institutional and economic environments in municipal decision making, Jacob and Hendrick contended that the choice of measurements should include some recognition and measurement of these dynamics. Justice and Scorsone (2013) reached similar conclusions and recommendations in their discussion of measuring fiscal stress.

Although neither of these two studies provided a clear approach to how fiscal health should be measured, they started a discussion within the literature that has been carried forward since then. The key takeaway of the discussion was that fiscal health may not be a one-size-fits-all concept but should be treated methodologically as an open system, allowing users to capture the dynamics of importance for their community without losing the benefits of following a measurement approach (see also Maher & Deller, 2011; McDonald et al., 2021).

Measurement pluralism aside, a key feature of fiscal health research from the post-recession period is that it has tried to sort through existing uncertainties and provide recommendations as to what approaches best capture the true condition of a municipality. Two notable contributions in this regard are Stone et al. (2015) and McDonald and Maher (2020). Stone et al. (2015) used Detroit as a case study to test the efficacy of several approaches in reflecting the city's now-recognized financial woes. They examined a disaggregated version of the FCT of Wang et al. (2007), the Kloha et al. (2005) variant of the 10-point test, and a series of financial ratios that reflect various financial aspects related to the municipality's assets, liabilities, and pension program. Although many of the approaches failed to reveal Detroit's worsening condition, financial ratios related to assets and liabilities as well as operating solvency did reflect the municipality's financial decline.

McDonald and Maher (2020) took this research one step further. Building on the approach, common within the business literature, of using a measure's ability to predict bankruptcy filings as a calibrator of what matters in measuring fiscal health (Altman, 1968; Horrigan, 1968; Wall, 1919), they tested how effective the different measurement systems were in predicting municipal bankruptcy. Using a dataset of the 150 largest cities over a 36-year period, McDonald and Maher identified years in which the cities experienced known financial hardship, as indicated by a bankruptcy filing or the imposition of an emergency board. Brown's (1993) 10-point test, the FCI (in both its aggregate and individual-dimension forms), and ratio analysis were used to see which approach best revealed the cities' actual condition. The results showed that Brown's test, some of the individual dimensions of the FCI, and the occasional financial ratio were effective in predicting the fiscal health of a municipality. Moreover, the results provide guidance on how to choose the methodological approach used to measure a municipality's fiscal health. For example, Brown's test can provide a useful understanding of fiscal condition when the comparison groups are sufficiently large. The findings based on the ratio analysis and the variants of the FCI showed that because of the complexity of a municipality's finances, fiscal health is best measured from a liquidity perspective—i.e., from the standpoint of whether it can pay its bills rather than what debt is outstanding or its other obligations.

What to Measure and How

In our approach to measuring fiscal health, we take to heart Jacob and Hendrick's (2013) assertion about the situational fluidity of fiscal health measurement. Furthermore, Justice and Scorsone's (2013) acknowledgement of the impact of institutional settings and socioeconomic conditions, fits our open-systems model. At the end of the day, however, we need some firm sense of how to think about measuring fiscal health. Here, we rely on the teachings of Maher, Ebdon et al. (2020), who suggest including an economic condition analysis that incorporates trends in socioeconomic metrics, along with a discussion of the political and institutional environment in which the community operates.

According to Maher, Ebdon et al. (2020), one should consider the following characteristics of the community of interest:

- Population patterns
- Economic base (major employers and industries)
- Recent unemployment rates

- Tax base and tax structure (what the major revenue sources are)
- Government structure (including TELs, other fiscal institutions, home-rule powers, and form of government)

As we note in our framework, these inputs are necessary antecedents for placing fiscal measures in the appropriate context. The specific fiscal measures selected will depend to some degree on the purpose and intended audience. That said, for those studies that have attempted to assess the efficacy of fiscal measures, one result is clear: an index approach such as those used by Brown (1993) and Wang et al. (2007) is incapable of capturing nuances associated with fiscal health. The measures most consistently associated with actual fiscal stress, and therefore with fiscal health and fiscal condition, include measures of revenues and expenditures, operating position, and long-term liability structure.

Students and practitioners are advised to calculate the following ratios and examine the trend or pattern of each ratio over time:

Revenues and expenditures

- Per-capita total general fund or government-wide revenues
- Per-capita total general fund or government-wide expenditures
- Property taxes relative to total governmental fund revenues
- Intergovernmental aid relative to total revenues (general fund or government-wide level)

Operating position

- General fund surplus (deficit) relative to general fund expenditures
- Unrestricted general fund balance as a percentage of general fund expenditures
- Total governmental cash, investments, and receivables relative to current liabilities
- Unrestricted net assets from governmental (or business-type) activities relative to total expenditures on these activities

Long-term liabilities

- General obligation debt relative to total assessed valuation
- Debt service expenditures relative to total governmental fund revenues
- Total governmental long-term liabilities relative to total assets

The next question is how to evaluate these measures: compared to other communities or over time? This decision must not be taken lightly and is complicated by the challenge associated with finding peer communities that have similar socioeconomic attributes, organizational structure, and fiscal institutions. Furthermore, professional organizations offer limited guidance on what is deemed best practice for debt levels, reserves, and other factors. Maher (2022) and Maher, Ebdon et al. (2020) suggest tracking five years of historical data to assess change over time. Finally, other measures may be useful based on the characteristics of your community, such as the degree of reliance on intergovernmental aid or the amount of pension and other post-employment benefit (OPEB) liabilities relative to assets.

Concluding Thoughts

The issue of how a municipality's fiscal health should be measured is far from resolved. Over the history of the United States, municipalities have struggled time and again to understand their financial position properly, and each series of struggles has brought an advancement in our methodologies. The measurement approaches from the 1980s and 1990s, notably the FTMS and 10-point test, may be the most effective systems in our arsenal. The more recent research on the measurement dilemma suggests why: the full financial position of a government is important, but it's the government's ability to manage its cash and pay its bills that matters for its continued solvency. By focusing on measuring that liquidity, whether in an aggregated form (such as the 10-point test) or on an individual basis (such as what a general ratio analysis and the FTMS allow), we can gain a true picture of the municipality's fiscal health.

As noted throughout this chapter, a number of considerations are involved in assessing a municipality's financial condition. The first one is the goals of the analysis. Is the aim to demonstrate to stakeholders that tax dollars are being spent wisely, or to demonstrate to rating agencies that the community is financially sound and capable of repaying debt? Is it an internal document used for management purposes and benchmarking, or a reporting document submitted for state monitoring? For students and academics, the operationalization of financial condition analysis is just as complicated.

The approach we have proposed in the preceding section requires the collection of data that, while time-consuming, can be obtained for case studies but are impractical for larger data analyses. Researchers must therefore make some important strategic decisions. Does the focus of the analysis consist of communities within a single state where the data collected will be relatively uniform? If not, researchers can use other data sources, including the Census Bureau's Annual Survey of State and Local Finance (see Appendix A for a discussion of its pros and cons), the GFOA's Financial Indicators Database (which contains data on local governments that seek recognition for their annual financial reporting), the Lincoln Institute of Land Policy's Fiscally Standardized Cities (FiSC) database (which contains annual financial data on the 150 largest U.S. cities for the 36-year period from 1977 to 2012), or customized datasets created by the researcher for a particular purpose. Regardless of the data collection strategy, there will be impediments that can affect the generalizability of findings.

Chapter 5

Outcomes

Measuring Fiscal Stress

Measuring the extreme of fiscal heath—fiscal stress—has taken on a unique understanding and conceptualization. Fiscal stress is more than just the extremely bad end of the fiscal health continuum. It can seriously impact service delivery (e.g., in Flint, Michigan), heighten creditor and retiree anxiety, and force state governments into difficult, complex interventions. Any attempt to understand the financial condition of a government requires that attention also be paid towards its level of stress. In this chapter, we extend our discussion of fiscal outcomes within our open-systems model to give added attention to fiscally distressed communities.

When times are good, municipalities tend to focus on new programs and service expansion, taking their healthy financial position for granted. With economic prosperity come increased tax revenue and a decline in demand for core government services. Budget surpluses allow municipalities to focus on what might be desirable rather than only on what is necessary. However, the U.S. economic cycle is in a constant swing. Along with times when the economy is good and fiscal health is a secondary concern, there will be times when the economy is unstable and municipalities experience fiscal challenges.

Fiscal stress is the condition that a municipality experiences when it is unable to meet its financial obligations. On definition alone, fiscal stress does not differ all that much from fiscal health. As previously discussed, fiscal health is "the extent to which [a government's] financial resources exceed its spending obligations" (Berry, 1994, p. 323). Although the difference in definition between the two might seem

DOI: 10.4324/9780429270765-5

trivial at first, the distinction has important implications for municipalities and their leadership.

Understanding Fiscal Stress

Fiscal stress, as a government's inability to meet its financial obligations, may take the form of an actual failure to meet an obligation or the significant risk of a potential failure. According to Danziger (1991, p. 169), "Fiscal stress is typically defined as a (usually growing) imbalance between the demands for a government's resources and its access to the private or public financial resources to meet those demands." This concept may appear straightforward, but its interpretation can vary widely. Clark and Ferguson (1983), for example, viewed stress in the context of fiscal strain. Through this lens of fiscal strain, fiscal stress is described as occurring when the financial structure of an organization is poorly aligned, leading to inappropriate choices and commitments on how to use available resources. This leads to an unsteady financial environment as the government's commitments become financially unsustainable, contributing to fiscal stress.

In practice, the understanding of fiscal stress has varied slightly, based on the definer's perspective on an organization's financial condition. Those with a primary interest in public budgeting and management tend to focus on decision making in the budget process.[1] Greene (1996), for example, defined fiscal stress as the pressure a city experiences when facing a budget deficit. This pressure may come as the result of poor planning or changes in circumstances. Morgan and Pammer (1988) also viewed fiscal stress in the context of a budget deficit, but they tied the understanding of stress to the question of why the deficit occurred in the first place. Municipalities exist in environments with economic, political, and institutional influences. Within such an environment, municipal leaders can make choices that improve or maintain a municipality's financial position, or they can make choices that extend the commitments of the municipality beyond its financial capacity. When the latter occurs, fiscal stress can emerge as the leadership struggles to close the budget gap.

A more comprehensive understanding of fiscal stress comes from the ACIR (1973), which authored one of the first studies to explore the financial condition of municipal governments. In this report, they defined fiscal stress in the context of a financial emergency. According to their definition, a municipality is in fiscal stress if it is unable to pay to maintain services due to a lack of cash, other liquid assets, or relevant appropriation authority. A financial emergency encapsulates the default process as municipalities fail to meet specific financial obligations. The level of the emergency may range from a small stressor, such as a delayed payment of an invoice, to complete failure, such as when a municipality does not make regularly scheduled debt service payments.

Despite the variety of the definitions of and perspectives on fiscal stress, the best understanding of fiscal stress comes from how it is defined in practice by municipalities around the United States. In practice, many municipalities view fiscal stress through a lens much like that of the ACIR. Poor management practices may contribute to a municipality's fiscal stress and good practices may help improve its condition, but the relationships are not mutually exclusive. Major events outside the municipality's control, such as the COVID-19 pandemic or the Great Recession, may influence the availability of tax revenue and the demand for public services, thereby producing fiscal stress. For example, the City of Long Beach, New York, was already experiencing some financial difficulty before the pandemic, but the onset of the pandemic in spring 2020 created severe fiscal strain (Yanes, 2021). A declining economy led to reduced tax revenues and increased unemployment and poverty. As Long Beach spent to meet the needs of the community, it began to run an operating deficit, which gradually gobbled up its fund balance. Opportunities for cities to reduce their financial obligations can be quite limited, as many states mandate the provision of certain services by municipal governments, effectively tying the hands of municipal leadership (Kim, Maher et al., 2018; McDonald, 2015). Financial policies or changes in management practices may slow down the rate of spending, but the fiscal stress that Long Beach was experiencing came as a result of a sizable divide between services provided and resources available.

Fiscal Stress Versus Fiscal Health

Any discussion of a municipality's fiscal stress must be connected to a broader discussion of fiscal health. To put it simply, the concept of fiscal health describes an organization's capacity on a spectrum of possible health conditions (Justice & Scorsone, 2013). It is a complex idea that concerns an organization's capacity to pay its bills and remain solvent (Honadle et al., 2004; McDonald & Maher, 2020). Municipalities with a high capacity to meet their obligations are referred to as fiscally healthy, whereas their counterparts with a low capacity are fiscally unhealthy.

According to Justice and Scorsone (2013), fiscal stress results from a government's failure to remain fiscally healthy. However, not all fiscally unhealthy municipalities should be considered fiscally stressed. The concept of fiscal health encompasses a government's ability to meet its financial obligations over both the short and long terms (Mallach & Scorsone, 2011). Fiscal stress, however, focuses solely on the short-term situation.

The case of Detroit, Michigan, helps us understand the distinction. Detroit declared bankruptcy in 2013, a sign that the city was facing extreme fiscal stress. Nevertheless, studies have noted that measurements of the city's financial condition at the time found the city to be generally fiscally healthy, or at least not seriously unhealthy (McDonald, 2018; Stone et al., 2015). How could a municipality be fiscally healthy while still needing to file for bankruptcy protection? From a long-term perspective, Detroit was solvent. The city maintained a large number of assets that could have been liquidated to pay bills, and other options were available for Detroit to either reduce its liabilities or improve its budgetary decision making. The challenge for Detroit was how to undertake these options as they take time to implement. It could have been years before the city might have seen any fiscal relief.

Unfortunately for Detroit, this relief could not come fast enough. While the city might have been able to address its long-term financial challenges without bankruptcy, immediate bills still needed to be paid and the city did not have the cash on hand to meet the needs. The short-term pressure to meet its financial obligations reflects the fiscal stress the city was facing. As we move away from the short-term perspective, any city appears less stressed even if unhealthy overall, because there remain options, or at least time to work on developing options, so as to solve the looming financial problems.

Measures of Fiscal Stress

Given the complexity of the broader concept of fiscal health and of fiscal stress, it is no surprise that there is no consistent, agreed-upon way to measure fiscal stress. Measurement attempts began in the 1970s with the report by the ACIR (1973), which was drafted in response to the bankruptcy of Penn Central in 1970—the largest bankruptcy in the United States at that time—and the federal bailout of Lockheed Corporation. Organizational failure was believed to be something that happened primarily to private corporations, but concerns spread to the public sector when Cleveland, Ohio, announced plans to shore up its financial stability. Cleveland, then one of the ten largest cities in the country, followed the private sector in its response to fiscal stress by announcing the layoffs of more than 2,000 public employees, a 22% reduction of its workforce.

Large municipalities had previously threatened major layoffs and service cutbacks to relieve fiscal stress, but Cleveland was the first actual instance since World War II (ACIR, 1973), and it led to wider recognition of the need to better understand the financial condition of municipalities. The ACIR report took a step in this direction, seeking to clarify the fiscal health of municipalities in order to isolate specific measures or factors contributing to their financial condition. The purpose was to then use those measures to determine warning signals for municipalities regarding a future financial emergency. After examining the financial behavior of the 33 largest U.S. cities, the ACIR (1973, p. 4) narrowed its recommended measures of fiscal stress to six factors:

- An operating fund revenue-expenditure imbalance in which current expenditures significantly exceed current revenues in one fiscal period
- A consistent pattern of current expenditures exceeding current revenues by small amounts for several years
- An excess of current operating liabilities over current assets (a fund deficit)
- Short-term operating loans outstanding at the conclusion of a fiscal year (or, in some instances, the borrowing of cash from restricted funds or an increase in unpaid bills in lieu of short-term operating loans)
- A high and rising rate of property tax delinquency
- A sudden, substantial decrease in assessed values for unexpected reasons

While recommending these six key measures, the ACIR acknowledged that this list was not all-inclusive. For example, unfunded pensions and poor budgeting and financial management practices may also influence the fiscal stress of a government.

One common set of measures within the fiscal stress literature involves socioeconomic, political, and institutional factors. The use of such factors within the fiscal health literature more generally has largely disappeared, but they continue to be included in examinations of fiscal stress remains because changes in these factors can substantially influence financial capacity. The factors may not influence a government's financial position directly, but they may be driving the environment in which the municipality operates. A decline in per-capita income, for example, may signal a forthcoming change in sales tax revenue and public service demands as residents adjust to their new economic means. An early example of the application of socioeconomic factors to measure fiscal stress came from Ladd and Yinger (1989), who used these factors to adjust revenues and expenditures in the calculation of their adjusted fiscal health index. Following their understanding that fiscal stress emerges as a result of poor management decision making, Morgan and Pammer (1988) relied on a single measure to account for the presence of stress—namely, the relative change over time in a municipality's debt burden (i.e., the ratio of total outstanding debt to revenue). Environmental rather than purely financial focus regarding fiscal stress was typical of the literature in the 1970s and 1980s as researchers struggled to understand the nature of a government's financial condition more fully (Clark & Ferguson, 1983; Levine et al., 1981; Rubin, 1982).

As research on fiscal health progressed over the decades, so did research on fiscal stress. Building on the work of Reschovsky (2004), Skidmore and Scorsone (2011) proposed a framework for measuring fiscal stress as a reflection of the relationship between spending and revenue. In their framework, fiscal stress is measured as the difference between the indexed cost of government services and its indexed revenues. The indexed cost of services includes the cost of government employees and capital. Indexed revenues were measured by taking the sum of revenue from all sources and calculating the percentage change from a base year.

The challenge produced by Skidmore and Scorsone's approach is one of complexity. Research on fiscal health has always sought to identify metrics that can be implemented effectively and easily by municipal governments. Measuring fiscal stress as the difference between service costs and revenues may appear simple, but calculating the indices necessary for this measurement can be challenging. Skidmore and Scorsone's solution was to rely on secondary data, which may not be available for all municipalities on a continuous basis. Moreover, using government services as a cost measure ignores operational costs. Wages do account for most of a government's noncapital expenses (Meyer-Sahling et al., 2021), but the non-wage-based operating expenses of a government can also be substantial (Hood & Piotrowska, 2021). Thus, the utility of the measurement Skidmore and Scorsone selected has been called into question.

A more recent study by Gorina et al. (2018) took an action-related approach to fiscal stress, focusing on whether a municipality experiences certain actions such as layoffs, large interfund transfers, or excessive across-the-board budget cuts. In their study of three states—California, Michigan, and Pennsylvania—over 30% of the communities in the sample reported at least one type of fiscal stress. The most common actions identified were across-the-board budget cuts in excess of 10% (present in 55% of distress episodes), followed by blanket reductions in employee salaries (15%), tax and fee increases (12%), and layoffs or furloughs (5%). Of the total of 565 reported distress episodes, only nine involved declarations of fiscal emergencies: six defaults on debt, two bankruptcies, and one takeover by the state.

As researchers debate the best approach to measure fiscal stress, a number of states have adopted their own approaches to tracking how municipal governments are doing and determining when to intervene if the fiscal stress becomes too great (Pew Charitable Trusts, 2016b). By monitoring its municipal governments for signs of fiscal stress, however, the state effectively removes the responsibility for maintaining fiscal health from municipal hands, along with establishing what fiscal stress means and how it will be measured within that state. Currently, 22 states have fiscal monitoring programs: Colorado, Connecticut, Florida, Iowa, Kentucky, Louisiana, Maryland, Michigan, Minnesota, Nevada, New Hampshire, New Jersey, New Mexico, New York, North Carolina, Ohio, Oregon, Pennsylvania, Rhode Island, South Dakota, Tennessee, and Washington. Eight states have early warning systems: Louisiana, Nevada, North Carolina, Ohio, Pennsylvania, Rhode Island, Tennessee, and Virginia.

How the states measure fiscal stress varies based on each state's particular concerns and its past experience with financial distress. Michigan, for example, maintains a Community Engagement and Finance Division within the Bureau of Local Government and School Services. This division is responsible for working with local governments to identify and resolve problems related to their financial condition. The division pioneered a monitoring system in 2002 that rated local governments based on a wide range of indicators (Kleine et al., 2003). The intent of this system was to provide "warning and preventative actions to avoid a fiscal crisis leading to a potential state takeover" (Plerhoples & Scorsone, 2010, p. 4). These concerns regarding municipalities' fiscal stress were grounded in state fears that they could have to step in and cover a municipality's expenses. To warn the state of impending fiscal stress that might require such a takeover, the monitoring system focused on variables from four dimensions that were viewed as causing fiscal stress: population and job market shifts, governmental growth, interest group demands, and poor management. However, Michigan's initial measurement system quickly encountered problems and was dropped within four years. Chief among the complaints was that the system took too broad an approach and thus did not accurately capture fiscal stress. Instead, many of the municipalities flagged by the system were not facing any sort of financial challenge.

Michigan instituted a new measurement system in 2006. The replacement system was more consistent with the intent to avoid state takeovers, as it contained nine indicators that focused on a municipality's capacity to meet its short-term financial obligations (Plerhoples & Scorsone, 2010). Much as in Skidmore and Scorsone (2011), the variables focused on the difference between revenues and expenditures and what might influence that balance. Eight of the variables were financially related, focusing on the balance in the general fund and other fund deficits, as well as changes in the taxable value of the community. The ninth variable concerned population growth, due to the expectation that changes in population can influence the balance of funds available to the municipality. A municipality is given a score of 0 or 1 on each indicator, and the nine ratings are then added together to create a total fiscal stress score. Municipalities with a score of 0 to 4 are labeled as *fiscally neutral*, those with 5 to 7 points are on *fiscal watch*, and those with 8 or 9 are considered in *fiscal stress*.

North Carolina's Department of State Treasurer contains a Local Government Commission that actively monitors the financial behavior of its local governments for signs of distress, with a focus on early detection. Rather than monitoring a municipality's current situation, the state monitors whether a municipality might fall into fiscal distress based on 14 financial ratios. These include many of the standard ratios used to assess a government's fiscal health more broadly, as discussed in the previous chapter, such as the operating ratio, debt service ratio, quick ratio, fund balance, and debt. Although they are not explicit measures of fiscal stress, like those used by the other approaches discussed in this chapter, they do reflect the state's desire for very early detection. Given the state's preemptive authority with respect to local government decisions (Goodman et al., 2021; McDonald et al., 2020), the broader measurements allow the state to step in, limit a municipality's access to debt, and provide advice on reducing expenses when the measures provide any hint of stress. Moreover, exactly how the state uses the ratios to decide when to intervene is generally not revealed publicly, so that state officials can become involved with municipal government finances quietly when they feel that doing so is necessary.

Pennsylvania's Department of Community and Economic Development monitors a variety of financial and socioeconomic variables to identify when local governments are moving toward a position of fiscal stress. Recently, Virginia adopted a plan to begin monitoring the condition of its local governments by looking at their revenue capacity and effort, as well as the median household income of their residents (Gilmore, 2017). These initiatives, however, mainly provide the state with information to help it manage its relationship with local governments, rather than supplying the local governments with information useful for their own administrative needs.

We should note that measurements of fiscal stress are often intertwined with the measurement of fiscal health. We can see this relationship in the measurement approaches discussed here, as well as in those considered in the previous chapter. The history of measuring the financial condition of an organization stems from measurements that sought to predict bankruptcy, a sign of extreme fiscal stress (Altman, 1968). Several recent attempts to clarify how fiscal health should be measured have used fiscal stress events, such as municipal bankruptcies or the assignment of an emergency manager, as benchmarks to establish the validity of the measurement used (McDonald, 2017; McDonald & Maher, 2020). Even though these studies focused on the broader concept of fiscal health, the direct connection between fiscal health and fiscal stress suggests that these measurement approaches should not be ignored when one is considering how to best capture the level of stress a municipality is facing. Rather, approaches to measuring fiscal health can be adopted and built on to suit the evaluation needs of a particular situation.

Concluding Thoughts

The intent of this chapter has been to provide an understanding of what fiscal stress is and how it relates to a municipality's fiscal health. We have seen that fiscal health is not a single measurement, but rather a spectrum of financial conditions that a municipality may experience. Fiscal stress is a position on that spectrum. It emphasizes a short-term perspective on financial condition, as the key question is whether municipalities have enough available revenue to meet short-term needs. Although the measurement of fiscal stress often reflects measurements of the broader concept of fiscal health, the implications for a government are very different. A government experiencing an unhealthy long-term fiscal condition may have the opportunity to improve its condition, whereas stress that emerges from unhealthy short-term conditions pose a very real threat to the municipality's continued survival.

Note

1. For a discussion of the distinction between public budgeting and financial management, see McDonald and Jordan (2021).

Chapter 6

Outcomes

Municipal Fiscal Condition Trends

As discussed in the previous two chapters, we have witnessed the remarkable development of new measures of fiscal condition over the last several decades. Although the existing measures still need work "to do what they are inherently meant to do—predict fiscal distress" (McDonald & Maher, 2020, p. 274), the developments thus far have provided significant benefits. For example, we now have specific tools to portray a municipal government's fiscal condition and compare it with peers and/or benchmarks. These tools can help municipal finance officers and decision makers better understand their jurisdiction's financial condition and proactively develop fiscal policies to deal with short- and long-term fiscal issues (Maher & Nollenberger, 2009). Building upon this practical benefit, the present chapter analyzes municipal average trends and variations on different fiscal condition measures. For students and practitioners, the most important part of this chapter is its discussion of how to interpret the ratios. We have found that whereas calculating ratios can be challenging for students with limited exposure to financial management, the greater challenge is to make meaningful sense of what the measures report within the context of a financial condition analysis.

We start with a comprehensive set of 29 fiscal condition measures, which can help us introduce and compare various fiscal condition measures used in previous studies, to understand average municipal trends. We then end up with a more focused set of ten measures that we use to illustrate municipal variations in fiscal condition. The selected measures are consistent with our suggestions in Chapter 4, with a few exceptions that were extensively covered in Chapter 3 (e.g., per capita revenues) or that have no available cross-state data (e.g., total governmental cash,

DOI: 10.4324/9780429270765-6

investments, and receivables). We have two particular expectations regarding the selected measures. First, they are expected to adequately capture the major dimensions of municipal fiscal condition including revenues and expenditures, operating position, and long-term liabilities (Brown, 1993; Maher & Nollenberger, 2009). Second, we expect the selected measures to contribute to the extant literature on assessing fiscal condition by enabling comparisons to different ways of measuring each fiscal condition dimension (see also McDonald & Maher, 2020).

The primary data source used in this chapter is the GFOA's Municipal Financial Indicators Database. Since 1945, the GFOA has awarded the Certificate of Achievement for Excellence in Financial Reporting to state and local government applicants that successfully attain high quality in their annual comprehensive financial reports. The GFOA digitalized the collected audited financial information for its county, municipal, and school district awardees for the years from 1995 to 2016, and it has made this information available for purchase on its website. Researchers have widely used the database to examine local fiscal outcomes (Brown, 1993; Honadle & Lloyd-Jones, 1998; Maher & Nollenberger, 2009; Park, 2018b; Shi & Tao, 2018).

The core merit of the GFOA database, with its cross-state collection of audited data, is that it addresses one of the most significant challenges in financial condition analysis: data accessibility. The database goes well beyond some other data sources, such as the Census Bureau Survey, which is often inconsistent with audited financial information and omits important financial categories needed for fiscal condition analysis (e.g., assets, fund balances), and individual annual comprehensive financial reports, which require enormous time for data entry. The GFOA data, however, also present their own challenges. They are not available for more recent years, because the GFOA stopped collecting data some years ago. Furthermore, the database is subject to sample selection bias, because the GFOA collected the financial data only from those municipal governments seeking its certificate. The database tends to be more representative of larger municipalities, particularly with populations of 25,000 or more, according to Park (2018a).

This chapter analyzes the GFOA municipal financial indicators data from 1996 to 2016, but with variations on a few fiscal condition measures due to data availability. We exclude the 1995 database as it includes several reporting errors. Each year has a different number of observations because a different number of municipal governments applied for the certificate each year.

Expenditure and Revenue Indicators

Expenditure and revenue indicators approximate a municipal government's service outputs and resource capacity (Nollenberger et al., 2003). To depict average trends in revenue and expenditure indicators, we first focus on four specific per-capita measures: total expenditures and revenues from governmental funds, total general fund (GF) expenditures, and total GF revenues.[1] Our focus is on the two different fund levels—governmental funds and GF—should capture both general government operations and a wider range of government activities. By comparing expenditures and revenues relative to population size, each measure reflects the unit cost of municipal service delivery. There are no clear benchmarks for per-capita expenditure and revenue measures because they depend on each municipality's particular environment and context. Maher (2013, 2022), along with Nollenberger et al. (2003), suggests that trending patterns, rather than single-year snapshots, of expenditures and revenues should be examined to understand municipal fiscal conditions better (see Appendix B).[2]

Table 6.1 shows that per-capita total governmental fund expenditures and revenues were $522.1 and $526.4, respectively, in 1996. Both governmental fund expenditures and revenues have generally been on an upward trend, reaching $1,661.7 and $1,573.4, respectively, in 2016. However, there was a slight decrease in both governmental fund expenditures and revenues in 2010. Here we can see the dampening impact of the Great Recession on municipal budgets (see also McFarland & Pagano, 2015). A similar pattern has been observed for per-capita total GF expenditures and revenues. Municipal governments experienced steady growth in GF expenditures and revenues from 1996 to 2008, then faced a recessionary period, and have recovered over the last few years.

One interesting observation is that total governmental fund expenditures have consistently exceeded total revenues each year, whereas the relationship has been the opposite at the GF level. This is typically the result of other governmental funds, such as special revenue, capital project, and debt service funds, being included as government expenditures. This difference between governmental funds and the GF has been a subject of discussion among researchers. Some have argued that GF expenditures and revenues should be a primary focus because they account for the most considerable portion of municipal services and are primarily supported by general tax revenues (e.g., Brown, 1993; Kloha et al., 2005; Rivenbark & Roenigk, 2011). In contrast, others counter that the GF is important but represents only a fraction of various governmental activities. Hence, the results of a fiscal condition analysis could be substantially different depending on whether one is looking at the governmental funds or the government-wide level (Crosby & Robbins, 2013; Maher, 2013). Which approach is more appropriate is still unresolved and depends on the context; each choice has distinct implications.

From the service-level solvency perspective, the steady increase in per-capita municipal revenues and expenditures could be a warning sign. It means lower service-level solvency because each taxpayer may encounter a higher level of fiscal burden for public services (Wang et al., 2007). However, from the fiscal health standpoint, these trends may bode well for municipal governments because revenues and expenditures have consistently grown in tandem. In other words, the

Table 6.1 Expenditures and Revenues: Governmental Funds and General Fund

	1996	*1998*	*2000*	*2002*	*2004*	*2006*	*2008*	*2010*	*2012*	*2014*	*2016*
Total governmental funds expenditures	552.1	640.4	747.4	889.2	972.6	1,172.4	1,390.1	1,378.0	1,431.4	1,533.8	1,661.7
Total governmental funds revenues	526.4	615.0	716.9	813.0	890.8	1,109.3	1,268.8	1,241.8	1,343.2	1,453.3	1,573.4
Total GF expenditures	351.4	398.7	465.6	561.9	614.7	734.0	868.6	863.4	947.5	1,031.3	1,103.4
Total GF revenues	378.7	436.1	510.7	582.0	637.6	779.7	904.3	878.6	986.5	1,085.1	1,175.9
N	1,390	1,498	1,564	1,466	1,693	1,727	1,778	1,850	1,927	2,008	2,055

Source: Government Finance Officers Association

Note: Average real per capita dollars are reported (adjusted for inflation using CPI; the base year is 2016)

average municipal government has successfully generated enough resources to cover increasing service demands. As a result, municipalities have generally managed to avoid large gaps between service needs and resources (Gorina et al., 2019).

Additional indicators are considered to capture more details on municipal revenue structures: total GF taxes relative to total GF revenues, property taxes relative to total governmental fund revenues, and total GF intergovernmental aid relative to total GF revenues. These ratio measures are expected to capture the extent to which a municipal government relies on traditional tax sources and external aid, respectively, for its GF or governmental fund operation. Relying heavily on tax sources, such as property taxes, can mean that municipal governments have lower resource flexibility due to their less diversified revenue structure (Carroll, 2009). Higher reliance on intergovernmental aid could also be detrimental, indicating a lower level of municipal own-source capacity (Chapman & Gorina, 2012). It is still unclear how much reliance on traditional taxes is too much; this variable should be understood in comparison to peers or based on trend patterns. In the case of intergovernmental aid, however, some sources suggest that more than 10% reliance (government-wide) or 25% at the GF level could be harmful (see Appendix B).

As presented in Table 6.2, for the average municipal government, the ratio of GF taxes to revenues was 0.616 in 1996. This means that GF taxes accounted for 61.6% of all GF revenues. The percentage decreased slightly until 2000, indicating the recessionary impact of the 2001–2002 economic downturn. GF taxes as a percentage of GF revenues have grown consistently since then, from 62.4% in 2002 to 67.6% in 2016, including a more than 2% increase around 2010. This pattern suggests that taxes have played a significant role in municipal GF operations even during the Great Recession (see also Tax Policy Center, 2021). From the financial condition perspective, this could be a warning sign because it may indicate a gradual increase in municipal reliance on tax sources rather than on other types of revenue sources (e.g., pay-as-you-go revenues).

As a percentage of total governmental fund revenues, property taxes have exhibited a similar but relatively more stable trend over the last two decades. This stability may have been due to state-imposed TELs, which were designed to curtail municipalities' ability to raise property taxes (Stallmann et al., 2017). Given that the ratio of property taxes to total governmental fund revenues has been greater than 0.3 (i.e., proportionally greater than 30% of total revenues) in more recent years, however, it could be argued that property taxes have remained an essential municipal revenue source despite state restrictions. Furthermore, the stability and reliability of property taxes through most periods of economic fluctuation may have made this source an attractive option to municipal finance managers seeking ways to sustain their fiscal resources (Gorina et al., 2019; Mikesell & Liu, 2013).

Table 6.2 Revenue Structures: Taxes, Property Taxes, and Intergovernmental Aid

	1996	*1998*	*2000*	*2002*	*2004*	*2006*	*2008*	*2010*	*2012*	*2014*	*2016*
Total GF taxes relative to total GF revenues	0.616	0.612	0.611	0.624	0.639	0.648	0.653	0.674	0.678	0.676	0.676
Property taxes relative to total governmental funds revenues	0.276	0.269	0.264	0.281	0.289	0.284	0.300	0.320	0.312	0.304	0.306
Total GF IG aid relative to total GF revenues	0.149	0.151	0.155	0.149	0.142	0.127	0.126	0.121	0.122	0.123	0.125
N	1,390	1,498	1,564	1,466	1,693	1,727	1,778	1,850	1,927	2,008	2,055

Source: Government Finance Officers Association

Note: Ratios are reported

Intergovernmental aid has followed the opposite trend thus far, rising from 14.9% of all GF revenues in 1996 to 15.5% in 2000 and then dropping steadily to 12.5% in 2016. As municipal governments have very little control over intergovernmental aid, such changes over time may be part of the reason why municipal governments have had to rely less or more heavily on tax sources during the 21-year period (Krane et al., 2004). This finding clearly supports the inclusion of intergovernmental aid as a percentage of GF revenues in fiscal condition analysis. In comparison with the benchmark of 25% used by some state governments (e.g., Colorado and Virginia) to detect their municipal governments' fiscal stress, the average municipal government has been far below that figure, meaning that municipalities generally may not be relying too heavily on external revenues.

Operating Position Indicators: Short-Term

Now we discuss short-term operating position indicators. Operating position has been of major interest to scholars and practitioners, as it captures core dimensions of government fiscal condition such as budget balances (i.e., budgetary solvency) and liquidity (i.e., cash solvency). It also includes those fiscal elements over which municipal officials have greater control (Hendrick, 2004). We employ several indicators, presented below, to analyze municipal deficits (or surpluses), fund balances, cash, and enterprise fund operations.

To measure municipal operating position in terms of annual surplus (or deficit), we focus on two specific indicators: total GF revenues relative to total GF expenditures, and total per-capita GF surplus. Following some prior fiscal condition studies (Brown, 1993; Rivenbark & Roenigk, 2011; Wang et al., 2007), we look at expenditures divided by revenues and the per-capita difference between expenditures and revenues to capture the level of municipal deficit. As shown in Appendix B, professional organizations and government entities generally follow the norm of balance (i.e., zero deficit) as a benchmark for detecting fiscal stress. GF expenditures more than either 2% (Scorsone & Pruettt, 2020) or 5% (Nollenberger et al., 2003) of revenues are often considered abnormally large deficits.

The average municipal government has consistently had larger revenues relative to expenditures in its GF operations (see Table 6.3). The revenues-to-expenditures ratio has generally ranged from 1.05 to 1.10, indicating revenues equal to 105% to 110% of total expenditures. This is generally a positive sign, particularly in comparison to the benchmark options of 2% or 5% deficits. The surplus gap was smaller in 2010 (approximately 3% surplus) when the impact of the Great Recession was ongoing and possibly worsening (McFarland & Pagano, 2015). Per-capita GF surpluses have generally ranged between $27 and $73. Again, the average was relatively smaller ($17) in 2010, similar to the result for the revenues-to-expenditures ratio as discussed above.

Table 6.3 Surplus (or Deficit)

	1996	*1998*	*2000*	*2002*	*2004*	*2006*	*2008*	*2010*	*2012*	*2014*	*2016*
Total GF revenues relative to total GF expenditures	1.09	1.10	1.10	1.06	1.05	1.09	1.05	1.03	1.06	1.07	1.08
Per capita surplus: GF	41.8	55.1	62.8	26.7	29.1	54.4	39.8	16.7	40.8	54.6	72.5
N	1,390	1,498	1,564	1,466	1,693	1,727	1,778	1,850	1,927	2,008	2,055

Source: Government Finance Officers Association

Note: Ratios and average real per capita amounts in dollars are reported (adjusted for inflation using CPI; the base year is 2016)

The next set of operating position indicators focuses on fund balances, which identify the difference between assets and liabilities and thus measure municipal slack fiscal resources (Marlowe, 2005). By doing so, fund balances are expected to capture municipalities' ability to mitigate fiscal contingencies or maintain economic stability. It makes sense from this standpoint that fund balances, and more broadly governmental fiscal savings, have garnered significant attention from academics and practitioners, especially since the Great Recession (Arapis & Reitano, 2018). Considering that municipal governments accumulate fund balances most often in the GF, our focus is there.

Before GASB Statement 54, which has been in effect since 2011, GF fund balances were reported in three categories: reserved, unreserved-designated, and unreserved-undesignated balances.[3] GASB Statement 54 has replaced those categories with five new ones: non-spendable, restricted, committed, assigned, and unassigned balances.[4] To focus on slack resources that are relatively free for use and not constrained by legal arrangements or management issues, we first focus on unreserved-undesignated GF balances for the years before 2011, and then on unassigned GF balances for the later years. After that, we expand our focus to a broader range of GF balances: unreserved (both designated and undesignated), assigned, and unassigned balances. The intent is to identify all GF slack resources that are not legally bound for specific purposes.

The general norm concerning GF balances is that the higher, the better (Rivenbark & Roenigk, 2011; Maher, 2013, 2022). Some professional sources offer more specific benchmarks. Perhaps the most widely known benchmark is the GFOA's (2015) two-months rule, which recommends that municipal governments should secure unrestricted GF balances (committed, assigned, and unassigned balances) equal to no less than two months (16.7%) of GF operating revenues or expenditures (see also Pennsylvania's Early Warning System in Appendix B). Other rules include GF unassigned balances no less than 5% of GF revenues (Kioko & Marlowe, 2016), GF assigned and unassigned balances no less than 10% (Office of the New York State Comptroller, 2017) or 15% (Virginia Auditor of Public Accounts [APA], 2020) of GF expenditures, and GF total balances no less than 13% of GF revenues (Kloha et al., 2005) or 20% of GF expenditures (Office of the New York State Comptroller, 2017).

As shown in Table 6.4, GF unreserved-undesignated balances, both relative to expenditures and revenues and per capita, experienced steady growth in general from 1996 to 2008. Possibly due to the Great Recession, however, there was a relatively stagnant trend between 2008 and 2010. From 2012 to 2016, GF reserves measured as unassigned balances relative to expenditures/revenues and per capita rose rapidly again (faster than the average inflation rate of 1.31% during the period). Thus, the average municipal government possessed reserves close to 40% of total GF expenditures or 36% of total GF revenues. This could signify solid

Table 6.4 Fund Balances: GF Unreserved-Undesignated and Unassigned Balances

	Before GASB 54								*After GASB 54*		
	1996	*1998*	*2000*	*2002*	*2004*	*2006*	*2008*	*2010*	*2012*	*2014*	*2016*
Total GF UU balances relative to total GF expenditures	0.260	0.294	0.301	0.300	0.304	0.340	0.318	0.314	–	–	–
Total GF UU balances relative to total GF revenues	0.232	0.260	0.267	0.281	0.285	0.304	0.294	0.301	–	–	–
Per capita total GF UU balances	82.1	104.7	121.5	149.8	164.5	222.9	245.3	236.7	–	–	–
N	1,390	1,498	1,564	1,466	1,693	1,727	1,778	1,850	–	–	–
Total GF UA balances relative to total GF expenditures	–	–	–	–	–	–	–	–	0.347	0.366	0.393
Total GF UA balances relative to total GF revenues	–	–	–	–	–	–	–	–	0.323	0.335	0.359
Per capita total GF UA balances	–	–	–	–	–	–	–	–	284.1	328.7	376.1
N	–	–	–	–	–	–	–	–	1,926	2,008	2,055

Source: Government Finance Officers Association

Note: Ratios and average real per capita amounts in dollars are reported (adjusted for inflation using CPI; the base year is 2016)

fiscal health for most municipal governments, because their unconstrained slack resources for GF operations exceeded the benchmarks discussed above.

The analysis results also highlight two other issues. First, what is the proper measure of GF balances? Researchers have measured GF balances in different ways: relative to total expenditures, total revenues, or population size. Our findings indicate that comparing fund balances with either expenditures or revenues could present a similar pattern, but using total revenues as a denominator tends to provide smaller values for fund balance indicators than an expenditure denominator. Per-capita GF balances offer essential information, but per-capita trend patterns could be largely different from those measured compared to expenditures or revenues. Second, what has the impact of GASB 54 been? Although there was an explicit increase in GF balances between 2010 and 2012, it was not an abnormal change compared to past years (see 2004 and 2006, for example), especially in view of the possibility of more robust municipal reserves as the nation emerged from the Great Recession. It is therefore reasonable to conclude that GASB 54 has had minimal effect on municipal fund balance reporting.

Table 6.5 shows a broader range of GF balances—unreserved, assigned, and unassigned balances. The trends are largely similar to those reported in Table 6.4. GF unreserved balances, however measured, generally rose from 1996 to 2006, except for GF balances relative to expenditures for the years from 2002 to 2004. This deviation can be attributed to the recession around 2001. During and after the Great Recession, there was a slight decrease in GF unreserved balances, particularly relative to total expenditures and population size. GF assigned and unassigned balances have increased continuously since 2012. As of 2016, the average municipal government had ratios of 0.423 or 0.464, respectively, for GF revenues and expenditures, meaning that it had GF balances corresponding to over 42% and 46%, again respectively, of total GF revenues and expenditures. These ratios were far above the benchmarks, suggesting a positive sign of municipal fiscal health.

The next operating position indicator focuses on municipal cash and investments. Cash and investments, readily convertible to cash or cash equivalents, have been of interest to researchers as a key measure of municipal liquidity (Maher, 2022; Turley et al., 2015; Wang et al., 2007). This liquidity measure has been evaluated either at the GF (e.g., Kioko & Marlowe, 2016) or government-wide level (e.g., Virginia APA, 2020). It also has been assessed compared to current liabilities (Maher, 2013, 2022; Rivenbark & Roenigk, 2011) or monthly expenditures (e.g., Office of the New York State Comptroller, 2017).

In this chapter, we measure the indicator as total GF cash and investments relative to total GF expenditures. Thus, it captures the extent to which a municipal government can cover its annual general operating expenditures using cash or cash equivalents. One advantage of this approach is that we can easily understand municipal liquidity as a sum of fund balances and cash because the ratio uses

Table 6.5 Fund Balances: GF Unreserved and Assigned and Unassigned Balances

	Before GASB 54								*After GASB 54*		
	1996	*1998*	*2000*	*2002*	*2004*	*2006*	*2008*	*2010*	*2012*	*2014*	*2016*
Total GF unreserved balances relative to total GF expenditures	0.351	0.394	0.405	0.393	0.382	0.419	0.401	0.398	–	–	–
Total GF unreserved balances relative to total GF revenues	0.315	0.348	0.359	0.367	0.359	0.376	0.371	0.382	–	–	–
Per capita total GF unreserved balances	167.6	206.6	230.6	260.9	258.1	321.4	340.4	330.7	–	–	–
N	1,390	1,498	1,564	1,466	1,693	1,727	1,778	1,850	–	–	–
Total GF assigned and unassigned balances relative to total GF expenditures	–	–	–	–	–	–	–	–	0.413	0.431	0.464
Total GF assigned and unassigned balances relative to total GF revenues	–	–	–	–	–	–	–	–	0.384	0.396	0.423
Per capita total GF assigned and unassigned balances	–	–	–	–	–	–	–	–	361.8	397.4	451.1
N	–	–	–	–	–	–	–	–	1,926	2,008	2,055

Source: Government Finance Officers Association

Note: Ratios and average real per capita amounts in dollars are reported (adjusted for inflation using CPI; the base year is 2016)

the same denominator as one of the frequently used fund balances indicators presented above. Because most municipal governments tend to have conservative cash management policies (Chaney, 2005), finding a higher value for this indicator is not a surprise. The general rule is that the higher it is, the less fiscal stress a municipal government should encounter (Rivenbark & Roenigk, 2011). Chaney (2005) suggested a ratio of 2.0 (i.e., 200%) as the norm for municipalities; the existing benchmarks in Appendix B also suggest specific thresholds such as 100% or 150%. The acceptable level, however, depends on fund levels and specific measurements.

Using our measure of municipal cash and investments, as presented in Table 6.6, the average municipal government had a cash and investments ratio of 0.435, equal to 43.5% of its total GF expenditures. This figure has grown steadily over the last two decades. The exceptions were again the years of 2002 and 2010, when municipal governments generally experienced the recessionary impact of economic downturns. As of 2016, the average municipal government had a ratio of 0.537, equal to 53.7% of its total GF expenditures and corresponding to the resources needed for 6.4 months of GF operations. This suggests that municipal governments have maintained ample liquidity, especially when one combines GF balances with cash and investments (which results in a total of more than 100% of annual GF expenditures).

Another commonly used indicator of municipal liquidity is the current ratio, measured as current assets relative to current liabilities (McDonald, 2018; Wang et al., 2007). Researchers have used the current ratio to understand municipal liquidity and cash solvency at the government-wide level (e.g., Wang et al., 2007) or at the level of a specific fund, such as enterprise funds (e.g., Nollenberger et al., 2003). Given our focus above on cash and investments as a measure of GF liquidity, we calculate the current ratio only for enterprise funds, which are a significant aspect of operations for many municipalities.[5] By doing so, the indicator captures "the enterprise fund's ability to meet the ongoing service needs as well as its ability

Table 6.6 Cash and Investments

	1998	*2000*	*2002*	*2004*	*2006*	*2008*	*2010*	*2012*	*2014*	*2016*
Cash and investments of GF relative to total GF expenditures	0.435	0.451	0.431	0.418	0.447	0.430	0.418	0.467	0.499	0.537
N	1,498	1,564	1,466	1,693	1,727	1,778	1,850	1,927	2,008	2,055

Source: Government Finance Officers Association

Note: Ratios and average real per capita amounts in dollars are reported (adjusted for inflation using CPI; the base year is 2016)

Table 6.7 Enterprise Fund Assets

	2004	*2006*	*2008*	*2010*	*2012*	*2014*	*2016*
Current assets of enterprise funds relative to liabilities	6.897	7.048	6.538	6.449	6.837	7.726	9.322
N	1,483	1,539	1,585	1,635	1,709	1,791	1,824

Source: Government Finance Officers Association

Note: Ratios and average real per capita amounts in dollars are reported (adjusted for inflation using CPI; the base year is 2016)

to withstand financial emergencies" (Maher & Nollenberger, 2009, p. 63). Nollenberger et al. (2003) suggested that a decreasing trend in the current ratio is a warning sign for municipal governments. The GFOA (2011) recommended that especially for heavily subsidized enterprise funds, current assets of enterprise funds should not be less than 45 days' worth of annual operating expenses (about 12.3%).

As shown in Table 6.7, the average municipal government had current assets of enterprise funds 6.9 times greater than current liabilities in 2004. This ratio rose to an even higher level of 9.3 in 2016. This is a strongly positive sign of municipal fiscal health (Nollenberger et al., 2003). The exceptions, once again, are those years around the Great Recession. The current ratio for the average municipal government went down from 7.0 in 2006 to 6.4 in 2010, with the recovery period starting in 2012. These findings are not directly comparable with the GFOA's benchmark because the GFOA focuses only on heavily subsidized enterprise funds, with expenditures as the denominator. However, the assets-to-liabilities ratio of 9.3 in 2016 seems sufficient to meet the threshold, indicating solid municipal ability to maintain working capital for enterprise funds.

Operating Position Indicators: Long-Term

A municipal government's operating position is determined not only by short-term fiscal elements, but also by its condition in the relatively long term. To capture the long-term side of municipal operating positions, we follow Maher's (2013) suggestion to use unrestricted net position (net assets before GASB 63 in 2011) divided by total expenses. More specifically, we focus on governmental and business activity net positions. In this way, our measure is expected to show the extent to which municipal resources, which extend beyond cash, are available to cover annual spending for any governmental and business-type purposes (Maher, 2013). Some researchers and practitioners have also used other measures of long-term operating position, such as changes in net position divided by total assets (Kioko & Marlowe, 2016) and unrestricted net position relative to total liabilities (Rivenbark & Roenigk, 2011), depending on their focus.

The general norm here is that a municipal government is likely to be more stressed when it has a lower level of unrestricted net position (Maher, 2013, 2022; Rivenbark & Roenigk, 2011). The Virginia APA (2020) offers a more specific threshold, stating that a municipal government may encounter greater fiscal risk when its unrestricted net position relative to total expenditures is less than 15%. However, it is not uncommon to find a negative unrestricted net position, because a municipal government may rely heavily on pay-as-you-go financing for capital projects or may have long-term debt in excess of assets.

Figure 6.1 shows that the impact of the Great Recession is visible for both types of activities. Although the pre- and post-recession levels of the ratios between unrestricted net position and expenditures were largely similar, there was a dip in both ratios around the recession. Specifically for governmental activities from 2004 to 2014, the highest average unrestricted net position ratio was 0.459 in 2006 and 2007, corresponding to 45.9% of total expenditures on governmental activities. This was significantly higher than Virginia's benchmark of 15%. The lowest average was 37.4% in 2011. The most recent two years of 2015 and 2016 experienced an abnormally lower level of unrestricted net position because of GASB Statement 68, which required government entities, as of 2015, to report unfunded pension liabilities in their government-wide financial statements. Those liabilities, which are substantial in most cases, have caused a large deficit in municipal unrestricted net position.

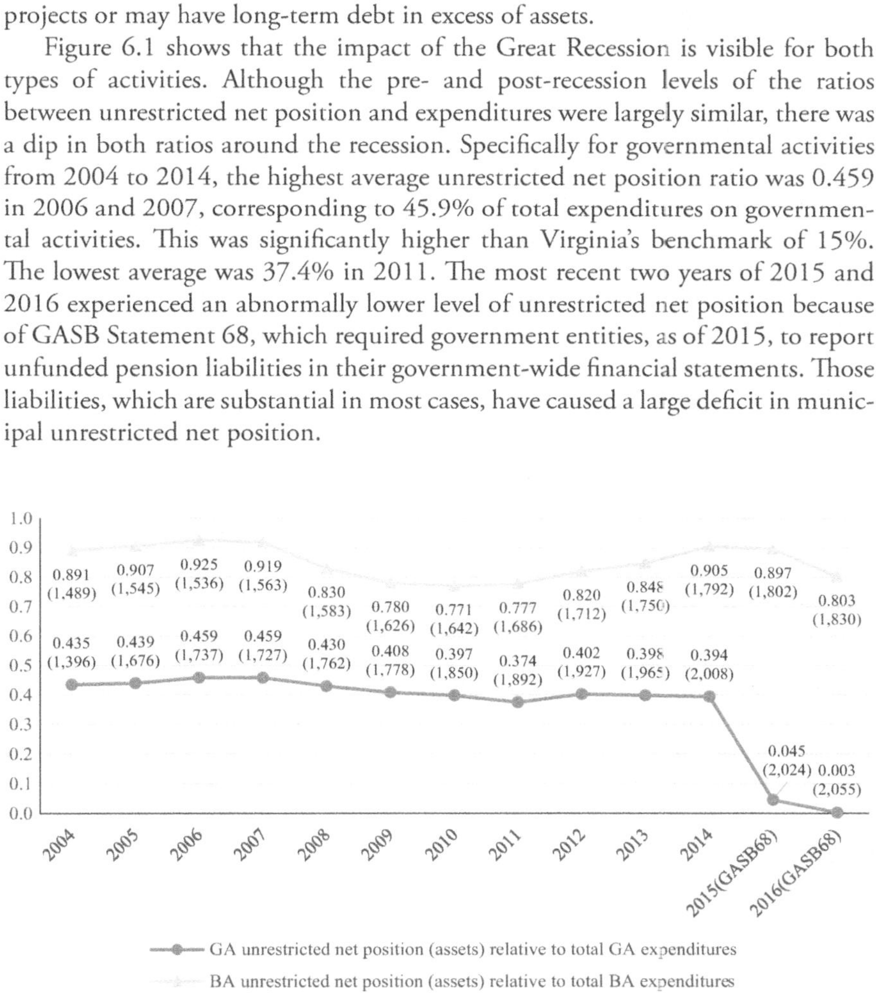

Figure 6.1 Unrestricted Net Position: Governmental and Business-Type Activities

Source: Government Finance Officers Association

Note: Ratios are reported. A total number of observations each year is reported in parenthesis

Not surprisingly, business-type activities, which tend to be capital-intensive, have a higher unrestricted net position ratio than governmental activities. The highest level of unrestricted net position for business-type activities was 92.5% of total business-type activity expenditures in 2006. The lowest was 0.771, or 77.1%, in 2010, after which it took several years to regain pre-recession levels in 2014 (at 0.905 or 90.5% of total expenditures). Over the study period, the average municipal government has maintained a unrestricted net position much higher than the benchmark suggested by the Virginia APA (2020), as another positive sign of overall municipal fiscal health.

Debt Indicators

Now we move to the last set of fiscal condition indicators, which focus on municipal debt, thereby capturing municipal ability to pay off existing long-term obligations (i.e., long-run solvency). We use four specific indicators: general obligation (GO) outstanding debt relative to assessed valuation, per capita GO outstanding debt, debt service expenditures relative to total governmental fund revenues, and per-capita debt service expenditures. The first two measures capture municipal debt levels in two ways: relative to assessed valuation (Maher, 2013, 2022) and population size (Wang et al., 2007). Higher debt levels mean that municipal governments are more fiscally distressed. The last two indicators focus on total debt service expenditures (i.e., principal and interest payments). Increasing debt service expenditures not only mean lower long-run solvency for municipal governments but also indicate less flexibility in spending (Nollenberger et al., 2003).

Professional sources offer varying benchmarks for debt indicators. The GFOA (2020) and Maher (2013, 2022) suggested that municipal outstanding debt relative to assessed valuation should be lower than the limits set by the state or the municipality (typically 2% to 4%), and that its trend patterns should also be assessed. Kloha et al. (2005) and the Virginia APA (2020) proposed that the ratio of debt to assessed valuation should be less than 0.06 or 0.03, respectively, for good fiscal health, meaning an amount of outstanding debt lower than either 6% or 3% of total assessed valuation. The Colorado Department of Local Affairs (2018) suggested that municipal governments in that state might encounter fiscal stress if they had per-capita debt larger than $1,778. For debt service expenditures relative to total revenues or expenditures, less than either 10% or 25% has been suggested as a threshold (Kioko & Marlowe, 2016; Virginia APA, 2020).

Our primary focus is on the ratio of GO outstanding debt to assessed valuation, because this ratio is typically the basis for state limits on permissible municipal GO debt (Park, 2018b). Over the last two decades, as reported in Table 6.8,

Table 6.8 Debt: GO Debt Outstanding and Debt Service Expenditures

	1996	*1998*	*2000*	*2002*	*2004*	*2006*	*2008*	*2010*	*2012*	*2014*	*2016*
GO debt outstanding relative to assessed valuation	0.009	0.008	0.008	0.009	0.008	0.008	0.008	0.008	0.009	0.009	0.008
Per capita GO debt outstanding	213.3	247.0	280.4	342.8	389.5	470.5	520.4	587.3	636.4	674.7	663.4
Debt service expenditures relative to total governmental funds revenues	0.089	0.082	0.074	0.079	0.065	0.089	0.094	0.103	0.104	0.095	0.090
Per capita debt service expenditures	45.8	50.2	52.5	67.9	57.8	97.0	119.2	129.2	139.1	133.9	138.4
N	1,390	1,498	1,564	1,466	1,693	1,727	1,778	1,850	1,927	2,008	2,055

Source: Government Finance Officers Association

Note: Ratios and average real per capita amounts in dollars are reported (adjusted for inflation using CPI; the base year is 2016)

the ratio has been consistently around 0.008 or 0.009, meaning that the average municipal government has maintained outstanding debt of 0.8% or 0.9% of assessed valuation. Based on the benchmarks of Kloha et al. (2005) and the Virginia APA (2020) cited in the previous paragraph, this is another positive sign, as it does not exceed either 6 or 3%. Per-capita GO outstanding debt grew steadily from 1996 ($213.3) to 2014 ($674.7); it then decreased slightly to $663.4 in 2016. Though the two figures are not directly comparable, this figure is significantly lower than Colorado's rule of $1,778.

Debt service expenditures relative to total revenues in governmental funds declined from 0.089 in 1996 (i.e., 8.9% of total governmental funds revenues) to 0.065 in 2004 (6.5%). The ratio rose to 0.089 (8.9%) in 2006 and 0.104 (10.4%) in 2012 before falling to 0.095 (9.5%) in 2014 and 0.090 (9%) in 2016. Except for those years right after the Great Recession, the average municipality has maintained a debt service expenditure ratio lower than 1—another positive sign of municipal fiscal health, according to Kioko and Marlowe (2016) and the Virginia APA (2020).

Municipal Variations in Fiscal Condition Measures: FY2016

Thus far, we have focused on identifying average trends in municipal fiscal conditions, using a large set of financial indicators. Now, looking only at 2016 data, we analyze municipal variations in fiscal condition by population size, region, and quartile. We also narrow our focus to ten of the 29 indicators discussed above. The ten prominent and representative indicators selected, shown in Table 6.9, are all ratio measures. Of those ten indicators, seven have a particular focus on short- and long-term operating positions, meaning that our analysis has an operating position bias. This is common in the literature, since fiscal sustainability or health is often closely related to budgetary balances and financial liquidity (Gorina et al., 2018; McDonald & Maher, 2020).

In Table 6.10, we first group the sample municipalities (N = 2,055) into six categories based on their population size. Then we analyze municipal variations in two ways: (1) calculating the average of each indicator for each of those six population groups for comparison purposes, and (2) calculating a cumulative index of municipal fiscal condition and using it to compare the different population groups.[6] Each population group includes a different number of sample municipalities. Some indicators are calculated based on unequal sample sizes within the same population group due to data availability.

The findings for indicators 1 to 4 show that smaller communities (with populations of 1 to 4,999, 5,000 to 9,999, and 10,000 to 49,999) were in a

Table 6.9 Selected Major Indicators

Indicator	*Dimension*	*Measure*
1	Revenue	Property taxes relative to total governmental funds revenues
2	Revenue	Total GF intergovernmental aid relative to total GF revenues
3	Operating position	Total GF revenues relative to total GF expenditures
4	Operating position	Total GF assigned and unassigned balances relative to total GF expenditures
5	Operating position	Total cash and investments of GF relative to total GF expenditures
6	Operating position	Current assets of enterprise funds relative to liabilities
7	Operating position (long-term)	GA unrestricted net position relative to total GA expenditures
8	Operating position (long-term)	BA unrestricted net position relative to total BA expenditures
9	Debt	General obligation debt outstanding relative to assessed valuation
10	Debt	Debt service expenditures relative to total governmental funds revenues

relatively worse position in 2016 than their counterparts with larger populations or the average municipal government. This is generally in line with our findings in Chapter 3. For example, municipal governments with populations between 5,000 and 9,999 had 0.317 on the first indicator, implying that their property taxes on average accounted for 31.7% of their total governmental fund revenues. Municipal governments with population less than 5,000 had 0.136 on the second indicator, meaning that their GF intergovernmental aid accounted for 13.6% of total GF revenues on average. This is larger than the sample mean of 0.125 and also the largest percentage of any population group. The same group had 1.051 on the third indicator. This result means that most municipal governments still had surpluses in their GFs (averaging 5%), but those surpluses were smaller when compared to the other population groups and to the sample mean.

The story is different for the remaining indicators, on which larger municipal governments were in a relatively worse position in 2016. This may suggest that smaller municipal governments could offset their stressed positions on the

Table 6.10 Municipal Variations in Fiscal Condition Measures by Population

	1–4,999	*5,000–9,999*	*10,000–49,999*	*50,000–99,999*	*100,000–499,999*	*500,000 or over*	*All municipalities (sample mean)*
Indicator 1	0.303	0.317	0.315	0.303	0.267	0.301	0.306
Indicator 2	0.136	0.125	0.134	0.109	0.105	0.106	0.125
Indicator 3	1.051	1.089	1.085	1.088	1.073	1.086	1.083
Indicator 4	0.746	0.534	0.490	0.394	0.299	0.171	0.464
Indicator 5	0.765	0.598	0.562	0.514	0.337	0.213	0.537
Indicator 6	15.070 (88)	12.524 (188)	9.778 (953)	7.821 (339)	5.549 (228)	3.149 (28)	9.322 (1,824)
Indicator 7	0.527	0.157	0.076	–0.133	–0.372	–0.960	0.003
Indicator 8	0.825 (90)	0.802 (187)	0.858 (957)	0.806 (341)	0.634 (227)	0.175 (28)	0.803 (1,830)
Indicator 9	0.006 (98)	0.008 (207)	0.008 (1,043)	0.007 (356)	0.011 (233)	0.013 (31)	0.008 (1,968)
Indicator 10	0.082	0.094	0.091	0.087	0.090	0.111	0.090
Cumulative z-score index	1.701 (80)	0.360 (177)	0.142 (910)	–0.249 (332)	–0.873 (217)	–2.041 (28)	0 (1,744)
N (otherwise specified in parentheses)	110	217	1,090	364	243	31	2,055

Source: Government Finance Officers Association

first three indicators with strong health on the remaining indicators. Municipal governments with populations of 500,000 or more, for example, averaged 0.171 (17.1% of total GF expenditures) and 0.213 (21.3% of total GF expenditures) on the fund balance and cash measures, respectively. Those figures were still higher than the existing benchmarks discussed above but far lower than the average for municipal governments with populations less than 5,000 (0.746 and 0.765, respectively). The sixth indicator suggests that smaller municipal governments' ratio of enterprise fund assets to liabilities was significantly greater than that for larger municipalities. Also, larger communities had relatively less unrestricted net assets relative to total expenses and higher debt and debt service burdens, according to the results of indicators 7 to 10.

The cumulative *z*-score index results show that overall, smaller municipal governments were in a better fiscal position than larger communities. In fact, municipal governments with populations less than 5,000 had a standard deviation of 1.701 from the sample mean, whereas those with at least 500,000 residents had a standard deviation of −2.041. This is in line with our observation above that smaller municipal governments had stronger operating and debt positions. Larger municipal governments were better on the revenue, expenditure, and deficit indicators, but these favorable results were not enough to compensate for their relative weakness on the other dimensions. We thus concur with Clark's (2015) concern about "cumulative errors" (p. 71); that is, generating a single index is useful to get an overall idea of municipal fiscal condition, but such an approach could mask some specific parts of the entire picture of municipal fiscal condition due to its cumulative nature.

In Table 6.11, we look at the same set of ten selected indicators and the cumulative *z*-score index by region. On indicator 1, municipal governments in New England and the Mideast had relatively higher ratios; on indicator 2, municipalities in the Great Lakes had a higher ratio. Municipal governments in those regions relied relatively more on property taxes or intergovernmental aid than the other regional groups—another pattern initially uncovered in Chapter 3. Municipal governments in the Plains, Southwest, and Southeast were in a relatively worse position on the surplus indicator, though each region still averaged 3% to 5% surpluses.

The fourth indicator concerns municipal fund balances. Municipal governments in the New England and Rocky Mountain regions had relatively lower ratios, or lower GF balances relative to GF expenditures than their counterparts in the other regions had. On indicator 5, municipalities in the Southwest region had a lower level of cash resources compared with the other regions. The results for New England were particularly ominous, as the average fund balance (0.166) and cash (0.284) ratios were lower than some of the existing benchmarks, such as the GFOA's 16.7% rule for fund balances.

Table 6.11 Municipal Variations in Fiscal Condition Measures by Region

	New England	*Mideast*	*Great Lakes*	*Plains*	*Southeast*	*Southwest*	*Rocky Mountain*	*Far West*	*All municipalities (sample mean)*
Indicator 1	0.637	0.397	0.278	0.327	0.323	0.296	0.149	0.213	0.306
Indicator 2	0.187	0.116	0.191	0.111	0.139	0.078	0.116	0.063	0.125
Indicator 3	1.064	1.105	1.158	1.030	1.048	1.033	1.121	1.111	1.083
Indicator 4	0.166	0.438	0.540	0.520	0.467	0.450	0.372	0.497	0.464
Indicator 5	0.284	0.737	0.552	0.539	0.566	0.469	0.471	0.600	0.537
Indicator 6	6.875 (101)	4.702 (46)	5.393 (348)	11.135 (193)	9.849 (459)	4.927 (255)	12.316 (98)	15.690 (324)	9.322 (1,824)
Indicator 7	–0.261	–0.058	–0.376	0.275	0.138	0.063	0.425	–0.005	0.003
Indicator 8	0.755 (101)	0.459 (47)	0.708 (349)	1.049 (194)	0.836 (461)	0.572 (255)	1.234 (97)	0.827 (326)	0.803 (1,830)
Indicator 9	0.021 (137)	0.009 (69)	0.011 (357)	0.010 (219)	0.005 (488)	0.013 (239)	0.002 (86)	0.002 (373)	0.008 (1,968)
Indicator 10	0.063	0.082	0.097	0.168	0.073	0.129	0.076	0.049	0.090
Cumulative z-score index	–2.491 (101)	–0.237 (46)	–0.539 (329)	0.234 (189)	0.102 (448)	–0.549 (231)	1.392 (83)	1.139 (317)	0 (1,744)
N (otherwise specified in parentheses)	137	69	379	225	500	263	101	381	2,055

Source: Government Finance Officers Association

The results for indicator 6 show that municipal governments in all regions were generally in a strong position in terms of enterprise fund assets relative to liabilities. However, municipal governments in the Mideast (4.702) and Great Lakes (5.393) regions had relatively lower ratios. The seventh indicator presents a warning for municipal governments in some regions, including New England, the Mideast, the Great Lakes, and the Far West, as their ratios were lower than zero. In contrast, municipal governments in all regions maintained a good level of unrestricted net position compared to their business-type activity expenses (greater than 45% on average).

Municipal governments in all regions had less GO outstanding debt relative to assessed valuation than the benchmarks of 3% or 6%. Municipal governments in New England and the Southwest had relatively higher debt ratios. Two regions—the Plains and Southwest—had average debt service expenditures relative to total governmental fund revenues that exceeded Virginia's benchmark of 10%, though they were below Kioko and Marlowe's 25% benchmark.

According to the cumulative *z*-score index, municipal governments in New England were overall in a worse position than any other region (−2.491) as of 2016. The Far West (1.139) and Rocky Mountain (1.392) municipal governments were at the favorable end of the spectrum. Their strong budgetary balances and enterprise assets appear to have been the main contributors to their strong fiscal positions.

In Table 6.12, we compare the selected fiscal condition indicators by quartile, with the fourth quartile indicating better condition in each instance. Two observations are noteworthy. First, there was a large gap between the first quartile and the fourth quartile on each indicator. For example, municipal governments in the first quartile averaged 0.581 on the first indicator, whereas their counterparts in the fourth quartile averaged 0.063. This means that the proportion of property taxes in total governmental revenues was 58.1% and 6.3%, respectively. The sixth indicator is another example. The ratio for the fourth quartile group was 16 times greater than that for the first quartile group. These high discrepancies may support the concern raised by Bradbury et al. (1984) about "fiscal disparities" between local jurisdictions (p. 151).

Second, much or all of the whole first quartile seems to be in a worrisome condition on several indicators. The second indicator has a ratio of 0.316 (or 31.6%) for the first quartile group, higher than the suggested benchmarks of 10% or 25%. Regarding budgetary balance (indicator 3), municipal governments in the first quartile had a value smaller than 1, suggesting that they tended to generate deficits at the GF level. Their fund balance, cash, and unrestricted net asset ratios were also lower than some comparable benchmarks. Their debt service expenditures relative to total revenues could also be a matter of concern, as the ratio exceeded the benchmark of 10%.

One crucial benefit of identifying different quartiles in municipal fiscal conditions is that it helps municipal officers not only to assess their entity's fiscal

Table 6.12 Municipal Variations in Fiscal Condition Measures by Quartile

	Quartile 1	*Quartile 2*	*Quartile 3*	*Quartile 4*	*All municipalities (sample mean)*
Indicator 1	0.581	0.361	0.220	0.063	0.306
Indicator 2	0.316	0.126	0.049	0.008	0.125
Indicator 3	0.890	1.024	1.094	1.323	1.083
Indicator 4	0.138 (514)	0.301 (514)	0.472 (514)	0.944 (513)	0.464
Indicator 5	0.164 (514)	0.335 (514)	0.535 (514)	1.113 (513)	0.537
Indicator 6	1.626 (456)	3.510 (456)	5.757 (456)	26.395 (456)	9.322 (1,824)
Indicator 7	-0.937 (514)	-0.150 (514)	0.216 (514)	0.885 (513)	0.003
Indicator 8	-0.113 (458)	0.452 (457)	0.843 (458)	2.030 (457)	0.803 (1,830)
Indicator 9	0.026 (492)	0.007 (492)	0.002 (385)	0 (599)	0.008 (1,968)
Indicator 10	0.207	0.090	0.050	0.014	0.090
Cumulative z-score index	-3.862 (436)	-1.708 (436)	0.113 (436)	5.456 (436)	0 (1,744)
N (otherwise specified in parentheses)	513	514	514	514	2,055

Source: Government Finance Officers Association

condition but also to compare their position with that of their peers. To further guide their self-assessment, we present the range of results on each indicator for each quartile by population size in Table 6.13. This table can be compared with information in Brown (1993, pp. 24–25) and Maher and Nollenberger (2009, p. 64) but contains more recent data, from 2016.

As an example of how to use this table, let us take the fifth indicator (fund balance ratio) and compare two mid-sized municipalities: the City of Azusa, California (population 48,498) and the City of Danville, Virginia (population 42,360). Azusa had assigned and unassigned GF balances worth $5.8 million in 2016, and the city's total GF expenditures were $32.5 million. Therefore, the fund balance ratio for Azusa was 0.179 in 2016. On the contrary, Danville's assigned and unassigned GF balances were $41.5 million while the city's GF expenditures were

Table 6.13 Quartile Ranges by Population Group

	Quartile 1	*Quartile 2*	*Quartile 3*	*Quartile 4*
<15,000				
Indicator 1	≥ 0.473	0.472 to 0.301	0.300 to 0.130	≤ 0.129
Indicator 2	≥ 0.203	0.202 to 0.086	0.085 to 0.027	≤ 0.026
Indicator 3	≤ 0.966	0.967 to 1.058	1.059 to 1.153	≥ 1.154
Indicator 4	≤ 0.308	0.309 to 0.491	0.492 to 0.755	≥ 0.756
Indicator 5	≤ 0.323	0.324 to 0.548	0.549 to 0.823	≥ 0.824
Indicator 6	≤ 2.254	2.255 to 4.467	4.468 to 7.698	≥ 7.699
Indicator 7	≤ –0.098	–0.097 to 0.215	0.216 to 0.600	≥ 0.601
Indicator 8	≤ 0.267	0.268 to 0.643	0.644 to 1.156	≥ 1.157
Indicator 9	≥ 0.0098	0.0097 to 0.0020	0.0019 to 0.0001	0
Indicator 10	≥ 0.111	0.110 to 0.059	0.058 to 0.025	≤ 0.024
15,000–29,999				
Indicator 1	≥ 0.480	0.479 to 0.317	0.316 to 0.172	≤ 0.171
Indicator 2	≥ 0.168	0.167 to 0.092	0.091 to 0.034	≤ 0.033
Indicator 3	≤ 0.991	0.992 to 1.051	1.052 to 1.130	≥ 1.131
Indicator 4	≤ 0.238	0.239 to 0.406	0.407 to 0.633	≥ 0.634
Indicator 5	≤ 0.273	0.274 to 0.445	0.446 to 0.704	≥ 0.705
Indicator 6	≤ 2.688	2.689 to 4.477	4.478 to 7.206	≥ 7.207
Indicator 7	≤ –0.285	–0.284 to 0.097	0.098 to 0.415	≥ 0.416
Indicator 8	≤ 0.310	0.311 to 0.685	0.686 to 1.197	≥ 1.198
Indicator 9	≥ 0.0121	0.0120 to 0.0038	0.0037 to 0.0003	≤ 0.0002
Indicator 10	≥ 0.128	0.127 to 0.070	0.069 to 0.041	≤ 0.040
30,000–49,999				
Indicator 1	≥ 0.427	0.426 to 0.266	0.265 to 0.148	≤ 0.147
Indicator 2	≥ 0.198	0.197 to 0.086	0.085 to 0.028	≤ 0.027
Indicator 3	≤ 0.987	0.988 to 1.060	1.061 to 1.152	≥ 1.153
Indicator 4	≤ 0.240	0.241 to 0.392	0.393 to 0.582	≥ 0.583
Indicator 5	≤ 0.266	0.277 to 0.419	0.420 to 0.661	≥ 0.662
Indicator 6	≤ 2.646	2.647 to 4.491	4.492 to 7.876	≥ 7.877
Indicator 7	≤ –0.380	–0.379 to 0.040	0.041 to 0.376	≥ 0.377
Indicator 8	≤ 0.313	0.314 to 0.649	0.650 to 1.100	≥ 1.101
Indicator 9	≥ 0.0104	0.0103 to 0.0035	0.0034 to 0.0001	0
Indicator 10	≥ 0.116	0.115 to 0.069	0.068 to 0.029	≤ 0.028

(*Continued*)

Table 6.13 (Continued)

	Quartile 1	*Quartile 2*	*Quartile 3*	*Quartile 4*
50,000–99,999				
Indicator 1	≥ 0.434	0.433 to 0.284	0.285 to 0.151	≤ 0.150
Indicator 2	≥ 0.161	0.160 to 0.062	0.061 to 0.017	≤ 0.016
Indicator 3	≤ 1.004	1.005 to 1.057	1.058 to 1.141	≥ 1.142
Indicator 4	≤ 0.194	0.195 to 0.338	0.339 to 0.497	≥ 0.498
Indicator 5	≤ 0.246	0.247 to 0.389	0.390 to 0.568	≥ 0.569
Indicator 6	≤ 3.157	3.158 to 5.170	5.171 to 7.804	≥ 7.805
Indicator 7	≤ –0.556	–0.555 to –0.090	–0.089 to 0.330	≥ 0.331
Indicator 8	≤ 0.276	0.277 to 0.646	0.647 to 1.107	≥ 1.108
Indicator 9	≥ 0.0106	0.0105 to 0.0029	0.0028 to 0.0001	0
Indicator 10	≥ 0.120	0.119 to 0.072	0.071 to 0.037	≤ 0.036
>100,000				
Indicator 1	≥ 0.382	0.381 to 0.252	0.253 to 0.143	≤ 0.142
Indicator 2	≥ 0.165	0.164 to 0.058	0.057 to 0.011	≤ 0.010
Indicator 3	≤ 0.997	0.998 to 1.055	1.056 to 0.129	≥ 1.130
Indicator 4	≤ 0.159	0.160 to 0.233	0.234 to 0.354	≥ 0.355
Indicator 5	≤ 0.164	0.165 to 0.270	0.271 to 0.400	≥ 0.401
Indicator 6	≤ 2.488	2.489 to 4.063	4.064 to 5.798	≥ 5.799
Indicator 7	≤ –0.905	–0.904 to –0.324	–0.323 to 0.072	≥ 0.073
Indicator 8	≤ 0.196	0.197 to 0.516	0.517 to 0.868	≥ 0.869
Indicator 9	≥ 0.0130	0.0129 to 0.0047	0.0046 to 0.0003	≤ 0.0002
Indicator 10	≥ 0.130	0.129 to 0.085	0.084 to 0.043	≤ 0.042

Source: Government Finance Officers Association

$90.0 million, resulting in a fund balance ratio of 0.462. According to Table 6.13, these data place Azusa in the first quartile and Danville in the third quartile. In other words, Danville was in a better fiscal position in terms of fund balances than Azusa. The same approach can be applied to the other indicators and with different population groups.

Concluding Thoughts

This chapter has built on the preceding two chapters by offering a set of financial condition indicators and then analyzing average municipal trends in fiscal conditions using those indicators. In addition, we also sought to understand municipal variations in fiscal condition by population size, region, and quartile. To accomplish this goal, we focused on ten selected measures of municipal fiscal condition. Overall, the average U.S. municipal government was in good shape in 2016, the most recent year available in the GFOA's financial indicators database. However, we also found some potential warning signs for the average municipality, including per-capita revenues and expenditures, tax ratios, and unrestricted net position for governmental activities. We also identified significant variations among municipal governments by population size, region, and quartile. Using our quartile analysis results, we offered the range on each indicator for each quartile by population size. These comparison data should assist municipal officers in conducting their own fiscal condition analysis.

Perhaps the most important finding in this chapter is the wide amount of variation in fiscal position across municipalities. From the policy standpoint, this means that municipal fiscal decisions and policies (discussed extensively in Chapter 3) often result in sharply different policy outcomes. These different policy outcomes can survive as part of the policy or system process, leading to different policy inputs through feedback loops. Therefore, it is natural for us to wonder what reactions and responses those policy outcomes may generate. In the following chapters, we will delve into this critical issue.

Notes

1. Researchers also use these indicators to measure service-level solvency, which denotes a municipal government's ability to deliver a necessary level of public services (Berne, 1992; Wang et al., 2007).
2. In Appendix B, we summarize different fiscal condition indicators used and/or suggested by selected studies, professional organizations, and government entities. We select these sources because they offer rather clear benchmarks of fiscal stress for each indicator or specific means of interpretation. We exclude some of their indicators (e.g., demographic conditions) that do not meaningfully align with the indicators we suggest in this chapter.
3. Reserved balances: resources legally constrained for specific purposes; unreserved-designated balances: resources not legally bound but still constrained by management for specific purposes; unreserved-undesignated balances: resources not constrained (GASB, 2022).
4. Non-spendable balances: resources not in spendable form or legally or contractually required to be maintained intact; restricted balances: resources legally bound by restrictions; committed balances: balances constrained by the limitations that the government imposes upon itself; assigned balances: resources intended for particular use by government committees or officials; unassigned balances: the remaining portion of fund balances (GASB, 2022).
5. One reason for this choice is data availability. The GFOA's Municipal Financial Indicators Database includes current liability information only for enterprise funds.

6. To generate the cumulative index, we first inversely calculated some of the ten measures so that higher values on all indicators would consistently imply better fiscal condition. Then we transformed each indicator value (i.e., ratio) into a z-score using the sample mean and standard deviation. Each z-score indicates the distance from the sample mean; a positive (negative) z-score indicates that the municipal government is in a better (worse) fiscal condition compared to the sample mean. Then we summed all z-scores to calculate a single cumulative score for each municipal government in the sample. This method allows the average municipal government to have zero in the cumulative index.

Chapter 7

Policy Actions

Municipal Responses to Fiscal Stress

Up to this point, we have offered a framework for studying municipal finances using an open-systems approach. We have put much effort into describing fiscal environments (inputs), fiscal decisions and structures (outputs), and fiscal condition (outcomes). Now we shift to responses to fiscal challenges or crises. The response that a municipality experiences to its fiscal condition creates a feedback loop through which local officials can learn to manage financial resources better and state officials can become aware of and address any instability that they see. In this chapter, we focus on the feedback loop at the local level by exploring how municipalities respond to periods of fiscal stress. In the next chapter, the loop will be expended to include responses observed at the state level.

Our exploration of municipal responses begins with a case study of Sidney, NE. Throughout much of the 21st century, the City of Sidney, a small (population 6,572) rural community in southwest Nebraska, was defying the odds and thriving. The city's economy was strong and the population was growing. According to the city's Comprehensive Development Plan (2012),

> Sidney's recent demographic revival began in the early 1990s with the rise in prominence of Cabela's, the expansion of their world headquarters, and a positive change in its economic strategies that has led to the development of one of the most (if not the most) attractive commercially prominent "Interchange Villages" in the state of Nebraska. (p. 5)

DOI: 10.4324/9780429270765-7

Unfortunately, like the experiences of such municipalities as Janesville, Wisconsin and Detroit, Michigan, the loss of a major employer had dramatic economic, demographic, and fiscal consequences for Sidney. In 2017, Cabela's was sold to rival Bass Pro Shop, meaning that the city's main corporate headquarters would not remain there. Despite assurances from Bass Pro that it would maintain a large footprint in Sidney, the former 2,000 jobs have now dwindled to about 200. The fiscal effects were felt almost immediately. The housing market was flooded with homes, causing prices to plummet. In 2018, more than 200 homes were on the market, compared to only 20 today. Average assessed home values peaked at $121,911 in 2017 and bottomed out at $90,320 in 2019.

As a result, property valuations also dropped—by 9% between FY2018 and FY2019 and another 11% the following year. This was after more than a decade of consistently positive valuation growth (averaging 5% from FY2006 to FY2018). Given the city's heavy reliance on property taxes for general revenues (20% in FY2018) and property tax rate limits, tax collections were affected. Between FY2017 and FY2018, property tax collections grew by 3%; following the drop in valuation, they dropped by 6% from FY2018 to FY2019 and 11.1% the next year. The city's other critical general fund revenue source, sales and occupation taxes, took a similar hit, falling by 4.8% between FY2017 and FY2018 and by 11.0% from FY2018 to FY2019.

City officials' responses to this fiscal and economic crisis appear to have been highly effective. According to Sidney's manager, David Scott, whom we interviewed in 2021, city officials first made some structural changes. They converted the clerk/treasurer position into two positions, maintaining the clerk position and turning the treasurer role into a new finance director position. The finance director was then charged with refinancing debt at lower costs and developing a five-year budget. These structural changes were not sufficient, however, so budget cuts were necessary. The cuts consisted of a combination of across-the-board and more targeted reductions. General fund expenditures dropped by 6.3% between FY2017 and FY2018, 6.4% from FY2018 to FY2019, and 4.1% from FY2019 to FY2020. The areas taking the largest hits were community and economic development (cut by 12.9% between 2018 and 2019), fire (10.6%), general administration (6.8%), and police (8.4%). Following best budgeting practices—especially for such difficult times—city officials also reached out to the public to help them explain the needed cuts, recruiting volunteers to participate in the decision processes. Mr. Scott also described the connections between service cuts and budget cuts so that residents would better understand these fiscal decisions.

Within the past few years, Sidney has experienced a leveling off of its decline. Aided by a relatively close proximity to Colorado, an influx of retirees, actions taken by city officials to stop the fiscal bleeding, and a commitment by residents and businesses to stay, Sidney is no longer hemorrhaging jobs or revenues. After bottoming out in 2019–2020, property valuations grew by 2.2% between FY2020 and FY2021. Property tax collections also grew during the same period, by 16%. Mr. Scott noted that the city has adopted an aggressive economic development strategy and has been successful in attracting new businesses. He added that one of the upsides of Cabela's departure is that wages are now competitive, allowing companies to tap into a highly skilled labor force at lower cost.

This case study highlights a few helpful points. First, although we frequently think about fiscal stress within the context of national or global recessions, fiscal stress can be inflicted on municipal governments at any time and for a number of reasons. Thinking back to the introductory chapter of this book, we can envision municipal fiscal health being affected by political changes (e.g., TELs), long-term demographic and economic decline, national and international economic trends, regional economic and demographic trends, sudden shocks caused by natural disasters, or (as in Sidney) the departure of a major employer. How communities react to events that cause fiscal stress and the degree to which response strategies are hindered by institutional constraints and/or aided by innovative methods have been topics of interest for both scholars and practitioners. This chapter highlights the different frameworks used to describe and explain fiscal stress response strategies.

Theoretical Descriptions of Municipal Responses to Fiscal Stress

The question of what actions municipalities take when confronted by fiscal distress has both practical and theoretical implications. Theoretically, one can expect the actions taken during this period to differ from the norm. For students of budgeting behavior, there is a sizable body of work that explains the actions taken by political actors. The most revered scholar in this field is Wildavsky (1966, 1974, 1986). Much of Wildavsky's seminal work on budgeting was written during a period of sustained growth in the public sector; he coined the phrase "incrementalism" to describe the fact due to the fragmented nature of political decision-making, budgetary changes from one year to the next would be only slightly different. However, such a framework is less defensible as resource scarcity forces non-incremental budgeting decisions, particularly in municipalities such as New York (Alcaly & Mermelstein, 1976; Berne & Schramm, 1986) and Detroit (Plerhoples & Scorsone, 2010). According to Levine (1978, p. 316):

> Almost all of our public management strategies are predicated on assumptions of the continuing enlargement of public revenues and expenditures. These expansionist assumptions are particularly prevalent in public financial management systems that anticipate budgeting by incremental additions to a secure base. Recent events and gloomy

> forecasts, however, have called into question the validity and generality of these assumptions, and have created a need to reopen inquiry into the effects of resource scarcity on public organizations and their management systems. These events and forecasts, ranging from taxpayer revolts like California's successful Proposition 13 campaign and financial crises like the near collapse into bankruptcy of New York City's government and the agonizing retrenchment of its bureaucracy, to the foreboding predictions of the *limits of growth* modelers, also relink issues of political economy of the most monumental significance to practices of public management.

Moving away from incremental budgeting decisions requires changes in the political environment (Wildavsky, 1986) and/or the economic and demographic environments. Fiscal stress has been shown to cause an inflection point at which budgetary policy changes occur at a rate that deviates from incremental change. Particularly since the 1970s, scholars have debated the extent to which we can explain and perhaps predict budgetary actions during periods of fiscal stress. Theoretically, those actions have fallen into three groups: decrementalist, rational, and garbage-can approaches.

Decrementalism

The decrementalist approach represents, in essence, a reverse model of incrementalism. Schick (1983) argued that sporadic fiscal stresses challenge the incremental approach to budgeting because "resources do not permit the government to continue doing all that it did in the past" (pp. 19–20). He proposed four stages of fiscal stress:

- Relaxed scarcity, which means that current operations can be continued and the organization forgoes any new commitments (thus, there is essentially no real fiscal stress)
- Chronic scarcity, described as "the normal budget situation" where the organization still has sufficient revenues to meet expenses but not all public demand
- Acute scarcity, when revenues are no longer sufficient to meet expenditures, therefore requiring spending limits with a short-term focus
- Total scarcity, where resources are grossly insufficient to meet public expenditure expectations, thus rendering unrealistic budget scenarios

Less clear than the stages in this decremental model are what response strategies will be selected or decisions made in response to fiscal stress. In general, it is expected that across-the-board cuts will occur in the early stages of cutback processes, with more targeted cuts occurring as stress levels grow. Across-the-board cuts generally cause little political conflict or risk and are most favorable to multiple actors (Lindblom, 1959).

However, this approach leaves further predictions of cutback strategies unclear (Nelson, 2012). After the early stages of cutback processes, worsening or unresolved fiscal conditions require governments to adopt riskier or more severe cutback strategies. Because of the political risk involved, entities might be reluctant to adopt strategies that reduce organizational growth or are more threatening (Downs, 1967; Jimenez, 2014; Niskanen, 1971). The decisions on cutback strategies that lead to more political conflict depend on each community's characteristics, including both financial and nonfinancial factors (Nelson & Balu, 2014; Overmans & Timm-Arnold, 2016). The variations in nonfinancial factors, such as socioeconomic status and politico-administrative systems, among local governments make it difficult to identify patterns in decisions regarding cutback strategies (Nelson, 2012).

Rational

The most prolific scholar on the topic of fiscal stress has been Levine (1978, 1979, 1980, 1984, 1985), whose rational approach (Levine, 1980) to budget decision making during periods of fiscal distress challenges the decremental explanation of municipal responses. Rather, according to Levine, budgetary actions during periods of fiscal distress are predicated on the of level of fiscal stress experienced. Under the least severe stress, governments tend to prefer short-term, band-aid solutions that offer little political risk, such as delaying capital spending and limiting discretionary spending. Cutback strategies that are more painful to the organization and politically controversial, such as salary and hiring freezes, increases in fees, and across-the-board or selected cuts, become more frequent under more severe stress. Finally, under the most severe fiscal stress, government services will need to contract, thus forcing the reduction and/or elimination of services, furloughs, and/or salary reductions. The rational approach predicts that identifiable step-by-step responses to fiscal stress will occur in most communities confronted by fiscal stress (Levine et al., 1981).

Following Levine's lead, Wolman and Davis (1979) focused on fiscal stress caused by economic and political challenges such as reductions in intergovernmental aid and growing imposition of TELs (e.g., California's Proposition 13 in 1978). Without laying out any sequence of actions, Wolman and Davis described response strategies based on the principal goals of "maintaining existing employment levels and budget total . . . [since] local governments, *ceteris paribus*, will prefer revenue-increasing to expenditure-reducing strategies" (1979, p. 233). This description assumes, of course, that revenue raising options are available given the proliferation of TELs. The available response strategies are described as follows:

Operating expenditure reductions

- Layoffs, hiring freezes, cutback of overtime, wage freezes or reductions in rate of salary growth, reduced operations expenditures (travel, equipment, supplies, etc.)
- Reduced maintenance, service delivery, administration
- Reduced spending on social, core (e.g., police and fire), optional (e.g., parks and recreation), and general (e.g., central administration) government functions
- Reduced participation in federal and state programs that require a matching contribution
- Transfer of functions to other levels of government
- Administrative and management reforms designed to create greater efficiencies
- Delay or nonpayment of bills
- Default

Capital expenditure reductions

- Freeze spending on new projects
- Defer nonessential projects
- Transfer costs to private capital

Increased revenues

- Tax rate increases or changes in tax structure
- Increased tax base (e.g., annexation, new construction)
- Increased fees or charges
- Borrowing
- Liquidation of assets
- Pursuing federal and state aid

Through a series of case studies, Wolman and Davis (1979) identified an array of actions taken by officials to address fiscal challenges. Initial actions tend to be short-term with limited political consequences; as the severity of stress increases, more politically challenging actions are taken. For instance, the authors note that pursuit of intergovernmental aid is often the first strategy pursued, along with actions that “buy time” (p. 234), including drawing down reserves, interfund transfers, and short-term borrowing. The authors even found that local governments were willing to make adjustments in programs previously funded at the local level to comply with federal funding requirements in order to save jobs and maintain overall spending levels. Other politically acceptable spending cuts included across-the-board reductions and cuts in capital improvement projects and maintenance.

Once these efforts were exhausted and/or proven ineffective, Wolman and Davis observed local governments shifting to more politically difficult strategies to raise revenues and limit spending. These included the imposition of new taxes, higher tax rates, actions to spur tax base growth, and increased fees and charges. Expenditure reductions were less common at this stage. When expenditure reductions were instituted, they tended to focus on preserving services by improving efficiency, such as through reorganization and contracting out for services. Other actions included freezes on travel, reductions in supplies and equipment, and reducing capital outlays. On the personnel side, efforts to lower payroll through attrition and freezes were easier than layoffs, especially in heavily unionized communities.

Writing at a time when most municipalities were constrained by TELs and on the heels of the Great Recession, Hendrick (2011) offered a more detailed and tiered set of municipal responses to fiscal stress. She broke down municipal budgetary actions based on four levels of distress:

Tier 1: Low stress; strategies focus on delaying and buying time

- Short-term notes and fund transfers
- Delaying capital expenditures
- Drawing down reserves
- Charging outlays to the next fiscal year
- Optimistic forecasts (higher revenues and lower expenditures)
- Charging internal services to fiscally healthy funds
- Limiting discretionary spending (e.g., travel)
- Pursuit of grants

Tier 2: Moderate stress; strategies focus on stretching and resisting

- Use of long-term debt for operating expenditures
- Salary and hiring freezes
- Reductions in employees, preferably through attrition
- Increasing the employees' share of retirement contributions
- Limiting service hours (e.g., library)
- Increasing fees and charges
- Efficiency reforms (service delivery, use of technology)

- Across-the-board or selected cuts
- Reductions in overtime
- Lower pension contributions

Tier 3: High fiscal stress; visible and dramatic cuts in services; revenue increases

- Selling assets
- Terminating programs and transferring services to other units of government
- Increasing visible taxes (e.g., property tax)
- Decreasing visible services (e.g., police)
- Layoffs, furloughs, and salary reductions
- Closing of facilities

Tier 4: Extreme fiscal stress; focus is on organizational survival

- Illegal, prohibited or dishonest actions (e.g., destroying records)
- Fake budgets based on unrealistic assumptions
- Non-budgets—i.e., operating without an adopted budget
- Focus on cash—not paying bills, defaulting on payments, and relying on transfers from other funds

Hendrick's hierarchical structure of response strategies based on fiscal stress severity was formed based on surveys she sent to municipal officials in the Chicago metropolitan area in 1993 and 1994. She found, consistent with the rational framework, that the response strategies were relatively consistent. Although she admitted some limitations of survey research in this context—such as having to assume that officials would respond honestly—Hendrick found convincing evidence of a "causal order" (p. 71) or consistent set of responses based on perceived levels of fiscal stress. This view is partially supported by several other studies that reported that high levels of fiscal stress increase the probability of service cuts, which are considered a severe response to fiscal stress (Jimenez, 2014; Maher & Deller, 2007). Presuming that cutback responses to fiscal stress occur in this straightforward, predictable, and rational manner, we should find a correlation between cutback strategies and the severity of fiscal stress (Nelson, 2012; Nelson & Balu, 2014).

Garbage-Can

In contrast to Levine and associated scholars, Morgan and Pammer (1988) and Pammer (1990) have asserted that the political environment of municipalities does not lend itself to systematic responses to fiscal stress. Rather, they drew on garbage-can theory to explain the unstructured behavior frequently observed in organizations under stress. First introducted by Cohen et al. (1972), garbage-can theory explains decision-making processes that disconnect problem identification, decision participants, and solutions from each other, leading to unstructured decisions. Pammer's (1990) seminal work on retrenchment strategies in 120 municipalities found little evidence of systematic and rational responses to fiscal stress.

Similarly, Bartle's (1996) study of fiscal responses to stress, measured as declines in revenues, found no consistent or systematic changes across municipalities on the expenditure side of the ledger. Bartle (1996) found that most responses were short-term—reducing capital spending and reserves, and increasing fees and taxes—leading him to conclude that municipalities look for "a path of least resistance" (p. 47) and that decision makers will focus on those actions over which they have the greatest control. These decisions follow the garbage-can policy process approach, according to which a municipal government's choices on cutback strategies are "confused and unstructured" (Pammer, 1990, p. 46). Thus, this view emphasizes that it is impossible to capture a clear logic in cutback management decisions. This view received earlier support from Miller (1983) and Downs and Rocke (1984), who found little or no evidence of any budgeting algorithm that would allow us to predict cutback strategies in a consistent and systematic way.

Survey of Fiscal Responses During a Pandemic

Although the bulk of the empirical evidence favors the framework that claims to find rational fiscal responses during periods of fiscal stress, the current environment may challenge those norms, in the sense that municipal revenue options have been curtailed by TELs and that the social and economic calamity caused by the COVID-19 pandemic could challenge conventional wisdom. In April 2020, Maher and his colleagues sent a survey to nonprofit and public-sector professionals to gauge the early fiscal effects of COVID-19 and how public officials had responded to these challenges (Maher, Hoang et al., 2020). The electronic survey received 297 responses from federal, state, county, municipal, special districts, and nonprofit or foundation representatives. In this chapter, we include only municipal government responses (N = 89). The respondents were predominantly from Nebraska and Wisconsin, but they also included a handful from Illinois, Florida, and Massachusetts.

Survey responses from municipal officials were tabulated based on their perceived level of fiscal stress and the identified response strategies. To gauge levels of fiscal stress, respondents were asked, "Please rate the current financial condition of your organization on a scale of 1 (perfect fiscal health) to 10 (fiscal crisis)." To measure response strategies, respondents were asked, "The suddenness and severity of the effects of COVID-19 are forcing many public and nonprofit organizations to face varying levels of fiscal stress. Please help us understand the means by which your organization has responded to these challenges." The respondents were also asked to "indicate the degree to which you agree with the following statements as they describe your organization's recent efforts to cope with fiscal stress." The respondents were then divided into categories of lower fiscal stress (those who rated their situation as 5 or less; n = 55) and higher fiscal stress (ratings of 6 or more; n = 34).

To the extent possible, Hendrick's response strategies were divided between those associated with low, moderate, and high fiscal stress and then compared with the responses. If municipal officials' responses to fiscal stress are erratic and show no patterns of systematic differentiation, then we should not find patterns in these responses. If, on the other hand, there are clear patterns in the data, we could surmise that officials do indeed follow a process in response to fiscal stress, like those proposed by Levine (1980) and Hendrick (2011).

The results revealed relatively consistent patterns, in that municipalities with higher fiscal stress were more likely to have implemented Hendrick's more advanced strategies (see Table 7.1). Compared to their counterparts with higher levels of stress, those with lower levels of stress were most likely to freeze discretionary spending (45%), seek financial assistance (40%), attempt to improve productivity (41%), and reduce employee work hours (35%). Officials in less stressed municipalities were least likely to engage in short-term borrowing (72% disagreed), reduce pension contributions (74%), raise property taxes (72%), or raise sales tax rates (74%).

The actions taken by leaders in more fiscally stressed municipalities differed in that they were more likely to delay capital expenditures (66%), freeze discretionary spending (59%), delay routine maintenance expenditures (56%), and seek federal assistance (50%). Officials in highly stressed municipalities were least prone to raise property taxes (74% disagreed), adopt or increase user fees and charges (73%), reduce pension contributions (71%), or raise sales taxes (71%).

The survey also asked an open-ended question: "Considering the actions needed to immediately cope with the fiscal effects of COVID-19, what were the five most important current actions taken?" The responses were similar between officials in municipalities with low to moderate fiscal stress and those with moderate to high fiscal stress. The results also vary from the typologies offered by Levine and Hendrick. Actions taken by most officials included closing facilities, such as city hall and libraries, and moving all meetings to virtual environments, which at the time incurred additional costs since most municipalities were not positioned to shift to remote work. For officials in less stressed municipalities, travel and non-critical expenditure limits were imposed, along with limits on capital expenditures and on hiring (especially part-time and seasonal employees). The open-ended responses from officials in more severely stressed municipalities were generally similar but cited each type of action more frequently.

Table 7.1 City Responses to Fiscal Stress

	Lower Fiscal Stress			*Higher Fiscal Stress*		
	Agree	*Neutral*	*Disagree*	*Agree*	*Neutral*	*Disagree*
Low fiscal stress						
Borrowed short-term	0.06	0.22	0.72	0.09	0.19	0.72
Delayed capital expenditures	0.34	0.21	0.45	0.66	0.16	0.19
Drew down cash reserves to meet daily operating expenses	0.13	0.28	0.59	0.24	0.15	0.61
Froze discretionary spending, e.g., travel	0.45	0.19	0.36	0.59	0.13	0.28
Refinanced outstanding debt	0.19	0.26	0.56	0.29	0.19	0.52
Delayed routine maintenance expenditures	0.32	0.21	0.47	0.56	0.19	0.25
Transferred funds to operating budget	0.15	0.28	0.57	0.26	0.19	0.55
Sought financial assistance through community/foundation relief grants, crowdfunding	0.19	0.26	0.55	0.28	0.22	0.50
Sought financial assistance (e.g., federal grants or FEMA)	0.40	0.21	0.40	0.50	0.09	0.41
Moderate fiscal stress						
Improved productivity through better management	0.41	0.43	0.17	0.21	0.47	0.32
Contracted out services	0.09	0.41	0.50	0.24	0.12	0.65
Pursued regional cooperation agreements	0.23	0.47	0.30	0.25	0.34	0.41
Consolidated departments	0.07	0.41	0.52	0.25	0.31	0.44
Made across the board budget cuts	0.13	0.28	0.58	0.33	0.13	0.53
Implemented targeted budget cuts	0.23	0.25	0.53	0.39	0.19	0.42

(*Continued*)

Table 7.1 (Continued)

	Lower Fiscal Stress			*Higher Fiscal Stress*		
	Agree	*Neutral*	*Disagree*	*Agree*	*Neutral*	*Disagree*
Froze hiring or reduced employment through attrition	0.23	0.15	0.62	0.34	0.38	0.28
Adopted or increased user fees and charges	0.11	0.19	0.70	0.12	0.15	0.73
Reduced pension contributions	0.02	0.25	0.74	0.03	0.26	0.71
Reduced hours for public access	0.35	0.15	0.50	0.34	0.22	0.44
Created or expanded enterprise funds	0.04	0.38	0.59	0.10	0.30	0.60
Severe fiscal stress						
Eliminated services	0.25	0.25	0.51	0.38	0.13	0.50
Raised property taxes	0.07	0.20	0.72	0.06	0.19	0.74
Raised sales taxes	0.00	0.26	0.74	0.06	0.23	0.71
Laid off workers, reduced employee's hours, or furloughs	0.26	0.15	0.58	0.23	0.10	0.68

Source: Maher, Hoang et al. (2020)

The survey results and comments received by municipal officials expressed the unique challenges associated with managing the COVID-19 pandemic. One unique complication was the need to provide for the health and safety of staff and citizens. To the extent possible, staff and services (including meetings) shifted to remote interaction. Doing so required additional costs associated with technology and equipment. Facilities such as libraries and city hall were closed. Municipal officials were also forced to invest in personal protective equipment (PPE). On the revenue side, sales tax collections were particularly hard hit due to the closing of restaurants and shops, in addition to people's apprehensions about venturing outside (see McDonald & Larson, 2020). Officials were also preparing for unpaid utility payments and potential property tax losses.

The response strategies discussed above, while consist with the rational framework, also highlight concerns expressed by Bartle (1996), meaning that regardless of the level of fiscal stress, response strategies tend to be short-term efforts to stop the bleeding. These include looking for management efficiencies, cutting discretionary spending, seeking financial assistance (not surprising, since the CARES Act provided some reimbursement for municipal expenses), and delaying capital expenditures. None of these responses, particularly avoidance of capital expenditures, are sustainable over a longer period of time.

There are also theoretical and practical challenges associated with cutback management (Levine, 1978; Pandey, 2010). For instance, state-imposed revenue and expenditure limits, debt limits, and balanced-budget requirements constrain municipal government response strategies (Goldberg & Neiman, 2014; Nelson, 2012; Pandey, 2010). Pandey (2010) also found that longer-term strategies can be challenging: "In hard times, public attention is focused, but in an impatient manner looking for and hoping for the impossible—solutions that are quick and easy" (p. 566). It also appears that budget processes based on annual allocations of resources encourage sacrificing long-term in favor of short-term goals (see also Bartle, 1996; Levine et al., 1981). Pandey (2010) further noted that ambiguity of public organization goals creates additional challenges for cutback management. For instance, program that benefit the disenfranchised are often the first ones cut due to recipients' lack of political influence (see also Clark & Walter, 1991).

Given the sizable share of public expenditures dedicated to personnel costs, it is not surprising that these costs are part of the retrenchment repertoire. Interestingly, retirement benefits in particular have become a focal point: "Deferring pension payments and issuing pension obligation bonds (POBs) has been a tool of last resort for cities that have cut spending to the bone and are looking for creative ways to finance their way out of looming insolvency" (Hinckley, 2015, p. 94). To give a sense of scale, Cournoyer (2012) identified 2,931 POBs issued by 236 governments through 2009. Pensions were a focus of reform strategies in Detroit (Hinckley, 2015) and in California municipalities (Goldberg & Neiman, 2014).

More recently, performance-based decision making has been considered an effective strategy for responding to fiscal distress. According to Goldberg and Neiman (2014), "Data transparency, innovation and legitimacy are important contributors to managing fiscal stress" (p. 22). Since the 1990s, a large amount of performance data has been collected, but there is limited evidence that these data are used meaningfully in decision-making process (Kim, Maher et al., 2018; Moynihan, 2008; Pandey, 2010). Kim, Maher et al. (2018), utilizing the ICMA survey data and municipal audit data, sought to determine the extent to which performance information was used during periods of severe fiscal distress. Although there was a correlation with the use of a couple response strategies (furloughs and layoffs), the authors failed to find evidence that performance information aided these decision-making processes.

Recovery Strategies

So what should municipal governments be doing? Putting aside the actual practice of response strategies, can we identify best practices? Interestingly, recovery strategies are not discussed widely in academia. Much of the work in this area comes from white papers and professional or trade publications. Following the Great Recession, the ICMA partnered with the Alliance for Innovation to produce a report on recovery strategies (Miller & Svara, 2009). The report encouraged municipal officials to seize the opportunity to eliminate outmoded and/or inefficient practices, increase revenues and/or draw down reserves, and sustain capital expenditures (p. 1). Interestingly, most of these suggestions run counter to the cutback strategies offered by Levine (1980). The National League of Cities conducted a five-year review of its surveys of city officials (from 2012 to 2017) and asserted that city recovery from recessionary shocks requires (1) a supportive relationship with the state, (2) alignment of budgetary practices with the community's economic base, and (3) demands from citizens that align with ability to pay (Yadavalli, 2018). In an NLC case study, the City of Lincoln, Nebraska was noted as a resilient community not heavily affected by the recession. The author notes the stability of public-sector jobs, a strong millennial base, and sound budgetary practices, which sustained budget surpluses (Wagner, 2019). Finally, the GFOA has produced a number of items to assist municipal policymakers, including trainings and a series of publications. Not surprisingly, the GFOA tends to focus more on budgeting processes and long-range planning.

Concluding Thoughts

When municipal governments are under fiscal stress, they can respond in any number of ways, from short-term, across-the-board budget cuts to the complete elimination of certain services. Common strategies include delaying capital improvements, such as the purchase of new equipment or replacement of existing infrastructure, as well as deferring regularly scheduled infrastructure maintenance programs. The responses by municipal governments, tend to vary depending on the severity of the fiscal stress and the amount of institutional flexibility determined by state and/or federal rules and regulations. Municipalities facing very severe stress, such as Flint, Michigan, or Sidney, Nebraska, must implement more draconian policies than a municipal government that was perhaps a little too optimistic in its revenue forecasts.

Also, municipal governments are increasingly facing restrictions as to how they can approach periods of fiscal stress. Most states now have some form of TELs that limit municipalities' ability to raise additional revenues in the short term. In addition, some services, such as police and fire protection, are mandated, further reducing the flexibility of many municipal governments. Nonmandated services that often improve residents' quality of life, such as parks and recreation or libraries, face disproportionate reductions if not total elimination. In the end, elected officials often wish to avoid as much political pain as possible and adopt the least controversial strategies in the short term, such as across-the-board reductions or delaying infrastructure investments or maintenance programs.

The lessons from Sidney, Nebraska, the small rural community that lost a major employer, may point to possible approaches moving forward. Keep the process as open as possible, informing citizens of current and possible future conditions and seeking public input into priority setting. Seek outside advice and counsel to the greatest extent possible, so as to gather as much information as possible. Be entrepreneurial in trying new ideas. Learn from mistakes and adapt as quickly as possible. Be willing to reach out to neighboring communities to form partnerships to help defer costs. Seek state and federal emergency funding, perhaps through one-time grants, to allow more time to plan and adopt strategies. Delaying implementation of long-term solutions in favor of short-term quick fixes, in essence pushing the problem down the road, will usually create greater difficulties in the long term. For example, deferring infrastructure maintenance programs or pension contributions will result in higher long-term costs. The challenge in such cases is whether the municipal leadership has the political will to make difficult decisions.

Chapter 8

Policy Actions

State Responses to Municipal Fiscal Stress

As we have discussed throughout this book, municipal fiscal decisions, fiscal condition, and the actions taken by municipal officials do not occur in a vacuum. Municipal finances are affected by a series of inputs over which municipal governments have little or no control, such as national recessions, natural disasters, or fiscal federalism. Therefore, to fully understand situations involving fiscal stress, we must also take state actions into account. Local governments, after all, are creations of the state and subject to its control and oversight. Not only are states part of the feedback loop within the open-systems model, but the rules and institutions they establish help to create the external pressure and institutional settings that impact a municipality's fiscal health. Moreover, given the consequences associated with municipalities experiencing fiscal stress, states are taking greater interest in municipal governments' financial management. In order to truly understand the financial condition of a municipality, we must also understand how its state responds to instability in local governments. What this chapter shows is that there is a surprising level of variation across states within their responses to municipalities in fiscal distress.

Harrisburg, Pennsylvania's capital city, was highly rated by *Forbes* in 2010 as the second-best place to raise a family (Levy, 2010) and was labeled recession-proof by *The Daily Beast* (*Patriot-News*, 2010). But in that same year, Harrisburg defaulted on $10.5 million in debt obligations. By the end of 2010, the city had amassed $73.2 million in claims, exceeding the city's $64 million operations budget. Unable

DOI: 10.4324/9780429270765-8

to meet these overwhelming debt obligations, city officials filed for state protection under Pennsylvania's Act 47, the Financially Distressed Municipalities Act. Act 47 provides an action plan that state and local officials can adopt in response to fiscal distress. As discussed in more detail later in this chapter, under Act 47 an analysis of the city's fiscal condition was conducted by Pennsylvania's Center for Local Government Services, which concluded that Harrisburg was financially distressed. The Pennsylvania Department of Community and Economic Development (DCED), which oversees financially distressed municipalities, concurred in this judgment due to the city's junk-bond credit rating that inhibited access to the credit market, a structural fiscal deficit forecast through 2015, worrisome economic and demographic shifts that were counterproductive to revenue growth (e.g., population decline, growing unemployment and poverty rates), and multiple lawsuits from creditors.

In response to Harrisburg's financial woes and its designation as fiscally distressed, the DCED Secretary appointed a coordinator to help manage the city back from financial ruin. The city's recovery plan included changes in the delivery of some city services (e.g., outsourcing commercial sanitary services), consolidating departments and staff, renegotiating contracts with employee unions, selling assets, and enhanced taxing authority. Key to Harrisburg's recovery were reducing its debt burden and an infusion of additional tax revenue. The former was aided by the sale of an incinerator that was at the heart of the city's debt problems and by working with creditors to lower debt payments.

After three years of trying to stabilize the city's finances, Harrisburg officials entered the five-year process for exiting the financial recovery plan as stipulated under Act 47. While the city was improving its financial position, including growing its reserves, the appointed coordinator recommended that Harrisburg remain in Act 47 for an additional three years, through 2021. The coordinator noted that the city had relied on the extraordinary revenue-raising authority granted under Act 47 and that if it exited distressed status, it would not yet be able to recover from its revenue losses. He recommended that during the additional three-year period, Harrisburg should focus on attaining home-rule powers that would give the city more administrative and revenue flexibility, lift caps on certain taxes including the property tax, and aid in restoring the city's credit rating so that officials would have access by needed capital. As of this writing, Harrisburg remains under Act 47 controls.

The story of Harrisburg's financial problems and the state's role in helping to address those problems exemplify the challenges associated with a federal system that tries to balance local control with state oversight. Pennsylvania is one of only a handful of states that have both the power and interest to become directly involved in municipal finance, and even for those states that do get involved in municipal financial matters, there is an important distinction been proactive and reactive measures. In most instances, state officials do not step in until a municipality is deemed financially distressed.

This chapter examines state responses (or the lack thereof) to municipal fiscal distress, with a focus on Chapter 9 bankruptcy filings, state monitoring systems, and the degree to which researchers have found these instruments effective in helping to improve municipal fiscal health.

State intervention dates back to the 1800s (ACIR, 1984) when more than one-quarter of local governments defaulted on bonds. Spiotto et al. (2016, pp. 24–25) found that in response to these defaults, states became more involved in setting policy for the issuance of municipal bonds and, in essence, forced restrictions on the municipal bond market. State requirements included the following:

- Debt limitations on municipal issuers to prevent excessive borrowing
- Clearly defined bondholder rights in the event of default, supported by statutory and case law
- Use of bond counsel to determine the legality of a bond issue before the sale, to avoid technical legal defects that could allow an issuer to repudiate the debt
- Development of credit rating agencies, as well as thorough credit review by investment firms and many institutional investors
- Statutory restrictions against municipal issuers borrowing in response to chronic deficiencies
- The use of indenture trustees, paying agents, and others who have certain duties in order to protect the rights and interests of bondholders

In addition to greater involvement in the bond market, state officials also became more involved in overseeing municipal finances. New Hampshire's takeover of Manchester in 1921 was the first recorded state takeover of a municipal government (Coe, 2008), but the Great Depression further spurred states to take a more active role in municipal finances. Today, about 30 states play at least some role in municipal finance, through either bankruptcy law, state monitoring, or some combination of the two. The other 20 states play a limited or no role in managing and or overseeing municipal finances.

Chapter 9 Bankruptcy

Although many states have enacted some "ground rules" for municipal government bankruptcy, some state statutes remain silent on the topic, creating potential confusion for municipal governments within those states. There are, however, laws at the federal level outlining municipal government bankruptcies, and judicial case law provides further clarification. In 1934, still reeling from the Great Depression, Congress passed the Municipal Bankruptcy Act, which laid the groundwork by which municipalities could claim bankruptcy. The law was later struck down by the U.S. Supreme Court, which determined that it encroached too much on states' rights. Accordingly, Congress amended the Municipal Bankruptcy Act in 1937 to address the legal impediments by prohibiting courts from interfering in municipal government affairs (a state function), including revenues, day-to-day operations, and the replacement or appointment of municipal officials (Watson et al., 2005). In essence, municipal bankruptcy courts are limited to supervising the debt restructuring plans offered by municipal governments and cannot interfere in matters of municipal governance. The law was revised again in 1976 following New York City's near-bankruptcy. This amendment removed the requirement of a preapproved debt restructuring plan and enabled affected municipalities to cancel collective bargaining agreements (Watson et al., 2005).

One of the most recent and frequently cited municipal bankruptcy filings occurred in 2013 in Detroit, Michigan, which became the largest municipality to pursue Chapter 9 bankruptcy, eclipsing Jefferson County, Alabama. Such a filing is rare in U.S. history and, similar to Chapter 11 bankruptcy filings, considered a last resort for municipalities struggling with debt payments on long-term liabilities. According to Moringiello (2014), there have been fewer than 700 municipal bankruptcy filings since the U.S. Supreme Court upheld the constitutionality of Chapter 9 bankruptcy in 1938. The process is complicated and time-consuming, affects access to credit, and leaves a poor impression of the community that can affect economic development.

From a legal standpoint, municipal bankruptcies are challenging in that they run up against state sovereignty and creditors' rights. Therefore, "The 10th Amendment limits the control that a federal court can exercise over a municipality and the Contracts Clause limits the ability of a state to force a creditor to a city to accept less than what it was owed" (Moringiello, 2014, p. 410). The intent of Chapter 9 bankruptcy is to provide some breathing room for municipal governments by requiring the formulation of a plan by which the municipality can fulfill its obligations to creditors. Development of the recovery plan typically falls on the shoulders of the municipality. Some states, as a stipulation for filing bankruptcy, have certain requirements that the municipality must fulfill. Interestingly, to avoid infringement on state sovereignty, Chapter 9 bankruptcy cannot require institutional changes in municipalities. This includes a prohibition on requiring the reorganization of municipal government officials, the sale of assets, or the impounding of general tax revenues. For these reasons, the option of Chapter 9 bankruptcy has been criticized:

> Chapter 9 is a solution in search of a problem . . . it does little to address the root causes of the deterioration of the city. . . . Chapter 9

> grants excessive powers to the debtor itself, reducing the chances of a successful reorganization because the same elected officials who ran the city poorly will continue in office during and after bankruptcy.
>
> (Moringiello, 2014, pp. 420–422)

Spiotto et al. (2016) added, "Merely reducing debt without addressing the systematic problems has proven to be a futile effort, and financial distress reappears shortly thereafter" (p. 129). Similarly, Mikesell (2002) identified several problems with Chapter 9 bankruptcy and offered the following policy changes for consideration:

- Provide more protection for creditors. Mikesell asserted that the law provides unbalanced protection of municipalities in comparison to creditors.
- Provide creditors with access to municipal revenues. Mikesell noted that with respect to general obligation (GO) debt (not the case with revenue bonds), once a municipality files for bankruptcy it can stop debt payments but can continue to collect revenues.
- Supervision of municipal affairs (based on previous court rulings, it would be difficult to obtain court approval for this action).
- Constraints on government policies. During bankruptcy proceedings, municipalities retain control over political and governmental decisions.

Currently, 27 U.S. states permit at least some municipalities to file bankruptcy, 21 states have no laws regarding bankruptcies, and two (Georgia and Iowa) expressly prohibit municipalities from filing bankruptcy (Pew Charitable Trusts, 2013). Some bankruptcy filings have occurred in the 21 states with no specific statutory language on the issue (Spiotto et al., 2016). Since the mid-1980s, municipal bankruptcies have occurred in ten states, including six filings in Tennessee (Spiotto et al., 2016). Most of them happened before 1994, when Congress tightened filing requirements, including state authorization.

Breaking down the 27 states that have legal authorization for municipal bankruptcy filings, 12 specifically authorize municipal bankruptcies and the remaining states provide either conditional authorization or limited authorization (See Table 8.1). For instance, Oregon allows only irrigation and drainage districts to file for Chapter 9 bankruptcy, while Illinois has statutory language only for the Illinois Power Agency.

For those states with conditional requirements (see Table 8.2), most require some form of approval, from either the Governor (Connecticut, Florida, Louisiana, Michigan, and Pennsylvania) or some other state oversight agency (Louisiana, North Carolina, Ohio, Pennsylvania, and Rhode Island). For instance, a Chapter 9 bankruptcy filing by a Louisiana municipality requires approval by the Attorney General, Governor, and State Bond Commission. California and

Table 8.1 State Bankruptcy Laws

Unconditional Bankruptcy Authorization	*Conditional or Limited Bankruptcy Authorization*
Alabama	California
Arizona	Colorado
Arkansas	Connecticut
Idaho	Florida
Minnesota	Illinois
Missouri	Kentucky
Montana	Louisiana
Nebraska	Michigan
Oklahoma	New Jersey
South Carolina	New York
Texas	North Carolina
Washington	Ohio
	Oregon
	Pennsylvania
	Rhode Island

Source: Pew Charitable Trusts (2013)

Table 8.2 Conditional Requirements for Chapter 9 Filing by Municipalities

State	*Requirement*
Alabama	Only for municipal bonded debt.
California	Municipality is required to participation in a "neutral evaluation process" and submit financial emergency resolution from the municipality stating that the financial condition "jeopardizes the health, safety, or well-being of the residents absent bankruptcy protection."
Connecticut	A filing requires the Governor's consent. The Governor is required to submit a report to the State Treasurer and General Assembly committee that deals with municipal finances.
Florida	Requires Governor approval.
Illinois	While there is no specific Chapter 9 authorization, a filing requires state authorization.
Kentucky	Authorization applies to all "taxing agencies", including municipalities

State	*Requirement*
Louisiana	Filing requires approval from the Attorney General, Governor and State Bond Commission
Michigan	Local Financial Stability and Choice Act requires Governor approval and a local resolution declaring a financial emergency
New York	Chapter 9 filing is only permissible for defaults on ARRA (American Recovery and Reinvestment Act) bonds.
North Carolina	Municipal filing requires approval by the Local Government Commission
Ohio	Requires approval by the Tax Commission
Pennsylvania	The municipality needs to meet certain conditions and receive approval from the Governor and State Department of Community and Economic Development.
Rhode Island	A municipality cannot file directly; filing must come from a receiver appointed by a budget commission. The Commission is created only after the municipality is deemed fiscally distressed by the State Department of Revenue.

Source: Pew Charitable Trusts (2013)

Michigan require an approved resolution by the municipality, declaring a financial emergency. Rhode Island does not permit municipalities to file directly for Chapter 9 bankruptcy; rather, the filing must be completed by a budget commission that is created after the state finds the municipality to be fiscally distressed.

Chapter 9 Bankruptcy and Long-Term Liabilities

Recent bankruptcies have involved two types of debt (GO and revenue bonds), employee contracts, and pensions. What distinguishes the treatment of revenue versus GO bonds is, in essence, the repayment arrangements during bankruptcy proceedings. According to Feldstein and Fabozzi (2008), revenue bonds must continue to be paid during the bankruptcy process because the bonds themselves are "secured by a pledge of revenues derived from the project or a special tax levy" (p. 166). GO bonds differ from revenue bonds because they are not linked to a specific revenue source; rather, they are backed by the full faith and credit of the municipality. This means that during the bankruptcy process, the municipality is not obligated to make these bond payments and has the power to restructure this debt in a manner more conducive to managing its fiscal distress.

There is also legal precedent for the rejection of "burdensome" labor contracts and unfunded pension liabilities. In *National Labor Relations Board v. Bildisco & Bildisco* (1984), the U.S. Supreme Court determined that it is permissible to cancel collective bargaining agreements if it is shown that the agreements are particularly burdensome (Spiotto et al., 2016). In the bankruptcy filings of both Central Fall, Rhode Island, and Vallejo, California, the courts permitted the abolishment of collective bargaining agreements (Spiotto et al., 2016). According to Spiotto et al. (2016), a court can reject such agreements if the municipality has made a good-faith effort to modify them, the modified proposal was rejected by the employee representatives, and the municipality is fiscally distressed.

Pension obligations were central to the bankruptcy filings in Stockton, California, and Detroit, Michigan. In both cases, the courts sided with the municipality since there was no state constitutional provision preventing plan alterations (Spiotto et al., 2016). The court involving Stockton's filing stated that "as a matter of law, the city's pensions administration contract . . . as well as the city-sponsored pensions themselves, may be adjusted as part of the Chapter 9 plan" (Spiotto et al., 2016, p. 156). In the end, Detroit pensioners recovered about 80% of their promised benefits and Stockton employees maintained some lifetime health benefits in exchange for a one-time payment of $5.1 million to a healthcare trust (Spiotto et al., 2016).

State Involvement in Municipal Finances Beyond Chapter 9

State efforts to avoid municipal bankruptcies consist largely of systems designed to monitor municipal finances (see Table 8.3). Features of these systems range from threats of losing state funding if bond payments are not made (e.g., Virginia) to monitoring of municipal financial data (usually audits) and tiered response strategies based on the identified level of fiscal distress (e.g., Michigan and Ohio). Over the past two decades, often guided by academic research, a number of states have adopted fiscal condition monitoring systems for their local governments, including New York (Office of the New York State Comptroller, 2021), North Carolina (Coe, 2007), Michigan (Crosby & Robbins, 2013; Kloha et al., 2005), Ohio (Clark, 2015), and Pennsylvania (Pennsylvania DCED, 2011).

Although the Pew Charitable Trusts (2016b) have identified 22 states with local government finance monitoring systems, the list expands to 36 states if we include those with statutory language covering responses to fiscal distress. Interestingly, only eight states have developed early warning systems to identify signs of fiscal distress before problems become serious (Louisiana, Nevada, New Jersey, North Carolina, Ohio, Pennsylvania, Rhode Island, and Tennessee). Of

Table 8.3 State Monitoring Approaches of Local Finances

State	*Monitoring System*
Colorado	Colorado Fiscal Stability Initiative. Municipalities annual submit budgets audits to State Department of Local Affairs (DOLA). DOLA examines a series of metrics to identify municipalities in fiscal distress. These metrics range from fiscal ratios (e.g., number of operating deficits over a three-year period) to education and population data. Using these data, DOLA ranks the fiscal vulnerability of municipalities.
Connecticut	Takes an ad-hoc approach to municipal fiscal distress, including the appointment of financial assistance boards. The state may also appoint a trustee if a municipality defaults for more than 30 days or does not comply with a repayment plan.
Florida	If the state deems a municipality in fiscal distress, the Governor is notified and the Governor can take several steps, including submission of a revised budget, inspection of financial records, prohibition on debt issuance and the creation of an advisory authority. State law allows modification of labor contracts if the municipality is financially distressed.
Georgia	Local governments exceeding 1,500 population or with annual operating expenditures exceeding $300,000 are required to submit an annual audit to the state auditor. If the auditor finds errors, the municipality must submit the changes to the State.
Illinois	The Illinois Finance Authority can provide assistance to local governments in order to ensure "basic municipal services, while permitting the distressed city to meet its obligations with creditors and bond holders." Under the Local Government Financial Planning and Supervision Act, local governments with populations greater than 25,000 and facing a financial emergency, can petition the Governor to establish a financial planning and Supervision Commission to help manage through the fiscal crisis.
Indiana	Municipalities can petition the State's Distressed Unit Appeal Board for designation as a distressed community. If deemed distressed (meeting at least 1 of 8 criteria), an emergency manager can be appointed. The Emergency manger can assume management responsibilities from the elected and management bodies, but does not have additional taxing authority. The Emergency Manager can prepare the budget, make expenditures, cancel contracts, renegotiate labor contracts, reduce or suspend salaries and engage in contracts of service provision.

(Continued)

Table 8.3 (Continued)

State	*Monitoring System*
Iowa	Under the Iowa Municipal Oversight Law, the State Auditor annually reviews municipal audits. The auditor's focus is on examining internal controls, cash and investments, debt management, fund balances, receipts, and disbursements.
Kentucky	The Department for Local Government does not monitor cities or towns, only counties. The Department conducts audits, quarterly financial analyses and approves county budgets. County officials can seek state assistance and the Department of Local Government has the authority to intervene in county operations.
Louisiana	The Office of the Louisiana Legislative Auditor collects and reviews municipal audits. The designation of a fiscally distressed municipality requires the unanimous consent of the Auditor, Attorney General and State Treasurer. If there is a finding of fiscal distress, the Attorney General has the power to petition for the appointment of a fiscal administrator.
Maine	The Board of Emergency Municipal Finance, comprised of the Commissioner of Finance, State Treasurer and State Auditor, has the authority to aid municipalities In fiscal distress, including taking over management of the municipality.
Maryland	The Office of Legislative Audits conducts annual audits of municipal finances. The focus is on monitoring local fiscal condition. State aid can be revoked if local governments do not comply with submission of audits.
Massachusetts	The state has rules in place to make bond payments if deemed necessary. More generally, the state takes an ad-hoc approach to municipal distress, including the creation of boards to oversee and turn around municipalities in fiscal distress.
Michigan	Each municipality files an annual audit. The Local Financial Stability and Choice Act has 19 different scenarios where the state is empowered to investigate municipal fiscal distress. If distress is identified, the state financing board is required to submit a report to the local emergency financial assistance loan board to determine the extent of the distress. The Governor is required to appoint a review team to help Governor determine if stress exists. If so, the local government must agree to either: (1) develop a plan, with state officials on how to achieve financial stability, (2) agree to appoint an emergency manager who also has the power to recommend Chapter 9 filing (e.g., Detroit), (3) agree on a neutral evaluator to resolve financial disputes, including filing Chapter 9, or (4) file for Chapter 9 with the Governor's consent.

State	*Monitoring System*
Minnesota	If a municipality is unable to make bond payments, local officials are required to report to the State Auditor who can provide a loan sufficient to satisfy the bond issuance.
Nevada	Local governments are required to submit annual audits to the Department of Taxation. If violations are found, the local government has 60 days to correct. If necessary, the Taxation Director, with consent of the Attorney General, to force compliance. The Local Government Financial Assistance program enables local governments to appeal to the Nevada Tax Commission for financial assistance. There are 27 "trigger events" where if the tax commission believe assistance is needed it can do so, including taking over management of the minimality. In 2015, legislation was added where the state now monitors municipalities and provides assistance before fiscal distress occurs.
New Hampshire	Any city in financial distress can apply to the State for assistance.
New Jersey	Special Municipal Aid Act. The law enables the state to facilitate loans and grants to municipalities in fiscal distress. Eligibility for support requires either being under the Local Government Supervision Act or being identified as facing severe fiscal distress. The Local Government Supervision Act allows that if the Local Finance Board of the State Department of Community Affairs finds an "irregular" event, the municipality can be placed under the Board's supervision. The Municipal Finance Commission was created to help municipalities unable to make bond payments. The Municipal Rehabilitation and Recovery Act requires that for municipalities that are heavily reliant on state support (more than 55% of operating budget) and have been subject to supervision for more than one year, the Governor has the authority to appoint a chief operating officer to manage the municipality.
New Mexico	Municipalities are audited by the State Auditor. Under situations where, "unforeseen occurrences or circumstances severely affect the quality of government services and require the immediate expenditure of money" the State Board of Finance can provide emergency loans.
New York	Fiscal Stress Monitoring System. The NY State Office of the State Comptroller annually monitors municipal audits for signs of fiscal distress. Following NY City's financial challenges in the 1970's, The New York Control Board and the Emergency Financial Control Boards and Fiscal Stability Authorizes were created so that the state legislature could establish one to oversee and oversee a municipality's finances.

(*Continued*)

Table 8.3 (Continued)

State	*Monitoring System*
North Carolina	The Local Government Commission has the power to authorize debt issuance and to assume the financial affairs of a local government that defaults on debt payments.
Ohio	The State Auditor has the power to place a municipality under either a fiscal caution or fiscal watch. A fiscal caution requires municipal officials devise a plan to matters of fiscal concern. A Fiscal Watch can be initiated by the State Auditor or locally-elected officials. There are a number of conditions that can trigger a watch ranging from having outstanding bill to budget deficits. A Fiscal Emergency can also be triggered by the State Auditor or locally-elected officials. Similar to a watch, a fiscal emergency has several possible triggering events ranging from lacking the cash to meet payroll to more severe budget deficits.
Oregon	The Audits Division of the Secretary of State biennially reviews county finances. The State does not monitor city finances.
Pennsylvania	Financially Distressed Municipalities Act (Act 47). The State Department of Community and Economic Development determines if a community is fiscally distressed. Fiscal emergencies can be declared by the Governor leading to action taken by the State Department, including appointment of a coordinator. The receiver is required to submit a recovery plan that could include filing Chapter 9.
Rhode Island	The Director of the State Department of Revenue can appoint a fiscal overseer if the municipality suffered two of the five events: projected deficit, failure to file audit, bond rating downgrade, inability to get access to credit or failure to respond to requests for financial information. The overseer can make policy recommendation, make fiscal decisions, create budgets and review contracts. The overseer is required to submit a 3-year recovery plan. If the overseer cannot see a path for fiscal sustainability, they can request a Budget Commission. The Commission has more extensive powers that include organizational restructuring, increasing revenues, making spending cuts, and recommending filing Chapter 9. If the Budget Commission cannot find a path to solvency, a municipal receiver can be appointed.
South Dakota	The State Department of Legislative Audits reviews county and larger cities' finances for signs of fiscal distress.

State	*Monitoring System*
Tennessee	Emergency Financial Aid to Local Governments. The State Funding Board can provide financial assistance to local governments if: (1) supported by a majority of locally-elected officials, (2) local officials accept actions recommended by the Comptroller of the Treasury, (3) local revenues are insufficient to cover debt service and, (4) the local government submits a plan to address its financial challenges.
Texas	In certain default situations, a municipality can apply to court for a receiver to take over its fiscal affairs.
Virginia	At the Governor's discretion, cities failing to make bond payments can lose state funding.
Washington	The State Auditor's Office reviews municipal finances at least once every three years. The Office reviews a set of indicators and offers advice, and training to local officials.

Sources: Spiotto et al. (2016) and Pew Charitable Trusts (2016b)

the larger set of 36 states, ten focus exclusively on municipal defaults (Alabama, Arizona, Arkansas, California, Idaho, Missouri, Montana, Nebraska, Oklahoma, and South Carolina). There is considerable variation even within this group. For instance, Arkansas law states that in certain default situations, a municipality can seek a court order for a receiver to take over municipal operations, whereas South Carolina law allows the state treasurer to revoke state aid for municipalities that fail to make bond payments. Seventeen states have laws on municipal defaults coupled with a fiscal monitoring system. Municipalities in Minnesota, for example, can receive state assistance to help in covering bond payments.

Most of the states listed focus more on monitoring municipal finances. The degree of involvement varies widely by state. According to Pew Charitable Trusts (2016b), there are four major stages of monitoring municipal fiscal health. First, states collect budgets, audits, or financial reports from municipal governments. For some states (e.g., Iowa and South Dakota), collecting and reviewing these financial documents is the extent of their involvement. These states may provide some training or require correction of inaccurate audit reports, but they do not directly define or identify stress. Second, some states use these financial data to establish a set of indicators of municipal fiscal distress (Colorado, Maryland, Michigan, Nevada, New Jersey, New York, Ohio, Pennsylvania, and Rhode Island). Revenues and expenditures, unrestricted or unassigned fund balances, GO debt, and debt service payments are among the more frequently used indicators. The third stage, identifying fiscally distressed entities, can be performed by either the state or municipalities themselves. For instance, Michigan has an extensive system for monitoring municipal government finances and assessing their degree of fiscal vulnerability; Illinois municipalities facing fiscal distress must petition the governor for assistance. The last stage, which consists of state measures to help municipal governments labeled as fiscally distressed, also contains various actions, from providing technical advice or helping with recovery plans to taking over operations.

Different states have different fiscal monitoring designs. For instance, New Mexico and Rhode Island state governments require municipal governments to submit quarterly financial updates. In this way, states can closely monitor municipal fiscal health and take timely measures to help municipal governments. Many states collect three to five years of data and conduct trend analyses to examine long-term patterns. Some states (e.g., Colorado, Minnesota, North Carolina, and Wisconsin) have created online platforms so that municipal governments can compare their fiscal condition with that of their peers and to help the public understand municipal governments' fiscal condition. Moreover, after identifying fiscally distressed entities, some states have enforcement authority to force those entities to make changes (e.g., Florida, Kentucky, Louisiana, Maine, Michigan, Nevada, New Jersey, New York, Ohio, Pennsylvania, and Rhode Island), whereas others do not (e.g., Colorado, Maryland, and Oregon).

States can gain several advantages from monitoring municipal fiscal health. First, with states' help, municipal governments can identify signs of fiscal distress at an early stage and implement preventive measures. Second, states may have better capacity to deal with fiscal distress than municipal governments. Thus, with their help, municipal governments can weather potential fiscal shocks. Third, since states may have a holistic view of municipal fiscal health, they can select best practices and foster training in accounting benchmarking. Finally, monitoring fiscal health can improve communication between state and municipal governments. States may realize the difficulties that municipal governments are facing, while municipal governments may be more willing to follow states' instructions.

States also face challenges when monitoring municipal fiscal health. In some cases, the fiscal monitoring systems may be inaccurate. For instance, Florida and Michigan labeled municipalities as fiscally distressed when, in fact, they were not (Pew Charitable Trusts, 2016b). State reliance on audits and financial reports also makes timely identification of fiscally distressed communities challenging due to the timing of those reports. Moreover, smaller municipal governments may not receive monitoring from such programs because they may not generate audit reports, yet small municipal governments are more susceptible to fiscal shocks because of their small tax bases. And in some states (e.g., Maryland and Washington), the fiscal monitoring systems lack enforcement authority. Thus, even though some municipal governments may be labeled as fiscally distressed, they are not subject to any state intervention and not required to make changes.

Pew Charitable Trusts (2013) identified five motivations for state intervention in local distress: avoiding stigma, concerns for credit rating downgrades, contagion (the domino effect), public health and safety, and economic stability. The stigma of fiscal distress, including bankruptcy, can cause serious damage to a municipality's economic development efforts, as illustrated in Vallejo, California, and Harrisburg, Pennsylvania. Obviously, bankruptcy filings will negatively affect ratings by agencies such as Moody's, S&P, and Fitch, thereby limiting access to capital. State intervention in Harrisburg's finances noted a concern for a possible domino effect, whereby if Harrisburg filed for bankruptcy, other municipalities would follow. Pew Charitable Trusts (2015) noted that if municipal officials need to cut services, including protective services, to balance budgets, some states fear that public safety could be negatively impacted. For instance, the Illinois Finance Authority can provide financial assistance to municipal governments to ensure the continuation of basic municipal services.

Does State Monitoring Matter?

Chung and Williams (2021) posed an important question: does labeling distressed municipalities affect their municipal fiscal condition? Few have studied the degree to which the identification of a community as fiscally distressed influences policy decisions that would be needed to rectify poor fiscal health. By comparing municipalities labeled as fiscally distressed to those not labeled as such over two time periods, Chung and Williams sought to determine if the labeling in period one (FY2013) affected their fiscal health in period two (FY2014). Studying fiscal metrics such as fund balance ratios and operating deficits, the authors found evidence that, at least for relatively less stressed municipalities, such labeling improved fiscal metrics in the following year. Not surprisingly, for those municipalities in more severe distress, the labels had no impact on subsequent fiscal health indices. This is either because municipalities did not pay attention to the labels or, more likely, because severely distressed communities are incapable of improving their fiscal health within a year and that being called out by the state, without material assistance, could not produce the intended results.

Berman (1995) offered a unique study of Pennsylvania, a state that monitors both municipal fiscal health and school districts' educational efficacy. Pennsylvania's 1987 Municipalities Financial Recovery Act authorized the Department of Community Affairs (since replaced by DCED) to collect and analyze municipal financial data. This department also has the power to declare a municipality fiscally distressed and to appoint a coordinator if deemed necessary. Berman found that the proactive monitoring approach Pennsylvania takes in relation to school districts is more effective than the reactive model used for municipalities.

Michigan's Local Financial Stability and Choice Act has been the focus of several studies. In testimony presented to the Michigan Senate Fiscal Agency, Plerhoples and Scorsone (2010) assessed the state's fiscal monitoring system that took effect in 2006 and compared it to the system in place from 2003 to 2006. They found that while Michigan's revised monitoring system was more able to identify fiscally distressed municipalities, errors were still occurring. This finding is concerning, since a false positive means that the model is identifying communities as fiscally distressed when in fact they are not. As previously discussed, a false positive could negatively affect the municipality's reputation in the eyes of developers, bond ratings, and possibly access to credit. On the other hand, a false negative means that municipalities that are truly fiscally distressed may not receive the support they need to improve their fiscal condition. To avert prediction errors, Plerhoples and Scorsone (2010) recommended the modification of specific metrics used for monitoring purposes, including the addition of general fund indices, a portal for municipal fiscal data, and an element that assesses change over time. Regarding this last recommendation, Plerhoples and Scorsone (2010) noted, "Both current and lagged ratios as well as percentage changes over the past few years are useful because they can together tell whether a unit is heading for stress or improving" (p. 8).

Crosby and Robbins (2013) also examined Michigan's monitoring system and the fiscal ratios used by state policymakers. Their concerns with the fiscal ratios were that rather than capturing the municipal government's entire fiscal picture, the existing system focused only on the general fund. Is so doing, Michigan's system was ignoring fiscal metrics regarding long-term liabilities and enterprise funds (see also Hendrick, 2011). Therefore, Crosby and Robbins recommended that state policymakers modify the system to include both governmental and business-type activities.

Taking a more comparative approach, Spreen and Cheek's (2016) study of Michigan's Fiscal Stress Indicator System found that it had no discernible effect on local governments' financial condition. Their analysis compared a sample of counties and municipalities in Michigan and neighboring states. Spreen and Cheek concluded, "Michigan's Fiscal Stress Indicator System has little effect on the monitored outcomes . . . state monitoring of local government financial conditions does not appear to affect the financial positions of local governments" (p. 742). In another comparative study involving Michigan, Justice et al. (2019) examined the predictability of the monitoring systems in both Ohio and Michigan. They found that Ohio's monitoring system was more able to predict bankrupt municipalities and had fewer false positives than the Michigan model.

Coe (2007) studied the North Carolina Local Government Commission, which monitors local government finances. Rather than examining improvements in specific fiscal metrics (Spreen & Cheek, 2016), Coe identified benefits in the monitoring system and asserted that the commission's oversight improved local bond ratings, which in turn lowers borrowing costs and improves local reserves. In Coe's (2008) subsequent essay on North Carolina's monitoring system, he identified three best practices for state oversight: monitoring local finances, actively assisting local governments in need, and, if necessary, forcing local governments to take remedial action.

In one of the few cross-state studies, Nakhmurina (2020) took advantage of the different state monitoring systems and the difference in the timing of their adoption. Her analysis consisted of over 20,000 observations from 2009 to 2017. Her quasi-experimental design found that state monitoring systems improve municipal health; more specifically, adoption of these systems was associated with lower municipal spending, larger fund balances, and greater assets relative to liabilities. She asserted that monitoring improves municipal fiscal health because it helps municipal officials better understand their financial condition (see also Maher & Deller, 2011). These findings are consistent with Rivenbark and Roenigk (2011), who noted that the North Carolina monitoring system made local officials and finance mangers more informed about their financial position and, perhaps more importantly, that local officials used these data to inform their policy actions.

Scorsone and Pruett (2020) studied the effectiveness of early warning systems in Colorado, Louisiana, Ohio, and Pennsylvania. Their focus was on the monitoring systems' predictive power and on the degree to which the systems affected municipal fiscal condition. Their recommendations essentially encouraged policymakers to think through their systems and determine whether it is better to have more false positives or false negatives (i.e., overestimation versus underestimation of municipal fiscal distress), as well as to include fiscal metrics that capture not only a value (e.g., fund balance as a percentage of general fund expenditures) but also change over time (see also Maher, Ebdon et al., 2020). Other recommendations focused on the number of ratios used, the timing of data collection, and benchmarking. The authors noted, "Each state operates amidst an individual context with an individual purpose . . . there is no one optimal system, only the right system based on the perceived policymakers in that particular location" (Scorsone & Pruett, 2020, p. 49).

Concluding Thoughts

Nearly all municipal governments within the United States exist because they are permitted under state law, whether the relevant provisions are statutory or constitutional. Most states, however, are less prescriptive in addressing matters of municipal government fiscal stress and, in extreme cases, bankruptcy. Nevertheless, a number of states play no role in monitoring the fiscal health of municipal governments or in addressing issues of municipal bankruptcy. Although municipal bankruptcy is rare, in states that have no or only vague statutory language on the issue, it can be very troublesome and can lead to unnecessarily chaotic and confusing reactions. Although federal Chapter 9 bankruptcy rules provide important guidance, the courts have stated clearly that since municipal governments are the creation of state governments, state law concerning municipal bankruptcy supersedes federal law. Indeed, more than half of all states either prohibit or significantly limit municipal bankruptcy filings under Chapter 9. Even among those states that allow bankruptcy filings, there is a substantial difference in state responses to those filings.

Perhaps state governments should be more proactive in helping municipal governments better understand their fiscal position. There is a growing movement toward the creation of state-designed systems to monitor municipal government finances. That said, for those states with municipal fiscal monitoring systems, the type of monitoring and, perhaps more importantly, state responses to municipal fiscal distress still vary widely from state to state. The research on the effectiveness of such monitoring programs, though mixed, is promising. There is growing evidence that these types of systems may provide the greatest help in the early stages of fiscal stress, when municipal governments are better positioned to be proactive. Monitoring systems that are more reactive and raise red flags when fiscal stress levels are high appeared to be less effective. Much of the current discussion both within academia and among practitioners concerns what should be included in those state monitoring systems. The challenges outlined in Chapters 4 to 6 regarding how to measure fiscal health or stress apply to state monitoring systems as well.

An equally challenging question is the degree to which the state should become involved in municipal government functions if evidence of fiscal stress is present. Should the state simply bring the analysis to the attention of municipal officials and offer suggestions, or should it take a more aggressive position? In an extreme case, should the state unseat democratically elected municipal officials and assume control of the municipal government? To what extent should these policies be codified in state statutes as opposed to the policies and regulations of the appropriate agencies? Naturally, each state will respond to these questions differently. In this chapter, we have highlighted the significance of context in studies of municipal fiscal conditions. Using our framework, not only can states affect inputs but, as we have shown in this chapter, they can also affect outcomes.

Foreword to Municipal Case Studies

The next five chapters apply our framework to the analysis of municipal fiscal health using case studies. The municipalities—Flint, Michigan; Wichita, Kansas; North Lauderdale, Florida; Havelock, North Carolina; and Commerce, California—were chosen based on several characteristics, including size, region, external factors, and management structure. We intentionally chose municipalities of small to medium size (ranging from Commerce's population of 13,000 to Wichita's 390,000), since most existing case studies focus on larger municipalities. Each municipality has experienced some type of significant economic challenge, and their states have various policies on such issues as TELs and state fiscal health monitoring.

The fiscal metrics used in the case studies are intended to capture the municipalities' ability to meet short and long-term obligations. Following our discussion of different fiscal condition measures, we particularly focus on each municipality's revenue and expenditure structures, operating position, and long-term liabilities (including debt). Revenue and expenditure structures indicate municipal reliance on different revenue sources. Operating position is operationalized using a variety of measures that capture budget surpluses, reserves, and cash and investments. We use GO debt relative to property valuation and/or debt service expenditures relative to total expenditures to measure municipal debt burdens. A broader measure of future obligations is total long-term liabilities for both governmental and enterprise funds. The most common way to measure these long-term liabilities is to divide liabilities due in more than one year by assets. A significant contributor to municipal long-term liabilities is pension and other post-employment benefits, which prior to GASB Statements 50, 67, and 68 may not have been fully disclosed in annual audited reports. For each case study, we rely on the municipality's audited annual financial report data from the early 2000s to the most current year available, typically 2019 or 2020.

Many studies of municipal financial condition overlook the attitudes and behaviors of the people responsible for fiscal policy suggestions, decisions, and implementation. This factor is particularly important in small to mid-sized municipalities, since the elected officials are usually part-time and rely heavily on the advice of professional staff. To address this common gap in the literature, the case studies in this book draw on interviews conducted with members of the municipalities' finance teams in 2015 and 2021.[1] The lone exception is Flint, Michigan, where we conducted an interview in 2015 but were unable to secure one in 2021.

Each interview was split into several distinct sections. The first section contained demographic questions about the respondent and his or her community, including length of time in the position, the government's structure, and the relationships of government officials within the community. The second section asked the respondent to describe how the community was impacted during by major economic shocks. The only questions that varied over the two time periods were in reference to these economic shocks: in 2015, the focus was on the Great Recession, whereas the 2021 interviews asked about the effects of COVID-19. In the third section, respondents were asked about the impact of various institutional constraints on their community during the Great Recession and the COVID-19 pandemic. Respondents were asked specifically about state-level constrains, self-imposed constraints, TELs, and home-rule powers, but the open-ended format allowed them to mention any other constraints they perceived to have impacted their community as well. Respondents were also asked about the role of formal and informal environments in the community's response to the external shocks. Finally, they were asked what lessons they and their community had learned from the Great Recession and COVID-19, what they would do differently if faced with another fiscal shock, and how they believed their community would fare if faced with another severe recession today.

Note

1. Interviews were transcribed and imported into MaxQDA for content analysis. Due to the explanatory nature of this study, directed content analysis was used during data analysis. Directed content analysis is more structured than a grounded theory approach (Hsieh & Shannon, 2005), using findings from previous research and/or theory to guide code construction prior to qualitative data analysis. A coding scheme was developed based on the areas of inquiry in the qualitative instrument.

Chapter 9

Case Study of Flint, Michigan

Since we have now presented our complete framework for understanding municipal fiscal health, it is time to put our model to work by applying it to case studies. We start with Flint, Michigan, a city that has been continuously challenged by declining economic and demographics, operating in a state with a strong monitoring system, and ravaged by water management issues that have had widely publicized detrimental consequences.

Inputs: Fiscal Environments

Institutional Settings/External Pressures

In 1978, Michigan voters approved the Headlee Amendment to the state constitution, which requires voter approval of any new taxes or tax increases and limits growth in property taxes. In addition, Michigan's state government is heavily involved in assessing municipal finances. Since 2001, as discussed below, the Michigan governor has twice intervened in Flint's fiscal and operational affairs.

Internal Structures

The City of Flint was incorporated in 1855 and currently occupies a land area of 32.8 square miles. Flint has operated under the strong mayor–council form of government since November 4, 1975, when the present charter was adopted.

DOI: 10.4324/9780429270765-9

Legislative authority is vested in a city council of nine members, one elected from each of the nine wards in the city and serving a four-year term. The city council is responsible, among other things, for passing ordinances, adopting the budget, approving resolutions, and appointing committees. The elected mayor serves as the city's chief executive officer for a four-year term of office and may be reelected for additional terms. The mayor appoints a city administrator as the chief administrative officer of the city, overseeing the government's day-to-day operations. The mayor also appoints the individuals responsible for budgeting, personnel, planning, legal counsel, and administrative services, representing up to ten principal staff members who serve at the mayor's pleasure. The city council and mayor are elected on a non-partisan basis.

Socioeconomic Conditions

In 2019, Flint's population was 95,943, down 24.5% from 2000 (see Figure 9.1). The city's population had been declining over the past 20 years (and beyond), but the Great Recession exacerbated the trend. The population declined by approximately 1% per year from 2000 onward, but by 8.1% between 2010 and 2011. The population decline reflects a long-term trend following a peak of nearly 200,000 in 1960. Flint was the 62nd-largest U.S. city in 1960 and ranks 335th as of the 2020 census.

Flint's economic indices have declined even more starkly than the city's population since 2000. The city's per-capita personal income in FY2000 was $22,899, but it dropped rapidly to $14,543 in 2006. By the end of the recession, in 2009,

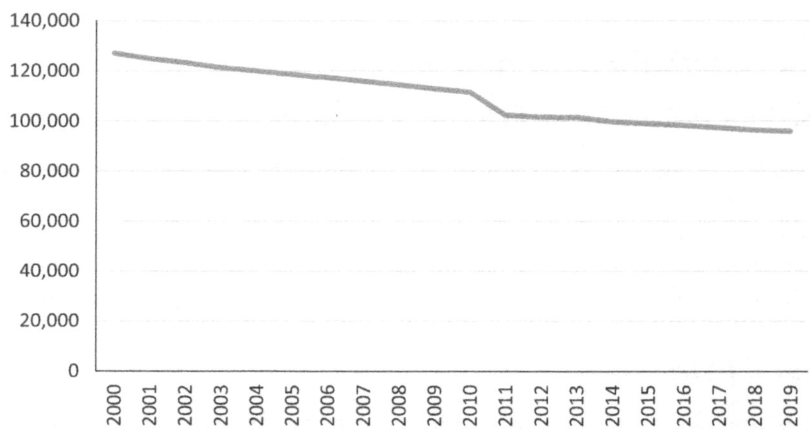

Figure 9.1 Population of Flint, Michigan, 2000–2019
Source: City of Flint (2021a)

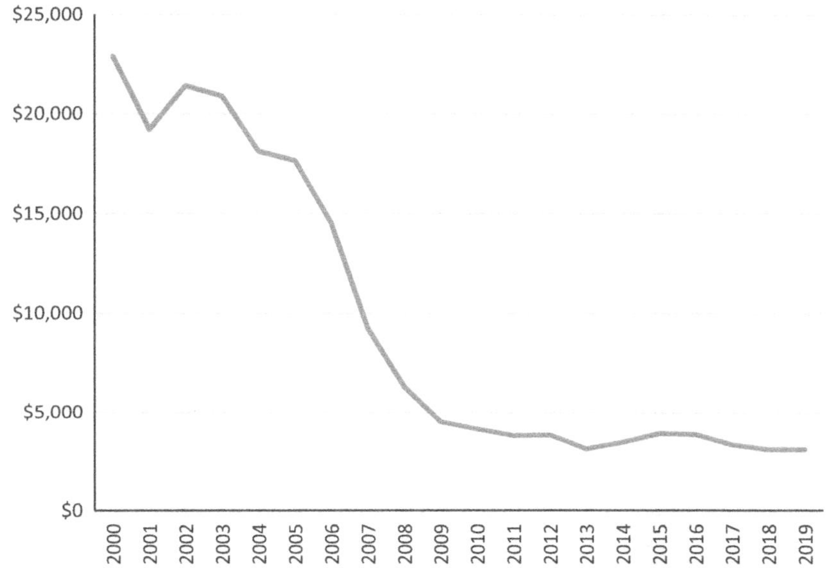

Figure 9.2 Personal Income of Flint, Michigan, 2000–2019 (Per Capita)
Source: City of Flint (2021a)

Flint's per-capita personal income was $4,536; in 2019, it was at about $3,000. Even with no adjustment for inflation, Flint's per-capita personal income plummeted by 72% from 2000 to 2019. An overview of Flint's per-capita personal income over time appears in Figure 9.2.

Despite Flint's population decline, the city continues to struggle with high rates of unemployment. The city's challenges have been apparent since the late 1970s and were largely attributable to the automobile industry. At its peak in the late 1970s, General Motors (GM) employed over 80,000 workers in the area; its employment dropped to 23,000 in 1990 and 8,000 in 2006 (Doidge et al., 2015). Those losses have also impacted the government sector (down 53% between 2003 and 2014) and the healthcare sector (down 38% over the same time period). In 2003, Flint had over 78,000 employees working in the city, but that number had fallen to just over 51,000 by 2014 (Doidge et al., 2015). More specifically, the city's unemployment rate was 8.1% in 2001 while the U.S. rate was 4%. The 2001 recession drove Flint's rate to 13.1% (the national rate was 6%), as shown in Figure 9.3. During the Great Recession, Flint's unemployment rise reached 24.4% in 2009 while the national rate was 9%. Flint still had an unemployment rate nearly triple the national rate in 2019 (10.3% versus 3.6%).

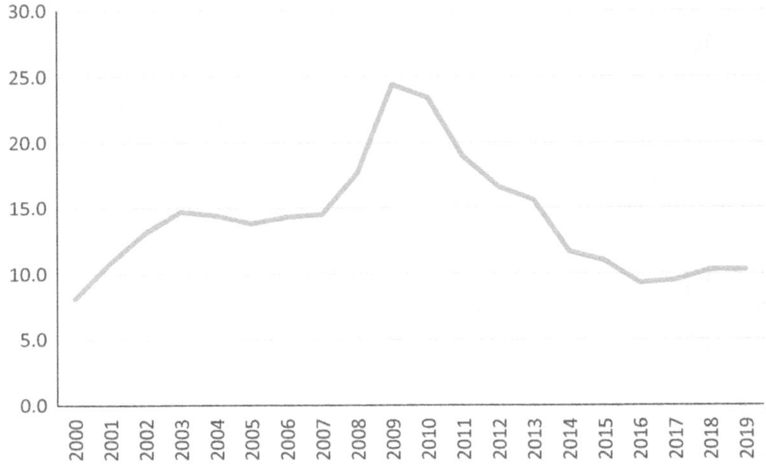

Figure 9.3 Unemployment Rate of Flint, Michigan, 2000–2019
Source: City of Flint (2021a)

The demographic and economic changes afflicted Flint's finances (discussed more in the next section) and its political environment to the point that Mayor Woodrow Stanley was recalled in 2002. In the same year, Michigan Governor John Engler declared a financial emergency, enabling the state to replace the city administrator with an emergency financial manager (ended in 2004). Flint was facing a $30 million deficit at that time. In late 2011, Flint was again placed under receivership until 2015 due to structural deficits and increasing debt. It was 2019 when the state returned complete city management to Flint officials.

Outputs: Fiscal Trends

Revenues

Flint's governmental revenues have been significantly affected by past recessions. For instance, in FY2000, Flint collected $117 million in total governmental revenues. But by FY2003, following the 2001 recession, those revenues were down by 9.5% to $106 million. Similarly, in FY2010, total governmental revenues were 10.2% lower than in FY2007 ($93.9 million versus $104.5 million).

The volatility of Flint's revenues is a reflection of both revenue structure and the effects of the economy on those revenue sources. In 2000, the combination of external funding from the state (29%) and federal (11%) governments accounted for 40% of Flint's total governmental revenues. The other major sources consisted of property taxes (23%), income taxes (20%), and charges for services (9%).

When the 2001 recession hit, property taxes and federal sources fell; property taxes were $26.4 million in 2000 and $24.7 million in 2002; federal sources provided $12.4 million and $8.6 million, respectively.

The overall revenue structure changed little between 2000 and 2010 (see Figure 9.4), but total governmental revenues were lower in 2010. Flint's $93.9 million in revenues included 30% from the state, 12% from the federal government, 20% from property taxes, 15% from income taxes, and 12% from fees and charges for services. Most major revenue sources were negatively affected by the Great Recession: property taxes fell by more than $1 million between 2007 and 2009, income tax collections dropped by $4.5 million, and federal sources were down $2.3 million. Revenues from state sources remained stable between 2007 and 2009 ($29.5 million vs. $29.8 million). Reflecting the city's efforts to rely more heavily on fees for services, the share of governmental revenues coming from fees and charges rose from 9% of total revenues in 2000 to 12% in 2010.

In FY2019, when city officials resumed management of Flint, the revenue structure revealed a problematic factor for those who study municipal financial condition: heavy reliance on state funding. More than one-third (36%) of Flint's total governmental revenues came from state sources, with another 11% coming from the federal government. According to Maher (2013), "The greater reliance a local government has on intergovernmental aid, the weaker its financial position" (p. 22). On a more positive note, Flint's total revenues grew in 2018 and 2019, including property taxes, income taxes, and federal and state sources. The only noticeable drop was in charges for services ($13.9 million in 2018 and $10.6 million in 2019).

Expenditures

During the 20 years reviewed (2000–2019), Flint's total governmental expenditures have changed dramatically due to economic shocks and forced restructuring under city emergency managers, as shown in Table 9.1. Consider the period from FY2000 to FY2003. Between FY2000 and FY2001, total governmental expenditures were cut by 10.9%; they fell another 3.8% the next year and then 14.5% between FY2002 and FY2003. Although no departments were spared, those most affected between 2000 and 2003 were public safety (–34%), parks and recreation (–36.3%), and public works (–34%).

While expenditures generally rose annually from FY2003 to FY2008 (except for FY2005), they fell again due to the Great Recession and following the appointment of an emergency financial manager from FY2011 to FY2015. Between FY2007 and FY2009, total governmental expenditures fell from $109.5 million to $104.1 million. The departments most affected were community development (−15.7%), parks and recreation (−13.7%), and judicial services (−12.4%). Those cuts, however, pale in comparison to the spending reductions imposed between FY2011 and FY2015. During that period, total spending was lowered by 13.8%

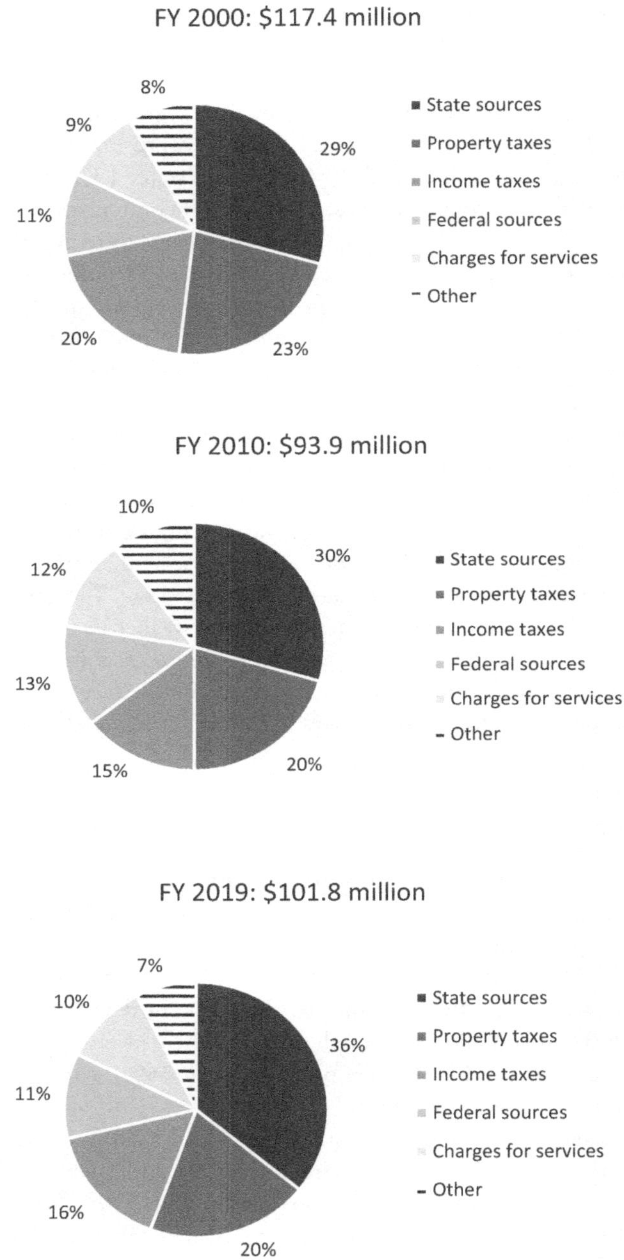

Figure 9.4 Governmental Revenues of Flint, Michigan
Source: City of Flint (2000, 2010, 2019)

Table 9.1 Governmental Expenditures of Flint, Michigan ($1,000)

Year	*Legis-lative*	*Judicial*	*General govern-ment*	*Public safety*	*Building inspec-tions*	*Public works*	*Parks & recrea-tion*	*Community develop-ment*	*Debt service*	*Other*	*Total*	*Annual pct change*
2000	1,078	5,503	20,912	56,325	0	22,044	7,841	11,783	3,637	6,058	129,123	–
2001	1,132	5,160	20,789	48,006	0	21,827	6,452	8,373	3,337	2,522	115,076	–10.9
2002	1,138	5,243	17,820	44,763	0	22,757	4,458	11,127	3,340	0	110,646	–3.8
2003	893	4,556	17,119	37,185	1,596	14,685	4,989	10,304	3,306	0	94,633	–14.5
2004	518	4,527	28,287	32,666	2,593	17,304	4,021	11,523	2,378	0	103,817	9.7
2005	916	5,156	12,388	41,437	2,884	23,065	3,810	4,015	1,941	0	95,612	–7.9
2006	1,275	5,325	12,386	44,068	4,669	20,743	4,254	9,391	3,281	0	105,392	10.2
2007	1,100	5,835	12,468	49,278	3,944	21,803	5,258	7,587	2,225	0	109,498	3.9
2008	1,165	6,368	13,095	57,196	4,625	34,463	6,000	5,974	2,815	0	131,701	20.3
2009	1,196	5,114	11,862	47,263	4,269	20,572	4,538	6,398	2,917	0	104,129	–20.9
2010	1,177	5,469	10,977	44,824	6,604	20,379	4,340	14,900	2,967	0	111,637	7.2
2011	1,226	5,293	16,876	42,520	7,336	16,951	9,279	8,285	2,664	0	110,430	–1.1
2012	1,214	5,596	10,905	41,398	7,013	15,775	15,384	8,428	1,778	0	107,491	–2.7
2013	334	4,955	8,000	44,195	4,171	15,286	8,328	9,379	1,935	0	96,583	–10.1
2014	339	5,181	7,467	42,372	2,445	14,609	2,729	6,750	2,422	0	84,314	–12.7
2015	558	5,294	11,034	38,758	1,574	15,801	2,981	5,583	13,568	0	95,151	12.9
2016	841	3,783	10,771	36,889	1,792	6,156	358	7,745	2,953	13,675	71,288	–25.1
2017	871	901	10,340	39,608	1,890	10,715	584	5,576	2,989	7,728	73,474	3.1
2018	901	859	12,688	43,075	1,701	11,106	360	5,585	3,909	8,613	80,184	9.1
2019	756	750	17,195	43,483	0	19,832	617	9,667	2,736	1,531	95,036	18.5
Annual avg pct change	4.7%	–6.3%	3.4%	–0.7%	–1.1%	5.4%	2.3%	9.7%	20.4%	–	–0.8%	

Source: City of Flint (2021a)

and all department budgets faced cuts. Those most dramatically affected were building inspections (−78.5%), parks and recreation (−67.9%), the legislative branch (−54.5%), general government (−34.6%), and community development (−32.6%). Even public safety expenditures were nearly 9% lower in FY2015 than in FY2011.

Transferring complete city management to Flint officials in 2019 resulted in an expenditure increase of 18.5% between FY2018 and FY2019. In an effort to restore sizable service cuts, expenditures jumped in public works (78.6%), community development (73.1%) and parks and recreation (71.4%). Despite these increases, most of the increases did not bring department expenditures close to FY2011 levels.

Outcomes: Fiscal Condition

Operating Position

Flint's operating position has been problematic for much of this 20-year period and was a primary reason for the state takeovers in 2002 and 2011. According to Flint's 2020 ACFR, a reserve policy does not currently exist, but officials are planning "establishment of a fund balance reserve, including establishment of a budget stabilization fund" (p. 5). An overview of the city's unreserved fund balance over time is provided in Figure 9.5.

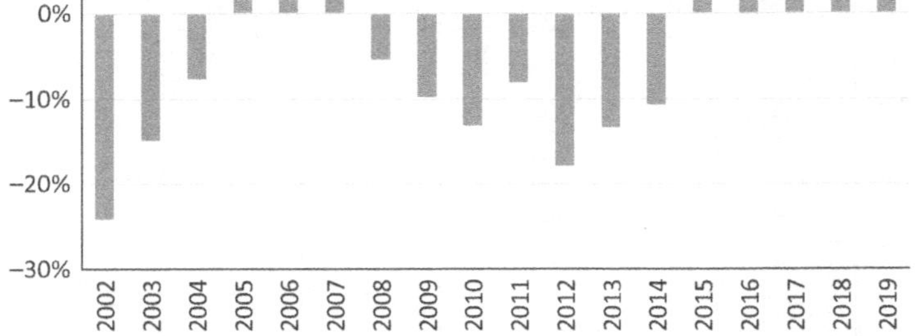

Figure 9.5 Unreserved Fund Balance as Percent of General Fund Expenditures, 2002–2019

Source: City of Flint (2002–2019)

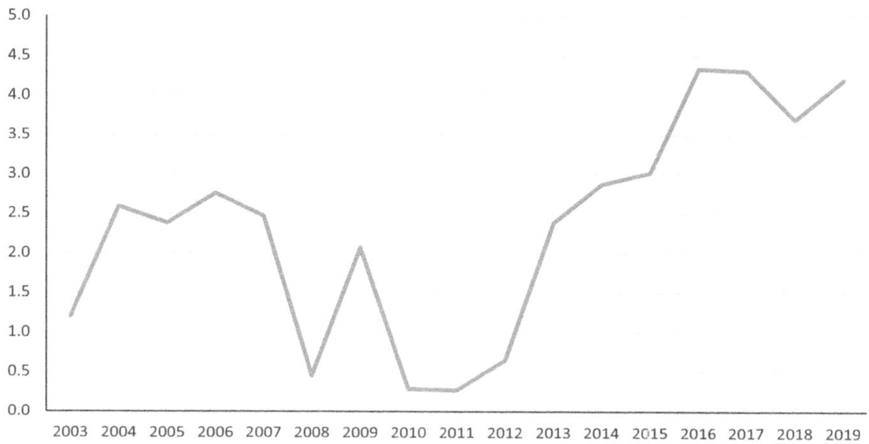

Figure 9.6 Cash, Investments, and Receivables Relative to Current Liabilities, 2003–2019

Source: City of Flint (2003–2019)

Once again, the effects of the recessions had serious fiscal consequences for Flint. Following the 2001 recession, Flint had negative reserves in FY2002 through FY2004. While the city experienced modest improvement in FY2005–FY2007, when it carried positive unreserved balances, the Great Recession wiped out those gains. From FY2008 to FY2014, Flint's unreserved fund balances were negative, falling as low as −17.8% of expenditures in FY2012. The return of positive unreserved general fund balances in 2015 coincided with the state's decision to remove the emergency manager. By FY2019, Flint's unreserved general fund balance equaled 25.3% of expenditures.

Similar patterns emerge from an examination of Flint's liquidity (cash, investments, and receivables), as shown in Figure 9.6. Recall that in 2001, Flint officials were transferring funds from other accounts to cover payments. By FY2003, the city's ratio of cash, investments, and receivables was at least equal to current liabilities, and from 2003 to 2007, the ratio was at the generally acceptable level of at least double current liabilities (Chaney, 2005). The Great recession quickly wiped out those gains, and it took until FY2013 for Flint to begin recovering. By FY2016, Flint's cash, investments, and receivables were four times its current liabilities, and this the ratio remained steady through FY2019.

Debt Position

Michigan law limits GO debt to 10% of assessed property valuation (City of Flint, 2020), which Flint falls well below (see Figure 9.7). Flint's GO debt peaked in FY2016 during this 20-year period at 1.3% of property value.

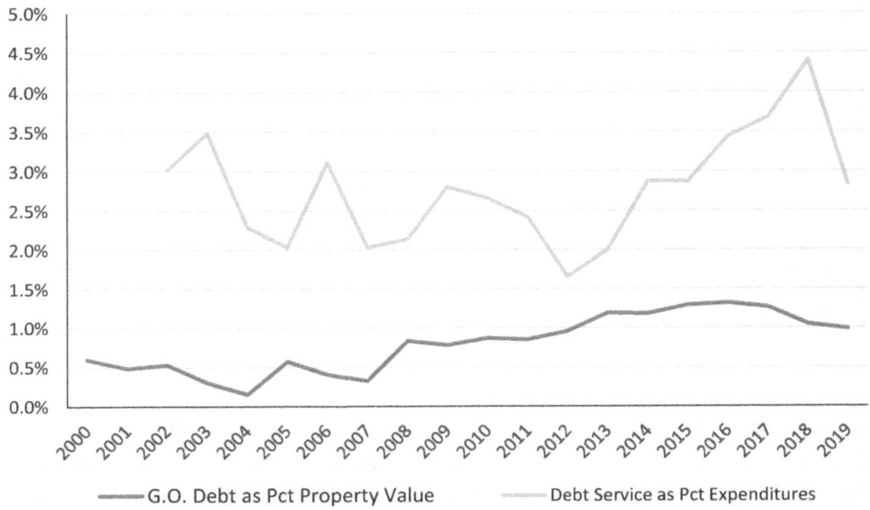

Figure 9.7 General Obligation Debt and Debt Service, 2000–2019
Source: City of Flint (2000–2019)

Flint's lower GO debt ratio is both a curse and blessing, because one reason for the low ratio is the lack of ratings from the bond rating agencies (City of Flint, 2020), making it virtually impossible to incur new debt. The rating agencies stopped assessing Flint's debt in the period leading up to state receivership. The last time Moody's rated Flint's GO bonds was in 2006, when they were rated Ba1—a rating that suggests significant credit risk.

To Flint's credit, debt service has consistently hovered around 3% of expenditures during this 20-year period. The ratio peaked in 2018 at 4.4% and was lowest in 2012 at 1.65%. This consistency also means that as governmental expenditures fluctuated, so too have debt service payments. Therefore, although the ratio has been generally stable, annual payments have varied from $1.8 million in FY2012 to $3.9 million in FY2018.

Long-Term Liabilities

Flint operates a hospital and sewer and water utilities through enterprise funds. As noted in the city's 2019 ACFR, Flint will be dealing with problems associated with its water crisis for years to come. This includes helping those citizens who have been adversely affected by the city's water crisis and providing much-needed infrastructure upgrades during a period of economic and financial recovery.

Government liabilities have been stable during this period, peaking at 19.3% of assets in FY2012. Long-term liabilities for business-type activities spiked in FY2009 and then dropped dramatically in FY2012. The latter change was caused by a sizable drop in business-type long-term liabilities ($139.8 million in FY2011 versus $23.8 million in FY2012). Total assets also dropped in FY2012 when compared to FY2011 ($438.2 million versus $142.6 million).

As noted above, Flint used to operate its own pension plans, but in 2014, the emergency manager shifted that responsibility to the Municipal Employees Retirement System (MERS). MERS is a statewide, multiple-employer pension system that administers various defined-benefit and defined-contribution pension plans for public safety and most non–public safety employees. New non–public safety employees hired after FY2013 are to be enrolled in a hybrid plan administered by MERS; similar plans for new public safety employees took effect in FY2014.

Each year, an independent actuary engaged by the pension system calculates the amount of the annual contribution the city must make to the pension system to ensure that the plan will be able to fully meet its obligations to retired employees. The city makes quarterly contributions to the system in accordance with the contribution rate determined by the independent actuary. Despite the city's funding activities, the overall retirement system was funded at 36.3% in 2017, and that ratio fell to 30.6% in 2018 (currently the latest actuarial evaluation date). In 2018, 443 active employees were paying into the city's retirement system, which was supporting 1,773 retirees (City of Flint, 2019).

The city has taken actions to reduce these legacy costs associated with healthcare and pensions. As of the end of FY2018, the city requested that *Welch v. City of Flint*, a class-action lawsuit resulting in the limitation of changes to retiree healthcare benefits, be reconsidered. Additionally, the city actively solicited the help of an outside consulting firm to review its current retiree healthcare benefits. The objective of all of these actions was to seek strategic and legal means to overhaul the city's retiree healthcare offerings and costs. The projected $17.9 million of costs for FY2019 was nearly insurmountable for a city in such a fragile financial state. The city's unfunded total liability for OPEB was $249.8 million. In addition, a pension plan provision was changed effective January 1, 2016, whereby surviving spouses and eligible dependents of a sworn Flint police officer or firefighter killed in the line of duty would be eligible to participate in the city's healthcare plan at no cost for life. Previous restructuring of health benefits has involved consolidating and updating plans, imposing premium sharing, limiting access of spouses and dependents, and eliminating the promise of retiree healthcare for new employees. Similar changes have taken place with respect to retirement benefits, with increased contributions, changes in multipliers, and enrollment of new employees into hybrid pension plans in lieu of traditional defined-benefit plans. Governmental activities showed a $393.8 million deficit in unrestricted net position. The $259.3 million total deficit was primarily driven by the pension and OPEB liability (City of Flint, 2019).

Policy Actions: State Oversight

The state's role in managing Flint's affairs is an important aspect of this case study. In 2002, when the first financial emergency was declared, the new emergency manager, Ed Kurtz, cut salaries of elected officials (e.g., the mayor's salary fell from $107,000 to $24,000), instituted controls on hiring, travel, and operational spending, cut pension benefits (an action later revoked by the courts), cut wages, and instituted some layoffs (Mostafavi, 2011). Although these actions made a dent in the city's deficit, Flint's longer-term fiscal problems remained. Nevertheless, the state takeover ended in 2004.

Later in 2011, Michigan's Treasury Department conducted an analysis of Flint's finances and found that the city officials had been running deficits in the general fund and were filling the cash shortages with transfers from other funds (Doidge et al., 2015). "Due to the City of Flint's structural deficit, increasing legacy costs, and accumulating debt," the review team recommended placing the city under emergency financial management a second time (Doidge et al., 2015, p. 13). The governor appointed four different emergency financial managers (Michael Brown was appointed on two separate occasions).

According to Doidge et al. (2015), actions taken by the emergency financial managers during this period of receivership were extensive, with a particular focus on both operating deficits and long-term liabilities. Initial actions included eliminating the salaries of the mayor and council (later restored), requiring council members to receive training in municipal governance, several position eliminations, and revisions of collective bargaining agreements so as to lower the salaries and wages of city employees. Additional budgeting actions included strict controls over expenses, expansion of user fees to cover service costs, fee rate increases (for water and sewer), and the requirement that all overtime work (except emergency overtime) be approved in advance. The emergency financial manager made significant changes to pensions and OPEBs. For pensions, the reforms included requiring higher contributions from employees (up 9.5%), changes to eligibility and payments, and a transfer of pension system management from the city to the state retirement system (Doidge et al., 2015). OPEB changes included eliminating spouses from healthcare benefits if they were covered by their own plan, shifts to more cost-effective plans (requiring higher employee contributions), and changes in employee coverage.

It can be argued that the emergency managers' focus on cost savings was the principal reason for Flint's water crisis (Jacobson et al., 2020). Despite sizable water and sewer rate increases (up by 25% in early 2011 and raised by an additional 35% in late 2011), Flint was unable to meet bond requirements associated with infrastructure improvements. In 2013, the emergency manager ended the city's contract with Detroit's Water and Sewerage Department and entered into an agreement with the Karegnondi Water Authority for the provision of city water. In so doing, the manager switched the city's water source from Lake Huron to the Flint River (Doidge et al., 2015). This conversion of water sources "created a major public health emergency and caused long-term harm to Flint residents' health, well-being, and trust in government" (Jacobson et al., 2020, p. 555). The effects of this action are still being felt today (Madani & Einhorn, 2021).

Flint's second financial emergency was declared "resolved" in April 2015, and the city was moved from control by the emergency manager to home rule, under the guidance of the Receivership Transition Advisory Board (RTAB). In 2018, Michigan Governor Rick Snyder ended the RTAB's participation, placing sole management of the city with its elected officials and management team. According to Flint's 2019 ACFR:

> The preparation and adoption of the FY13, FY14, and FY15 budgets were under the control of the Emergency Manager. Under the direction of these Emergency Managers, considerable progress was made in reducing the City's June 30, 2012 accumulated General Fund deficit of $19.2 million. As of June 30, 2013, the deficit had been reduced to $12.9 million, and by June 30, 2016 a positive fund balance in the amount of $10.0 million was achieved. The FY18 budget was adopted under the guidance of the newly elected Mayor, City Administrator and Charter-designated leaders along with State receivership transitionary advisory board oversight. Under their guidance, the FY17 fund balance of the General Fund has increased to $17.0 million. Steps have also been taken to reduce long-term liabilities such as OPEB unfunded accrued liability, which stand at $249 million at the end of FY19, compared to more than $862 million seven years ago. Starting in FY15, all municipalities were required under Governmental Accounting Standards number sixty-eight (68) to record the City's net pension liability. Starting with FY18, all municipalities were required to account for OPEB liabilities using the General Accounting Standards number seventy-five (75) as opposed to forty-five (45). The $249 million liability was recorded using this standard. The City recorded a $346 million net pension liability on the government wide financial statements in FY 18. The total net pension liability increased to $372.0 million at the end of FY 19.
>
> (p. 4)

Despite this optimistic assessment of Flint's financial picture, concerns remain. For instance, Michigan law requires the reporting of underfunded retirement benefits; Flint's pension system is funded at only about 37%, and there is no pre-funding of OPEB liabilities (Colomer, 2018). Flint's water infrastructure remains in disrepair, and the city is now dealing with lawsuits stemming from the contamination of the water supply. In 2021, a partial civil lawsuit settlement of $641 million was reached between state and local government officials and residents (Egan, 2021). In addition, concerns have been raised about state support of local governments, which is the largest source of Flint's governmental revenues. According to Dan Gilmartin, executive director and CEO of the Michigan Municipal League, "the biggest problem Flint faces now is what all cities in Michigan face, and that is the state's system of municipal financing, which simply doesn't work" (Colomer, 2018).

Policy Actions: Input from Interviews with Finance Members

At the time of the 2015 interview, Flint was being managed by an emergency finance manager and the locally elected body had been dissolved. Flint's receiver was interviewed by telephone.

Effects of the Recession and Response Strategies

Regarding the recession's fiscal impact in 2008, the receiver stated, "Flint was already in a downward spiral, but the recession accelerated it. I would say that if it were not for the recession, Flint still was going to go over the cliff, but it got to the cliff a lot quicker." A series of response strategies were pursued, including tax and fee increases, plus reducing expenses significantly by eliminating services and cutting the workforce. As noted earlier, strategies focused on labor contracts (compensation and benefits, even—through litigation—for retired professionals). To the extent possible, the city also outsourced services and service delivery.

Fiscal Health and Fiscal Stress Measurement

When asked about fiscal health measurements, the Flint receiver focused on spending: were service needs equal to revenues generated? With regard to measuring fiscal stress, the receiver said

> Basically, fiscal stress would be the inability to provide even the minimal level of service on a sustainable basis . . . fiscal stress is when you do not have the resources to provide the level of services, even

minimal level of services, that are needed. Then you are forced into making decisions that reduce services immediately. Or, in some cases I suppose, you kick the can down the road by ignoring long-term liability.

Lessons Learned

Looking to the future, a discussion ensued about Flint's capacity to handle another recession. One step Flint was taking involved adjusting long-term costs so as to establish a balanced budget well into the future. The city was also partnering with entities such as the Greater Regional Flint Chamber of Commerce and the State of Michigan to promote economic development. Strong support—financial and otherwise—for a variety of activities and programs in Flint had been demonstrated by the Mott Foundations, the Kellogg Foundation, and the Ford Foundation. Diversification of Flint's economic base, especially in higher education and healthcare, was a major focus; cutting back on retiree healthcare plans was a more controversial action.

Final Assessment

In Flint, policymakers are guiding a municipality with limited access to borrowing and considerable legacy costs—demographic, economic, and fiscal—that present an enormous challenge to overcome. One of the city's greatest challenges is to overcome decades of decline, compounded by public frustration with previous actions, including the water crisis. Historically, Flint has been dominated by GM manufacturing. However, as plants have closed, so too have the employment opportunities. Loss of these opportunities has resulted in population outmigration (down 24.5% since 2000) and wealth decline, as personal incomes fell 75% after 2000 and property valuation dropped by 60%.

The impacts of this challenging environment have been visible on all fiscal metrics. The city's emergency financial manager focused on spending cuts, both operating and long-term (pensions and OPEBs). These actions resulted in improved operating position (cash and reserves) and the termination of state oversight of city financial management. The remaining question is whether the city's current socioeconomic composition can sustain its finances, particularly when state and federal aid accounts for nearly half of the city's governmental revenues. The COVID-19 pandemic seemed like just the next crisis to ravage Flint. According to the mayor's FY2021 and FY2022 transmittal letters, the pandemic caused serious disruption to the city economy. In summer 2020, the city's unemployment rate hit 44%; in the following year, it fell back to 12%, still higher than before the pandemic (City of Flint, 2021b). The FY 2021 transmittal letter went on to state that the city would face a structural general fund deficit of $16 million in FY2022 and another $18 million deficit in FY2023. Interestingly, the letter placed much of the blame for the city's current financial challenges on the state, citing property tax limits, insufficient state aid (including a claimed $100 million shortfall in revenue sharing), and the state takeover that resulted in pension funding degradation and the water crisis.

The pandemic's impact represents the continuation of a serious of fiscal challenges that have confronted Flint for decades. As with the 2001 recession and the Great Recession, just as the city seemed to be making positive strides, another shock hit the system and the city has struggled to rebound. Flint's unemployment rate was improving, and personal income was stabilizing through 2019. As a result, the city's operating position was also improving, in terms of both cash and reserves. The pandemic appears to have wiped out those gains.

Discussion Questions

Questions to consider regarding the Flint case study:

- What economic and demographic data are most useful to examine over time when considering city fiscal condition? Discuss what a city can/should do when these external forces have long-lasting effects on fiscal condition as is the case for Flint, Michigan.
- What fiscal trends or condition ratios best reflected Flint's financial struggles?
- The State of Michigan has a fiscal monitoring system and a process in place to take over city governance. How would you assess these mechanisms? To what extent and how did they aid or hinder the city's fiscal condition?
- With respect to the previous question, review the management team's response to the city's fiscal stress. Compare those response strategies to Chapter 7. Discuss the degree to which the response strategies for Flint were similar/different from the strategies discussed in Chapter 7.
- What state and municipal policy actions or management strategies would you suggest for the city's financial future?

Chapter 10

Case Study of Wichita, Kansas

Wichita, Kansas, a mid-sized city in the Great Plains, offers a case study in which the external environment, both politically and economically, has seriously threatened the city's financial condition. Wichita's economy was hit hard by the Great Recession. Its manufacturing sector alone lost approximately 15,000 of its nearly 68,000 jobs. Its aerospace industry was further hit when Boeing suspended production of the 737 Max in early 2020, and the subsequent COVID-19 pandemic further affected the aviation industry. Despite these challenges, Wichita officials have been able to avoid fiscal calamity, largely because of a strong management team, political buy-in and policies that both provided guidelines and sufficient maneuverability.

Inputs: Fiscal Environments

Institutional Settings/External Pressures

Following the Great Recession, Kansas Governor Sam Brownback and his tax consultant, Arthur Laffer, developed the framework for HB 2117, known as the Great Experiment, under which most business income taxes were eliminated, and personal income tax rates were cut. Governor Brownback signed the bill into law in 2012, and additional income tax cuts were passed in 2013. Specifically, the state's three personal income tax brackets were reduced to two, and the top rate was reduced from 6.45% to 4.9% (Mazerov, 2018). The legislation resulted

DOI: 10.4324/9780429270765-10

in severe state revenue shortfalls, however, and it was repealed in 2017. The lost revenue forced the state to draw down reserves and cut spending. Areas affected by the spending cuts included K-12 education and highway projects, both of which had a direct impact on local governments.

In the realm of municipal finance, Kansas state policymakers have imposed statutory TELs on municipalities. The most recent one, which took effect in 2017, limits property tax growth to the average inflation rate from the preceding five years. Exceeding the TEL requires voter approval. Furthermore, in 2006, the Kansas legislature passed a law exempting commercial and industrial equipment from personal property taxes. This resulted in an estimated $2 million annual revenue loss (City of Wichita, 2010). This latter change was of greater concern than the state-imposed TEL, as it directly affected the city's revenue-raising capacity.

Internal Structures

Wichita has one of the oldest manager-council government structures in the United States. In 1917, the city adopted a commission-manager form of government. Currently, it has a manager, mayor, and six-member council. The manager develops the city's budget and is responsible for day-to-day operations. The finance division has a director, budget officer, and several analysts. Wichita is also the largest city in Kansas by population. Wichita's fiscal policies include a general fund reserve of no less than 10% of expenditures and a GO debt limit of 30% of equalized assessed valuation.

Socioeconomic Conditions

In 2019, Wichita had a population of 389,255 (see Figure 10.1); since 2000, the population has grown by 10.6%. Much of that growth occurred between 2005 and 2010 (8%). Since 2010, Wichita's population has been stagnant, growing by fewer than 7,000 residents. The city's economy, more specifically the aerospace industry, had much to do with these population trends.

By any metric, the city's economy, particularly its manufacturing sector, was significantly affected by the Great Recession. In 2000, the city's top employers were Boeing (17,300 employees or 6% of total city employment), Cessna Aircraft Company (11,156, 4%), and Raytheon Aircraft Company (9,200, 3%). Wichita's manufacturing sector peaked in 2008 with 67,700 jobs (City of Wichita, 2019). Total personal income in the Wichita metropolitan statistical area (MSA) jumped by 49% between 2000 and 2008. During the same period, per-capita personal income grew by 37% (see Figure 10.2). The city's unemployment rate in 2008 was 4.8%, down from 6.7% just four years earlier (see Figure 10.3). The Wichita MSA's unemployment rate in 2008 was even lower—4.4% in 2008.

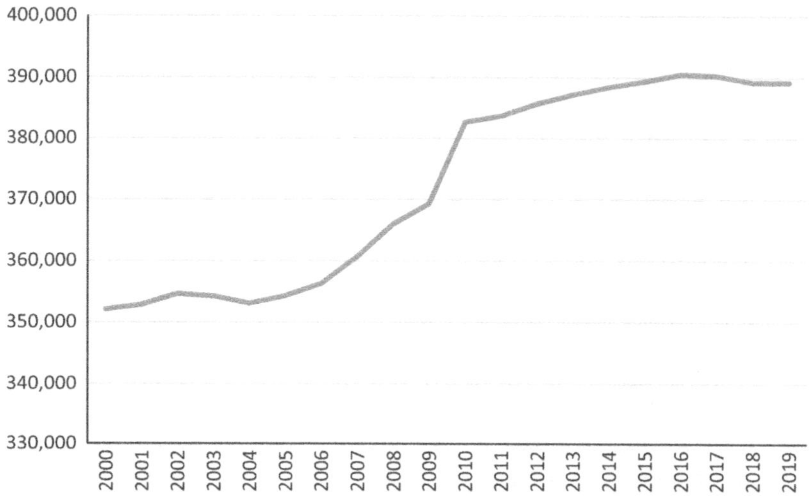

Figure 10.1 Population of Wichita, Kansas, 2000–2019
Source: City of Wichita (2020)

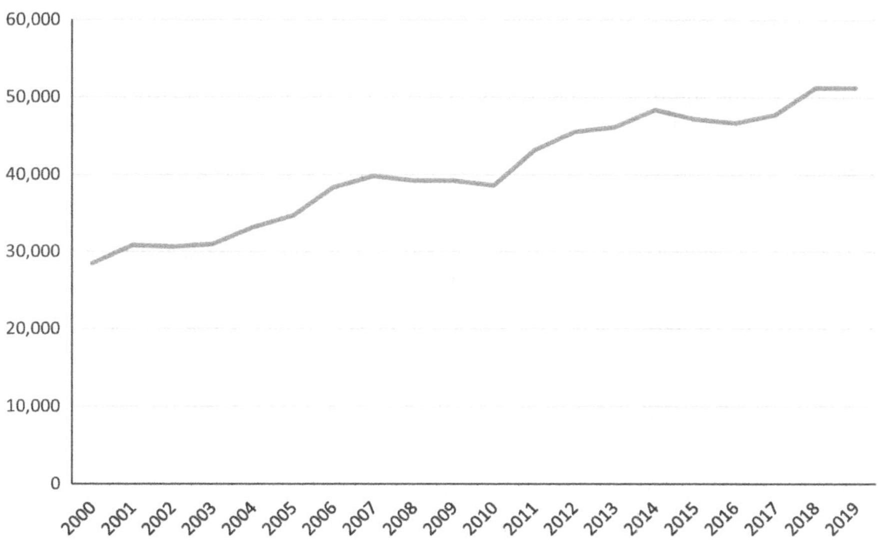

Figure 10.2 Personal Income of Wichita, Kansas, 2000–2019 (Per Capita)
Source: City of Wichita (2020)

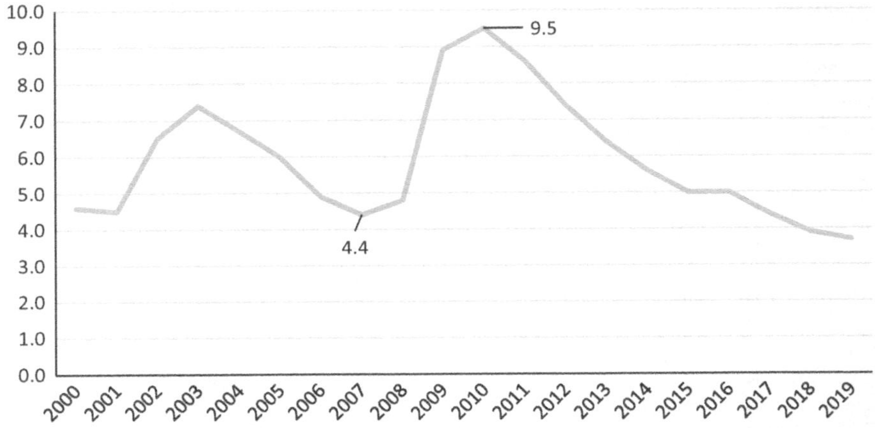

Figure 10.3 Unemployment Rate of Wichita, Kansas, 2000–2019
Source: City of Wichita (2020)

The Great Recession's effects on Wichita's economy were immediate. Boeing, the city's leading employer in 2000, ranked tenth by 2009 with 2,500 employees (0.78% of total employment). Cessna Aircraft Company had barely half the number of employees in 2009 (5,994) that it had in 2000. According to the city's 2019 ACFR, Wichita lost 15,000 manufacturing jobs between 2008 and 2010. The city's unemployment rate nearly doubled in those years, from 4.8% to 9.5%. Per-capita personal income in nominal dollars also fell, from $39,207 in 2008 to $38,598 in 2010.

Since peaking in 2010, Wichita's employment picture has gone through a bit of a transformation. For instance, while the top ten employers in 2000 accounted for 22% of the city's workforce, by 2019 they represented only 17% of total employment. The biggest change was Boeing's decision to pull its manufacturing work out of Wichita in 2013, ending an 85-year presence. There was also a consolidation of aircraft manufactures, as Textron Aviation now manufactures Beechcraft and Cessna aircraft. All told, aircraft manufacturing in 2019 employed approximately 22,000 people in Wichita, compared to over 41,000 in 2000. Despite these losses, total employment is up, and the city's employment base is more diverse. In 2019, Wichita's top ten employment sectors included aircraft manufacturing (7.3% of total employment), an Air Force base (1.9%), government agencies (3.7%), and healthcare (15).

Despite the shift in employment, total employment in 2019 was up slightly (at 305,000) compared to 2000 (299,138). Furthermore, unemployment rates have consistently fallen each year, from the peak in 2010 to 3.7% in 2019, the lowest rate during the period of study. Personal income has also grown during the 10-year period. For the Wichita MSA, personal income grew by 36% while per-capita personal income for the MSA grew by 33%.

Outputs: Fiscal Trends

Revenues

Wichita's revenue sources have been transformed between 2000 and 2019, as the city has become less reliant on intergovernmental revenues and more reliant on taxes (including property and franchise), licenses, and permits. In 2000, nearly half of the city's revenues came from property and motor vehicle taxes (25%) and intergovernmental revenues (24%). By 2009, intergovernmental revenues represented only 11% of the total, and that proportion dropped further to 9% in 2019 (see Figure 10.4).

Aided by 3.7% average annual growth in assessed valuation during the period, taxes (predominantly property) grew as a portion of total government revenues from 25% in 2000 to 33% in 2009 and 34% in 2019. There was similar growth in franchise taxes collected from utilities (water and sewer), which represented 10% of total government revenues in 2000, 16% in 2009, and 21% in 2019. Finally, income from licenses and permits, included in the "other revenues" category, grew from $5 million in 2000 to over $21 million in 2019.

From the perspective of a financial condition analysis, Wichita's revenue mix has several positive attributes. For instance, although it is an important source of revenue, intergovernmental revenues pose challenges because municipal governments lack control over the funding. Wichita's reduced reliance on intergovernmental revenues means that when the next fiscal shock hits the city, cuts in intergovernmental revenue like those experienced from FY2009 to FY2012 will be less impactful. Also, the city's overall revenue mix is more diverse in 2019 than in 2000, and Wichita is more reliant on less elastic revenues (property and franchise taxes, and fees and charges) than on sales taxes and intergovernmental revenues.

Expenditures

Wichita's total revenues experienced considerable annual variability during the 20 years examined (2000–2019). For instance, between FY2000 and FY2001, governmental expenditures jumped by 15.6%, followed by another 15.2% increase the next year. These increases were predominantly driven by capital outlays (up 47% between 2000 and 2001) and debt service expenditures (up 58% between 2001 and 2002). The Great Recession also had visible effects on spending.

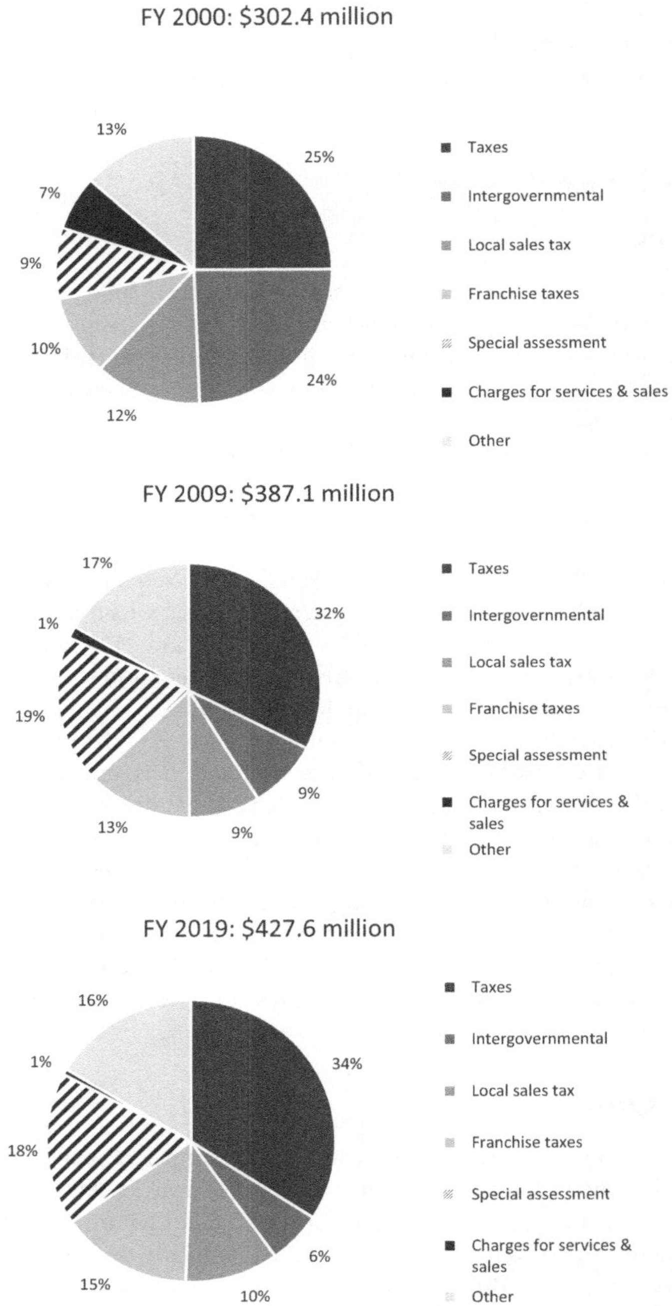

Figure 10.4 Governmental Revenues of Wichita, Kansas
Source: City of Wichita (2000, 2009, 2019)

Between 2008 and 2009, total governmental expenditures dropped by 5.4%; they then fell by another 4.2% and 8.1%, respectively, in the following two years.

There was much less change in the annual distribution of expenditures by source than with revenues. In 2000, debt service and capital outlay expenditures accounted for 39% of Wichita's total spending; they represented 42% of expenditures in 2009 and 45% in 2019. The second-largest expense, public safety, accounted for 23% of expenditures in 2000, 25% in 2009, and 28% in 2019. The slight percentage growth in these expenditure categories meant that other programs accounted for a smaller share of the pie, including highways, streets, and sanitation (7% in 2000, 5% in 2009, and 4% in 2019) as well as health and welfare (11.5%, 8%, and 7%, respectively). An overview of the city's expenditures is provided in Table 10.1.

Outcomes: Fiscal Condition

Operating Position

Wichita's fund balance policy requires sufficient reserves to meet or exceed 10% of the next year's budgeted expenditures (City of Wichita, 2019). When general fund unassigned and assigned balances are combined and divided by general fund expenditures, Wichita's reserves show a high degree of consistency and upward growth following the Great Recession. The city's low point was 2018, when fund balance levels were 4.6% of expenditures. Interestingly, despite the economic difficulties that Wichita sustained through 2010, the city's reserves grew to 7.3% of expenditures in 2011. Since then, Wichita's reserves have peaked at 9.6% of general fund expenditures in 2016 and have remained around 8% in subsequent years. An overview of the unreserved fund balance over time appears in Figure 10.5.

The crucial question of whether a municipality's reserves are adequate is often difficult to answer because it generally requires an understanding of the internal and external environments that directly impact reserves. In the case of Wichita, the period studied includes two recessionary periods, including the Great Recession. As described earlier, the city's economy was severely impacted by the recession of 2007–2009. The city's fiscal response included significant expenditure reductions, coupled with relatively stable revenues that enabled policymakers to sustain fiscal shocks without the need to draw down reserves. Comparing Wichita's reserves in the years prior to the Great Recession to the most recent years studied—just before the fiscal shock caused by the COVID-19 pandemic—suggests that the city has a stronger operating position. Reserves in 2007 represented 5% of expenditures, compared to 8% in 2019.

Buttressing Wichita's strong operating position is the city's strong liquidity. Figure 10.6 shows governmental cash, investments, and receivables relative to

Table 10.1 Government Expenditures of Wichita, Kansas ($1,000)

Year	*General government*	*Public safety*	*Hwys, streets & sanitation*	*Health & welfare*	*Culture & education*	*Debt service*	*Capital outlay*	*Total*	*Annual pct change*
2000	23,980	76,700	22,017	37,618	24,386	62,858	78,920	326,479	
2001	25,496	78,639	24,499	38,741	25,098	68,993	115,792	377,258	15.6
2002	29,644	84,887	23,125	36,822	27,271	108,847	123,828	434,424	15.2
2003	25,343	86,742	21,317	38,100	25,987	70,888	171,333	439,710	1.2
2004	29,836	91,576	22,388	34,741	27,883	80,086	146,568	433,078	–1.5
2005	30,524	94,352	24,651	32,900	29,256	86,009	126,314	424,006	–2.1
2006	34,193	103,315	26,138	33,482	29,650	80,284	170,129	477,191	12.5
2007	31,576	110,745	26,392	31,758	30,171	78,828	150,383	459,853	–3.6
2008	36,064	116,580	26,710	31,864	32,720	80,673	165,767	490,378	6.6
2009	32,855	117,087	25,309	35,986	31,892	98,454	122,187	463,770	–5.4
2010	34,640	120,792	24,387	40,109	31,720	108,821	83,658	444,127	–4.2
2011	36,588	122,930	26,714	35,379	30,793	72,672	82,901	407,977	–8.1
2012	34,643	126,734	21,908	32,134	31,061	85,949	109,959	442,388	8.4
2013	36,414	129,574	20,450	31,854	30,379	82,574	108,380	439,625	–0.6
2014	37,368	129,934	22,782	31,656	31,044	68,057	76,412	397,253	–9.6
2015	37,601	131,496	25,278	33,035	33,391	70,369	91,671	422,841	6.4
2016	39,113	136,049	24,319	36,431	36,592	67,561	93,163	433,228	2.5
2017	38,243	136,336	24,888	35,388	37,018	73,623	118,071	463,567	7.0
2018	39,409	144,224	22,570	35,896	37,042	67,989	134,089	481,219	3.8
2019	42,163	147,100	22,665	36,836	40,463	71,595	165,779	526,601	9.4
Annual avg pct change	4.0%	4.8%	0.2%	–0.1%	3.5%	0.7%	5.8%	3.2%	

Source: City of Wichita (2020)

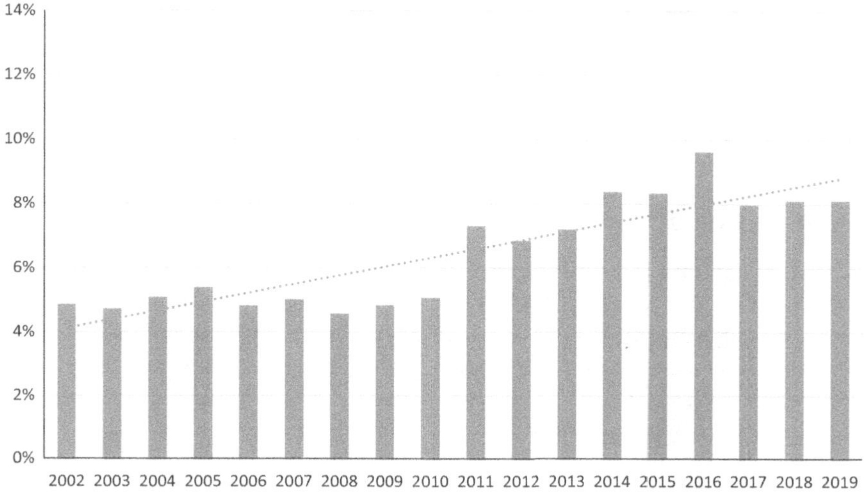

Figure 10.5 Unreserved Fund Balance as Percent of General Fund Expenditures, 2002–2019

Source: City of Wichita (2002–2019)

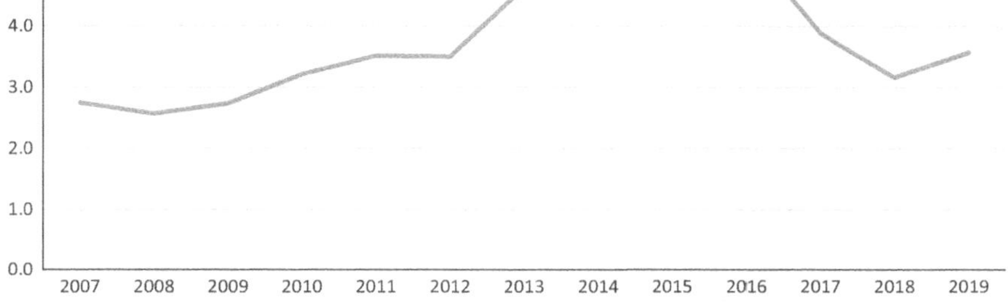

Figure 10.6 Cash, Investments, and Receivables Relative to Current Liabilities, 2007–2019

Source: City of Wichita (2007–2019)

current liabilities. Compared with Chaney's (2005) suggestion of 2.0 as a threshold, Wichita exceeded it in each year studied. FY2008 was Wichita's low point at 2.6, and the ratio then grew annually to 6.95 in FY2015. This means that Wichita had nearly seven times as much cash, investments, and receivables as short-term liabilities.

Debt Position

Wichita's debt limit is linked to property value; it cannot exceed 30% of equalized assessed valuation. Wichita's GO debt as a percentage of assessed valuation has remained stable during this 20-year period (see Figure 10.7). It peaked at 19% in 2015 and has fallen each year since then. Even during and after the Great Recession, when property valuation was stagnant (2008–2012), GO debt grew only from 12% to 16% of valuation, still well below the statutory limit.

Debt service spending has averaged 14.3% of governmental expenditures during the 2000–2019 period. As Wichita cut spending in response to the Great Recession, debt service relative to governmental expenditures inched up from 12.8% in 2008 to 16.9% in 2011. Following this peak, GO debt service declined back to 12.8% in 2019.

Long-Term Liabilities

Wichita operates water, sewer, and stormwater utilities and an airport. Figure 10.8 demonstrates the minimal effects of the Great Recession on Wichita's long-term

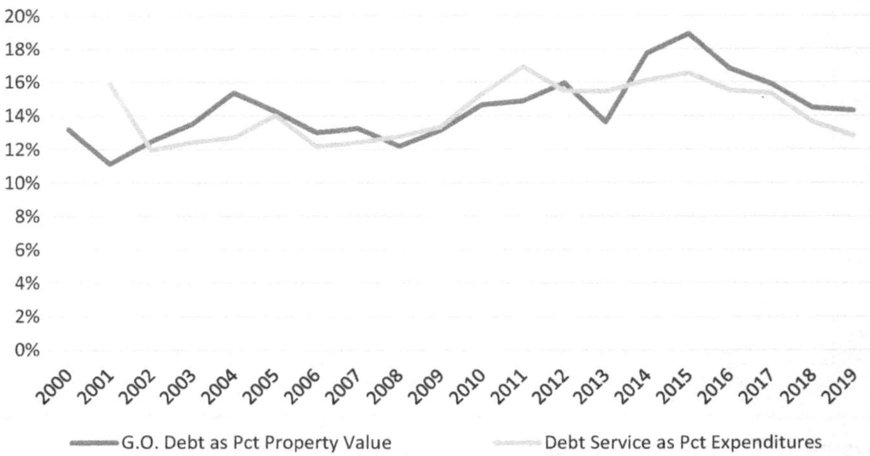

Figure 10.7 General Obligation Debt and Debt Service, 2000–2019
Source: City of Wichita (2000–2019)

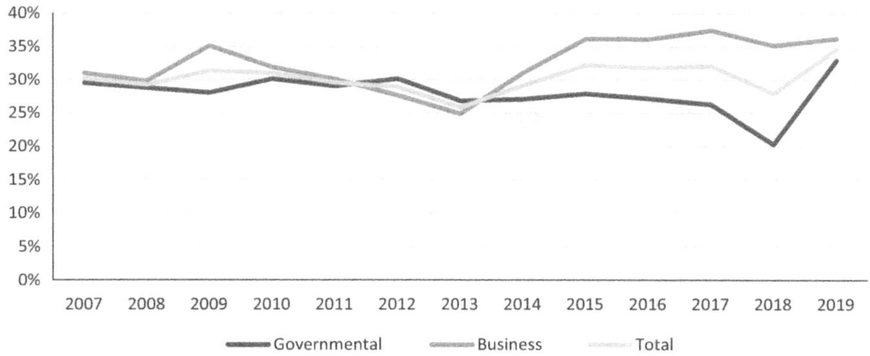

Figure 10.8 Long-Term Liabilities as Percent of Total Assets, 2007–2019
Source: City of Wichita (2007–2019)

liabilities. From FY2007 to FY2019, liabilities averaged 28% of assets for governmental funds, 33% for business-type activities, and 30% overall. Following the Great Recession, long-term liabilities for business-type activities steadily declined from 25% of assets in 2008 to 35% in 2013. This was followed by a jump to 36% of assets in 2015, and the ratio has since been stable since then. Governmental long-term liabilities were generally stable from FY2007 to FY2017, dipped in 2018, and jumped in 2019. The drop in 2018 was the result of a 19% drop in long-term liabilities, followed by a 64% jump in 2019 that appears to be attributable to a $219 million pension liability.

According to Wichita's 2010 ACFR, the city's pensions are well endowed, with a funded ratio of 96%. Additional detail is provided in later financial reports. In the city's 2019 ACFR, two pensions are reported: (1) police and fire and (2) other Wichita employees. The latter fund's total pension liability was $671.7 million at the end of 2019, and the plan's fiduciary net position was $546.7 million, resulting in a ratio of 81.4%. This net position as a percentage of pension liability was well below FY2018 (98.3%) and was caused largely by a $39.5 million loss in investment income. A similar pattern affected the police and fire pension fund, as a $44 million loss in net investment income dropped the net position as a percentage of pension liability from 100% in 2018 to 82.7% in 2019.

Policy Actions: Input from Interviews with Finance Members

In 2015, Wichita finance managers were interviewed over the telephone; a follow-up interview was conducted in June 2021. The 2015 interview enabled us to better understand how the city managed the Great Recession, whereas the 2021 interview asked about the fiscal effects of COVID-19 pandemic.

Relations with Elected Officials

Under the city manager structure, meetings occur weekly, but the finance team is generally insulated from elected officials. "Interaction directly with city council is pretty minimal, except at presentations at the council meetings or some other special circumstances." Interviewees also noted that they did not observe much conflict between council members that inhibited the team's ability to "move forward." They acknowledged that this had not always been the case, but at this point, relations are positive.

Effect of the Recession and Response Strategies

With regard to the Great Recession, Wichita officials noted that problematic signs first started appearing near the end of 2008 and continued into 2009. The city experienced layoffs from aircraft manufacturers, builders stopped new development, and valuation and sales tax collections flattened. As reflected in the budget data, "City officials implemented short-term strategies that focused on spending cuts, including freezing and holding positions, reducing street maintenance funding, and slowing hiring. Medium to longer-term strategies focused on prioritizing programs, staffing adjustments and cost recovery." Interviewees were asked in 2015 if the city had recovered by 2009 and the responses were a definitive no, but "we are just starting to" now. Another informant stated, "We are recovering, but we're a long way from recovery." They noted that sales tax collections were improving, building activity was picking up, and unemployment was down, but there was still no progress with aircraft manufacturers. The focus was now on trying to diversify the business sector.

Institutional Constraints

Interviewees were asked about the impact of institutional fiscal constraints. There was unanimity in their response: none have impacted decision making. "We have to publicize increases in tax levies so this is no biggie . . . also, we have a debt limit but we are not up to the maximum." One interviewee mentioned the state's statutory limitations on the size of revenue increases but affirmed that existing TELs "had no relevance." More restrictive than state TELs are self-imposed constraints such as having had a stable mill levy for 20 years; politically, officials now feel unable to deviate from that mill rate. Other guidelines that affect policy include the requirement that general fund reserves must be 10% of expenditures. When asked about the value of home-rule powers, respondents replied, "I don't know that it gives us much more autonomy than anyone else."

Fiscal Health

One frequent pattern in the fiscal condition literature is the lack of consistency between local officials' self-assessments of their fiscal condition and objective measures used by professionals and scholars. To help in interpreting the situation, city professionals were asked how they assess fiscal health. Wichita's finance team said they assess fiscal health in terms of fund balances (drawing on reserves or having a balanced budget) and forecasts of future debt, bond ratings, and pension funding. An interviewee said, "We are very conscious of our debt levels, and that's it."

When asked how they define a fiscally stressed community, these finance officers described Wichita's situation during the recession. They focused on freezing hiring for vacant positions ("we had vacancies that were held for quite a while"), drawing down reserves, and/or service cuts. They noted that they were forced to take all these steps, except that they avoided drawing down the fund balance. One interviewee added, "Underlying trends for our primary revenues were not good. I'm talking primarily about property valuations. We had about three years of flat and decreasing property valuation, so I would say that was a definite sign of fiscal stress."

Lessons Learned

Looking to the future, a discussion ensued about Wichita's capacity to handle another recession. It was noted that they now have "more of a prioritization model in place . . . so I think we understand what's important, what services are the most important, which makes it easier to cut the ones you've determined are the least important." Interestingly, the statement was followed up with, "but at the same time, they've already done all their cuts . . . the next crisis, you know, there's not a whole lot left that we didn't think was very important." When asked about lessons learned, the response was to "figure out what we want to do and try to do that well and cut everything else."

The last question asked whether in hindsight, the professionals interviewed might have done anything differently. The initial response was no, as they felt that the city took a very strategic approach to weathering the recession's effects. Upon further reflection, they noted that some initiatives, such as a home buyer rebate program, were not as successful as hoped. Overall, however, the team members were proud of their efforts, because they didn't rely on one-time fixes, took the fiscal challenges seriously every year, and didn't expect things to improve for some time.

Final Assessment

Wichita policymakers operate in an environment that, despite some state-imposed restrictions, tends to give municipal governments the capacity to manage their affairs effectively. This situation is reflected in terms of both the relatively weak TELs and the strong home-rule powers granted to local governments.

One of the city's greatest challenges is to manage fiscal policies in a volatile economic environment. Historically, Wichita has been dominated by the aerospace industry, which is particularly susceptible to economic variability. In 2000, Boeing was the largest employer (17,300 employees); by 2019, the company had left Wichita completely. While the city's population grew by 10.6% between 2000 and 2019, total employment grew by only 2%. The city's economy is more diverse in 2019 than in 2000, but it is also less poised for growth. In 2019, while aerospace remains the largest employer, government, the service sector, and healthcare constitute a larger share of the base.

The impacts of this dynamic environment have been visible in certain fiscal metrics and not others. Policymakers' response to fiscal shocks such as the Great Recession has focused on spending cuts. The city's reserves, cash, debt, and other liabilities have been held relatively stable. Therefore, the financial condition analyses generally rate Wichita as in good or strong fiscal health. The same applies to Moody's rating agency, which has rated the city's GO bonds (and most revenue bonds) as Aa1, the second-highest rating possible.

How prepared was Wichita for the COVID-19 pandemic? For the most part, when comparing Wichita's preparation for the pandemic to the years around the Great Recession, the city is in stronger position. At the state level, the Brownback income tax cuts were rescinded, and existing TELs remain relatively weak. The city's economy is more diverse and so should not experience job cuts as it did from 2008 to 2010. Interestingly, however, Moody's downgraded Wichita from Aa1 to Aa2, citing "acute economic weakness due to the downturn in the aerospace sector . . . below-average resident income levels, low wealth, elevated fixed cost burden, above-average debt burden with below-average payout, and an elevated pension burden" (Moody's, 2020, p. 1). On the positive side, the rating agency noted "Wichita's sizable tax base and importance as the regional economic center of south-central Kansas along with healthy reserve levels and quarterly financial reporting" (Moody's, 2020, p. 1). Factors that could improve Wichita's future ratings, according to Moody's, include lower debt and pension burdens, growth in reserves, and a more diversified and stronger economy. Conversely, further downgrades could occur if the city's economy continues to decline and negatively affect its tax base (and thus its ability to make debt payments).

Discussion Questions

Questions to consider regarding the Wichita case study:

- Discuss the effects of the changing manufacturing sector, particularly the aviation industry, on Wichita's fiscal condition. How did these changes shape the city's finances?

- In Chapter 2 we discussed a series of state-imposed constraints that included debt limits and TELs. Discuss the Wichita interviewee's response that these constraints had no effect on their fiscal decisions and what mattered were self-imposed limits. To what degree should self-imposed limits be part of fiscal condition analysis? How could/should one best measure these self-imposed limits?
- The expectation in financial literature is that during periods of economic decline, reserves are to be used when revenues decline so that expenditures can be sustained. Wichita policy caps reserves at 10% of expenditures and during the study period reserves never quite hit the limit. Yet, when the Great Recession negatively impacted city revenues, policymakers made the conscious decision to sustain reserves and cut expenditures. Discuss whether you think reserve policy needs reconsideration in light of Wichita's responses to fiscal stress.
- When asked how fiscal stress was defined, interviewed Wichita officials focused on property valuation. This appears to be in response to the political challenges associated with raising mill rates. Discuss the extent to which fiscal constraints caused by political motives, rather than formal policy that limits actions, should be included in the fiscal stress literature.

Chapter 11

Case Study of North Lauderdale, Florida

North Lauderdale, Florida, is a small to mid-sized city (population 41,000) in Broward County. The city makes for an interesting case study due to its size, location (as part of the Miami MSA and vulnerable to threats from hurricanes) and commission-manager form of government. North Lauderdale is largely residential and relies on property taxes from residential homes, condominiums, and apartments to fund services.

Inputs: Fiscal Environments

Institutional Settings/External Pressures

Florida state lawmakers have imposed several restrictions on municipal governments, particularly with respect to property taxes. The state's constitution imposes limits on both property tax rates and property tax assessments. Currently, municipal property taxes cannot exceed ten mills without voter authorization. Florida's recent history of property tax limits dates back to the early 1990s. According to the Lincoln Institute of Land Policy (2020, p. 3):

> In 1992, Florida adopted the "Save Our Homes" amendment, which imposed constitutional limits on growth in homestead assessments, with no override provision. Under "Save Our Homes," home values may not increase more than the lesser of 3 percent of the prior year's

DOI: 10.4324/9780429270765-11

> assessment or the percentage change in the consumer price index. In 2008, Florida voters approved another constitutional amendment, Amendment 1, which further restricted property taxation. . .. Florida's Truth in Millage (TRIM) statute requires cities and towns to calculate and issue notice of prior year millage rate, proposed millage rate, and the rollback rate . . . and to issue notice of a tentative budget hearing. Once a tentative budget and millage are approved, local governments must issue notice of and advertise the final budget and millage hearing. . .. Florida provides both homestead exemptions and exemptions for active military, disabled veterans, the blind and disabled, and widows and widowers. The state also offers a homestead property tax deferral program for permanent residents. Some exemptions are subject to income limits. The state has no property tax circuit breaker program.

Internal Structures

North Lauderdale was incorporated in 1963 and operates under a commission-manager form of government. According to the NLC (2022), the commission form of government is rare (used in fewer than 1% of cities) yet one of the oldest in the United States. The commission consists of five elected officials, of whom four represent districts while the mayor is elected at-large. The commission sets policies, adopts legislation, and appoints the manager, clerks, and attorney. The city manager is charged with day-to-day operations. The finance team consists of a director, controller, purchasing and contracts manger, purchasing coordinator, and payroll specialist.

Socioeconomic Conditions

By most measures, North Lauderdale has recovered from the Great Recession, but by officials' own account, the recovery has been relatively slow. As the finance team noted, "Between 2009 and 2013, the city experienced an unprecedented reduction in property values which forced the city staff to review operations and institute innovative and proactive cost cutting measures that helped the city weather the effects of the recession" (City of North Lauderdale, 2020, p. ii).

In 2019, North Lauderdale had a population of 44,481 (see Figure 11.1), up 9.3% from 2009 and up 35.6% compared to 2002. According to the U.S. Census Bureau (2021), 8.2% of the population is under age 5 and 8.9% are age 65 or older. The city's racial composition is 55.6% Black/African American, 32.0% White, and 28.5% Hispanic or Latino (Hispanics can be of any race). Compared to the overall makeup of Florida (which has only 5.3% of the population under age 5, 20.9% age 65 or older, 77.3% White, 26.4% Hispanic or Latino,

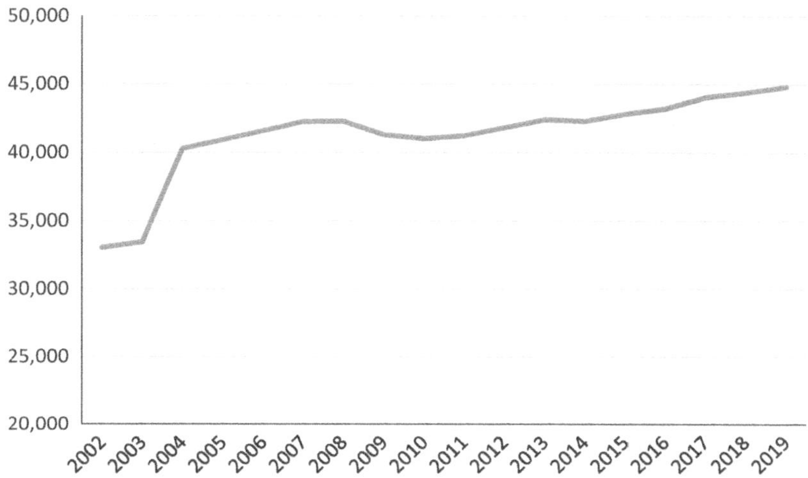

Figure 11.1 Population of North Lauderdale, Florida, 2002–2019
Source: City of North Lauderdale (2020)

and 16.9% Black or African American), North Lauderdale is younger and more racially diverse. In 2019, the city's per-capita personal income ($20,325) lagged well behind Broward County ($32,909) and the nation ($34,103).

The commercial and real estate industries drive North Lauderdale's economy. In 2020, half of the top ten taxpayers were rental apartment companies or mobile home parks. The others were commercial, a public utility company, and a call service center. By comparison, in 2011, 8 of the top ten taxpayers in North Lauderdale were rental apartment companies. In 2020, the county's top ten employers consisted of government (Broward County School Board, 36,575 employees; Broward County, 12,246), education (Nova Southeastern University, 6,114), healthcare (Memorial Healthcare Systems, 13,500; Broward Health, 8,477), services (four companies combined, 14,140), and Spirit Airlines (3,391).

The city's unemployment rate has trended similar to the statewide figure. In 2020, North Lauderdale's unemployment rate was 7.8% while Florida was at 7.7%; in 2019, the rates were 2.8% and 3.3%, respectively. The impacts of the Great Recession and COVID-19 on employment are readily apparent. In 2007, North Lauderdale's unemployment rate was 3.8%, but it jumped to 6.4%, 10.9%, and 10.2% in the next three years. Similarly, the unemployment rate was 2.8% in 2019 and then spiked to 7.8% in 2020. The city's unemployment trend over time is shown in Figure 11.2.

Although unemployment jumped during the Great Recession, per-capita personal income remained stable (see Figure 11.3). Part of that stability may be a

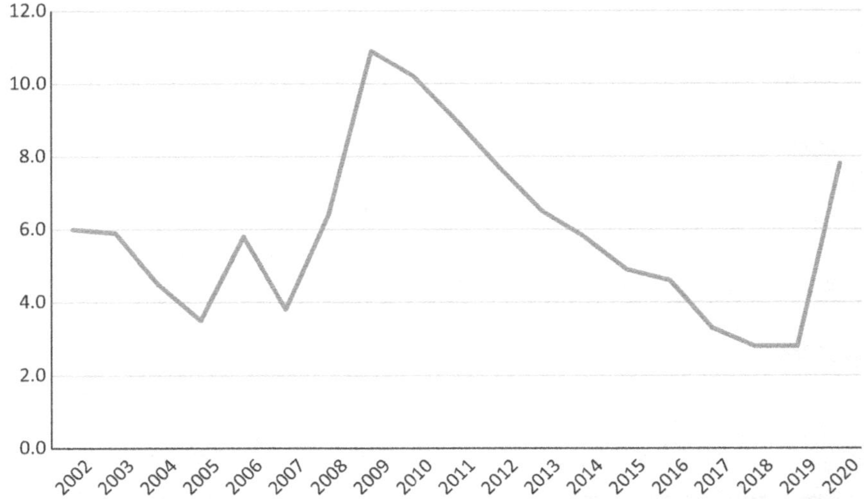

Figure 11.2 Unemployment Rate of North Lauderdale, Florida, 2002–2020
Source: City of North Lauderdale (2020)

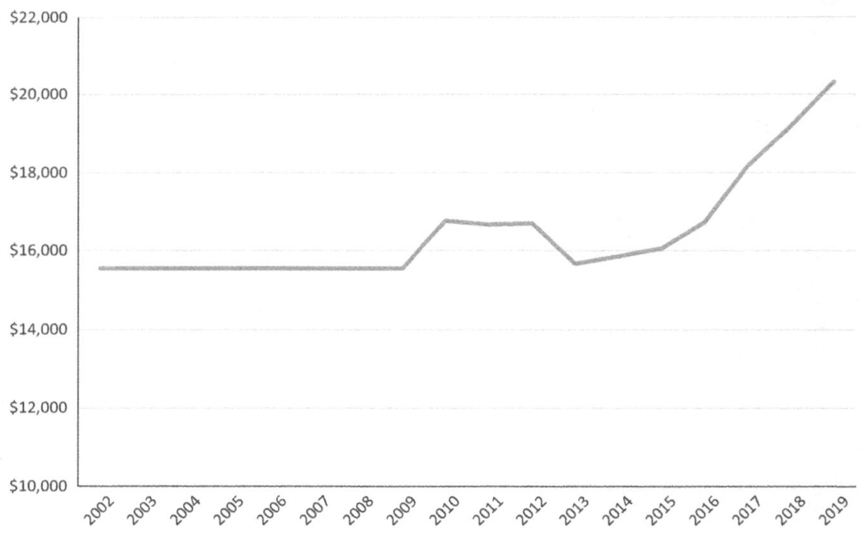

Figure 11.3 Personal Income of North Lauderdale, Florida, 2002–2019 (Per Capita)
Source: City of North Lauderdale (2020)

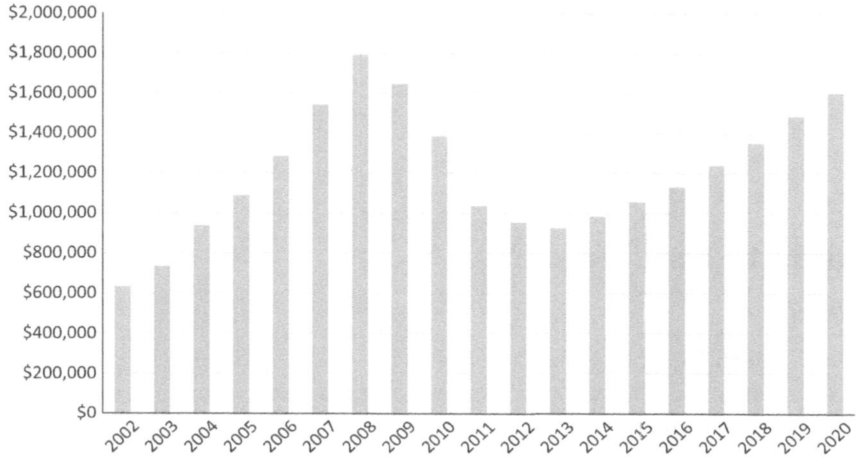

Figure 11.4 Assessed Property Values of North Lauderdale, Florida, 2002–2019 ($1,000)

Source: City of North Lauderdale (2020)

function of data collection methodology, as the figures from 2002 through 2010 were based on the same U.S. Census count (City of North Lauderdale, 2011, p. 83). Following the Great Recession, per-capita personal income grew from $16,667 in 2011 to $20,325 in 2019.

For a municipality heavily reliant on residential and commercial industries, property valuation is an important economic benchmark. Figure 11.4 paints a vivid picture of the struggles North Lauderdale faced following the Great Recession. In 2008, assessed property valuations peaked at $1.8 billion; they then plummeted to $925 million (a 48% drop) by 2013. According to North Lauderdale's 2020 ACFR, "The city experienced an unprecedented reduction in property values which forced the city staff to review operations and institute innovative and proactive cost cutting measures that helped the city weather the effects of the recession" (p. ii). Although property values are rebounding, with an average annual growth of 8.2% from 2014 to 2020, valuations remain below 2018 levels.

As noted, the Great Recession caused significant damage to North Lauderdale, where the economy is heavily driven by real estate. Property valuation has steadily recovered to near 2008 levels, and the city's unemployment rate fell annually for ten years after 2009, to 2.8% in 2019. Similarly, personal income rose steadily from $15,557 per capita in 2009 to $20,325 per capita in 2019. That amount, however, remained far below the statewide figure of $31,629.

COVID-19 had less of an effect on North Lauderdale's finances than expected. According to the city's revised 2021 budget, revenues from sales and gas taxes were projected to be down by $1 million, but an 8.5% increase in property valuation enabled the city to retain its millage rate of 7.4 mills and still raise an additional $868,000 in property taxes. Reading through the 2021 budget, there is little indication that the pandemic impacted fiscal decision making (City of North Lauderdale, 2021).

Outputs: Fiscal Trends

Revenues

North Lauderdale government revenues have shifted between 2003 and 2020, meaning that the city has become less reliant on intergovernmental aid and more reliant on property taxes, fees and charges, and special assessments (see Figure 11.5). In FY2003, North Lauderdale's $26.8 million in governmental revenues included, as main revenue sources, intergovernmental aid (32%), taxes (26%—predominantly property but also sales, charges for services (17%), and special assessments (8%), which are charged for solid waste, stormwater, and fire and rescue services.

Still reeling from the Great Recession, North Lauderdale's total governmental revenues in FY2011 were $30.6 million (only 13.8% higher than in FY2003). State cuts due to the recession meant that proportionally, those funds accounted for only 18% of the total (down 14 percentage points from 2003). Taxes (property, utility, franchise fees, and other taxes) accounted for 43%. Special assessments were another 17% of total revenues (up from 8% in 2003). North Lauderdale's revenue composition changed little between FY2011 and FY2020. In FY2020, taxes accounted for 43%, intergovernmental aid 20%, special assessments 18%, and charges 10% of the total.

As previously noted, the Great Recession had two direct effects on North Lauderdale revenues: lost intergovernmental aid and declining property tax revenues, for which the city could not compensate due to the restrictions imposed on Florida municipalities. Figure 11.6 shows the 18-year trend in property tax collections and property taxes as a percentage of total taxes. Following the drop in property valuations, property taxes fell by 32%, from $10 million in 2009 to $6.8 million in 2013. It took until FY2019 to regain pre–Great Recession property tax collection levels. The second part of the story is North Lauderdale's significant loss of intergovernmental aid which declined from 32% of governmental revenues in 2003 to just 18% in 2011. To compensate for these lost revenues, city officials grew increasingly dependent on property tax collections. As already noted, since 2003, taxes have accounted for a growing share of total revenues. Although utility taxes are included in the figures above, property taxes account for more than three-fourths of total tax collections, up significantly from 2003 when property

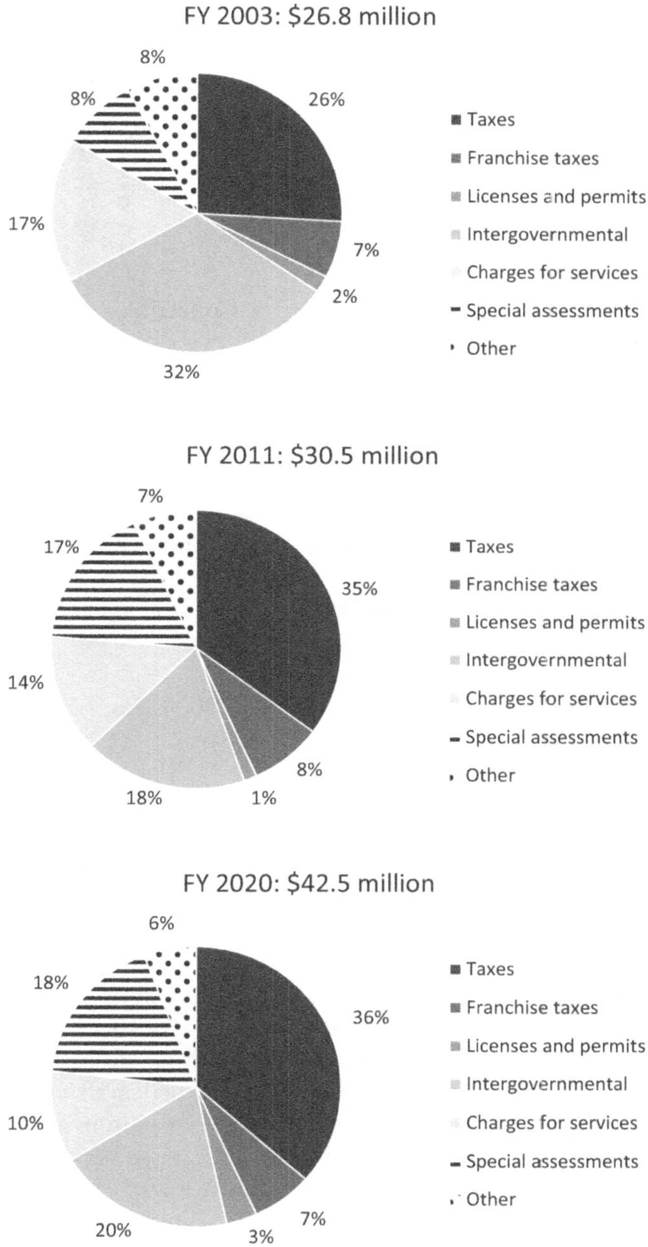

Figure 11.5 Governmental Revenues of North Lauderdale, Florida
Source: City of North Lauderdale (2003, 2011, 2020)

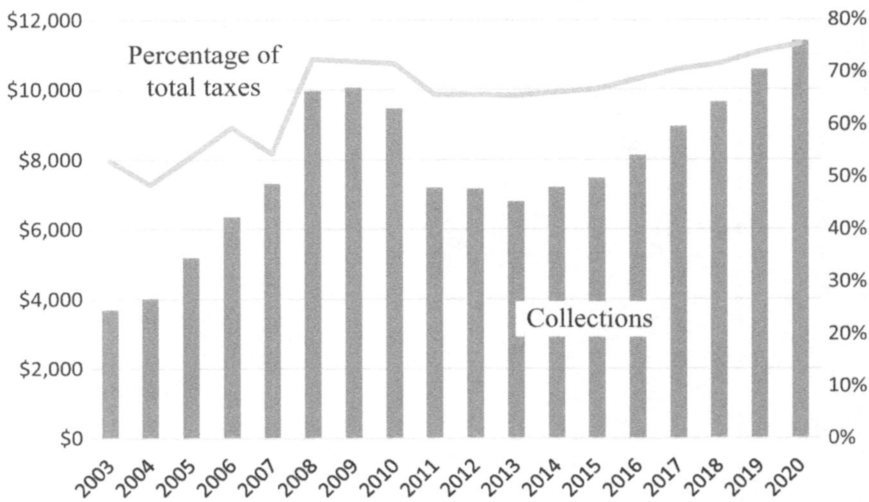

Figure 11.6 Property Tax Collections in Thousands and as Percent of Total Taxes, 2003–2020

Source: City of North Lauderdale (2020)

taxes accounted for only 53% of total taxes. Since 2008, property taxes have represented at least 65% of total tax collections every year.

Expenditures

During these 18 years (2003 to 2020), North Lauderdale's total expenditures grew at an annual average rate of 1.7%. That figure, however, masks a significant degree of annual variability. For instance, between FY2005 and FY2006, expenditures jumped by 14.2%, followed by three consecutive years of total expenditure reductions. North Lauderdale's total expenditures in FY2009 were lower than in any of the prior six fiscal years. From the perspective of total expenditures, the recovery from the Great Recession has been mixed. Between 2011 and 2012, total expenditures jumped by 16.9%, and FY2018 experienced a similar increase over 2017 (15.5%). Excluding those two periods, expenditure growth has been weak between 2011 and 2020; total expenditures decreased between FY2012 and FY2013, FY2016 and FY2017, and FY2019 and FY2020.

Despite this annual variability in total government expenditures, North Lauderdale officials sustained commitments to public safety, community development, and public works. Public safety expenditures increased each year from 2003 to 2020, growing by 84.7% over that period. While on not quite as consistent a trajectory as public safety, public works expenditures grew by 175% from 2003 to 2020, and community development expenditures increased by 157.6% during the same period. As is common for a fiscally stressed municipality, expenditures on capital outlays were down 51.3% from 2003 to 2020, and (as will be discussed below) principal and interest payments fell by 79.3% during this period, reflecting the city's commitment to eliminating GO debt. An overview of the city's expenditures is provided in Table 11.1.

Outcomes: Fiscal Condition

Operating Position

North Lauderdale does not currently have formal policies that guide the city's use of fiscal measures such as fund balances or debt. When general fund unassigned and assigned balances are combined and divided by expenditures (excluding capital spending), North Lauderdale's reserves have been markedly high since FY2006, averaging 110% of expenditures from 2007 to 2020. In 2020, the city had an unassigned fund balance equal to 145.7% of operating expenditures (see Figure 11.7). The city's 2011 ACFR stated that the city's unassigned fund balance grew, "mainly due to higher-than-expected revenues" and "various operational savings as a direct result of planned cost containment measures" (p. 11). Even amidst the city's economic and fiscal challenges during the Great Recession, North Lauderdale's reserves grew from 59.3% of expenditures in 2007 to 95.9% of expenditures in 2010.

In addition to these sizable reserves, North Lauderdale also has strong liquidity. Figure 11.8 shows of governmental cash, investments, and receivables relative to current liabilities. In each year studied, North Lauderdale maintained a sufficient level of liquidity (i.e., higher than 2.0). Given the unavailability of electronic audited financial reports, the data begin in 2011, at which time the city's combined cash, investments, and receivables equaled 16 times North Lauderdale's current liabilities. That ratio has since grown to 21 in 2016, 27.8 in 2019, and 48.3 in 2020. Given the city's strong liquidity, management was able to invest $48.6 million in FY2020. Just under half of those investments ($21 million) were set to mature within the year, and the balance will mature within five years. All investments were either U.S. Treasury notes or highly rated by Moody's (predominantly AAA rated).

Debt Position and Long-Term Liabilities

Under state law, North Lauderdale's GO debt cannot exceed 10% of total assessed value (City of North Lauderdale, 2020, p. 87). The city adopted a commitment

Table 11.1 Government Expenditures of North Lauderdale, Florida ($1,000)

Year	*General government*	*Public safety*	*Community development*	*Public works*	*Parks & recreation*	*Educational programs*	*Capital outlay*	*Principal & interest*	*Total*	*Annual pct change*
2003	3,430	9,593	1,196	1,856	2,846	4,643	3,024	1,732	28,320	
2004	3741	10,547	1,403	1,743	3,369	4,062	3,358	1,821	30,044	6.1
2005	3,617	11,498	1,517	1,690	3,678	3,903	1,447	2,053	29,403	–2.1
2006	4,808	11,745	1,868	4,775	3,651	3,201	1,499	2,038	33,585	14.2
2007	4,166	12,295	1,914	2,022	3,472	3	3,868	2,051	29,791	–11.3
2008	3,070	12,575	1,765	2,310	3,190		4,174	2,047	29,131	–2.2
2009	2,866	13,122	1,860	2,504	3,386		1,359	2,087	27,184	–6.7
2010	2,739	13,558	4,239	2,757	3,530		118	1,657	28,598	5.2
2011	2,852	13,577	2,290	2,730	3,555		1,265	1,025	27,294	–4.6
2012	2,871	13,886	1,930	3,288	3,850		1,278	4,816	31,919	16.9
2013	2,910	13,946	2,157	4,471	3,859		1,354	715	29,412	–7.9
2014	2,868	14,658	2,369	3,897	3,976		1,410	715	29,893	1.6
2015	2,911	14,821	2,244	3,946	4,084		2,780	715	31,501	5.4
2016	2,803	15,438	2,711	4,520	4,483		1,089	715	31,759	0.8
2017	2,906	15,634	2,362	4,520	4,536		718	715	31,391	–1.2
2018	2,907	16,413	3,128	7,303	4,541		1,261	716	36,269	15.5
2019	3,089	17,021	2,783	6,620	4,629		1,444	715	36,301	0.1
2020	4035	17723	3081	5107	4101		1474	359	35,880	–1.2
Annual avg pct change	1.8	3.7	10.1	13.9	2.4		61.3	11.5	1.7	

Source: City of North Lauderdale (2020)

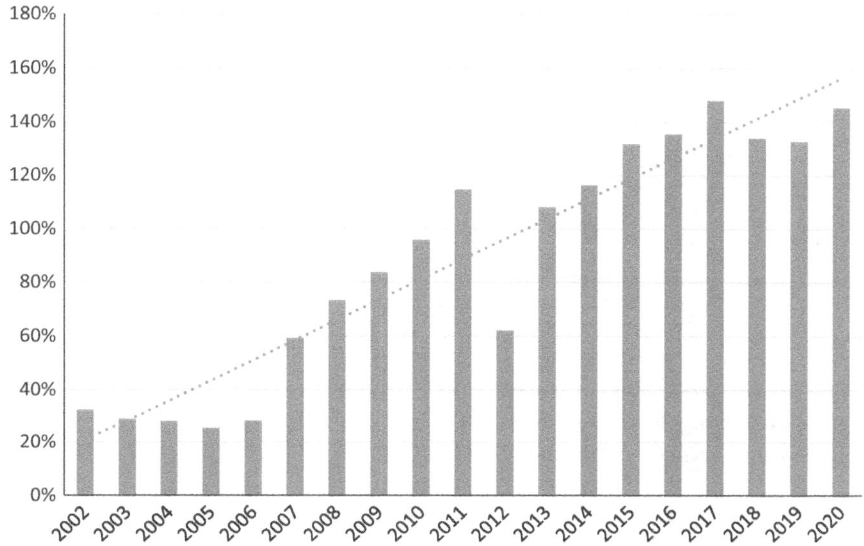

Figure 11.7 Unreserved Fund Balance as Percent of General Fund Expenditures, 2002–2020

Source: City of North Lauderdale (2002–2020)

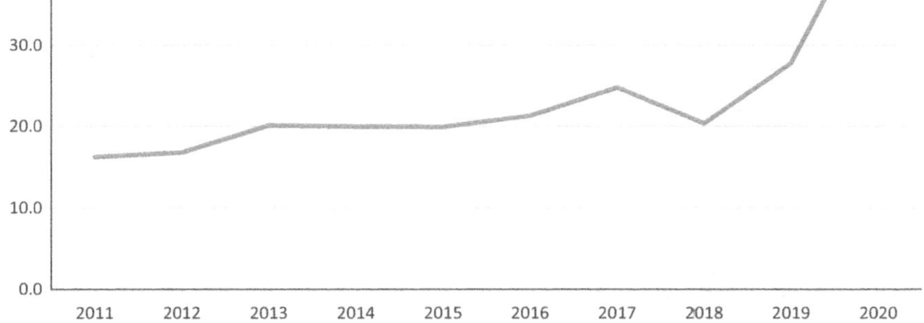

Figure 11.8 Cash, Investments, and Receivables Relative to Current Liabilities, 2011–2020

Source: City of North Lauderdale (2011–2020)

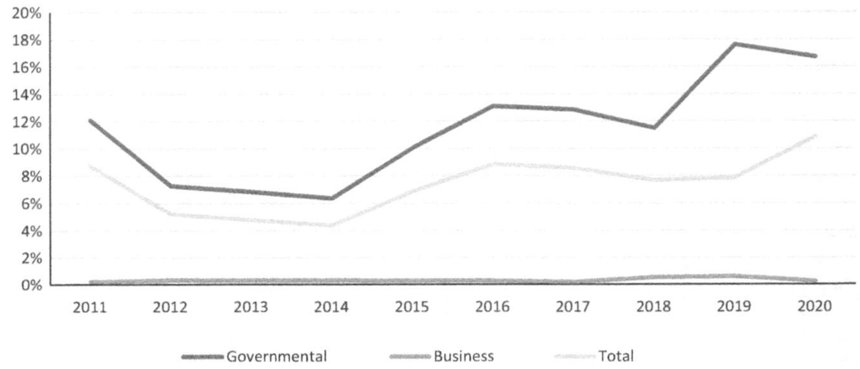

Figure 11.9 Long-Term Liabilities as Percent of Total Assets, 2011–2020
Source: City of North Lauderdale (2011–2020)

to eliminating its GO debt, which it fulfilled by 2012. North Lauderdale operates water, sewer, and stormwater facilities. Figure 11.9 reflects the city's general aversion to debt accumulation. During these ten years, long-term liabilities averaged 11% of assets for governmental funds, 0.3% for business-type activities, and 7.4% overall. Overall, North Lauderdale carries less debt than most cities. For governmental funds, the greatest long-term liabilities are pensions ($11.7 million) and OPEBs ($4.3 million). These two in combination account for 93% of the city's governmental long-term liabilities and 92% of total long-term liabilities.

North Lauderdale offers several retirement plans to employees. All full-time employees are offered a defined-contribution retirement plan administered by the ICMA Retirement Corporation (City of North Lauderdale, 2020). The city also offers a deferred compensation plan, whereby employees can defer a portion of their salary "until termination, retirement, death or unforeseeable emergency" (City of North Lauderdale, 2020, p. 45). This plan is also administered by the ICMA. In 2003, North Lauderdale firefighters joined the state's Florida Retirement System, which is a defined-benefit plan. North Lauderdale's reported pension liability is related to this plan. OPEBs offered by North Lauderdale include a retiree health insurance subsidy program available to employees and their beneficiaries to "obtain medical, dental, vision, and life insurance benefits upon retirement" (City of North Lauderdale, 2020, p. 54). The plan is pay-as-you-go and fully funded by employees. Although a long-term liability of $4.3 million was reported in 2020, the current ratio of those paying into the plan (active employees) to those receiving benefits was very healthy at 145 to 13.

Policy Actions: Input from Interviews with Finance Members

Relations with Elected Officials

In 2015 and 2021, North Lauderdale finance officials were interviewed by telephone. Relations with the five commissioners were described as positive, with frequent interaction throughout the year. During the 2015 interview, a respondent described a colleague's long-established working relationship with the commissioners: "They would come into my office almost daily and chat with me about finance matters . . . [there was a] positive relationship once a level of confidence in his abilities was established." During the 2021 interview, the relationship appeared more transactional. The interviewee said that the commissioners were removed from day-to-day operations and that commissioners had different objectives and expectations: "Some want to see more grants to residents . . . free programs, etc." In both years, the relationship with the city manager was described as positive: "very open—good communication." Approaches to fiscal management were well aligned. The interviewee said of the finance team and the city manager, "Both are fiscally conservative."

Effects of the Recession and Response Strategies

The fiscal effects of the recession hit around 2010. In 2015, the interviewee described a significant drop in taxable assessed value: "At the bottom of what we considered the recession, the city had lost almost 50% of its taxable assessed value . . . [which] accounted for about 40% of the city's revenue." They continued to have high millage, but when the taxable assessed value dropped, it affected city revenues. Response strategies, interestingly, included delaying adoption of state legislative property tax reforms before the recession. "I mean, how many communities can lose 50% of their taxable value and not miss a beat?" By delaying the Property Tax Act directive to cut taxes, North Lauderdale had "substantial surpluses in the general funds." Actions taken were limited to outsourcing "unneeded" services to cut expenses.

COVID-19 hit North Lauderdale in March 2020 and a state of emergency was declared. As in most places, the pandemic forced a change in city operations and revenues dropped. Revenue losses consisted of shared state sales taxes (intergovernmental aid), return on investments due to lower interest rates, and utilities because of customers paying late or not at all. Understanding their residents' plight, city officials suspended late fees and service disconnections for failure to pay utility bills, and they also stopped charging emergency medical services transportation fees. All recreation programs were halted, including park and facility rentals. Spending was frozen and focused on essential services; although staff were reallocated, there were no layoffs. To help those in need, officials offered food giveaway programs and some financial assistance. In the longer run (as officials expect revenues to recover by 2023), there will be a reassessment of capital projects due to price increases and labor shortages, and spending will be more scrutinized, but the official we interviewed called North Lauderdale lucky because it is not a heavy tourist destination and is 96% residential without a large commercial base.

Institutional Constraints

Interviewees were asked about the impact of institutional fiscal constraints. City officials pay close attention to millage rates. Between 2002 and 2011, North Lauderdale's city millage rate grew from $5.84 to $7.23 per $1,000 of assessed value. The millage rate peaked at $7.75 in 2012 and has remained at $7.40 since 2018. As a result, the state's millage rate cap has had "no real effect" on North Lauderdale. Similarly, although the state imposes a cap on GO debt, which is not to exceed 10% of total assessed property value, that does not matter to North Lauderdale, which has not had any GO debt since 2011.

Fiscal Health and Fiscal Stress

North Lauderdale's finance officials assess fiscal health in terms of fund balance as a percentage of operating revenues and debt. The official we interviewed was very proud of both metrics in relation to North Lauderdale. When asked how a fiscally stressed community is defined, the interviewee cited three types of evidence: having to increase the millage rate to the state cap of ten mills, not meeting obligations, and not being able to maintain or replace assets.

Lessons Learned

When asked about lessons learned from the Great Recession, the interviewee stated, "They didn't learn any lessons because they had already started preparing, based on a different bogeyman being there . . . the state property tax restriction was the bogeyman in this case." The city had already started outsourcing and slimming government down before the recession came. "The mindset was already there," our informant explained. COVID-19's impact was much more immediate than that of the Great Recession. Lessons from the pandemic were yet to be determined, other than reinforcing the city's commitment to holding millage rates steady, minimizing debt, and sustaining strong reserves.

Final Assessment

In North Lauderdale, Florida, policymakers operate in a unique fiscal environment. North Lauderdale, while heavily dependent on its property tax collections in a state that limits property taxes and assessment increases, has managed to place itself in a very strong financial position. The city is able to make fiscal decisions without concern for state fiscal constraints, because it has low debt and very strong liquidity, in terms of both cash and reserves.

One of the city's greatest challenges may be long-term planning. Officials have noted problems with aging infrastructure; given the city's commitment to minimizing debt, addressing these infrastructure needs will require drawing down cash and/or reserves. Furthermore, given North Lauderdale's geographic location in southeastern Florida, threats from hurricanes and tropical storms require planning and preparation. Since 1851, Broward County has been hit by 27 hurricanes, of which Hurricane Wilma in 2005 was the worst (National Hurricane Center, 2022). The city's website provides detailed information on preparation for and assistance following a hurricane (City of North Lauderdale, 2022). City officials have set aside $3.5 million in reserves for disaster recovery.

Discussion Questions

Questions to consider regarding the North Lauderdale case study:

- Discuss the short and long-term effects of The Great Recession on North Lauderdale. To what extent has the city recovered? Is North Lauderdale in a better financial position to respond to the next fiscal shock?
- North Lauderdale has a sizeable reserve (greater than 140% of expenditures in 2020) and cash, investments and liabilities (48 times current liabilities in 2020). Often discussed is a policy establishing a minimum reserve. Does North Lauderdale reserves suggest establishment of a policy that caps reserves? If so, what criteria should be considered if establishing such a policy?
- North Lauderdale officials committed to the elimination of general obligation debt. From a financial point of view, this would be perceived as positive. What are the potential downsides from such a policy? Discuss the tradeoffs of making such a commitment.
- North Lauderdale introduced the threat of natural disasters to the city's fiscal condition. Review other city policies that address natural threats and devise a fiscal policy for North Lauderdale.
- Similar to Wichita, North Lauderdale officials discussed sustaining millage rates as a measure of fiscal stress. Discuss why this comes up in these interviews. Can/should political calculations be an element of fiscal stress analysis or is it important to stick with objective fiscal metrics?
- Also similar to Wichita, TELs and state-imposed debt limits were inconsequential to fiscal decisions because of local commitment to minimizing debt and sustaining millage rates. Does this say anything about the role of state-level fiscal controls? Is it possible to incorporate local political commitment to fiscal outcomes as a measure of fiscal condition?

Chapter 12

Case Study of Havelock, North Carolina

Havelock is a smaller-sized coastal city (population 20,000) in Craven County, North Carolina. This city is an interesting case study due its dependence on two military bases, Marine Corps Air Station Cherry Point and the 2nd Marine Aircraft Wing. Havelock is largely residential and relies on property, sales, and franchise (utilities) taxes to fund services.

Inputs: Fiscal Environments

Institutional Settings/External Pressures

North Carolina state lawmakers have imposed several restrictions on local governments, particularly with respect to property taxes and debt. Currently, combined county and municipal property tax levies cannot exceed 15 mills. Havelock's legal debt limit is 8% of its assessed property value. Since much of the community is connected to the Marine bases, including civil service employees, their families, and service-oriented business providers, federal policies directly impact the city. For example, the federal government shutdown in early 2018 resulted in employee furloughs, including approximately 1,000 people associated with providing services to nearby Camp Lejeune and Cherry Point (Stiglitz, 2018).

DOI: 10.4324/9780429270765-12

Internal Structures

The city was incorporated in 1959 and operates under a council-manager form of government. The governing body comprises a mayor and five commissioners who are elected at large. All board members including the mayor serve four-year, staggered terms. The board of commissioners has legislative authority and establishes policies for the city. The board appoints the city manager and the city attorney. The city manager is the chief executive officer and is responsible for implementing board policies and ordinances, managing daily operations, and appointing department directors. The city manager is also responsible for preparing the annual operating budget.

Socioeconomic Conditions

By most socioeconomic measures, Havelock was unaffected by the 2001 recession and the Great Recession. Population, assessed valuation, and unemployment rates do not appear to have been affected by these economic events. Havelock's population was stable from 2000 to 2005, took a modest dip in 2006, and then grew steadily from 2007 to 2010 (see Figure 12.1). The city's population dropped by 12.7% from 2010 to 2011 and has remained between 20,000 and 21,000 through 2019.

According to the U.S. Census Bureau (2021), 8.3% of the population was under age 5 and 5.3% was age 65 or older as of 2019. These percentages differ

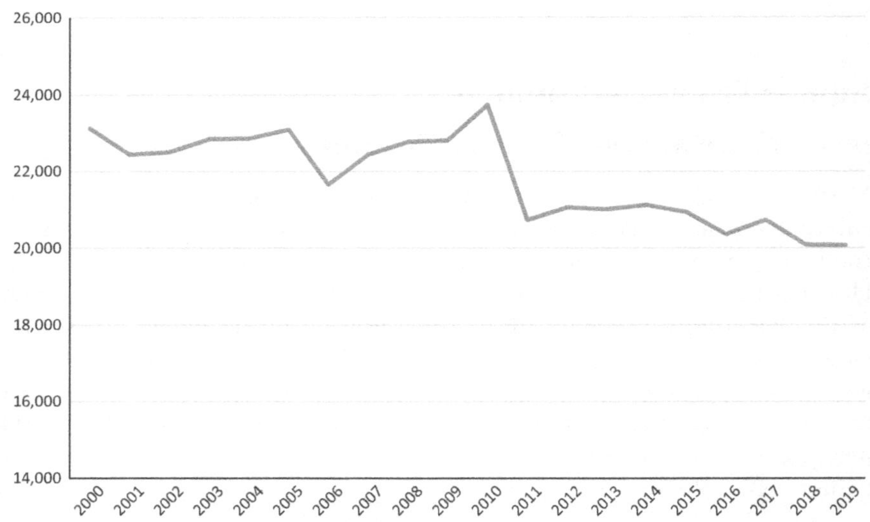

Figure 12.1 Population of Havelock, North Carolina, 2000–2019
Source: City of Havelock (2019)

noticeably from those for Craven County (6.2% and 19.7%, respectively) and the state of North Carolina (5.8% and 16.7%). The racial composition of the city is 67% White, 22% Black/African American, and 14% Hispanic. It has a racial makeup similar to the county and state, except that it has more Hispanic or Latino residents (14%; 8% and 10% for Craven County and North Carolina, respectively). Reflecting the impact of the military families living in Havelock, the city's owner-occupied housing rate of 40% is significantly lower than that of Craven County (63%) and the statewide average (65%), and its population density per square mile (1,231) is substantially higher than that of Craven County (146) or the state (196).

The scope of the military's presence within the city's economy is perhaps best illustrated by employment figures. In 2016, Havelock's top five employers were as follows (City of Havelock, 2016):

- The 2nd Marine Aircraft Wing: 7,698 employees
- Fleet Readiness Center East: 3,425 employees
- Marine Corps Air Station Cherry Point: 2,160 employees
- MCCS (Marine Corps Community Service facility): 951 employees
- Havelock School District: 451 employees

Following these five are Wal-Mart (254 employees) and the City of Havelock (122 employees). No other businesses employed more than 100 people. Housing military personnel, their families, and those providing services to the military bases is the basis for property tax collections in Havelock. Nine out of the top ten property taxpayers have been property management or development corporations, at least for the past decade (City of Havelock, 2010–2019).

A look at the city's unemployment rate reveals three distinct periods from 2000 to 2019 (see Figure 12.2). From 2000 to 2008, Havelock's hovered around 5%; from 2009 to 2013, it was around 10%; and since 2013, it has declined annually to a low of 4.2% in 2019. Interpreting the higher unemployment figure, Havelock's 2009 ACFR stated,

> The local economy did not suffer as bad as the national economy during the economic downturn although it is recovering slightly slower than the state and the nation. The local economy has also been negatively impacted due to significant oversees troop deployments.
>
> (pp. 4–5)

Although the city's unemployment rate jumped following the Great Recession, per-capita personal income remained stable (see Figure 12.3). That apparent stability may be partly a function of the available data, as the figures come from the U.S. Census Bureau's five-year estimates. According to those estimates, Havelock's per-capita personal income changed little from 2010 to 2018 (essentially

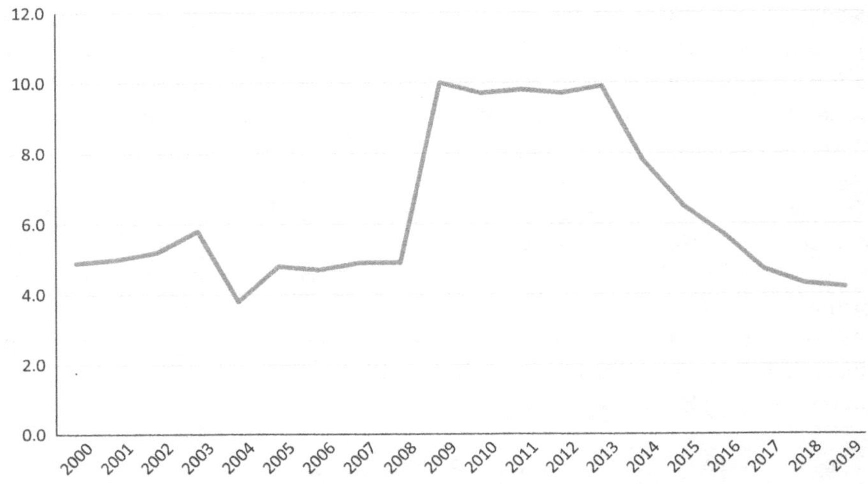

Figure 12.2 Unemployment Rate of Havelock, North Carolina, 2000–2019
Source: City of Havelock (2019)

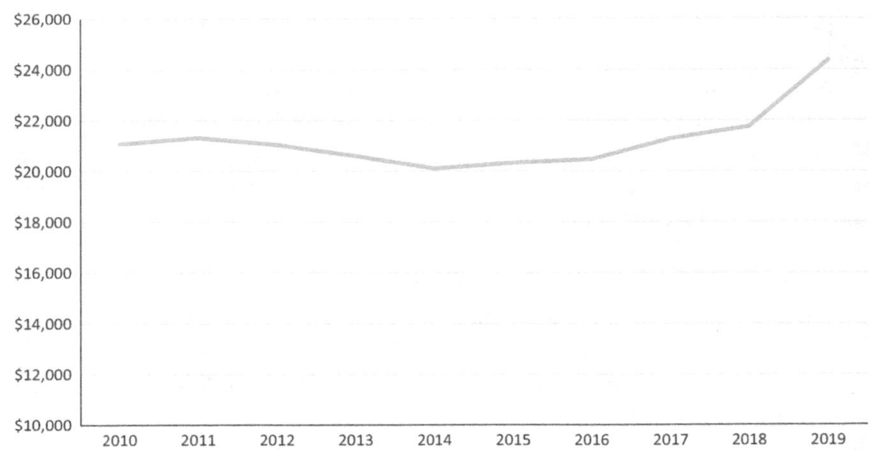

Figure 12.3 Personal Income of Havelock, North Carolina, 2000–2019 (Per Capita)
Source: City of Havelock (2019)

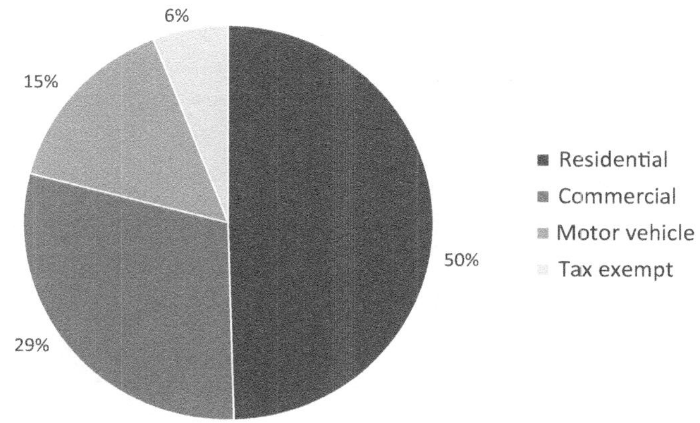

Figure 12.4 Property Valuation by Class of Havelock, North Carolina, 2019
Source: City of Havelock (2019)

around $21,000) and then jumped to $24,359 in 2019. The 2019 figure lags behind Craven County ($29,521) and North Carolina ($30,783).

Property valuation is an important economic benchmark for a municipality, especially when it relies heavily on residential housing. Based on 2019 figures, half of the city's total assessed valuation is residential, followed by commercial real estate and motor vehicles (see Figure 12.4). Reflecting the large portion of publicly owned facilities, 6% of the city's valuation is tax-exempt. Since 2000, there was a shift in the proportion of assessments between commercial property and motor vehicles. In 2000, commercial property accounted for only 16% of valuation (less than half of its share in 2019) and motor vehicles accounted for 23% (nearly double their 2019 share). The portions attributable to residential (53% in 2000) and tax-exempt (9%) property changed little.

During the 20-year period of study, Havelock's assessed valuation grew at an average annual rate of 5.4%. However, that average does not reflect recent trends (see Figure 12.5). The city's assessed valuation grew steadily from 2000 to 2010, jumped by 48% from 2010 to 2011, was flat from 2011 to 2016, and has been declining since 2016. Assessed valuation fell 20% from 2016 to 2017, another 26% the following year, and 16% from 2018 to 2019. These recent declines were caused by revaluations and general declines in the real-estate market.

As noted, the Great Recession had little effect on Havelock. The city's economic and fiscal success is tied to its military bases. Therefore, when the federal government shuts down and furloughs employees and/or when it becomes involved in major international military operations, Havelock is affected. Whereas COVID-19 greatly affected most municipalities, it also appears to have limited effect on Havelock's finances, due to the city's economic and fiscal structures. The

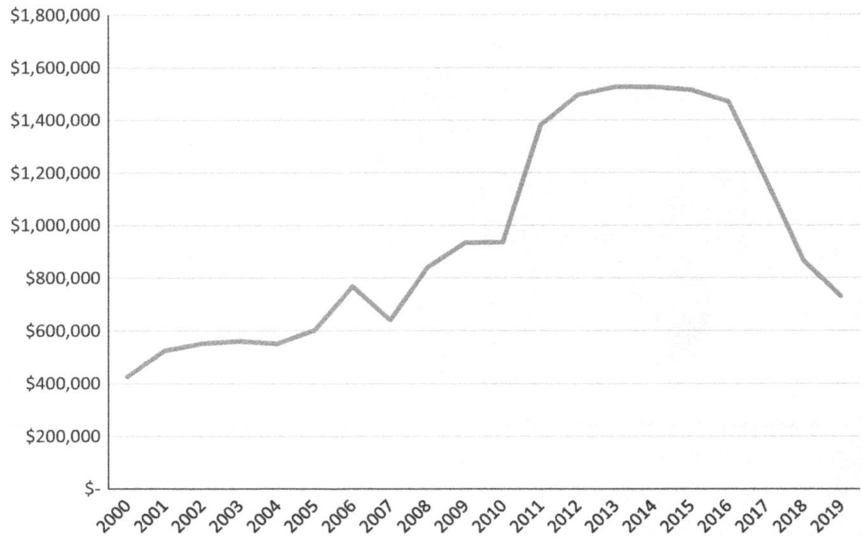

Figure 12.5 Assessed Property Values of Havelock, North Carolina, 2000–2019 ($1,000)

Source: City of Havelock (2019)

community is largely residential and driven by military base activity, so business closures were few. Because the city is largely dependent on property taxes, sales taxes, and motor vehicle registrations, it was also spared on the revenue-side.

The greater challenge for Havelock has been to recover from Hurricane Florence and prepare for similar natural disasters. Hurricane Florence, a Category 4 storm carrying winds close to 130 miles per hour, hit Havelock in mid-September 2018. According to a news story (Buday, 2018), Havelock Mayor Will Lewis said, "I've lived in Havelock my whole life and I've never seen a storm do that much damage. I've never seen so many trees down with power lines spaghetti-strapped around them. . . . Everything we do as a city has major damage." According to Havelock's 2019 ACFR (p. 21), the hurricane crippled the city's tourist and events center for six months, and budgeted expenditures rose by $3.3 million.

Output Measures

Revenues

Havelock governmental revenues have been relatively consistent over the 20-year study period. Property taxes account for over one-third of total revenues, followed by sales and motor vehicle taxes at just under one-third, charges for services (12% to 15%), and grants. The significant factor affecting FY2019 figures was Hurricane Florence, which resulted in a jump in grants and contributions. Capital grants jumped from $312,171 in 2018 to $1.1 million in 2019 and operating grants more than doubled between 2018 ($1.2 million) and 2019 ($2.8 million) due to disaster recovery assistance.

In FY2004, Havelock collected $6.2 million in revenues (see Figure 12.6). Property taxes accounted for 37% of this total, or $2.3 million. Other taxes (i.e., sales and motor vehicle taxes) represented 31%, or $1.9 million. The sales tax is levied and collected at the county level, remitted to the state, and then redistributed by the state. Similarly, effective in 2013, the state assumed responsible for billing and collection of property taxes on registered motor vehicles on behalf of all municipalities and special tax districts.

In FY2010, government revenues totaled $8.7 million, up 42% (or an average annual increase of 6.8%) compared to 2004. Over those six years, the proportion of revenues coming from the property tax increased to 43% while the percentage coming from sales and motor vehicle taxes remained unchanged. Grants and investments, as a proportion of total government revenues, were lower in 2010 than in 2004. The 2019 fiscal picture for Havelock is different from that in FY2010 largely due to the influx of federal disaster relief funding. Operating and capital grants combined to account for 25% of governmental revenues in 2019, compared to 12% in 2010 and 16% in 2004.

Expenditures

Havelock's governmental expenditures are predominately for public safety (police and fire), streets, and general government management. From 2000 to 2019, expenditures grew at an average annual rate of 6.3%; however, if FY2019 (which incorporates the response to Hurricane Florence) is excluded, the average annual growth rate drops to 4.1%. Interestingly, during the Great Recession, expenditures jumped by 18.4% from FY2008 to FY2009, dropped 9.7% in the next year, and then rose by 11.9% from FY2010 to FY2011. Hurricane Florence caused expenditures to increase by 37.8% from FY2018 to FY2019. This increase was reflected in the general government budget—up from $2.2 million in 2008 to $5.0 million in 2019—and covered operating expenditures associated with recovery and cleanup. An overview of the city's expenditures is provided in Table 12.1.

Outcome Measures

Operating Position

Havelock does not currently have formal policies that guide the use of fiscal measures such as fund balances. However, according to the city's 2019 ACFR,

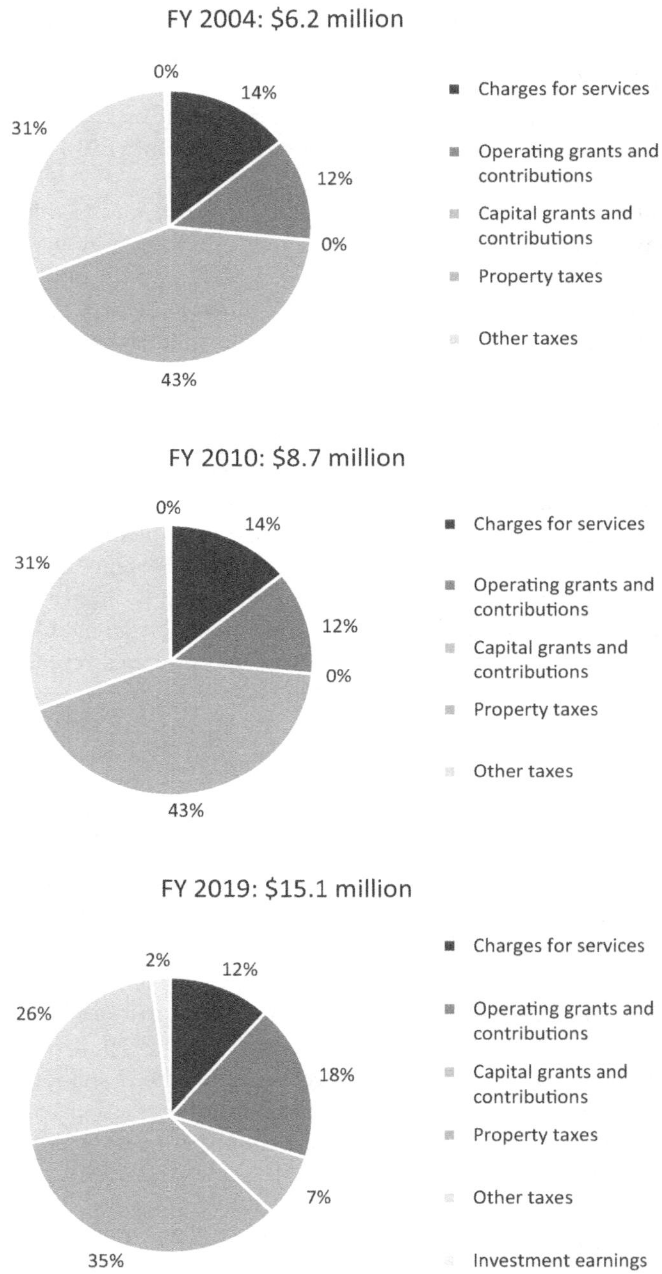

Figure 12.6 Governmental Revenues of Havelock, North Carolina
Source: City of Havelock (2004, 2020, 2019)

Table 12.1 Government Expenditures of Havelock, North Carolina ($1,000)

Year	*General government*	*Public safety*	*Highways & streets*	*Environmental protection*	*Cultural & recreation*	*Interest*	*Total*	*Annual pct change*
2004	1,209	2,687	1,269	98	627	22	$5,912	
2005	1,116	2,685	1,266	82	699	32	5,880	–0.5
2006	2,184	3,001	1,202	169	120	34	6,710	14.1
2007	1,827	3,063	1,228	151	740	30	7,039	4.9
2008	1,767	3,683	1,110	145	912	55	7,672	9.0
2009	2,914	3,789	1,295	165	836	83	9,082	18.4
2010	1,990	4,065	1,220	0	864	64	8,203	–9.7
2011	2,171	4,807	1,134	0	868	200	9,180	11.9
2012	2,454	4,672	1,546	0	854	398	9,924	8.1
2013	2,270	4,719	1,479	0	1,048	245	9,761	–1.6
2014	2,305	5,059	1,214	75	815	237	9,705	–0.6
2015	2,069	4,877	1,156	214	833	254	9,403	–3.1
2016	2,239	4,911	967	166	847	178	9,308	–1.0
2017	2,582	5,069	887	12	886	175	9,611	3.3
2018	2,228	4,703	1,560	72	1,241	162	9,966	3.7
2019	5,004	5,378	1,207	960	1,031	154	13,734	37.8
Annual avg pct change	16.1	5.0	1.9		33.0	25.6	6.3	

Source: City of Havelock (2019)

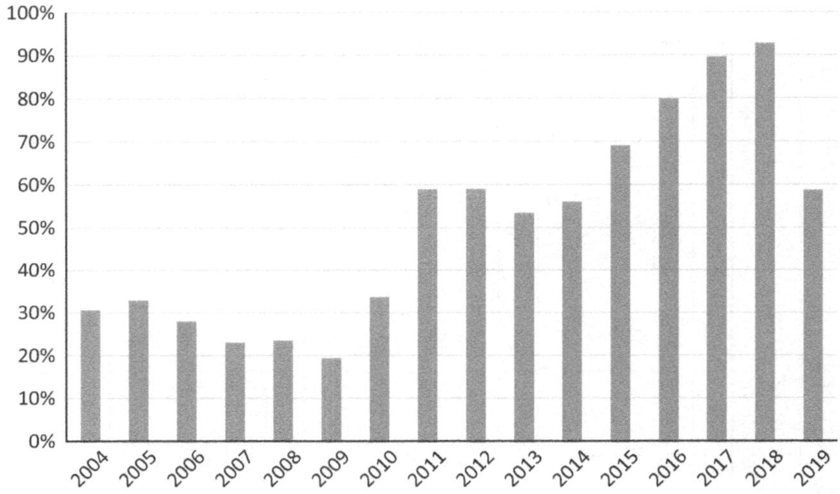

Figure 12.7 Unreserved Fund Balance as Percent of General Fund Expenditures, 2004–2019

Source: City of Havelock (2004–2019)

"The Board of Commissioners' goal [is] to maintain 32 percent in general fund balance" (p. 13). GO debt is limited by state statutes to 8% of total assessed valuation.

When general fund unassigned and assigned balances are combined and divided by expenditures, Havelock's reserves have been markedly high since FY2011, averaging 69% of expenditures from 2011 to 2019 (see Figure 12.7). The jump in reserves from 2010 to 2011 (from 33.6% of expenditures to 58.9%) appears to be a result of changes in reporting requirements. In 2009, GASB issued Statement 54, which, in essence, changed the language regarding the classification of reserve funds. Prior to the related reporting changes, Havelock carried an undesignated reserve in the general fund that ranged from 19% of expenditures (2009) to 33.6% (2010). From 2011 to 2019, assigned and unassigned general fund balances ranged from 53.4% of expenditures (in 2013) to 92.7% (in 2018). The drop in 2019 was caused by the unanticipated expenses compelled by Hurricane Florence. Despite this drop in reserves, the city was able to maintain a balance (58.7%) well above the goal of 32% of expenditures.

In addition to its large fund balances, Havelock also has strong liquidity. Figure 12.8 shows governmental cash, investments, and receivables relative to current liabilities. Because of the unavailability of electronic audited financial reports, the data begin in 2009. For the most current year available, FY2019, the city's

Figure 12.8 Cash, Investments, and Receivables Relative to Current Liabilities, 2009–2019

Source: City of Havelock (2009–2019)

combined cash, investments, and receivables equaled 13.4 times Havelock's current liabilities. That ratio was lowest in 2014 (3.3) and highest in 2012 (21.2). The city invests much of this money in a variety of funds managed primarily by the North Carolina State Treasurer. According to Havelock's 2019 ACFR,

> The City has no formal investment policy regarding interest rate risk. As a means of limiting its exposure to fair value losses arising from rising interest rates, the city's internal investment policy limits at least half of the city's investment portfolio to maturities of less than 12 months. Also, the city's internal management policy requires purchases of securities to be laddered with staggered maturity dates and limits all securities to a final maturity of no more than three years.
>
> (p. 47)

Debt Position

As noted above, under state law, Havelock's GO debt cannot exceed 8% of total assessed value. In 2019, this limit was equivalent to $50.2 million (City of Havelock, 2019). Havelock has taken a position of not incurring GO debt and has not carried such debt during the period of study. Havelock carries installment loan debt ($6.2 million in 2019) and revenue bond debt for its sewers ($11 million in FY 2019) and water system ($3.5 million) (City of Havelock, 2019).

Long-Term Liabilities

As shown in Figure 12.9, during these 11 years (2009–2019), long-term liabilities averaged 31.6% of assets. The average ratio was 31.8% for governmental funds and 30.9% for business-type activities. As long-term liabilities include debt issuance, it is not surprising to find annual variability. The ratio for governmental activities was largely stable from 2009 to 2015, followed by an annual decline through 2019. Business-type activities spiked in 2013, reflecting major capital investments in sewer plant work ($1.9 million). Overall, Havelock carries less debt than most municipalities.

For governmental funds, the greatest long-term liabilities are pensions ($2.0 million). Havelock participates in North Carolina's Local Governmental Employees' Retirement System (LGERS), a defined-benefit plan. State statutes require city employees to contribute 6% of their compensation to the retirement plan, and the city's share is actuarially determined; in 2019, it was 8.5% for law enforcement and 7.8% for firefighters and general employees (City of Havelock, 2019). The previously noted $2.0 million liability was actuarially determined based on "a projection of the city's long-term share of future payroll covered by the pension plan, relative to the projected future payroll covered by the pension plan for all participating LGERS employees" (City of Havelock, 2019, p. 52). Havelock also carried OPEB liability of $2.8 million in 2019. This liability is based on the city-administered, defined-benefit Healthcare Benefits Plan, which "provides post-employment healthcare benefits to retirees of the city, provided they participate in the North Carolina LGERS" (City of Havelock, 2019, p. 60).

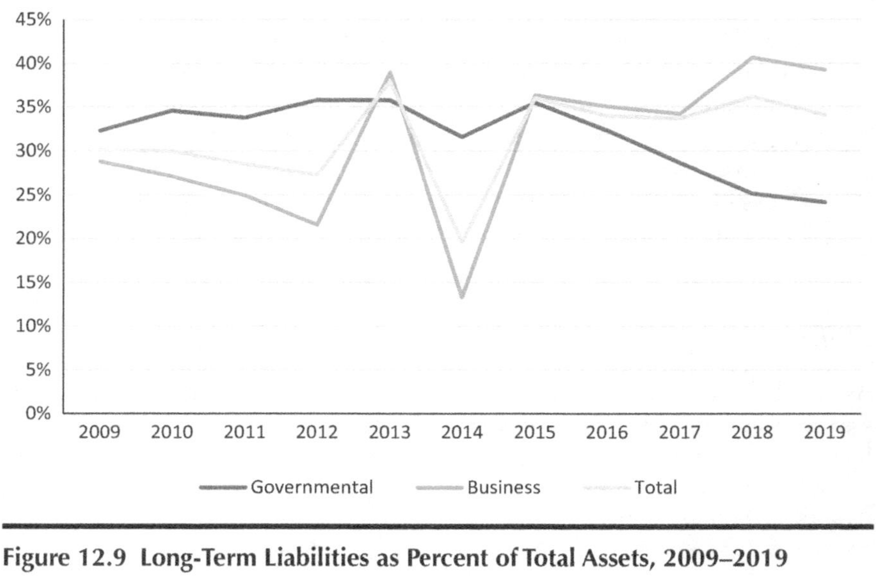

Figure 12.9 Long-Term Liabilities as Percent of Total Assets, 2009–2019
Source: City of Havelock (2009–2019)

Policy Actions: Input from Interviews with Finance Team Members

Relations with Elected Officials

In 2015 and 2021, Havelock finance officials were interviewed by telephone. Relations with the commissioners and mayor were described as positive, with frequent correspondence throughout the year. During the 2015 interview, informants referred to some conflict prior to 2013, but with the election of a new mayor, the degree of hostility subsided. Similar sentiments were expressed in 2021, when the response to the question about conflict was "some conflict but expected with multiple backgrounds." Internally, the relationship with the city manager is "very good," and elected officials respect his professional opinion. Having spent more than 20 years in the position has earned the finance official a certain level of respect, which is aided by the council-manager form of government. Without providing much detail, the respondent stated that the city's form of government enabled everyone "to work together through the [hurricane] crisis . . . it allows a middle-ground approach."

Effects of the Recession and Response Strategies

The fiscal effects of the Great Recession were observed in late 2009, in the form of declining sales tax revenue and the Marine airbase sequestration. The interviewee noted that although Havelock did not prosper, neither did it suffer as badly as many other communities. However, "Recovery has been less than other communities." Regarding the fiscal effects of COVID-19, the response was "very little on the revenue side, but did increase expenses." Those expenses were, however, largely reimbursed by the CARES Act.

Post-Great Recession response strategies consisted of "knee-jerk reactions—[we] tried to defer things." In the medium term, there were some layoffs and delayed hires. The focus was on spurring new development by "trying to get upbeat about upcoming projects." As for recovery from the Great Recession, the response was that the city was in worse shape in 2015 and had still not fully recovered. One lesson from the recession was that the city needs to diversify beyond its dependence on the military bases. Given the limited effect of COVID-19 on Havelock's finances, no special actions were required at that time.

Institutional Constraints

Interviewees were asked about the impact of institutional fiscal constraints. City officials pay particular attention to millage rates, and the 2015 interviewee expressed angst about an upcoming revaluation that was expected to increase tax rates. During the 2021 interview, a respondent noted that North Carolina's revenue restrictions were "hurtful" because they prevent Havelock from "raising local revenue from a variety of sources," resulting in greater reliance on property tax revenues.

Fiscal Health and Stress

As noted previously, to probe for possible lack of consistency between self-assessments of the city's fiscal condition and objective measures recommended by professionals, we asked interviewees how they assess fiscal health. In 2015, Havelock's finance official replied:

> I'm going to look at property tax value. I'm going to look at property tax, sales tax, and utilities collections. We have a water and sewer utility system, so when sequestration was coming and we had people who went from 40 hours (full employment) to 32 hours, my first [question] was, "Did my cutoffs go up? Am I increasing my days that are receivable?" How can we be a strong business utility, but yet be customer service–friendly? In fact, we played around with our policy for a little while, so if somebody came in and they honestly couldn't pay the bill because they weren't working anymore, we tried to give them some flexibility.

The response regarding how to assess fiscal health was quite different in 2021. The interviewee stated, "Havelock's major economic engine is Marine Corps Air Station Cherry Point, so monitor military and federal defense spending."

The 2015 interviewee explained that fiscal stress "is when my expenses are outpacing my revenues. I don't just mean the fact that that happens every August, but I worry more on an annual basis." When we asked this question in 2021, the response was similar: "Inability to fund required services . . . unable to respond to changing economic conditions while still maintaining core services." A fiscally sound community was defined as one with healthy reserves and the ability to react to changing situations.

Final Assessment

In Havelock, North Carolina, policymakers operate in a unique fiscal environment that is driven by one very important source: U.S. Marine Corps bases. The top four city employers are directly tied to these bases. One of the city's greatest challenges may be long-term planning. The 2015 interviewee pointed out that the city needs to diversify its economy and tax base, but both actions are difficult to achieve. Regarding the former, how does a coastal city redefine its economy when the military base, Cherry Point, has played such a prominent role? The base, in fact, precedes the city, dating back to the mid-1800s, whereas the city was incorporated in 1959 (Byers, 2020). Meanwhile, diversifying the tax base is challenging due to the city's economic structure and state policies.

Discussion Questions

Questions to consider regarding the Havelock case study:

- The Havelock case study introduces a new dimension to our examination of financial condition analysis—federal policy. Discuss how this case study adds to the discussion of municipal fiscal health.
- Havelock does not have a formal reserves policy and has maintained sizeable liquidity in the forms of reserves and cash. Consider the city's environment—a coastal community affected by hurricanes and dependent on a primary employer—and design a reserves policy.
- To what extent and how did the city's internal management and decision-making structure (e.g., form of government) affect the city's finances? In the case of Havelock, consider the importance of longevity for financial managers.
- The interview with the finance team revealed a dimension of financial condition not previously discussed—business-type activities. The interviewee noted that a dimension of fiscal condition was water and sewer revenues, and the number of cutoffs to those services. Discuss how business-type activities could be incorporated into a financial condition analysis.
- The finance team discussed the need to diversify the city's tax base which means expanding the city's economy and revenue sources. Discuss challenges associated with attempting to diversify a city's tax base, particularly in a state with restrictive TELs.

Chapter 13

Case Study of Commerce, California

Commerce is a relatively small city (population 12,868) in Los Angeles County, California. The city is about six miles from downtown Los Angeles and 20 miles from the Pacific Ocean. Its size, location, and economic base make it an interesting case study. Commerce relies heavily on tourism and, as the city's name implies, commercial industries. Consumers are drawn to the city for shopping and gambling. Commerce's estimated population during the day is about four times its official population, as about 40,000 people work within the city boundaries.

Inputs: Fiscal Environments

Institutional Setting/External Pressures

All California municipalities operate under tax limitations. Proposition 13, adopted in 1978 through a citizen initiative, is commonly described as the beginning of the popular tax revolt, particularly with respect to property taxes. California limits property taxes to 1% of a property's full-market valuation. To prohibit property taxes from growing through increases in property valuation, Proposition 13 froze valuations at the levels set according to 1975–1976 market rates, unless the property is sold or "significantly modified" (Spiotto et al., 2016, p. 199). Debt is also limited to the income and revenue for that year. Voter approval is required to override these limitations. As described in Chapter 8, California does permit municipal bankruptcies. The state also engages in municipal government financial

DOI: 10.4324/9780429270765-13

monitoring through the California state auditor. The auditor's office created a web-based system for assessing high-risk municipalities (discussed in more detail below). There are currently no policies, procedures, or actions that arise from this monitoring system.

Internal Structures

Commerce was incorporated in 1960 and operates under the council-manager form of government. The city council appoints the manager, who is responsible for the day-to-day administration of city business and the coordination of all departments. Policymaking and legislative authority are vested in the city council, which consists of the mayor, mayor pro tern, and three council members. The city council is responsible for setting policy, adopting the budget, and committee appointments. The city manager and assistant city manager are responsible for "implementing the vision, broad policy goals and ongoing strategic programs of the city council" as well as overseeing day-to-day government operations (City of Commerce, 2022). The five-member city council is elected on a biennial cycle with four-year alternating terms, at large, on a nonpartisan basis. The mayor is selected by the city council from among its members, serving a one-year term.

Socioeconomic Conditions

By most measures, Commerce has recovered from the Great Recession, but the recovery has been relatively slow. According to Commerce's 2019 ACFR, the "economic environment continues to grow at a moderate pace. The city council continues to focus on diversifying its economic base, along with the maintenance of its arterial streets and/or roadways, public safety enhancements and beautification of our neighborhoods/business districts" (p. iii).

In 2020, Commerce had a population of 12,868 (U.S. Census Bureau, 2021; see Figure 13.1). Over the past 20 years, the city's population appears to have gone through three phases: steady growth from 2003 to 2008, decline from 2008 to 2012, and stability from 2012 to 2020.

Commercial industries dominate Commerce's economy. In 2020, the city's top employers were the California Commerce Club, Inc., also known as the Commerce Casino (4,750 employees and 9.9% of total employment); Los Angeles County (1,100 employees, 2.3%); and Parsec, Inc., an intermodal shipping company (1,036 employees, 2.2%). Those same organizations were the top employers in 2011: Commerce Casino, 2,191 employees, 3.8%; Los Angeles County, 910 employees, 1.6%; Parsec, 890 employees, 1.6%).

The Great Recession's effects on Commerce were neither immediate nor of short duration. The city's unemployment rate was already relatively high—8.5% in 2008, compared to the U.S. average of 5.8% (see Figure 13.2). It jumped to 13.8% in 2009 and peaked in 2011 at 23.3%, while the U.S. average was 8.9%.

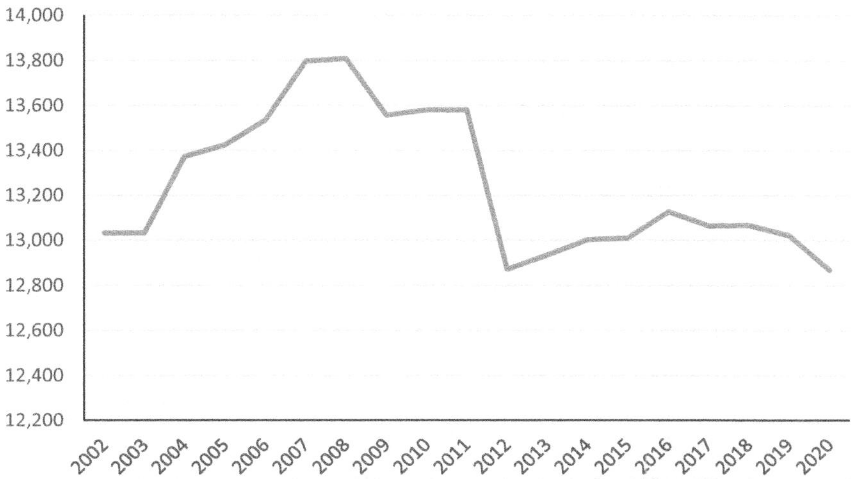

Figure 13.1 Population of Commerce, California, 2002–2020
Source: City of Commerce (2020)

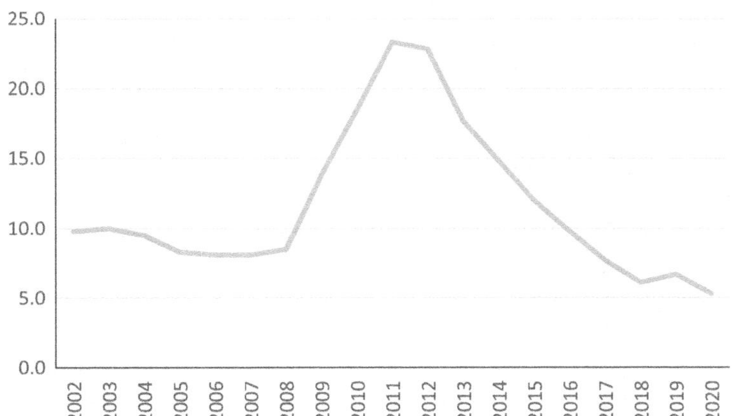

Figure 13.2 Unemployment Rate of Commerce, California, 2002–2020
Source: City of Commerce (2020)

Heading to the pandemic, the city's unemployment rate was 8.2% in 2018, 6.1% in 2019, and 5.6% in 2020.

While unemployment soared during the Great Recession, per-capita personal income remained stable (see Figure 13.3). From 2004 to 2008, the city experienced annual growth in personal income, from $14,164 to 16,059 per capita. From 2008 to 2019, per-capita personal income has fluctuated between $15,444

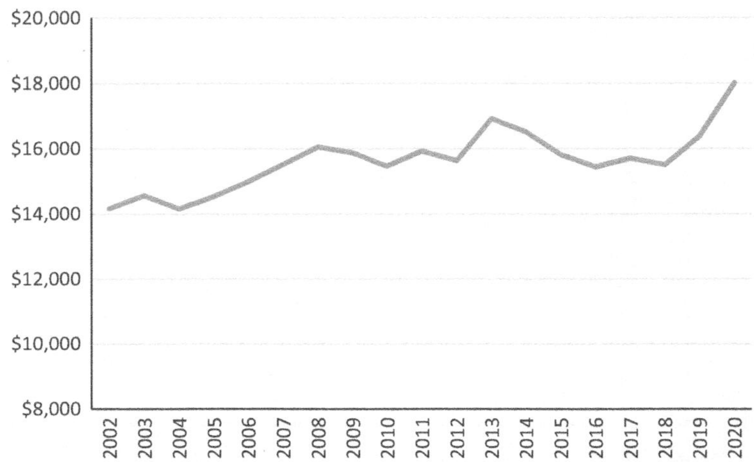

Figure 13.3 Personal Income of Commerce, CA, 2002–2020 (Per Capita)
Source: City of Commerce (2020)

(in 2016) and $16,925 (in 2013). In the most recent year for which data are available, 2020, per-capita personal income jumped to $18,021.

Since the city relies heavily on a commercial tax base, property valuation can be an important economic benchmark. Fortunately for Commerce, the city's property valuation has been relatively well insulated from economic shocks (see Figure 13.4). Between 2002 and 2012, assessed valuation grew annually from $947,000 to $1.3 million. Between 2012 and 2013, it was more than tripled to $4.3 million. Since 2013, the city's property values have continued to grow steadily, reaching $5.8 million in 2020.

As noted, the Great Recession was slow to impact Commerce, but the effects were long-lasting. The city's economy is heavily dependent on the commercial sector, including a casino and shopping center. The city lost population during the 19-year analysis period, and much of that loss occurred after the Great Recession. While personal income and property valuations have been stable, the city wrestles with unemployment rates and per-capita personal income levels that remain significantly less favorable than the national averages.

Although the socioeconomic impacts of COVID-19 are not as clear as those of the Great Recession, the pandemic's fiscal shock has, not surprisingly, directly affected Commerce's financial position particularly due to the city's reliance on commercial activities. California has been severely ravaged by the COVID-19 pandemic. The state reported its first coronavirus death in March 2020, and in response, Governor Gavin Newsom was the first to impose a shelter-in-place requirement. This meant the closing of casinos, bars, restaurants, and other businesses. The

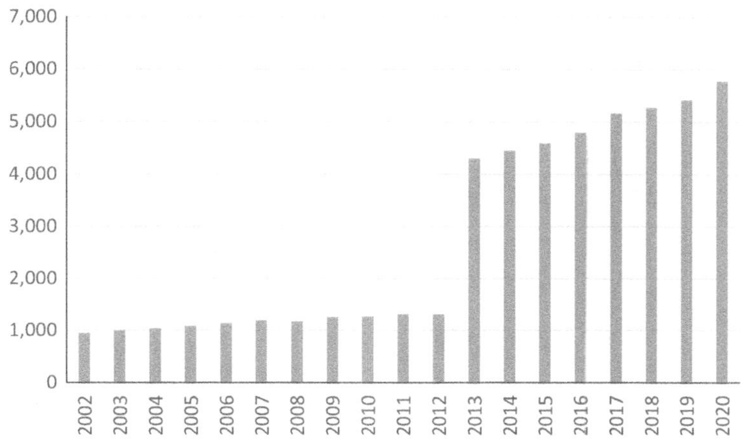

Figure 13.4 Assessed Property Values of Commerce, California, 2002–2020 ($1,000)

Source: City of Commerce (2020)

lockdown began in April 2020; businesses reopened for a few weeks in the summer but were then essentially closed from July 2020 through January 2021.

Outputs: Fiscal Trends

Revenues

Over the last several years, the city has become less reliant on property taxes and more reliant on sales taxes (see Figure 13.5). Nevertheless, the casino remains a dominant source of revenue. In 2003, one-quarter (28%) of the city's revenues were collected from property taxes. In FY2011, property taxes represented 29% of total revenues. However, by 2020, that share had dropped to 7%. In FY2011, the city collected $17.3 million in property taxes, but in 2012, that figure had dropped to $9.4 million, and it was down to $4.5 million by FY2020.

This plunge in property tax collections was the result of a concerted effort by policymakers to lower the city's property tax burden. Sales tax revenues helped to fill the void. Whereas sales taxes accounted for 24% of total government revenues in 2002 and 22% in 2011, they provided 42% in 2020. Sales tax collections grew from $10.6 million in 2003 to $13.1 million in 2011 and $27 million in 2020.

The most important single source of revenue for Commerce is the casino. The city collects a monthly fee of $10,000 plus a share of card game revenues monthly from the casino. During the period from FY2003 to FY2020, casino revenues

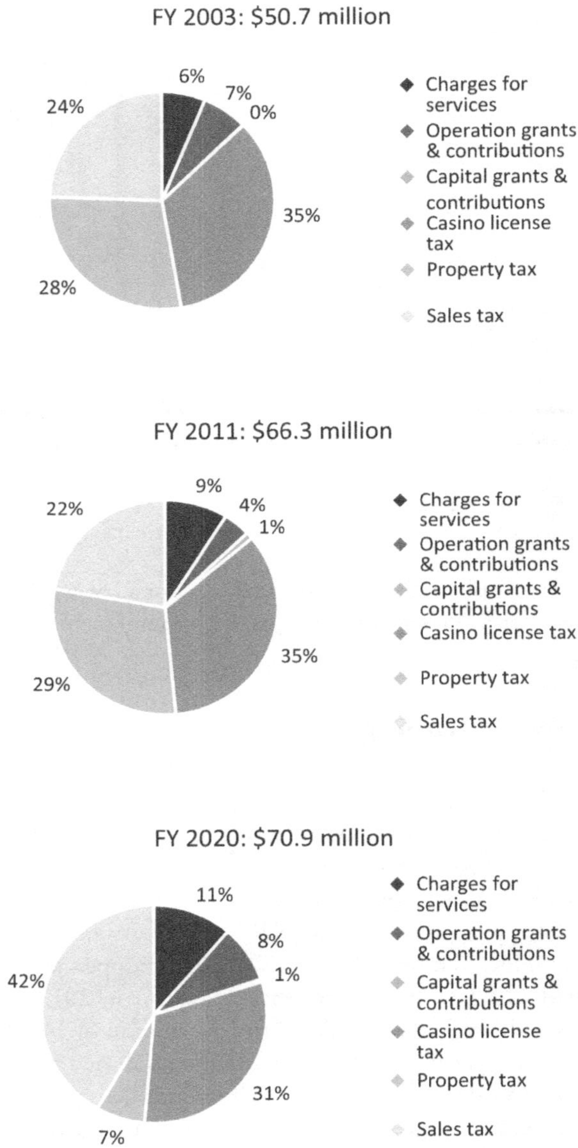

Figure 13.5 Governmental Revenues of Commerce, California
Source: City of Commerce (2003, 2011, 2020)

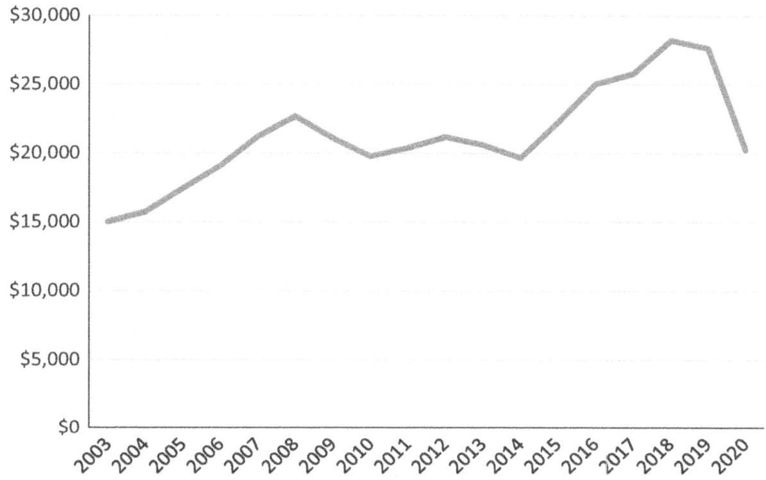

Figure 13.6 Casino License Tax Collections, 2003–2020 ($1,000)
Source: City of Commerce (2020)

have consistently accounted for approximately one-third of total government revenues. The cyclical nature of those revenues can be seen in Figure 13.6. When the economy grows, so too do casino license taxes. However, during periods of decile, casino tax revenues fall.

From the standpoint of financial condition analysis, Commerce's government revenue mix requires careful monitoring. On one hand, although property taxes have negative connotations, they also tend to be the most stable. Commerce is now much less reliant on property taxes than it was even ten years ago. In FY2020, 73% of Commerce's governmental revenues came from two volatile sources: sales and casino taxes.

Expenditures

From 2003 to 2020, Commerce's total government expenditures exhibited substantial annual variability, as shown in Table 13.1. For instance, between FY2003 and FY2004, government expenditures jumped by 10.6%, they rose another 7.8% the following year, then fell 10.1% between 2005 and 2006. Similarly, total expenditures grew by 8.8% from 2008 to 2009, followed by a 20% spike from 2009 to 2010, but then fell 16.1% from 2010 to 2011. Interestingly, the fluctuations in expenditures were primarily driven by changes in general government and community development expenditures. The Great Recession had little effect on overall expenditures, as they rose by 3.6% from 2007 to 2008, 8.8% from 2008 to 2009, and 20% from 2009 to 2010.

Table 13.1 Government Expenditures of Commerce, California ($1,000)

Year	*General government*	*Community development*	*Public safety*	*Public works*	*Library*	*Parks & recreation*	*Interest on debt*	*Total*	*Annual pct change*
2003	13,139	7,784	12,251	2,156	2,476	8,754	7,144	53,704	
2004	17,736	5,890	13,556	2,110	2,462	9,121	8,514	59,389	10.6
2005	19,216	6,575	13,695	2,319	2,403	9,388	10,444	64,040	7.8
2006	14,441	6,035	12,799	2,120	2,554	10309	9,300	57,558	–10.1
2007	16,891	6,430	13,742	2,864	2,862	10,158	9,101	62,048	7.8
2008	15,824	7,029	14,672	3,198	3,220	10,634	9,685	64,262	3.6
2009	21,404	3,257	16,198	4,900	3,216	10,950	9,997	69,922	8.8
2010	16,399	21,051	16,358	7,285	2,472	10,516	9,813	83,894	20.0
2011	17,652	11,021	16,206	5,868	3,970	8,152	7,510	70,379	–16.1
2012	17,997	2,270	15,584	6,465	3,001	8,808	10,055	64,180	–8.8
2013	16,664	2,026	16,495	6,954	2,799	9,123	5,554	59,615	–7.1
2014	18,217	2,085	17,466	6,903	1,361	9,744	4,847	60,623	1.7
2015	18,681	2,582	17,826	9,574	1,201	9,299	5,394	64,557	6.5
2016	16,097	4,551	18,994	10,080	3,211	9,917	4,196	67,046	3.9
2017	17,143	3,111	20,529	7,754	3,775	11,936	1,871	66,119	–1.4
2018	19,706	3,189	21,462	13,955	4,276	12,836	2,036	77,460	17.2
2019	19,893	2,112	21,457	13,706	3,627	13,083	366	74,244	–4.2
2020	14,924	2,444	22,514	16,343	4,720	12,837	348	74,130	–0.2
Annual avg pct change	2.3	23.9	3.8	15.5	10.8	2.7	–9.1	2.3	

Source: City of Commerce (2020)

Looking at the annual distribution of expenditures by source, public safety was the most stable, growing by 3.8% annually. General government expenditures experienced a surprising amount of variability during the period, rising by more than 10% between FY2003 and FY2004 (35%), FY2006 and FY2007 (17%), FY2008 and FY2009 (35%), and FY2017 and FY2018 (15%). General government expenditures dropped by more than 10% on four occasions: between FY2005 and FY2006 (−25%), FY2009 and FY2010 (−23%), FY2015 and FY2016 (−14%), and FY2019 and FY2020 (−25%). There was also a high level of annual variability in community development (average annual increase of 23.9%), public works (15.1%), and libraries (10.8%).

Outcomes: Fiscal Condition

Operating Position

According to the city's fund balance policy, adopted in 2009, Commerce needs to "maintain a designated general fund working capital reserve equivalent to 15% of the general fund's operating budget and a designated emergency reserve equivalent to 5% of the general fund's operating budget" (p. 2). When general fund unassigned and assigned balances are combined and divided by general fund expenditures, Commerce's reserves greatly exceed city policy requirements (see Figure 13.7). The city's low point was 2006, when fund balance levels were 15.1%

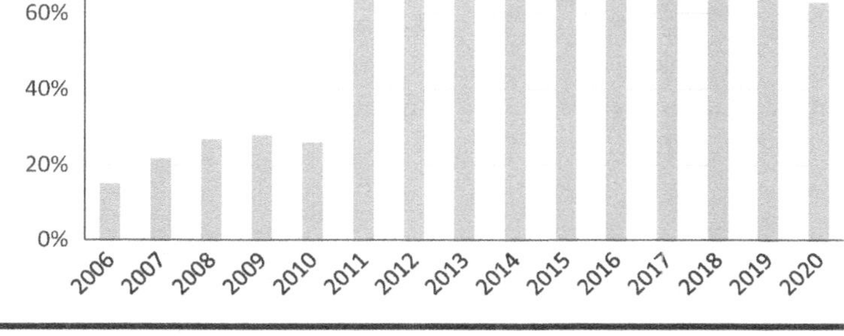

Figure 13.7 Unreserved Fund Balance as Percent of General Fund Expenditures, 2006–2020

Source: City of Commerce (2006–2020)

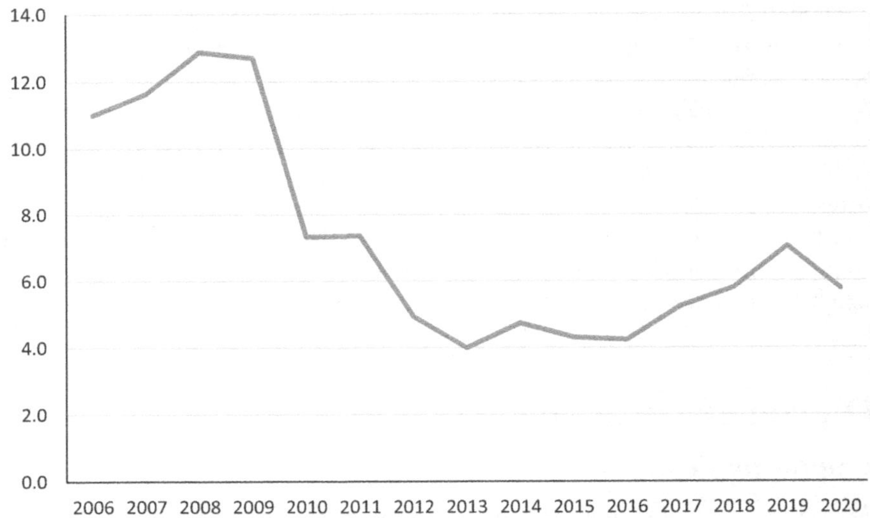

Figure 13.8 Cash, Investments, and Receivables Relative to Current Liabilities, 2009–2020

Source: City of Commerce (2009–2020)

of expenditures. Interestingly, the economic impact sustained by Commerce through 2010 had no effect on the city's reserves. In 2011, reserves increased to 71.8% of expenditures, and by 2018 they had reached 97.5% of expenditures. Despite recent declines, the city retained a reserve balance in 2020 equal to 62.9% of expenditures.

In addition to carrying sizable reserves, Commerce also has strong liquidity. Figure 13.8 presents governmental cash, investments, and receivables relative to current liabilities. Commerce had the ratio higher than 2.0 in each year studied. Prior to the Great Recession, Commerce was carrying cash and investments more than 11 times current liabilities. Beginning in FY2010, the ratio dropped each year, falling to 4.0 (still double the norm) in 2013. After that, the ratio of cash and investments to current liabilities grew annually, to 7.0 in FY2019, before falling slightly in 2020 to 5.8.

Debt Position

Commerce has adopted a commitment to eliminating their GO debt. The city's 2009 policy states, "We will use long-term financing methods or cash accumulated in excess of policy requirements for major capital improvements and acquisitions." In 2002, Commerce carried $16.4 million in GO debt; in 2003, GO debt was still $15.9 million. But by 2006, it was down to $1.8 million, and 2011 was the last year of recorded GO debt. This drop in GO debt is consistent with the city's decline in cash and investments relative to current liabilities, and with Commerce's policy statement.

Long-Term Liabilities

Commerce operates water, transit, and cable television services. Figure 13.9 reflects the city's general aversion to debt accumulation. From FY 2006 to FY2020, liabilities averaged 51% of assets for governmental funds, 32% for business-type activities, and 50% overall. These averages, however, mask two very important trends. Prior to 2014, Commerce business-type liabilities were minimal, representing 1% to 3% of total assets. Business-type long-term liabilities jumped to 25% of total assets in 2015 and to 151% in 2018, reflecting revenue bond issuances. In late 2014, the city issued $10 million in lease revenue bonds to pay off more costly outstanding debt on its Community Center. In 2018, the city issued $30 million in Tax Allocation Refunding Bonds to pay off more costly outstanding bonds. Governmental long-term liabilities were consistent from 2006 to 2015, ranging between 53% and 58% of total assets. Governmental long-term liabilities dropped to 40% of total assets in 2016 and have remained below pre-2015 levels.

The city is a member of the California Public Employees Retirement System (CalPERS), which sets the contribution rates for the city's represented and

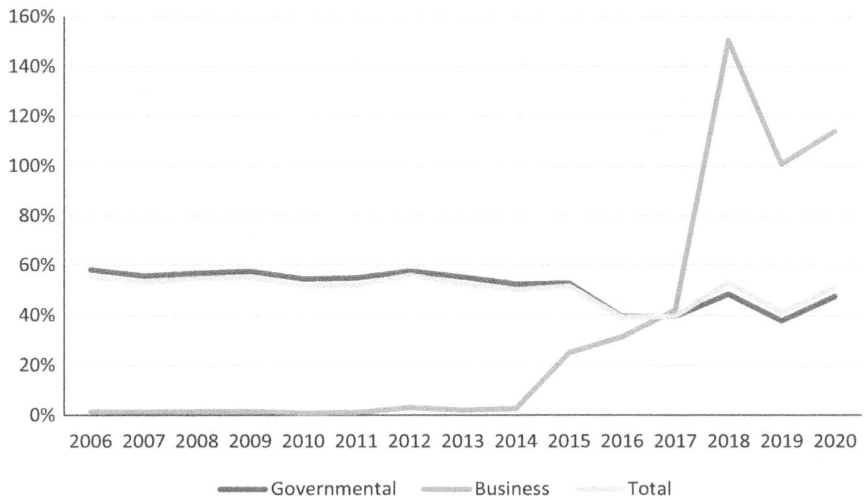

Figure 13.9 Long-Term Liabilities as Percent of Total Assets, 2009–2019
Source: City of Commerce (2009–2019)

non-represented employee groups. Participants were required to contribute 7% of their annual covered salary until July 1, 2015; previously, the city made a portion of the contributions required of city employees into their account on their behalf. The city is required to contribute the actuarially determined remaining amounts necessary to fund the benefits for its members. The actuarial methods and assumptions used are those adopted by the CalPERS board of administration. The contribution requirements of plan members are established by state law; the employer contribution rate is established and may be amended by CalPERS. In early 2018 the city council approved the establishment of an irrevocable trust for employee pension benefits. The pension trust fund allows the city to set aside funds for future employee pension costs and potentially earn a higher rate of return on these funds. To date, $2.6 million has been deposited in the trust to fund future pension costs.

Policy Actions: Input from Interviews with Finance Team Members

Relations with Elected Officials

Relations with the board have, at times, been strained. An interviewee stated, "On some days and some issues, [the council] hear me very clearly. On some days and some issues, they don't care. They don't care what I have to say." The board has also been riddled with controversy and conflict. For example, the California district attorney had investigated some Commerce council members for misappropriation of funds. Then, a council member was elected after being barred from holding office for three years due to convictions for obstruction of justice and perjury. The interviewee said that this man (the council member elected after previously being barred from office) and

> the lady who controls the majority . . . basically hate each other. She knew that coming in. It's like it's a state of normalcy in the whole southern Los Angeles basin area. . .. They do things and take things very personal. They involve staff members, put them in the middle of things.

During the 2015 interview, the informant's comments throughout the conversation suggested a somewhat contentious relationship, as he tried to advise council members and they ignored or downplayed his suggestions. In the 2021 interview, it was noted that younger council members were doing a better job at trying to disassociate policymaking from policy implementation.

Effects of the Great Recession and COVID-19 and Response Strategies

The fiscal effects of the Great Recession hit in 2007. Of the $50 million general fund budget, $40 million comes from the casino, but at the height of the recession, those revenues dropped to $22 million. Sales tax revenue also fell precipitously, from $14 million to less than $10 million. COVID-19 had a similarly major impact. Given the city's heavy reliance on the casino and shopping mall, the closing of businesses in April 2020 and then again from July 2020 to January 2021 meant significant revenue losses.

During both interviews, the descriptions of response strategies focused on budget cuts rather than revenue expansion. During the Great Recession, finance officers urged making cuts through hiring freezes and attrition. According to the interviewee, the city "started looking at doing things differently with less . . . at this time none of the employees were paying into their retirement. The city was picking up the entire tab." Policymakers began exploring changes to the city's pension funding model and created an early retirement program that led to the voluntary retirement of 27 of 150 full-time workers. An interviewee also noted that while the recession was felt in fall of 2008 another large impact was in 2011 due to change in governors and state requirements—"Jerry Brown announced the end of redevelopment, and that put us . . . that basically was a significant setback for us."

The effects of COVID-19 were more rapid and severe. The interviewee explained that Commerce "scrapped the budget process as it faced a $12 million deficit." The city council was committed to not cutting any full-time employees, so the cuts included approximately 200 part-time positions, a voter-approved sales tax increase, and getting employees to cover a larger share of pension and OPEB costs.

The interviews also discussed the longer-term policy implications of both events. It was believed that the events had served as learning experiences for staff policymakers:

> The mindset has changed, not only from a staff perspective but from elected officials' perspective. They totally understand what needs to be done. I think they're better prepared because of the last recession, and they're not overstepping their bounds as they had prior to the last recession.

The interviewee added with respect to the elected officials, "I think they actually heed a lot of the things that staff is telling them, which has made our relationship a lot better." Municipal employees have agreed to take on a larger share of pension and OPEB costs, the city is planning two or three years ahead, and there is a concerted effort to diversify revenue, which includes considering user fees, utility taxes, the sales tax, and the parcel tax. Parcel taxes only exist in California, and they are a tax on parcels of property, not the valuation of property which is most common. This is, arguably, a way to get around Proposition 13 but its adoption requires two-thirds voter approval. The parcel tax was proposed and rejected by voters in 2021.

Institutional Constraints

Interviewees were asked about the impact of institutional fiscal constraints. Given the attention received by California's Proposition 13, bankruptcy filings by Stockton and other cities, and the state's fiscal health monitoring system (California State Auditor, 2022), it is not surprising that state policies are seen as dictating many municipal fiscal decisions. With respect to the state monitoring system, the state examines the following categories and Commerce received the scores indicated in the parentheses for 2018–2019 (the most current year for which data were available):

- General fund reserves: Low risk (30 out of 30 possible points)
- Debt burden: Low (15/15)
- Liquidity: Low (10/10)
- Revenue trends: Moderate (3.5/5)
- Pension obligations: Low (9.4/10)
- Pension funding: Moderate (3.65/5)
- Pension costs: Low (4.17/5)
- Future pension costs: Low (3.61/5)
- OPEB obligations: Moderate (7.52/10)
- OPEB funding: High (0.25/5)

On nearly all these measures, Commerce was at low risk of fiscal stress or crisis. Interestingly, Commerce, like most municipalities in the Los Angeles region, is at greatest risk due to OPEB funding and obligations. According to the state website, Commerce has a OPEB fiduciary net position equal to 5% of total OPEB liabilities.

When we asked about these state policies, the general response was that they have little impact on Commerce's fiscal decisions. Little attention is paid to the state's monitoring website, and Proposition 13 means little to Commerce because the city does not rely heavily on property taxes. The greatest frustration was expressed about population-based formulas for grants and other forms of aid. As noted earlier, the city's population more than triples on weekdays due to its commercial sector, which affects core services such as infrastructure and public safety, yet the only population figure used to calculate aid is residential, which underrepresents service demands.

Fiscal Health and Stress

Commerce's finance officials assessed fiscal health in terms of a "visceral feeling" about the community. They specifically mentioned the city's relationship with the casino. Casino management is very involved in the community, sponsoring programs, and funding events. When hard economic times hit the casino, the community suffers.

When asked how he defines a fiscally stressed community, one interviewee placed relatively little emphasis on fiscal metrics and a much greater emphasis on community appeal and core services. He mentioned public safety and the ability to provide those services. He discussed metrics such as the number of calls received regarding burglaries and grand theft. During the 2015 interview, he stated:

> I guess it depends on who you're asking. If you are asking the residents, I think that they are happy with the way things are as long as they're taken care of. For me, it does not matter if we've got a $50 million budget and we have $50 million in reserves; when I look at the city, there's a lot of dilapidation that should be addressed. I think aesthetically, for me that falls under that umbrella. It doesn't tell you the whole story, but for me, the effect is paramount.

Lessons Learned

When asked about lessons learned from the Great Recession, the interviewee stated,

> I think when the recession hit and people worked together to get through it, bonds became stronger. I think certain levels in government understood what the end goal was. . .. I honestly feel that the family bond is there and if we are pushed up against the wall in the future, we know what we went through and what needs to be done.

This attitude was also clearly reflected in Commerce's response to the COVID-19 pandemic. There was a commitment to preserving full-time employees, although to do that, employees needed to assume a larger share of pension and OPEB costs, departments had to endure sizeable budget cuts (up to 23%), and the city council had to convey to constituents why these actions were necessary.

When asked, in hindsight, if they would do anything differently, a 2015 interviewee referred to "creating a joint management-employee group to meet on a weekly basis to address everything under the sun." Nothing similar was stated during the 2021 interview. Rather, the discussion centered around the opportunities afforded by the COVID-19 crisis: lowering long-term costs associated with pensions and OPEBs, educating elected officials about the city's financial position, and cutting personnel via attrition and reduction of part-time positions while committing to preserving the positions of full-time personnel.

Final Assessment

In Commerce, California, policymakers operate in a unique fiscal environment in which the commercial and gambling sectors insulate them from the impact of strict, state-imposed property tax limits yet leave the city vulnerable to significant revenue losses during periods of economic decline.

One of the city's greatest challenges is to manage its fiscal policies in a volatile economic environment. In FY2019, Commerce collected 31% of its revenues from the casino and 42% from sales tax collections, making the city susceptible to economic variability. The management team and city officials have confronted this challenge and deserve credit for adopting policies and making fiscal decisions designed to protect the city from core service and personnel cuts. These actions include growing cash and reserves during periods of economic growth so that the city can not only navigate economic downturns but also cover capital expenditures using a pay-as-you-go model. As a result, the city has not carried any GO debt since 2011.

Although these fiscal metrics are encouraging, external challenges—particularly economic and demographic ones—will continue to plague the city of Commerce. As previously noted, the city struggles with high unemployment and low per-capita personal income. An interviewee also described southeastern Los Angeles County as "pretty volatile." Commerce's population is smaller in 2020 (12,868) than it was in 2002 (13,033). How the city sustains its fiscal position despite these economic and demographic challenges will determine its long-term success.

Discussion Questions

Questions to consider regarding the Commerce case study:

- Commerce experiences a tripling of its population on a daily basis as a result of its commercial and gambling sectors. Discuss how this can skew comparative per capita measures used in financial condition analysis.
- Commerce has a formal reserve policy and an emergency fund. Discuss the merits of these policies in light of the city's revenue volatility.
- As a follow-up to the discussion above, Commerce's reserves have consistently exceeded its formal policy requirements. Discuss the pros and cons of designing a reserve policy that sets both minimum and maximum amounts.

- Commerce, like Havelock and North Lauderdale, carries no general obligation debt. Discuss the differences in their use as well as and pros and cons of capital projects funding using revenue bonds versus general obligation bonds.
- Commence officials discussed economic development as a means of responding to fiscal stress. Discuss this strategy within the context of previously discussed response strategies.
- Commerce officials consistently discussed challenges associated with pension and OPEB funding. The latter is also an area where California's fiscal monitoring system rated the city as moderately vulnerable. Discuss the merits and challenges associated with including pension and OPEB liabilities in an analysis of city financial condition.

Chapter 14

Academic and Professional Approaches to Financial Condition Analysis

In this chapter, we summarize the previous case studies using our framework and then for the sake of comparing approaches, we present other, more common approaches to the examination of the financial condition of public-sector entities. The three methods of assessing financial condition described come from Kloha et al. (2005), Wang et al. (2007), and Moody's (2009), respectively. The first two sources are among the most frequently cited studies in the field of financial management, and the Moody's model assesses financial risk for prospective borrowers and lenders.

Open-Systems Framework for Municipal Financial Condition

Our approach to municipal financial condition requires an assessment of the municipality, including understand the inputs (institutional settings, external pressures, socioeconomic conditions, and internal management), outputs (fiscal structures), policy decisions, outcomes (fiscal health measures) and feedback loops. For each of the five case studies we can see the value in such an approach.

DOI: 10.4324/9780429270765-14

Flint, Michigan

Inputs: The most striking inputs affecting Flint during the period of study include the decades of economic decline and demographic changes. The loss of industrial base centered around automobile manufacturing resulted in declining incomes, growing unemployment, and declining population. The economic shocks caused by the Great Recession and COVID-19 exacerbated these existing fiscal challenges. Outputs and outcomes: These economic and demographic problems resulted in the significant loss of revenues, deficit spending and loss of access to capital (more specifically, GO bonds).

Policy actions: Actions taken in response to Flint's fiscal challenges included state takeovers of city operations in 2002 and 2011. The city's emergency financial manager focused on cutting operating expenditures (salaries, wages, personnel cuts, etc.) and reducing pension liabilities. The most egregious action taken was changing contracts for municipal water drawn from Lake Huron to the Flint River. This decision exposed residents to dangerous levels of lead and outbreaks of Legionnaire's disease. This health crisis led to loss of life, sickened many more residents and is still being litigated. Other results caused by these policy decisions have helped the city's bottom line. Flint's pension liabilities have been lower since employees started paying a greater share of the associated costs, operating spending has been down, reserves have grown, and some revenues have increased (principally fees due to significant rate increases). Flint remains financially challenged—pensions remain poorly funded and infrastructure needs are great—to the point where the city remains heavily dependent on state revenues.

Wichita, Kansas

Inputs: During the period of study, Wichita experienced significant economic change, particularly in the aeronautics industry where thousands of jobs were lost. The Great Recession resulted in significant job losses, decreased per capita personal income, and increased unemployment. In addition, state policies constrained city revenues. These policies included sizeable income tax rate reductions that resulted in lower intergovernmental aid, limits on property tax growth and exemptions from personal property taxes. Other important inputs include a stable demographic environment—population remained stable—and a commission-manager form of government where the management team is well respected by stakeholders.

Outputs and outcomes: The economic and state policy decisions resulted in revenue losses that included intergovernmental aid. Policy actions: Actions focused on shifting the city's revenue structure and cutting spending. Wichita has become less dependent on intergovernmental revenues and more reliant on fees, charges, and permits. Expenditure reductions were well-documented in the case-study chapter and were as substantial as an 8.1% drop from FY2010 to FY2011. Local policy means that Wichita carries relative low fund balances (less than 10%), and the city's debt cannot exceed 30% of equalized valuation. The results of these policy actions include carrying sizeable amounts of cash, investments, and receivable (perhaps to offset the fund balance policy). Wichita has been also performing well on long-term liabilities measures, including a well-funded pension.

North Lauderdale, Florida

Inputs: Relevant inputs for North Lauderdale include operating under a commission-manager form of government and, on the finance-side, under strict property tax limits imposed by the state. City management has a good working relationship with commissioners. The city's economy, largely driven by real estate, was affected by the Great Recession that reduced property values (and therefore, property tax collections) and intergovernmental aids. Outputs and outcomes: The outputs and outcomes from these environmental effects resulted in revenue declines from FY2009 to FY2013, and subsequent fiscal distress. Policy actions: Responses included reductions in total expenditures for FY2009, FY2011, and FY2013. City officials also committed to eliminating GO debt, which was accomplished in 2012. The results of these fiscal policies and actions have positioned the city well—strong reserves and cash balances, and low long-term liabilities. That said, long-term planning will be challenged by officials' commitment to minimize debt, which is resulting in aging infrastructure and by natural disasters, more specifically hurricanes and tropical storms. Setting aside $3.5 million for disaster recovery may not be sufficient if/when the city experiences a direct hit.

Havelock, North Carolina

Inputs: The state imposes property tax and debt limits on municipalities, including Havelock. The city operates under a council-manager form of government interactions with elected officials and city management are generally positive. There do not currently exist local policies regarding reserves or debt management. Other important inputs include the city's vulnerability to natural disasters, the most recent being Hurricane Florence in 2018, and the significance of two military bases that drive the local economy. The latter means that while Havelock was relatively insulated from the Great Recession, federal policies and inactions (e.g., federal government shutdowns) affected the community. Outputs and outcomes: The federal government shutdown in 2013 resulted in revenue losses; total revenues in FY2012 and FY2013 were lower than in 2011. Hurricane Florence damaged city infrastructure and resulted in inflows of federal dollars.

Policy actions: In response to the hurricane, officials drew down reserves, but few other policy actions were taken during the period. The interviewed official commented that the reliance on the military bases was concerning, and that Havelock needs to diversify its economy, but no formal policies/actions were documented. As a result, Havelock carries sizeable liquidity, including reserves that averaged 50.5% of expenditures during the study period and cash and investments that averaged 137% of current liabilities. The city carries no GO debt and other long-term liabilities have been stable/declining during the study period. Preparing for future natural disasters will still challenge Havelock.

Commerce, California

Inputs: Commerce operates under Proposition 13, the state monitors local finances and allows for bankruptcy filings. The city's economy is dominated by commercial sector, including a casino which draws a sizeable non-resident population. Commerce's economy and finances are susceptible to fiscal shocks, including the Great Recession and COVID-19. The city operates under a manager-council form of government and the relationship between management and elected officials has varied over time. Outputs and outcomes: Revenue volatility has been a key feature throughout the study period. This includes variation in total revenues from year to year, and pivoting from revenue sources (e.g., from property taxes to sales taxes).

Policy actions: Reflecting the volatility in revenues, expenditures also fluctuated, particularly in community development. As mentioned above, there was also a commitment to reduce reliance on property taxes and pivot to casino license, sales and to some degree transient occupation taxes. The fiscal effects of the Great Recession and COVID-19 forced spending cuts and offered opportunities to increase taxes (sales tax) and shift a larger share of pension and OPEB costs onto employees. Officials have also committed to reducing GO debt, which was eliminated in 2011. As a result, Commerce's long-term liabilities have fluctuated over time and given the policy toward GO bonds, debt has shifted to revenue obligation bonds. The city has strong liquidity, both in terms of reserves, and cash and investments.

Leading Approaches to Fiscal Condition Analysis

Our logic-model approach and its application to the five case studies reveals the complexity of assessing financial condition. Having some historical understanding of the context in which fiscal decisions are made, from our perspective, is essential when studying municipal fiscal condition. Our approach is not necessarily novel and it can be placed with a vast number of studies that have struggled with the same question—how to measure municipal financial condition. The following is a demonstration of three important approaches to financial condition analysis applied to our five case studies. An overview of the tools is provided in Table 14.1.

Table 14.1 Overview of Financial Condition Analytic Tools

Indicator/ Category	*Kloha et al. (2005)*	*Wang et al. (2007)*	*Moody's (2009)*
1	Two-year population growth	Cash ratio: (Cash + cash equivalents + investments)/Current liabilities	Institutional framework (10%)
2	Two-year real taxable value growth	Quick ratio: (Cash + cash equivalents + investments + receivables)/Current liabilities	Economy (30%)
3	Large drop in real taxable value decrease over a two-year period	Current ratio: Current assets/Current liabilities	Management (20%)
4	Current general fund expenditures as a percentage of taxable value	Operating ratio: Total revenues/Total expenses	liquidity (10%)
5	Current general fund operating deficit relative to general fund revenues	Surplus (deficit) per capita: Total surpluses (deficits)/Population	Budgetary performance (10%)
6	Prior general fund operating deficit (for two previous years)	Net asset ratio: Restricted and unrestricted net assets/Total assets	Budget flexibility (10%)
7	Current general fund balance as a percentage of general fund revenues	Long-term liability ratio: Long-term (non-current) liabilities/Total assets	Debt and contingent liabilities (10 %)
8	Current or previous year deficit in major fund	Long-term liability per capita: Long-term (non-current) liabilities/ Population	
9	General long-term debt as a percentage of taxable value	Tax per capita: Total taxes/ Population	
10		Revenue per capita: Total revenues/Population	
11		Expenses per capita: Total expenses/Population	

Kloha et al. (2005)

Kloha et al. (2005) provided the impetus for Michigan's initial financial monitoring system. The measures suggested by the authors incorporate a series of economic, demographic, and fiscal indicators. Also, this is one of the few financial health systems that include measures of change over time (see also Maher, Oh et al., 2020). It encompasses population change, assessed valuation change, expenditures as a percentage of valuation, operating deficits, fund balance, and long-term debt. Generally, it expects that municipalities experiencing declining population and valuation, running deficits, and carrying a large amount of debt are in financial distress.

Like Brown (1993), Kloha et al. used a scoring system that weights each measure equally and aggregates the scores associated with each measure to arrive at a total value that assesses financial condition. Using a 10-point scale, the authors classified a score of less than 5 as indicating that a municipality is "fiscally healthy," while a score of 5 suggests a "fiscal watch," 6 or 7 means "fiscal warning," and a score above 7 suggests "fiscal emergency" (Kloha et al., 2005, p. 321).

Applying this model to our case studies (see Table 14.2), we find that Flint was the only city in the fiscal warning position during the Great Recession. As discussed in Chapter 9, the reasons for Flint's poor fiscal health score included declining population (–2.1%) and property valuation (–2.2%), coupled with operating deficits (–15.9% in 2008) and negative fund balances (–15.8% in 2009). Interestingly, the city's financial challenges around the Great Recession prevented Flint from incurring more debt and forced governmental expenditures down relative to valuation (from 4.3% in 2008 to 3.9% in 2009). Comparing Flint's ratios heading into the pandemic (2017 to 2019), however, tells a different story. For instance, the city's summative score was just 3, suggesting a fiscally healthy city. While population continued to decline from 2017 to 2019 (by 1.3%), assessed valuation grew (by 4.0%) and general fund balances were 35% or more of general fund revenues. Nevertheless, despite this favorable rating by the Kloha et al. model, the city continued to run general fund operating deficits (–1.4% in 2009), government expenditures relative to valuation were substantially higher (9.0% in 2009), and long-term debt as a percentage of valuation was higher (3.6% in 2019).

North Lauderdale fared the best among our case studies (0 points) during both time periods. On all measures, North Lauderdale fared well: growth in population (e.g., 3.9% from 2007 to 2009) and assessed valuation (e.g., 20.0% from 2017 to 2019), low spending relative to valuation (e.g., 0.9% in 2009), no deficits, very strong fund balances (e.g., 117.9% in 2020), and low debt (zero since 2012). Commerce received scores of 2 in 2008 and 1 in 2020. For both periods, declining population was the source of a point and the second point in 2008 was GO debt relative to valuation. Wichita received a score of 3, representing

Table 14.2 Financial Condition of Case Studies Using Kloha et al.'s Measurements

		Flint	*Wichita*	*North Lauderdale*	*Havelock*	*Commerce*
Population change (two-year)	Great Recession	■ 2007 to 2009: –2.1% (1)	■ 2007 to 2009: 2.0% (0)	■ 2007 to 2009: 3.9% (0)	■ 2007 to 2009: 1.6% (0)	■ 2007 to 2009: –1.7% (1)
	COVID-19 pandemic	■ 2017 to 2019: –1.3% (1)	■ 2017 to 2019: 0.2% (0)	■ 2017 to 2019: 1.0% (0)	■ 2017 to 2019: –3.2% (1)	■ 2018 to 2020: –1.5% (1)
Assessed valuation growth (two-year)	Great Recession	■ 2007 to 2009: –2.2% (1)	■ 2007 to 2009: 6.8% (0)	■ 2007 to ■ 2009: 3.4% (0)	■ 2007 to ■ 2009: 22.6% (0)	■ 2007 to 2009: 10.1% (0)
	COVID-19 pandemic	■ 2017 to 2019: 4.0% (0)	■ 2017 to 2019: 7.4% (0)	■ 2017 to 2019: 20.0% (0)	■ 2017 to 2019: –37.7% (1)	■ 2018 to 2020: 4.9% (0)
Large real taxable value decrease	Great Recession	■ No (0)	■ No (0)	■ No (0)	■ No (0)	■ No (0)
	COVID-19 pandemic	■ No (0)	■ No (0)	■ No (0)	■ Yes (1)	■ No (0)
Governmental expenditures as a percentage of valuation	Great Recession	■ 2007: 3.4% (0) ■ 2008: 4.3% (0) ■ 2009: 3.9% (0)	■ 2007: 13.6% (1) ■ 2008: 13.8% (1) ■ 2009: 13.1% (1)	■ 2007: 0.9% (0) ■ 2008: 0.8% (0) ■ 2009: 0.9% (0)	■ 2007: 0.9% (0) ■ 2008: 0.8% (0) ■ 2009: 0.9% (0)	■ 2007: 1.7% (0) ■ 2008: 1.6% (0) ■ 2009: 1.7% (0)
	COVID-19 pandemic	■ 2017: 14.1% (1) ■ 2018: 10.2% (1) ■ 2019: 9.0% (1)	■ 2017: 12.2% (1) ■ 2018: 12.3% (1) ■ 2019: 12.9% (1)	■ 2017: 2.7% (0) ■ 2018: 2.5% (0) ■ 2019: 2.4% (0)	■ 2017: 1.1% (0) ■ 2018: 1.2% (0) ■ 2019: 1.5% (0)	■ 2018: 1.5% (0) ■ 2019: 1.4% (0) ■ 2020: 1.3% (0)
General fund operating deficits	Great Recession	■ 2007: –2.4% (1) ■ 2008: –15.9% (1) ■ 2009: –4.1% (1)	■ 0 (0)	■ 0 (0)	■ 0 (0)	■ 0 (0)
	COVID-19 pandemic	■ 2017: –7.7% (1) ■ 2008: –1.3% (1) ■ 2009: –1.4% (1)	■ 0 (0)	■ 0 (0)	■ 0 (0)	■ 0 (0)

(Continued)

Table 14.2 (Continued)

		Flint	*Wichita*	*North Lauderdale*	*Havelock*	*Commerce*
Prior general fund operating deficits	Great Recession	■ Yes (1)	■ No (0)	■ No (0)	■ No (0)	■ No (0)
	COVID-19 pandemic	■ No (0)	■ No (0)	■ No (0)	■ No (0)	■ No (0)
Size of general fund balance as a percentage of general fund revenues	Great Recession	■ 2007: 3.0% (1) ■ 2008: –10.3% (1) ■ 2007: –15.8% (1)	■ 2007: 6% (1) ■ 2008: 5.7% (1) ■ 2009: 5.8% (1)	■ 2007: 47.2% (0) ■ 2008: 62.9% (0) ■ 2009: 76.5% (0)	■ 2007: 69.3% (0) ■ 2008: 63.1% (0) ■ 2009: 66.6% (0)	■ 2007: 21.8% (0) ■ 2008: 26.8% (0) ■ 2009: 27.8% (0)
	COVID-19 pandemic	■ 2017: 34.8% (0) ■ 2018: 40.0% (0) ■ 2019: 45.9% (0)	■ 2017: 8.0% (1) ■ 2018: 8.1% (1) ■ 2019: 8.1% (1)	■ 2019: 111.4% (0) ■ 2020: 117.9% (0)	■ 2018: 75.1% (0) ■ 2019: 58.4% (0)	■ 2019: 84.7% (0) ■ 2020: 62.9% (0)
Deficits in major funds	Great Recession	■ Yes (1)	■ No (0)	■ No (0)	■ No (0)	■ No (0)
	COVID-19 pandemic	■ No (0)	■ No (0)	■ No (0)	■ No (0)	■ No (0)
General long-term debt as percentage of valuation	Great Recession	■ 2007: 0.3% (0) ■ 2008: 0.7% (0) ■ 2009: 0.3% (0)	■ 2007: 13.2% (1) ■ 2008: 12.2% (1) ■ 2009: 13.1% (1)	■ 2007: 0.3% (0) ■ 2008: 0.2% (0) ■ 2009: 0.2% (0)	■ 0 (0)	■ 2007: 47.1% (1) ■ 2008: 37.6% (1) ■ 2009: 25.0% (1)
	COVID-19 pandemic	■ 2017: 3.8% (0) ■ 2018: 3.9% (0) ■ 2019: 3.6% (0)	■ 2017: 15.9% (1) ■ 2018: 14.5% (1) ■ 2019: 14.3% (1)	■ Zero since 2012 (0)	■ 0 (0)	■ Zero since 2012 (0)
Total fiscal stress score	Great Recession	6	3	0	0	2
	COVID-19 pandemic	3	3	0	3	1

Source: U.S. Census Bureau; Each municipality's Annual Comprehensive Financial Reports

good fiscal health, for each of the two time periods. Wichita accrued points for government expenditures as a percentage of property valuation (more than 12% in each time period), general fund balances (less than 9% in each year), and debt relative to valuation (e.g., 14.3% in 2019). Interestingly, Havelock earned a score of zero during the Great Recession but three points leading up to the COVID-19 pandemic. The change was attributable to population change (growth from 2007 to 2009, but a 3.2% decline from 2017 to 2019) and valuation change (increase from 2007 to 2009, but a 37.7% decrease from 2017 to 2019).

Looking at Havelock and Wichita reminds us that the economic fluctuations caused by the Great Recession and COVID-19 had greatly varying impacts. In the case of Havelock, for example, the economic variability had less impact; what really mattered to the financial viability of this port city was federal policy regarding military operations and personnel, along with natural disasters (in this case, a severe hurricane). Sequestration had a ripple effect on Havelock because it not only affected property valuation but also shaped employment, sales, and residents' ability to make utility payments. Wichita had to endure shocks especially during the Great Recession due to the city's relationship with the aviation sector. These impacts are clearly different from what Commerce experienced during the same economic shocks, in view of the city's heavy reliance on casino revenues. Kloha et al. acknowledged that their scoring system puts very different cases in the same category of fiscal condition, masking important variation across municipalities.

These case studies also call into question the process of weighting measures and then aggregating them into a summative score. Flint illustrates the problem. During the Great Recession, Flint was clearly in fiscal crisis yet was rated only at the "fiscal warning" level. Although the city was running deficits in major funds and carrying negative fund balances, those obvious fiscal problems were offset by low debt (itself a by-product of Flint's fiscal challenges) and lower expenditures. Ironically, heading into the pandemic, Flint received a score indicating good fiscal health despite having continued general fund operating deficits, higher debt, and higher expenditures relative to property valuation.

Wang et al. (2007)

Wang et al. (2007) is one of the most cited examinations of fiscal condition and one of the first to incorporate government-wide financial statements into an analysis. Although the study focused on state-level fiscal condition analysis, it has also been widely cited and adopted in the municipal fiscal condition literature (see McDonald & Maher, 2020). Like many fiscal condition analyses (including ours), the authors focused on liquidity, operating position, and long-term liabilities (Table 14.1). Unlike Kloha et al. (2005), the Financial Condition Index (FCI) consists of fiscal metrics and intentionally omits economic indices. The authors asserted that "socioeconomic factors may affect financial condition, but they are not financial condition itself" (p. 5). Finally, similar to Kloha et al. (2005), Wang et al. (2007) standardized their 11 ratios and then collapsed them to arrive at one score.

Cash Ratio

The authors suggested several measures of cash solvency, including a cash ratio, quick ratio, and current ratio. Although each ratio captures slightly different attributes, there exists a high degree of correlation across them according to Stone et al. (2015). In fact, the cash ratio is a subset of values used to calculate the quick ratio, and the quick ratio is a subset of values used to calculate the current ratio.

Focusing on the quick ratio, in our first case study, Flint carried cash, investments, and receivables at dangerous levels during the Great Recession (in 2008, the ratio was 0.88). Heading into the COVID-19 pandemic, however, the city was in stronger position with a quick ratio of 11.5 in 2019, up from 5.63 in 2018 (see Table 14.3). Wichita carried cash, investments, and receivables at levels more than double current liabilities during the Great Recession. In 2019, the city's quick ratio was 3.8. Commerce is an interesting case because its liquidity scores were much stronger during the Great Recession than in the pre-pandemic years. In 2008, Commerce had a quick ratio of 12.9, only slightly higher than in 2007 and 2009 (11.1 and 12.5, respectively). In 2019, Commerce's cash, investments, and receivables were down to 6.6 times current liabilities.

The other two cities analyzed were flush with cash just before the pandemic (see Table 14.4). North Lauderdale reported cash, investments, and receivables 20.6 times current liabilities in 2017, and the city's quick ratio grew further to 24.3 in 2019. In 2017, Havelock carried cash, investments, and receivables 10.7 times current liabilities; in 2019, the city's quick ratio was even stronger at 12.4.

Budgetary Solvency

To capture budgetary solvency, Wang et al. (2007) suggested examining total revenues relative to total expenditures, as well as per-capita surpluses. Interestingly, missing from their analysis is one of the most common measures of financial condition: general fund balances. According to the assessment by Stone et al. (2015), "surplus per capita seems to be more prone to year-to-year fluctuations" (p. 99) and is not necessarily an effective measure of budgetary solvency.

With regard to comparing government revenues to expenditures, the expectation is that the ratio should be at least 1.0, meaning that revenues should be at least equal to expenditures. We can also conceive of a connection between municipal reserves and/or cash balances—which we can categorize as liquidity—and the revenues-to-expenditures ratio. Since municipalities are required to balance budgets, liquidity goes down when revenues are less than expenditures (to balance

Table 14.3 Financial Condition of Case Studies Using Wang et al.'s Measurements

Measurement	*2008*			*2019*		
	Flint, Michigan	*Wichita, Kansas*	*Commerce, California*	*Flint, Michigan*	*Wichita, Kansas*	*Commerce, California*
Cash ratio	0.45	0.85	12.44	5.65	1.89	6.12
Quick ratio	0.88	2.50	12.90	11.49	3.75	6.56
Current ratio	0.99	2.56	24.29	11.83	3.84	9.83
Operating ratio	0.91	1.09	1.12	1.41	1.02	1.02
Surplus (deficit) per capita	-450.53	132.09	605.85	595.88	31.13	1,336.18
Net asset ratio	0.09	0.13	0.60	-0.80	0.12	0.01
Long-term liability ratio	0.23	0.34	0.56	1.36	0.38	0.46
Long-term liability per capita	1,345.50	2,617.12	10,253.41	7,894.23	3,778.61	7,162.32
Tax per capita	372.03	564.00	4072.26	378.34	651.41	5,252.83
Revenue per capita	4,429.34	1,538.92	5,583.89	2,065.55	1,640.24	6,475.87
Expenses per capita	4,879.87	1,406.83	4,978.04	1,469.67	1,609.11	6,318.50

Source: Each municipality's Annual Comprehensive Financial Reports

Table 14.4 Financial Condition of North Lauderdale, Florida and Havelock, North Carolina

Measurement	*2017*		*2018*		*2019*	
	North Lauderdale, Florida	*Havelock, North Carolina*	*North Lauderdale, Florida*	*Havelock, North Carolina*	*North Lauderdale, Florida*	*Havelock, North Carolina*
Cash ratio	19.90	10.12	18.26	7.19	23.40	10.85
Quick ratio	20.56	10.73	18.94	7.70	24.26	12.40
Current ratio	22.33	11.15	20.44	8.38	24.45	13.07
Operating ratio	1.16	1.10	1.11	1.08	1.17	1.06
Surplus (deficit) per capita	161.06	85.43	122.19	68.29	188.41	67.17
Net asset ratio	0.61	0.34	0.63	0.30	0.65	0.30
Long-term liability ratio	0.09	0.35	0.08	0.39	0.08	0.40
Long-term liability per capita	262.87	1,026.19	244.41	1,272.19	273.28	1,278.78
Tax per capita	350.11	421.42	365.11	439.74	383.09	454.03
Revenue per capita	1,143.83	901.04	1,216.07	938.04	1,301.25	1,131.84
Expenses per capita	982.77	815.61	1,093.88	869.75	1,112.84	1,064.67

Source: Each municipality's Annual Comprehensive Financial Reports

the budget) and increases when revenues exceed expenditures. Flint, once again, stands out as the municipality with expenditures in excess of revenues throughout the Great Recession. In 2008, Flint's total governmental revenues were only 91% of expenditures. Prior to the pandemic, Flint's operating ratio improved sufficiently that in 2019, revenues were 140% of expenditures (and the city's reserves were growing). All the other case-study municipalities had strong operating positions (i.e., ratios greater than 1.0) during the periods analyzed.

Wang et al. (2007) also included a measure of surplus (or deficit) per capita to complete their operationalization of budgetary solvency. Contrary to the observation by Stone et al. (2015) cited above, this measure exhibited a high amount of consistency in our five case studies, in comparison to the revenues-to-expenditures ratio. In years when revenues exceeded expenditures, the per-capita surplus measure was positive. In contrast, when the revenues-to-expenditures ratio was less than 1.0 (Flint in 2008), the per-capita surplus measure was negative.

Long-run Solvency

Wang et al. (2007) identified three long-run solvency ratios, which "paint a similar picture" according to Stone et al. (2015, p. 100). These ratios included restricted and unrestricted net assets as a percentage of total assets, long-term liabilities as a percentage of total assets, and per-capita long-term liabilities. Focusing on long-term liabilities, whether they are measured relative to assets or population, there were only marginal changes during the years studied in most instances, especially for Wichita, Havelock, and North Lauderdale. For Flint, however, long-term liabilities were lowest during the Great Recession and markedly higher during the years immediately before the pandemic. Does this mean that Flint's financial health was in worse condition around 2019? Obviously not. But this growth in long-term liabilities can be construed as positive since the city had regained creditworthiness something it lacked during the Great Recession.

Service Solvency

According to Wang et al. (2007), "Service-level solvency refers to an organization's ability to provide and sustain a service level that citizens require and desire." They operationalize service solvency with per-capita measures of revenues, expenditures, and taxes. Our five case studies offer interesting perspectives on these measures. Comparing the measures across the municipalities yields very different results that call their interpretation into question. In 2019, per-capita revenues ranged from $1,301 (North Lauderdale) to $6,476 (Commerce). For the same year, per-capita expenditures ranged from $1,065 (Havelock) to $6,318 (Commerce), while per-capita taxes were lowest in North Lauderdale ($383) and highest in Commerce ($5,253). A quick assessment of these data would suggest that

Commerce has weaker service solvency than the other four municipalities since its per-capita figures are much greater. As our case study noted, however, Commerce's population triples during the day due to its casino and shopping center. In this case, therefore, understanding the context is critical to interpreting the results. Furthermore, using Flint as an example, how would tracking per-capita revenues, expenditures, and taxes truly reflect service solvency? Flint's per-capita expenditures were $4,880 in 2008 and only $1,470 in 2019. Does that make Flint's service solvency stronger in 2019 than in 2009? The city's crippling water crisis calls into question the appropriateness of such an interpretation.

Validity Analysis

To the credit of Wang et al. (2007), they expended considerable effort on assessing the validity of their measurement system. They asserted, "In cases where a measure consists of multiple indicators, a method to estimate random measurement errors is to assess a measure's internal consistency. . .. Large variation (or lack of correlation) among indicators indicates large random errors" (p. 10). We will apply this approach to our case studies for FY2019.

Using Pearson correlations[1] (see Table 14.5), we find, not surprisingly, that the cash, quick, and current ratios are highly correlated across the five cities (0.97 to 0.99). The cash ratio is also correlated with the net asset ratio (0.66) and negatively correlated with long-term liabilities (–0.51). The operating ratio is negatively correlated with the net asset ratio (–0.66) and positively correlated with long-term liabilities (0.78). The net asset ratio is strongly correlated with long-term liabilities (–0.98), and the surplus ratio is strongly correlated with per-capita taxes (0.90), revenues (0.95), and expenses (0.92). These latter correlations reflect the similarity between the denominators; for both the net asset ratio and long-term liabilities, the denominator is total assets, whereas for the surplus ratio, taxes, revenues, and expenses, the denominator is population.

We also examined the correlation between the 11 indicators used by Wang et al. (2007) and socioeconomic measures (per-capita personal income, unemployment rate, assessed valuation, and population). These results show a lack of consistency. For instance, the cash, quick, and current ratios are negatively associated with unemployment rate and population, suggesting that where unemployment is high and population is large, municipalities tend to have a lower cash solvency. The operating ratio, however, is negatively associated with per-capita personal income and positively associated with unemployment, implying that in municipalities with lower levels of personal income and higher unemployment, operating ratios will be higher.

The framework constructed by Wang et al. (2007) has received much academic attention. As discussed above, it has the capacity to offer considerable explanation of a municipality's fiscal condition. The authors' approach is also conceptually

Table 14.5 Pearson Correlation Among Wang et al.'s Measurements

	Cash ratio	*Quick ratio*	*Current ratio*	*Operating ratio*	*Surplus (deficit) per capita*	*Net asset ratio*	*Long-term liability ratio*	*Tax per capita*	*Revenue per capita*	*Expenses per capita*	*Per capita personal income*	*Unemployment rate*	*Assessed value per $1000*	*Population*
Cash ratio	1.00													
Quick ratio	0.97	1.00												
Current ratio	0.97	0.99	1.00											
Operating ratio	0.11	0.35	0.30	1.00										
Surplus (deficit) per capita	–0.25	–0.28	–0.13	0.03	1.00									
Net asset ratio	0.65	0.45	0.46	–0.66	–0.37	1.00								
Long-term liability ratio	–0.51	–0.28	–0.31	0.78	0.27	–0.98	1.00							
Tax per capita	–0.26	–0.40	–0.25	–0.42	0.90	–0.04	–0.11	1.00						
Revenue per capita	–0.32	–0.42	–0.27	–0.27	0.95	–0.19	0.05	0.99	1.00					
Expenses per capita	–0.31	–0.43	–0.28	–0.37	0.92	–0.11	–0.04	1.00	0.99	1.00				
Per capita personal income	–0.27	–0.40	–0.46	–0.68	–0.49	0.44	–0.55	–0.14	–0.22	–0.14	1.00			
Unemployment rate	–0.42	–0.20	–0.20	0.80	0.39	–0.96	0.99	–0.01	0.15	0.05	–0.67	1.00		
Assessed value per $1000	–0.24	–0.27	–0.39	–0.28	–0.64	0.20	–0.26	–0.45	–0.48	–0.43	0.89	–0.40	1.00	
Population	–0.52	–0.52	–0.63	–0.21	–0.44	–0.08	–0.02	–0.31	–0.30	–0.27	0.83	–0.16	0.95	1.00

Source: Each municipality's Annual Comprehensive Financial Reports

consistent with most studies, in that it applies fiscal metrics that capture budgetary, operating, long-term, and service-level solvencies. One key contribution of this model is to incorporate government-wide financial information rather than relying on fund-based metrics that can vary widely across entities. However, to what degree does this framework help us better understand fiscal health in our case studies? The results seem to be mixed. Some metrics (e.g., long-term liabilities) are consistent with our knowledge of the cities' status. However, the tracking of per-capita taxes, revenues, and expenditures as proxies for service-level solvency proves to be unpersuasive. Not only do the measures inaccurately capture service solvency, but we are left wondering about how to interpret them. The assumption appears to be that high per-capita values are a sign of poor fiscal health, but there is little justification for such an assertion.

Interestingly, the authors ignored reserves and instead focused on cash, receivables, and investments. This decision runs counter to most academic and professional guides used to assess fiscal health. Our analysis revealed that except for Flint during the Great Recession, the case-study cities carried large cash ratios. Whether that is a sign of budgetary solvency remains open to debate. The same idea applies to the operating and long-term solvency measures suggested by Wang et al. Lower measures of long-term solvency can be indicative of strong fiscal health or of poor long-term planning and inadequate attention to infrastructure.

One important takeaway from this exercise is an appreciation of context. Relying solely on fiscal metrics can lead to misunderstandings of the circumstances driving those numbers. In the case of Commerce, for instance, a lack of appreciation of the daily population flow into the city due to its casino and shopping centers, which leads to increased costs, distorts per-capita figures and suggests a fiscal condition inconsistent with reality. Similarly, without a meaningful standard or benchmark for most of these ratios, we are left making comparisons to other entities, on the assumption that relative comparisons can indicate fiscal health or weakness. Such an assertion without an understanding of context leaves much to be desired.

Our correlation analyses revealed inconsistent associations or lack of association between a number of fiscal condition and socioeconomic measures. As Wang et al. noted, a lack of correlation calls into question the internal validity of the measures. From our perspective, the lack of consistency in the correlation analysis confirms our assertion that a composite measure can mask important variations in aggregate fiscal metric scores, and that therefore the more appropriate strategy is to consider fiscal condition analysis as a dynamic process that requires assessment across various fiscal, economic, demographic, structural, and political elements.

Moody's (2009)

Moody's rating process is proprietary, but the company provided a framework for understanding it following the Great Recession. In a 2009 report, Moody's explained that its assessment of municipal fiscal health is broken down into the following categories: institutional framework (10%), economy (30%), management (20%), liquidity (10%), budgetary performance (10%), budget flexibility (10%), and debt and contingent liabilities (10%). Moody's tax base analysis incorporates absolute valuation and historic growth rates, a qualitative assessment of the stability of the local economy, and the community's relative sociodemographic strength (Moody's, 2009).

Economy

Since GO bonds are generally repaid by property tax collections, Moody's examines five-year trends in assessed valuation, full valuation, and housing permits. The economic analysis involves the type of economy—e.g., urban versus rural, industrial types, and diversity of sectors. Baseline wealth and demographic assessment can include population trends, income trends, and, in comparison, to the surrounding region, unemployment rates, and associated trends.

We know that Flint has struggled with population retention and economic degradation for years. In Chapter 9, we learned that Flint's assessed property valuation fell from $1.7 billion in 2000 to $743 million in 2019. Similarly, the city's population dropped from 127,100 to 95,943 during the same period. Other socioeconomic metrics fared no better, including increased unemployment and loss of personal income.

The demographic and socioeconomic characteristics of the other four case studies are mixed. Wichita experienced growth in valuation during the 20-year study period, but some sectors of the economy struggled. For example, the city's unemployment rate more than doubled between 2007 (4.4%) and 2010 (9.5%), and per-capita income fell during that three-year period. North Lauderdale's valuation took a hit following the recession, yet its per-capita personal income grew significantly during those years. Havelock's assessed valuation has dropped precipitously from 2013 to 2019, and the city's population fell by 15.4% from 2010 to 2019. On the positive side, Havelock's unemployment rate remained below county and state rates, and its median household income was consistent with that of the county and state (U.S. Census Bureau, 2021). While valuation grew in Commerce nearly every year over the last several years, other sectors of the economy have been highly susceptible to economic downturns. Furthermore, the city's unemployment rate remained high and was in double digits from 2009 to 2015, peaking at 23.3% in 2011. Per-capita personal income was very low ($16,380 in 2019) compared to the national average ($56,490) and California ($66,619), and it was also stagnant—$16,059 in 2008 and $16,380 in 2019.

Financial Strength

From Moody's perspective, financial strength is largely driven by general fund reserves. The rating agency also considers liquidity (cash and cash position) and, interestingly, the degree to which municipal officials have control over financial operations. The latter can include matters such as TELs,[2] requirements for voter approval of revenue increases, and reliance on intergovernmental revenues. The ability to adjust expenditures also plays a role in Moody's assessment. This includes both the capacity and "demonstrated willingness to do so" (Moody's, 2009, p. 9).

Moody's (2009) noted that "a strong government management team prepares well for economic downturns, maintains strong controls during boom times, and manages well during all phases of an economic cycle" (p. 12). Much of this assessment is qualitative and thus does not yield the level of scrutiny required for more quantitative econometric analyses of financial condition. Moody's assessment covers the management team's ability to accurately forecast revenues and expenditures, the existence and use of long-term planning including debt management and capital planning, adherence to policies such as those governing fund balances, and the validity of said policies based on the revenue structure of the community.

As previously noted, Flint's cash reserves have been weak but improved within the past few years, reaching 25% of governmental expenditures in 2019. Flint remains heavily reliant on intergovernmental aid from both state and federal sources, and the state-imposed TEL is stricter than those in many other states (Stallmann et al., 2017). A review of Flint's ACFRs finds a commitment to policy development and longer-range requirements for the creation and maintenance of a strategic plan. These requirements include the adoption of a biennial budget and five-year financial projections, along with a budget stabilization fund (City of Flint, 2020).

Wichita's cash reserves are lower than generally expected but are consistent with the city's policy, and they remained stable during the Great Recession. City management appears solid, in that appropriate financial management policies are in place and the city operates under a manager-council form of government. At the state level, Wichita has little reliance on intergovernmental aid, and its state-imposed TEL is much less strict than those in many other states. As an interviewee noted, "TELs had no impact" on their fiscal decision making.

Moving to the Havelock case, the city's cash balances were strong, and its reserves remained high. City management has a good working relationship with elected officials, and the commissioners appear to be listening to the management team's fiscal advice. State-level policies focused on limiting property tax rate growth and GO debt. The city's declining assessed property valuation could pose challenges for Havelock under state-imposed TELs. The state's debt limits have no impact on Havelock, however, since officials have been committed to avoiding the issuance of GO debt.

Commerce was in a strong position in terms of cash balances and reserves. The city has financial policies, a manager-council form of government, and a solid management team. Importantly, the finance department has remained stable while the city has gone through the Great Recession and the COVID-19 pandemic. The finance department successfully implemented short- and long-term strategies to respond to these external shocks, such as spending cuts, position eliminations, keeping business taxes low to help with retention and attraction, minimizing debt by using pay-as-you-go financing strategy for capital projects, and diversifying the city's revenues. California's Proposition 13 is known for limiting property taxes and property valuation growth. The state also monitors municipal finances with an online dashboard (California State Auditor, 2022). The most recent dashboard data show Commerce to be in solid fiscal position, and the city's heavy reliance on casino and sales tax revenues means that property taxes are low and unaffected by Proposition 13.

Debt Profile

Moody's focuses on debt relative to full valuation. The actual debt level calculation becomes quite specific; for instance, is the debt secured from revenues other than property taxes? Does it include enterprise funds? Does it include school districts? The level of debt and repayment scheduling also receive scrutiny from Moody's. The debt analysis extends beyond GO debt and includes pension liabilities and OPEBs, as these can be considered constraints on financial maneuverability.

Flint has had limited access to GO bonds over the past decade, because rating agencies lost faith in the city's ability to repay the debt. As a result, the city's infrastructure has been deteriorating (City of Flint, 2014). Flint's pension and OPEB liabilities are another area of concern. Not only has the city poorly managed those funds, but they have also been underfunded, and today a far greater number of retirees are receiving benefits than there are employees paying into those plans.

As discussed in Chapter 10, whether measured in terms of GO debt relative to property valuation, debt service, or long-term liabilities relative to assets, Wichita is in fine shape. Wichita officials noted that they are well within existing debt limits. With regard to pension and OPEB liabilities, Wichita manages two pensions: one for general employees and the other for police and fire. In both cases, the pension systems are well-funded. In 2019, Wichita's general employee net pension liability relative to pension assets was 81.4%, down from 98.3% in 2018. This difference was largely the result of poor returns on investments (down $39.5 million in 2019). The police and fire pension's ratio of liabilities to assets was 82.7% in 2019 and 99.95% in 2018. This fund lost $44 million in investment value in 2019, compared to a gain of $103 million in 2018. In 2018 and 2019, Wichita carried $35 million in OPEB liabilities, but there was sufficient coverage for these liabilities.

Currently, North Lauderdale does not carry any GO debt. If the city can sustain its infrastructure while using this pay-as-you-go approach, it should not have any fiscal problems. Long-term planning, does however, appear to be a concern. As noted in the city's 2020 ACFR:

> The risk of hurricane loss is a continual concern for the city. As a smaller local government located in South Florida, immediate access to resources in an emergency is critical. Therefore, city administration has assigned $3,500,000 of general fund balance for disaster recovery. In addition, aging infrastructure is in need of repair and replacement. Resources included in the general fund balance will help funding some of the costs of renovating the aging infrastructure.
>
> (p. iii)

Currently, Commerce does not carry any GO debt, and its most recent large ($30 million) revenue bonds were incurred to pay down existing revenue bonds. As of 2020, however, Commerce was carrying a net pension liability of $32.6 million, which represented 46% of total governmental revenues. OPEBs for Commerce employees consist of medical insurance benefits for employees and their spouses. This covers the gap between retirement and Medicare coverage at age 65. In 2019, 164 active and 153 inactive employees had OPEB coverage. The city uses a pay-as-you go model to fund OPEBs, and in 2020, it contributed $6.7 million for premiums. The city's net OPEB liability was $59.9 million. According to the state's financial dashboard, OPEB funding is Commerce's greatest fiscal risk.

Moody's Rating

Prior to the pandemic, Flint's creditworthiness was highly suspect, and in late 2006, Moody's withdrew its rating completely. As of 2020, Moody's had yet to offer a rating for the city. In the Wichita case, the city's creditworthiness was rated Aa1 prior to the COVID-19 pandemic, meaning that the city demonstrated "very strong creditworthiness relative to other U.S. municipal or tax-exempt issuers or issues" (Moody's, 2009, p. 23). The rating agency typically cites Wichita's tax base and its importance to the Kansas region as positives. Favorable feedback by Moody's has also been expressed regarding the size of the city's reserves and management capabilities. Notably, although some comparison benchmarks are used, such as reserves relative to in-state peers, Moody's analysis tends to be more community-specific. Since North Lauderdale, Havelock, and Commerce do not carry any GO debt, they are not rated by Moody's.

The approach used by Moody's is informative and is consistent with our open-systems framework. The main challenges associated with broader application of Moody's methodology is its proprietary nature, which prevents us from knowing how it could be used to evaluate different municipalities in a consistent manner. In addition, it is used only for entities seeking to borrow; thus, three of our five case-study cities are not assessed by Moody's at all.

Concluding Thoughts

Kloha et al. (2005), Wang et al. (2007), and Moody's (2009) are typical of the array of assessment options available to students, academics, and practitioners. These particular tools were discussed and compared with our open-systems framework and case study results because they demonstrate the importance of connecting the appropriate fiscal condition analysis methodology with the intent of the analysis. For instance, the model presented by Wang et al. (2007) is designed for academic audiences interested in conducting quantitative analyses with large datasets. The key to such an analysis is data reliability. One reason why researchers appreciate government-wide financial statements in ACFRs is that they provide apples-to-apples comparability, regardless of the type of government. Similarly, conducting a financial condition analysis is much more efficient if its operationalization can be condensed into just one measure (Wang et al., 2007). Some downsides of this approach have been highlighted (see McDonald & Maher, 2020), including potential measurement error. From a practitioner's perspective, these measures can also be difficult to explain to the community's stakeholders.

For those who are more interested in understanding potential causes of fiscal position in conjunction with the financial condition analysis, Kloha et al. (2005), Moody's (2009), and our model may be more appropriate. Each of these models focuses on both fiscal condition metrics and the community's socioeconomic, structural, and demographic attributes that are most known to interact with municipal finances. Studies of the approach proposed by Kloha et al. have found that using a set of metrics to identify and predict fiscally distressed communities is very challenging because, as we have observed throughout this book, no two communities are alike. Being able to predict fiscal distress is the holy grail of this research, but more work is needed to get there. Consider, for instance, the rating agencies that exist for the very purpose of assessing fiscal risk. Although relatively few municipalities have ever filed for bankruptcy or defaulted on debt payments, the level of fiscal distress caused by the Great Recession forced rating agencies such as Moody's to recalibrate their models (Adelino et al., 2017).

Notes

1. Pearson correlation coefficients measure the relationship between two continuous variables. The absolute value of the coefficient can range from 0 to 1.0, where 1.0

represents perfect correlation between two variables and 0 represents no correlation, also known as covariation, between two variables. The Pearson correlation can be negative or positive, indicating the direction of the relationship between the variables.

2. Maher et al. (2016) demonstrated, for instance, that local bond ratings are stronger—if all other factors are held constant—when expenditure limits are imposed and weaker under revenue limits.

Chapter 15

Conclusions and Lessons Learned

Municipal finances are constantly evolving, so any useful examination of their fiscal picture must be comprehensive. Multiple events over the past couple of decades have kept academics and practitioners focused on financial condition analysis. These events include economic shocks such as the Great Recession and the fallout of the COVID-19 pandemic, as well as bankruptcies that befell such cities as Detroit, Michigan, and Stockton, California. State involvement in municipal fiscal affairs has escalated beyond TELs, balanced-budget requirements, and debt limits to monitoring of local finances and, in some cases, takeovers of municipal operations. To help municipal governments prepare for and anticipate these challenges, scholars, practitioners, policymakers, and think tanks alike have paid considerable attention to efforts to develop models to assess the fiscal condition of municipalities and, hopefully, predict fiscal stress before it occurs.

This book has sought to contribute to the discussion by offering an open-systems framework that can be used to assess municipal financial health. The framework we provide emphasizes the impacts of the environment, settings, and structures in which municipalities operate. Fiscal environments include economic and demographic patterns along with external pressures from stakeholders including federal and state governments, interest groups, and citizens. Institutional settings are also crucial; for example, nearly every state now imposes TELs. These environmental factors can build over time. For instance, the economic and demographic shifts occurring in cities such as Flint and Detroit, Michigan, have

DOI: 10.4324/9780429270765-15

been present for decades, yet appropriate response strategies to ensure financial stability have been elusive.

Municipalities are increasingly affected by events beyond their control. Although federal and state governments have helped offset some costs through emergency declaration powers, the immediate costs are borne by municipal governments. Tornadoes, hurricanes, wildfires, and other disasters require rapid assistance to those affected and can have crippling consequences on revenues. Similarly, while municipalities have always been affected by economic fluctuations, the experiences of the Great Recession and the COVID-19 pandemic have been unprecedented. More than a decade after the Great Recession, its depth and breadth have left many municipalities still in worse shape. The suddenness of COVID-19, which forced entire municipalities to impose lockdowns and close businesses while imposing unprecedented demands on public services—including health monitoring, vaccination management, mask mandates, and the associated political strains associated with each of these measures—has left officials reeling across the country.

These events all function as fiscal environments affecting a municipality's fiscal health. In turn, they necessitate effective internal management. Internal structures include the form of government, policies, and procedures related to financial management, and the administrative team's ability to gain respect among stakeholders. This is where we diverge from most academic studies of fiscal health. Many scholars make a demarcation between the assessment of financial information and the factors that may impact those fiscal metrics. Although this difference may seem unnecessary, it is a very important part of an assessment process. When scholars have included variables designed to capture features of management structure and capacity, the results have been underwhelming. This may be a result of the relatively blunt instruments at scholars' disposal, such as categorizing the form of government. As we noted in the Wichita case study, the actual impacts of internal structures are more subtle and nuanced. This may also explain rating agencies' focus on management structure and capacity in their assessments of governments' creditworthiness.

What We Have Learned

We observed in Chapter 2 that the degree of heterogeneity in municipalities across the states, in terms of fiscal environments under which municipalities operate, makes studying municipal fiscal health and strategies to promote it quite complicated. An attribute or external event that affects the fiscal health of one municipality may not apply to other municipalities within the same state, let alone in other states. Although this heterogeneity across municipalities and states creates challenges for scholars of government finance, policymakers, and practitioners can still learn from a set of best practices. Our aim is to help these municipal policymakers and practitioners make the most informed decisions possible. Applying lessons learned in other communities can help to promote the fiscal health of individual municipalities, even if the contexts differ somewhat.

In Chapter 3, we described how municipal finances have changed over time. Important changes have included growth in demand for municipal services since the 1970s, although this growth has varied by region, at least partly due to differences in ideological perspectives. The municipal revenue picture has also shifted, in the sense that sales taxes and, to a lesser extent, income taxes now represent a larger share of municipal revenues. Fees have also grown as a percentage of total revenues. This shifting revenue picture was driven by declining intergovernmental revenue and property taxes, the latter source being constrained by TELs and political pressure. One perspective on this revenue shift is positive, in that municipal revenues have become more diversified (Carroll, 2009; Hendrick, 2002), a development that can better insulate cities from external shocks. Conversely, greater reliance on elastic revenues means that economic changes will have a greater impact on revenue collections. We saw this dynamic play out following the onset of the COVID-19 pandemic (McDonald & Larson, 2020). The empirical evidence on the effects of revenue diversification, however, remains inconclusive (Park & Park, 2018).

Chapter 3 also pushed us to think about unresolved fundamental questions regarding municipal finances. For example, what is the optimal level of government size and growth? From a public-choice perspective, growth in municipal government expenditures is a sign of inefficiency. Interestingly, the cause of this inefficiency is a fundamental principal-agent problem: government officials have more information about the community's finances than taxpayers, and this unequal distribution of information enables government officials to tax more than would be the case if taxpayers were fully informed. In this case, we have policy divergence between scholars, practitioners, and taxpayers. Public-choice scholars assert that the principal-agent problem could be minimized with a more salient tax structure that focuses on property taxes and fees for services. Ironically, however, municipal revenue structures are becoming more, not less, complicated for reasons that include voters' and state policymakers' disapproval of property tax growth and calls by professional associations (and some academics) for more diversified revenue structures.

We suggest that more community-level analysis of municipalities' financial condition could help resolve some of these questions at both the community and theoretical levels. For instance, are current fiscal restrictions on municipal governments effective or not? Should they be sustained, revised, or removed? Second, is the current American municipal revenue system appropriate to meet increasing service needs and spending? Do municipal revenue structures add to the principal-agent problem by being unnecessarily complicated? Are they resilient enough to address such needs? Third, what would be the long-term outcomes of increasing municipal reliance on debt financing? Can municipal governments afford greater debt with improved economic conditions? If not, should they be subject to stricter controls in addition to the recent GASB requirements? All these questions deserve further attention from scholars and practitioners.

Following thorough examination of these inputs and outputs contained in our open-systems model, we shifted to the assessment of financial condition, as a system outcome. As noted in Chapters 4 and 5, this is nothing new. However, the data and techniques have changed over time. Our approach emphasizes the importance of understanding financial information within a given municipality's context. In other words, the inputs and outputs we identified are necessary antecedents for placing fiscal measures in the appropriate context. The specific fiscal measures used depend to some degree on the purpose of the analysis and the intended audience. That said, students of financial condition analysis and practitioners interested in assessing their community's financial health are advised to calculate the following ratios and examine the trend pattern of each ratio.

Revenues and expenditures

- Per-capita total general fund or government-wide revenues
- Per-capita total general fund or government-wide expenditures
- Property taxes relative to total governmental fund revenues
- Intergovernmental aid relative to total revenues (at the general fund or government-wide level)

Operating position

- General fund surplus (deficit) relative to general fund expenditures
- Unrestricted general fund balance as a percentage of general fund expenditures
- Total governmental cash, investments, and receivables relative to current liabilities
- Unrestricted net assets from governmental (or business-type) activities relative to total expenditures on these activities

Long-term liabilities

- General obligation debt relative to total assessed valuation
- Debt service expenditures relative to total governmental fund revenues
- Total governmental long-term liabilities relative to total assets

These ratios are most consistently associated with fiscal stress measures and are most salient among community stakeholders. One key decision point is how to analyze these metrics—compared to other communities or over time. This is not a decision to be taken lightly and is complicated by the challenges associated with identifying peer communities that have similar socioeconomic attributes, organizational structure, and fiscal institutions. Furthermore, professional organizations offer limited guidance on what is deemed best practice for debt levels, reserves, and other measures. Maher (2022) and Maher, Ebdon et al. (2020) suggested tracking five years of data to assess change over time. Finally, assessing other measures may be useful based on the characteristics of a particular community. Such additional measures may include reliance on intergovernmental aid, as well as pension and OPEB liabilities relative to assets.

There are a wide range of potential measures or indicators of fiscal health, ranging from simple (such as the ratio of expenditures to revenues) to complex. Some of the various approaches we have reviewed could become a source of information overload, resulting in "paralysis by analysis." One must keep in mind the audience for the analysis. Does it consist of professional administrators and finance officers of the government, or elected members of the government board or council? Are the audience representatives from the various credit rating agencies or investment bankers who are assisting in the issuance of public debt? A detailed analysis of the municipality's fiscal health in the form prepared for credit agency representatives would likely overwhelm and confuse most elected officials or concerned citizens. A practitioner may want to consider using different sets of fiscal health measures or indicators depending on the intended audience.

One word of warning about making direct comparisons between municipalities: institutional differences that distinguish municipal governments can result in some unexpected results. For example, it was noted previously that some municipalities such as Anchorage, Alaska, and Boston, Massachusetts, are responsible for K-12 education and therefore have sizable education spending. Most other cities in the United States have school districts rather than the municipalities that are responsible for K-12. Ignoring these service provision distinctions could lead to incorrect inferences. When making direct comparisons between two local governments, we must be careful to consider the capability and responsibility of each government.

Care should also be taken to incorporate unique institutional differences at the municipal level to avoid incorrect interpretations. For example, one municipal government may be performing contract work for neighboring governments. Alternatively, state statutes may or may not mandate certain services that are embedded within the fiscal data. Comparing a municipality under such mandates to another that does not face such mandates could result in incorrect interpretations of the analysis. In addition to being diligent in selecting suitable comparison municipalities, one could make comparisons to group-wide averages. These groups could be based on population, geographic location, or even industrial bases.

Chapter 6 offered an assessment of municipal fiscal condition that focused on ten selected measures. We noted that in 2016, municipalities were generally in good shape but there were some potential warning signs. The study showed significant variation among municipal governments by population size, region, and quartile. Using an analysis based on quartiles (see also Brown, 1993), we also indicated a distribution by population size, which can help municipal officers in conducting fiscal condition analyses. Perhaps the most important finding in this chapter was the great deal of variation in fiscal position. From a policy standpoint, this means that municipal fiscal decisions and policies (discussed extensively in Chapter 3) often result in varying policy outcomes. Such different policy outcomes can survive as part of the policy or system process, leading to different policy inputs through feedback loops.

We also explored the important role of states in understanding municipal finances (Chapter 8). This includes fiscal policies such as TELs, balanced-budget requirements, and debt limits. In addition, we discussed state policies regarding bankruptcy filings and state monitoring systems. It is perhaps not well understood that while the majority of states allow municipal bankruptcies, exactly what steps are or are not allowed can vary greatly, along with the state's role in these filings. Beyond bankruptcy filings, there has been a growing trend toward state monitoring of local government finances. Most states merely collect financial information, but some have taken more aggressive positions that can even include takeover of municipal management operations. Michigan is the best-known example in the latter category, since the state government assumed management of Detroit and Flint. The effects of state monitoring systems and takeovers are important but underexplored. Interestingly, existing results are inconclusive.

One notable feature of our open-systems model is that it does not end with presenting the municipality's fiscal picture but requires understanding the strategies adopted by municipal policymakers during periods of fiscal distress (Chapter 7). We focused on the most recent major fiscal challenge, COVID-19, and reviewed survey results and comments received from municipal officials. Response strategies were generally short-term in nature and included looking for management efficiencies, cutting discretionary spending, seeking financial assistance (not surprising since the CARES Act provided some reimbursement for local expenses), and delaying capital expenditures. But none of these responses are sustainable over the longer term, particularly deferral of capital expenditures. Professional associations such as the NLC and GFOA have offered suggestions for communities reeling from fiscal shocks. These recommendations include realigning budgetary practices with the community's economic base, adopting sound budgetary practices, and long-range planning. The most effective communities view fiscal shocks as a unique opportunity to pursue major changes in fiscal practices that can better position themselves for the long run and would not be possible under normal fiscal circumstances.

Our presentation of five case studies in Chapters 9 to 13 demonstrated how different environmental factors impacted municipal finances, along with how management can mitigate some of those effects. In Flint, Michigan, city officials had been dealing with decades of economic and social decline, resulting in a misalignment between fiscal inputs and outputs. This misalignment meant increased reliance on intergovernmental aid, drawing down reserves, and taking on debt in an unsustainable manner. Although Flint did not declare bankruptcy, Michigan's governors declared financial emergencies in 2002 and 2011. The state takeover of Flint's political and fiscal decision making resulted in significant developments, including fee increases, pension reforms, and a water crisis. While the city's fiscal picture improved to the point at which management was returned to city officials in 2015, fiscal challenges remain.

Wichita, Kansas, is another example of a municipality impacted by economic decline. The city lost a sizable number of aerospace manufacturing jobs over the past 20 years. In addition, extensive income tax cuts led to reduced intergovernmental aid. Yet despite these external shocks, the city's financial picture remained stable. Commerce, California, offered an example of a suburban municipality that relies heavily on commercial activities and a casino to insulate the city from property tax limits; unfortunately, these revenue sources can drop precipitously in times of economic decline, such as during the business shutdowns caused by COVID-19. In the longer term, Commerce continues to struggle with population decline, high unemployment, and low per-capita personal income. How the city sustains its fiscal position despite these economic and demographic challenges will determine its long-term success.

North Lauderdale, Florida, is a municipality heavily dependent on property taxes in a state that limits property taxes and assessment increases. Furthermore, its location in southeast Florida presents the ongoing threat of hurricanes and tropical storms that require planning and preparation. This context poses unique long-term planning challenges. The Havelock, North Carolina, case study diverges from the others because its fiscal environment is driven by one very important source, U.S. Marine Corps military bases. Havelock was among the few municipalities largely unaffected by the Great Recession but was significantly impacted when Marines were deployed oversees. One of the city's greatest challenges is overreliance on the military bases for its economy and revenues. Finance officials noted that the city needs to diversify its economy and its tax base, but both are difficult steps to achieve.

Final Thoughts

There is an extensive body of work on municipalities' fiscal condition and fiscal stress. We have explored a large portion of it in this book. What remains to be studied or understood? The exploration of a municipality's fiscal health is as much an art as a science. Each of the models that have emerged from the literature provides its own snapshot of financial condition. In essence, they treat fiscal health as a science, using measures and models in an attempt to discern definitive answers regarding a municipality's condition. But any exploration of financial condition should be undertaken and interpreted with care. No single measurement or model provides the full picture of what is happening within a municipality. To understand a municipality's condition, we must take a step back and view the situation more broadly, interpreting the data and making conclusions based on the story that the data tell.

In this book, we have offered a new way to structure the approaches offered by our predecessors. We also emphasize the need to conduct thorough fiscal condition analyses that focus on the features of the municipality of interest that most directly affect its fiscal health. The fundamental, pervasive challenge in municipal financial condition analysis is data availability, at two levels. First, our approach poses serious challenges for scholars (including ourselves) who are interested in testing hypotheses with large datasets, since the information we recommend obtaining is simply not available for large quantitative analyses. The second problem is timing. Scholars and practitioners have focused primarily on retrospective examination of financial data due to lags in reporting. There is no easy way to resolve these challenges, which call for finding new, innovative methods of data collection at the local, state, and national levels.

Appendix A

Pros and Cons of the Census Bureau's Survey of State and Local Government Finances

Using data from the Census Bureau's Survey of State and Local Government Finances (hereafter the Census Finance Survey) for research and policy analysis has been subject to debate due to the pros and cons of this source. Here, we suggest guidelines for the proper use of the Census Finance Survey.

Among the benefits of the Census Finance Survey, it covers a more comprehensive range of municipalities and years than other existing financial databases. The Census Bureau has conducted this nationwide voluntary survey every year since 1967. Although it has collected information only on selected municipalities (relatively larger municipalities in general) in most years, a complete census has been conducted in years ending 2 and 7. For those years, the Census Finance Survey provides the only database that covers all municipalities in the United States. Another positive feature of the Census Finance Survey is its broad coverage of different financial information. The survey includes almost 130 revenue categories, more than 270 expenditure categories, and over 100 categories for other activities such as debt, cash, and investment securities.

Despite these merits, the use of the Census Finance Survey requires caution for several reasons. First, the information reported is statistical in nature and may not correspond to actual financial statements or accounting measures. This makes it hard to match or compare the data in the Census Bureau categories with those available in financial or accounting statements. For a similar reason, whether the Census Finance Survey can precisely capture a balance sheet for each municipal government is questionable, even though it includes information on municipal assets (e.g., cash and security holdings) and liabilities (e.g., debt and retirement system contributions). Also, the goal of the Census Finance Survey is to uniformly measure local finances at a certain point in a year. Municipal officials, however, may vary as to how they interpret the questions and report answers in the 600 uniform categories offered by the Census Bureau. Even if municipal officials do interpret those categories properly, there is still a possibility of data entry error or lack of individual capacity to report all financial categories in a precise manner.

Given these pros and cons, we recommend the Census Finance Survey only for descriptive purposes. To further clarify our suggestion, we have selected three particular cities as examples and have compared each city's financial information available in the Census Finance Survey from 2010 to 2019 with those in the city's Annual Comprehensive Financial Reports (ACFRs) and the GFOA's financial indicators database in Table A.1. The cities chosen are Hot Springs, Arkansas (2019 population 38,559), Victoria, Texas (67,055), and Bakersfield, California (377,917). From the Census Finance Survey, we collected each city's general direct expenditures, defined as total expenditures except utility spending. From the ACFRs and the GFOA database, we gathered each city's information on total direct expenses for governmental activities, as this figure is closer to general direct expenditures in the Census Finance Survey than other accounting categories are.

In doing so, we demonstrate that the financial information available in the Census Finance Survey differs from that in the cities' ACFRs and the GFOA database. For example, Hot Springs's total general direct spending in 2010 was $59.3 million, while the city's total governmental activity spending reported in its ACFR (and in the GFOA database) was $34.6 million. The gap was smaller for Victoria in 2018, but it was still about $1 million. The problems with the Census Finance Survey discussed above may contribute to these differences.

Despite significant variations between the financial data sources examined, we found relative similarities when looking at each city's annual or 10-year spending trends. For example, Bakersfield's average annual percentage changes in general direct expenditures (on the Census Finance Survey) and in direct expenses on governmental activities (in the ACFRs) were 1.4% and 1.7%, respectively. The city's 10-year average percentage changes according to the two data sources were quite close to each other at 10.8% and 11.2%, respectively. Furthermore, we found that the Census Finance Survey does not necessarily distort relative budget sizes between the cities. Hot Springs and Bakersfield have the smallest and largest budget sizes, respectively, among the three cities according to all three data sources.

Table A.1 Comparison of Three Financial Data Sources

	Hot Springs City, Arkansas			*Victoria City, Texas*			*Bakersfield City, California*		
Year	*Census*	*GFOA*	*CAFRs*	*Census*	*GFOA*	*CAFRs*	*Census*	*GFOA*	*CAFRs*
2010	59,287,000	34,633,000	34,633,627	89,455,000	56,541,000	56,540,936	418,360,000	305,246,000	305,245,579
2011	63,123,000	35,468,000	35,468,291	74,625,000	69,548,000	69,547,926	373,272,000	302,290,000	302,289,698
2012	67,711,000	36,303,000	36,303,742	88,905,000	62,708,000	62,707,978	374,327,000	326,459,000	326,549,256
2013	70,055,000	35,395,000	35,395,829	78,390,000	61,827,000	61,826,690	382,998,000	331,040,000	331,039,502
2014	69,785,000	38,204,000	38,204,089	76,133,000	64,301,000	64,300,625	375,251,000	275,650,000	275,650,295
2015	69,070,000	51,622,000	51,622,205	74,192,000	65,575,000	65,574,751	428,907,000	331,869,000	331,868,612
2016	73,178,000	37,906,000	37,906,676	75,481,000	69,045,000	69,044,972	450,991,000	360,400,000	360,400,169
2017	80,613,000	–	42,272,728	83,900,000	–	73,293,062	467,932,000	–	374,476,956
2018	81,360,000	–	47,260,750	70,862,000	–	71,893,989	443,144,000	–	356,000,126
2019	76,268,000	–	44,973,294	114,175,000	–	68,207,592	463,509,000	–	339,350,533
Average annual percentage change (%)	2.95	3.13	4.14	4.86	3.84	2.46	1.37	3.45	1.67
10-year average percentage change (%)	28.64	–	29.85	27.63	–	20.63	10.79	–	11.17

Our findings indicate that the Census Finance Survey may not capture or correspond to actual accounting information, but that it can still help us understand municipal financial trends over time and generally analyze differences between municipalities or groups of municipalities. It may not be a reliable source if researchers are seeking to identify a specific budget or financial figure and probe its policy implications. However, the Census Finance Survey may still be useful for the purpose of describing fiscal trends and variations at the municipal level.

Appendix B

Selected Benchmarks

Table B.1 Overview of Selected Benchmarks

Indicator	*Source*	*Measure*	*Fiscal stress benchmark/ interpretation*
Expenditure and revenue indicators			
Expen-ditures	ICMA's FTMS (Nollenberger et al., 2003)	Per capita total operating expenditures	Increasing trend
	Kloha et al. (2005)	GF expenses/Current taxable value	> 0.05
	Maher (2013, 2022)	Per capita total expenses	Trending patterns particularly in conjunction with per capita revenues should be examined.
Revenues	ICMA's FTMS	Per capita total operating revenues	Decreasing trend
	Maher (2013, 2022)	Per capita total revenues (program revenues + total general revenues + transfers)	Trending patterns particularly in conjunction with per capita expenditures should be examined.

(*Continued*)

Table B.1 (Continued)

Indicator	*Source*	*Measure*	*Fiscal stress benchmark/ interpretation*
	California's Local High-risk Program (California State Auditor, 2022)	Average annual change in GF revenues during the past three fiscal years	Moderate or high risk when ≤ 10%
Revenue sources	ICMA's FTMS	Elastic tax revenues/ Operating revenues	Declining trend
		Total property taxes	Declining trend
		Total intergovernmental aid/Total revenues	Decreasing trend; overdependence
	Kioko and Marlowe (2016)	Total primary government operating grants and contributions/Total primary government revenues	≥ 10%
	Rivenbark and Roenigk (2011)	Total intergovernmental revenues/Total revenues	Higher stress when higher
	Maher (2013, 2022)	Operating and capital grants + contribution + unrestricted aid reported with general revenues/ Total revenues	Higher stress when higher
	Colorado's Fiscal Stability Initiative (Colorado DOLA, 2018)	Total intergovernmental revenue/ Total revenue (government-wide)	> 25%
	Virginia's Early Warning System (Virginia APA, 2020)	Total GF intergovernmental aid/Total GF revenues	Potential risk when ≥ 25%

Indicator	*Source*	*Measure*	*Fiscal stress benchmark/ interpretation*
Operating Position Indicators			
Deficit or surplus	ICMA's FTMS	GF deficit	Two consecutive years of operating deficits; current operating fund deficit greater than that of the previous year; operating deficit in two or more of the last five years; abnormally large deficit (more than 5 to 10% of net operating revenues) in any one year
	Kloha et al. (2005)	Current or previous year deficit in major funds	> 0
		(GF expenditures-GF revenues)/GF revenues	<-0.01
	Kioko and Marlowe (2016)	(Net revenue or expense for governmental activities/Total governmental activities expenses)*-1	Negative
	Rivenbark and Roenigk (2011)	Total revenues (program revenues + total general revenues + transfers)/ Total expenses	< 1.0
	Pennsylvania's Early Warning System (Scorsone and Pruettt, 2020)	Total GF expenditures/Total GF revenues	> 1.02
		Total GF public safety expenditures/Total revenue	< 0.5

(*Continued*)

Table B.1 (Continued)

Indicator	*Source*	*Measure*	*Fiscal stress benchmark/ interpretation*
	Colorado's Fiscal Stability Initiative	Count number of operating deficits in current year and two prior years (government-wide)	Two years or more
	New York's Fiscal Stress Monitoring System (Office of the New York State Comptroller, 2017)	(Total revenues—total expenditures)/ Total expenditures	Potential risk when < 0% in one of the last three years
	Virginia's Early Warning System	Total GF expenditures/Total GF revenues	Potential risk when > 100%
Fund balance	ICMA's FTMS	Unrestricted balances/GF revenues	Decreasing trend
	GFOA	Unrestricted GF balances/ GF revenues or expenditures	Less than two months of regular GF operating revenues or expenditures (16.7%)
	Kloha et al. (2005)	GF balances/GF revenues	< 0.13
	Kioko and Marlowe (2016)	Total GF unassigned balances/Total GF revenues	≤ 5%
	Rivenbark and Roenigk (2011)	Available fund balances/Total expenditures	Higher stress when lower
	Maher (2013, 2022)	Total GF assigned and unassigned balances/Total GF expenditures	Higher stress when lower
	Pennsylvania's Early Warning System	Unrestricted GF balances/Total GF revenues	< 0.167
		Unrestricted balances/Total GF assets	< 0.586

Indicator	*Source*	*Measure*	*Fiscal stress benchmark/ interpretation*
	California's Local High-risk Program	Unrestricted GF balances/Total GF expenditures	Moderate or high risk when less than six months of regular GF expenditures (50.0%)
	New York's Fiscal Stress Monitoring System	Total GF assigned and unassigned balances/Total GF expenditures	Potential risk when ≤ 10%
		Total GF fund balances/Total GF expenditures	Potential risk when ≤ 20%
	Virginia's Early Warning System	Change in GF unassigned fund balance	Potential risk when ≤ -0.01%
		Total GF assigned and unassigned balances/Total GF expenditures	Potential risk when ≤ 15%
		Total GF fund balances/Total GF expenditures	Potential risk when ≤ 10%
Cash	ICMA's FTMS	Total cash and investments/ Current liabilities	Declining trend
	Kioko and Marlowe (2016)	Total GF cash and investment/GF current liabilities	≤ 1.0
	Rivenbark and Roenigk (2011)	Total cash and investments/ Current liabilities	Higher stress when lower
	Maher (2013, 2022)	Cash, investments, and receivables/ Current liabilities	Higher stress when lower
	Pennsylvania's Early Warning System	Total cash and investments/ Total outstanding debt	< 0.089

(*Continued*)

Table B.1 (Continued)

Indicator	*Source*	*Measure*	*Fiscal stress benchmark/ interpretation*
	California's Local High-risk Program	Total GF cash and investments/ GF current liabilities	Moderate or high risk when < 150%
	New York's Fiscal Stress Monitoring System	Total cash and investments/ Total monthly governmental fund expenditures	Potential risk when ≤ 150%
		Total cash and investments/Current liabilities	Potential risk when ≤ 100%
	Virginia's Early Warning System	(Cash and cash equivalents + investments - current liabilities)/(Charges for services + general revenues) (Government-wide)	Potential risk when < 15%
		(Cash and cash equivalents + investments)/ Total (current and noncurrent) liabilities (Government-wide)	Potential risk when < 60%
Enterprise funds	ICMA's FTMS	Current assets of enterprise funds/ Liabilities	Decreasing trend
	GFOA	Current assets of enterprise funds/ Operating expenses	Less than 45 days' worth of operating expenses (12.3%)
	Kioko and Marlowe (2016)	Enterprise funds operating revenues/ Enterprise funds interest expense	≤ 0.5
Net position	Kioko and Marlowe (2016)	Change in governmental activities net position/Beginning governmental activities net position	Negative

Indicator	*Source*	*Measure*	*Fiscal stress benchmark/ interpretation*
	Rivenbark and Roenigk (2011)	Change in net position/Net beginning assets	Negative
	Maher (2013, 2022)	Change in net position/Total assets	Negative
	Virginia's Early Warning System	Change in net position (ending—beginning)/Net position beginning (Government-wide)	Potential risk when < -0.01%
	Rivenbark and Roenigk (2011)	Unrestricted net position/Total liabilities	Higher stress when lower
	Maher (2013, 2022)	Unrestricted net position/Total expenses	Higher stress when lower
	Virginia's Early Warning System	Unrestricted net position/ Total expenses (Government-wide)	Potential risk when < 15%
Debt Indicators			
Debt amount	ICMA's FTMS	GO debt outstanding/ Assessed valuation	Increasing trend
	GFOA	GO debt outstanding/ Assessed valuation	Under the limit set by state/ municipality (typically 2 to 4%)
	Kloha et al. (2005)	GO debt outstanding/ Assessed valuation	> 0.06
	Kioko and Marlowe (2016)	Primary government non-current liabilities/Population	Higher stress when higher
	Rivenbark and Roenigk (2011)	Long-term debt/Total assets	Higher stress when higher
		Tax-supported, long-term debt/Assessed value	Higher stress when higher

(*Continued*)

Table B.1 (Continued)

Indicator	*Source*	*Measure*	*Fiscal stress benchmark/ interpretation*
	Maher (2013, 2022)	GO debt outstanding/ Assessed valuation	Should be evaluated relative to state-imposed debt limits along with patterns in trends over time
	Pennsylvania's Early Warning System	Total outstanding debt/Total government wide revenues	> 1.27
	Colorado's Fiscal Stability Initiative	Per capita GO debt outstanding	> $1,778
	California's Local High-risk Program	Long-term debt/Total government wide revenues	Moderate or high risk when 40% or greater
	Virginia's Early Warning System	Total tax supported debt/Assessed valuation	Potential risk when ≥ 3%
Debt service	ICMA's FTMS	Debt service expenditures/Total revenues	Increasing trend
		Per capita debt service expenditures	Increasing trend
	Kioko and Marlowe (2016)	Governmental funds principal and interest on long-term debt/ GF expenditures	≥ 0.25
	Rivenbark and Roenigk (2011)	Debt service expenditures/Total expenses	Higher stress when higher
	New York's Fiscal Stress Monitoring System	Debt service expenditures/ Total governmental expenditures	Potential risk when ≥ 10%
	Virginia's Early Warning System	Debt service expenditures/Total revenues	Potential risk when > 10%

Bibliography

Adelino, M., Cunha, I., & Ferreira, M. A. (2017). The economic effects of public financing: Evidence from municipal bond ratings recalibration. *The Review of Financial Studies, 30*(9), 3223–3268.

Adrian, C. R. (1952). Some general characteristics of nonpartisan elections. *American Political Science Review, 46*(3), 766–776.

Advisory Commission on Intergovernmental Relations. (1973). *City financial emergencies: The intergovernmental dimension*. Advisory Commission on Intergovernmental Relations.

Advisory Commission on Intergovernmental Relations. (1974). *Changing public attitudes on governments and taxes*. Advisory Commission on Intergovernmental Relations.

Advisory Commission on Intergovernmental Relations. (1984). *Regulatory federalism: Policy, process, impact and reform*. Advisory Commission on Intergovernmental Relations.

Advisory Commission on Intergovernmental Relations. (1993). *State laws governing local government structure and administration*. Advisory Commission on Intergovernmental Relations.

Afonso, W. (2018). Time to adoption of local option sales taxes: An examination of Texas municipalities. *Public Finance Review, 46*(4), 558–582.

Ahn, M. J. (2011). Adoption of e-communication applications in U.S. municipalities: The role of political environment, bureaucratic structure, and the nature of applications. *The American Review of Public Administration, 41*(4), 428–452.

Alcaly, R. E., & Mermelstein, D. (Eds.). (1976). *The fiscal crisis of American cities: Essays on the political economy of urban America with special reference to New York* (Vol. 193). Vintage Books.

Almond, G. A., & Powell, G. B. (1978). *Comparative politics: Systems, process, and policy* (2nd ed.). Little, Brown and Company.

Altman, E. I. (1968). Financial ratios, discriminant analysis and the prediction of corporate bankruptcy. *Journal of Finance, 23*(4), 589–609.

Anderson, T. (2010). *Federal data show how far Great Lakes economy has shrunk*. Council of State Governments. https://knowledgecenter.csg.org/

Andrews, R., & Boyne, G. A. (2010). Capacity, leadership, and organizational performance: Testing the black-box model of public management. *Public Administration Review, 70*(3), 443–454.

Arapis, T., & Reitano, V. (2018). A glimmer of optimism in government savings accumulation? An empirical examination of municipal unassigned fund balance in Florida. *Public Finance Review, 46*(3), 389–420.

Auerbach, A. J., & Slemrod, J. (1997). The economic effects of the tax reform act of 1986. *Journal of Economic Literature, 35*(2), 589–632.

Bahl, R., & Duncombe, W. (1993). State and local debt burdens in the 1980s: A study in contrast. *Public Administration Review, 53*(1), 31–40.

Bank Management Committee. (1963). *A guide for developing municipal bond credit files.* American Bankers Association.

Barnekov, T., & Rich, D. (1989). Privatism and the limits of local economic development policy. *Urban Affairs Quarterly, 25*(2), 212–238.

Bartle, J. R. (1996). Coping with cutbacks: City response to aid cuts in New York State. *State & Local Government Review, 28*(1), 38–48.

Becker, T. (2020, June 16). A first look at the 2020–2021 proposed budget. *Mohawk Valley Compass.* https://mohawkvalleycompass.com/2020/06/a-first-look-at-the-2020–2021-proposed-budget/

Bendor, J., Taylor, S., & Van Gaalen, R. (1987). Politicians, bureaucrats, and asymmetric information. *American Journal of Political Science, 31*(4), 796–828.

Bennett, J. T., & DiLorenzo, T. J. (1982). Off-budget activities of local government: The bane of the tax revolt. *Public Choice, 39*(3), 333–342.

Bergstrom, T. C., & Goodman, R. P. (1973). Private demands for public goods. *The American Economic Review, 63*(3), 280–296.

Berman, D. R. (1995). Takeovers of local governments: An overview and evaluation of state policies. *Publius: The Journal of Federalism, 25*(3), 55–70.

Berne, R. (1992). *The relationships between financial reporting and the measurement of financial condition.* Governmental Accounting Standards Board.

Berne, R., & Schramm, R. (1986). *The financial analysis of governments.* Prentice Hall.

Berry, F. S. (1994). Innovation in public management: The adoption of strategic planning. *Public Administration Review, 54*(4), 322–330.

Berry, F. S., & Berry, W. D. (2018). Innovation and diffusion models in policy research. In P. A. Sabatier & C. M. Weible (Eds.), *Theories of the policy process* (pp. 253–297). Routledge.

Bhattacharyya, D. K., & Wassmer, R. W. (1995). Fiscal dynamics of local elected officials. *Public Choice, 83*(3–4), 221–249.

Bland, R. L., & Overton, M. R. (2019). *A budgeting guide for local government* (2nd ed.). International City/County Management Association.

Bogart, E. L. (1912). *Financial history of Ohio.* University of Illinois.

Booms, B. H. (1966). City governmental form and public expenditure levels. *National Tax Journal, 19*(2), 187–199.

Booth, D. E. (1978). The differential impact of manufacturing and mercantile activity on local government expenditures and revenues. *National Tax Journal, 31*(1), 33–43.

Borcherding, T. E., & Deacon, R. T. (1972). The demand for the services of non-federal governments. *The American Economic Review, 62*(5), 891–901.

Boustan, L. P., Kahn, M. E., Rhode, P. W., & Yanguas, M. L. (2020). The effect of natural disasters on economic activity in U.S. counties: A century of data. *Journal of Urban Economics, 118*, 103257.

Bradbury, K. L., Ladd, H. F., Perrault, M., Reschovsky, A., & Yinger, J. (1984). State aid to offset fiscal disparities across communities. *National Tax Journal, 37*(2), 151–170.

Brennan, G., & Buchanan, J. M. (1979). The logic of tax limits: Alternative constitutional constraints on the power to tax. *National Tax Journal, 32*(2), 11–22.

Brennan, G., & Buchanan, J. M. (1980). *The power to tax: Analytic foundations of a fiscal constitution.* Cambridge University Press.

Brown, K. W. (1993). The 10-point test of financial condition: Toward and easy-to-use assessment tool for smaller cities. *Government Finance Review, 9*(6), 21–26.

Brown, T. (2000). Constitutional tax and expenditure limitation in Colorado: The impact on municipal governments. *Public Budgeting & Finance, 20*(3), 29–50.

Buchanan, J. M. (1967). *Public finance in democratic process.* University of North Carolina Press.

Buchanan, J. M., & Tullock, G. (1962). *The calculus of consent.* University of Michigan Press.

Buday, K. (2018, September 17). Florence called one of the worst storms to hit Havelock. *Sun Journal.* www.newbernsj.com/story/news/local/havelock-news/2018/09/17/florence-called-one-of-worst-storms-to-hit-havelock/10280755007/

Bunch, B. S., & Strauss, R. P. (1992). Municipal consolidation: An analysis of the financial benefits for fiscally distressed small municipalities. *Urban Affairs Quarterly, 27*(4), 615–629.

Bureau of Economic Analysis. (2021). U.S. economy at a glance. www.bea.gov/news/glance

Byers, K. (2020, September 14). Havelock has grown and changed through the decades. *Sun Journal.* www.newbernsj.com/story/news/local/havelock-news/2020/09/14/havelock-has-grown-and-changed-through-decades/42619993/

Cabral, M., & Hoxby, C. (2012). *The hated property tax: Salience, tax rates, and tax revolts.* National Bureau of Economic Research. www.nber.org/papers/w18514.pdf

California State Auditor. (2022). *Fiscal health of California cities.* www.auditor.ca.gov/local_high_risk/dashboard-csa.html

Camp-Landis, S. (2020). *The future of fiscal oversight in Philadelphia: The state agency that monitors city finances may soon disappear.* The Pew Charitable Trusts.

Carelton, W. T., & Lerner, E. M. (1969). Statistical credit scoring of municipal bonds. *Journal of Money, Credit and Banking, 1*(4), 750–764.

Carr, J. B. (2015). What have we learned about the performance of council-manager government? A review and synthesis of the research. *Public Administration Review, 75*(5), 673–689.

Carroll, D. A. (2009). Diversifying municipal government revenue structures: Fiscal illusion or instability? *Public Budgeting and Finance, 29*(1), 27–48.

Carroll, D. A., & Goodman, C. B. (2011). The effects of assessment quality on revenue volatility. *Public Budgeting and Finance, 31*(1), 76–94.

Chaney, B. A. (2005). Analyzing the financial condition of the City of Corona, California: Using a case to teach the GASB 34 government-wide financial statements. *Journal of Public Budgeting, Accounting & Financial Management, 17*(2), 180–201.

Chapman, J., & Ascanio, K. (2020). State websites offer fiscal data on local governments. *The Pew Charitable Trusts.* www.pewtrusts.org/en/research-and-analysis/articles/2020/10/20/state-websites-offer-fiscal-data-on-local-governments

Chapman, J., & Gorina, E. (2012). Effects of the form of government and property tax limits on local finance in the context of revenue and expenditure simultaneity. *Public Budgeting & Finance, 32*(4), 19–45.

Cheng, Y. (2019). Nonprofit spending and government provision of public services: Testing theories of government–nonprofit relationships. *Journal of Public Administration Research and Theory*, *29*(2), 238–254.

Chernick, H., Langley, A., & Reschovsky, A. (2011). The impact of the great recession and the housing crisis on the financing of America's largest cities. *Regional Science and Urban Economics*, *41*(4), 372–381.

Chernick, H., & Reschovsky, A. (2001). *Lost in the balance: How state policies affect the fiscal health of cities.* Brookings Institution Center on Urban and Metropolitan Policy. www.census.gov/programs-surveys/gov-finances/about/glossary.html#par_textimage_1669110194

Chernick, H., & Reschovsky, A. (2017). The fiscal condition of U.S. cities: Revenues, expenditures and the Great Recession. *Journal of Urban Affairs*, *39*(4), 488–505.

Chicoine, D. L., Walzer, N., & Deller, S. C. (1989). Representative vs. direct democracy and government spending in a median voter model. *Public Finance—Finances Publiques*, *44*(2), 225–236.

Christian, C., & Bush, J. (2018). Municipal response to the great recession. *Journal of Public Budgeting, Accounting & Financial Management*, *30*(4), 384–401.

Chung, I. H., & Williams, D. (2021). Local governments' responses to the fiscal stress label: The case of New York. *Local Government Studies*, *47*(5), 808–835.

City of Commerce, California. (2003–2020). *Annual comprehensive financial reports.* www.ci.commerce.ca.us/city-hall/finance/adopted-budget-financial-reports/-folder-1050

City of Commerce, California. (2022). *Administration/city manager.* www.ci.commerce.ca.us/city-hall/administration-city-manager

City of Flint, Michigan. (2000–2021a). *Annual comprehensive financial reports.* www.cityofflint.com/finance/finanical-reports/

City of Flint, Michigan. (2021b). *Fiscal year 2021–2022 and 2022–2023 proposed budget.* www.cityofflint.com/wp-content/uploads/A-FY2022-Budget-Book-Proposed.pdf

City of Havelock, North Carolina. (2004–2019). *Annual comprehensive financial reports.* www.havelocknc.us/Archive.aspx?AMID=36

City of New Orleans, Louisiana. (2009). *Annual comprehensive financial report.* www.nola.gov/accounting/files/comprehensive-annual-financial-report/ACFR2009/

City of North Lauderdale, Florida. (2002–2020). *Annual comprehensive financial reports.* www.nlauderdale.org/departments/finance/comprehensive_annual_financial_reports_(ACFR).php

City of North Lauderdale, Florida. (2021). *FY 2021 Proposed and adopted budget.* https://www.nlauderdale.org/departments/finance/annual_budgets.php

City of North Lauderdale, Florida. (2022). *Hurricane information.* www.nlauderdale.org/quick_links/hurricane_information/index.php

City of Sidney, Nebraska. (2012). *Comprehensive development plan 2012.* https://cityofsidney.org/DocumentCenter/View/180/Comp-Plan-Appendix-3-Demographics?bidId=

City of Wichita, Kansas. (2000–2020). *Annual comprehensive financial reports.* www.wichita.gov/Finance/Pages/FinancialDocs.aspx

Clark, B. Y. (2015). Evaluating the validity and reliability of the financial condition index for local governments. *Public Budgeting & Finance*, *35*(2), 66–88.

Clark, C., & Walter, B. O. (1991). Urban political cultures, financial stress, and city fiscal austerity strategies. *Western Political Quarterly*, *44*(3), 676–697.

Clark, T. N. (1994). Municiapl fiscal strain: Indicators and causes. *Government Finance Review*, *10*(3), 27–30.

Clark, T. N., & Ferguson, L. C. (1983). *City money: Political processes, fiscal strain, and retrenchment*. Columbia University Press.

Coe, C. K. (2007). Preventing local government fiscal crises: The North Carolina approach. *Public Budgeting & Finance, 27*(3), 39–49.

Coe, C. K. (2008). Preventing local government fiscal crises: Emerging best practices. *Public Administration Review, 68*(4), 759–767.

Cohen, M. D., March, J. G., & Olsen, J. P. (1972). A garbage can model of organizational choice. *Administrative Science Quarterly, 17*(1), 1–25.

Colomer, N. (2018, August 28). Michigan emergency manager program may not survive the mess it made in Flint. *The Bond Buyer*. www.bondbuyer.com/news/flint-crisis-may-seal-fate-of-michigan-emergency-manager-law

Colorado Department of Local Affairs. (2018). *Colorado fiscal stability initiative*. www.canr.msu.edu/center_for_local_government_finance_and_policy/uploads/files/cofiscalstability2018.pdf

Committee for the Study of the Future of Public Health. (1988). *The future of public health*. National Academies Press.

Cope, G. H., & Grubb, W. N. (1982). Restraint in a land of plenty: Revenue and expenditure limitations in Texas. *Public Budgeting & Finance, 2*(4), 143–156.

Cournoyer. (2012, December 20). Pension obligation bonds: Risky gimmick or smart investment? *Governing*. www.governing.com/archive/gov-pension-obligation-bonds-risky-or-smart.html

Crawford, S. E., & Ostrom, E. (1995). A grammar of institutions. *American Political Science Review, 89*(3), 582–600.

Crosby, A., & Robbins, D. (2013). Mission impossible: Monitoring municipal fiscal sustainability and stress in Michigan. *Journal of Public Budgeting, Accounting & Financial Management, 25*(3), 522–555.

Dahlberg, J. S. (1966). *The New York Bureau of municipal research, pioneer in government administration*. New York University Press.

Danziger, J. N. (1991). Intergovernmental structure and fiscal management strategies: A crossnational analysis. *Governance, 4*(2), 168–183.

Das, B., & Skidmore, M. (2017). *Asymmetry in municipal government responses in growing vs. shrinking counties with focus on capital spending*. Working Paper WP17BD1, Lincoln Institute of Land Policy. www.lincolninst.edu/sites/default/files/pubfiles/das_wp17bd1.pdf

De Benedictis-Kessner, J., & Warshaw, C. (2016). Mayoral partisanship and municipal fiscal policy. *Journal of Politics, 78*(4), 1124–1138.

Decker, J. W. (2021). An (in)effective TEL: Why county governments do not utilize their maximum allotted property tax rate. *Public Administration*. Published online first. https://doi.org/10.1111/padm.12756

Deller, S. C. (1998). Local government structure, devolution, and privatization. *Review of Agricultural Economics, 20*(1), 135–154.

Deller, S. C., & Maher, C. (2009). Government, effectiveness, performance, and local property values. *International Journal of Public Administration, 32*(13), 1182–1212.

Deller, S. C., & Rudnicki, E. (1992). Managerial efficiency in local government: Implications on jurisdictional consolidation. *Public Choice, 74*(2), 221–231.

Deno, K. T., & Mehay, S. L. (1987). Municipal management structure and fiscal performance: Do city managers make a difference? *Southern Economic Journal, 53*(3), 627–642.

Doidge, M., Scorsone, E., Taylor, T., Sapotichne, J., Rosebrook, E., & Kaminski, D. (2015). *The Flint fiscal playbook: An assessment of emergency manager years (2011–2015)*. MSU extension paper. http://ippsr.msu.edu/research/flint-fiscal-playbook-assessment-emergency-manager-years-2011–2015

Downs, A. (1967). *Inside bureaucracy*. Little Brown.

Downs, G. W., & Rocke, D. M. (1984). Theories of budgetary decisionmaking and revenue decline. *Policy Sciences, 16*(4), 329–347.

Dye, R., & McGuire, T. (1997). The effect of property tax limitation measures on local government fiscal behavior. *Journal of Public Economics, 66*(3), 469–487.

Ebdon, C. (2000). The effects of voter control on budget outcomes. *Journal of Public Budgeting, Accounting & Financial Management, 12*(1), 22–42.

Ebdon, C. (2002). Beyond the public hearing: Citizen participation in the local government budget process. *Journal of Public Budgeting, Accounting & Financial Management, 14*(2), 273–294.

Ebdon, C., & Franklin, A. (2004). Searching for a role for citizens in the budget process. *Public Budgeting & Finance, 24*(1), 32–49.

Egan, P. (2021, January 21). Historic $641M Flint water crisis class-action settlement just got closer to approval. *Detroit Free Press*. www.freep.com/story/news/local/michigan/flint-water-crisis/2021/01/21/flint-water-crisis-lawsuit-settlement-michigan/4242611001/

Farmer, E. (2018, May 24). Governments haven't had rules for revealing their private debt—until now. *Governing*. www.governing.com/archive/gov-gasb-government-bank-loans.html

Farmer, L. (2016, February 1). The evolving job description (and requirements) of a CFO. *Governing*. www.governing.com/archive/gov-chief-financial-officer-job-description.html

Farnham, P. G. (1985). Re-examining local debt limits: A disaggregated analysis. *Southern Economic Journal, 51*(4), 1186–1201.

Feldstein, S. G., & Fabozzi, F. J. (2008). *The handbook of municipal bonds*. John Wiley & Sons.

Figlio, D. N., & O'Sullivan, A. (2001). The local response to tax limitation measures: Do local governments manipulate voters to increase revenues? *The Journal of Law and Economics, 44*(1), 233–257.

Finkler, S. (2001). *Financial management for public, health, and not-for-profit organizations*. Prentice Hall.

Foote, A. R. (1911). A state tax on local government incomes proposed as a practical substitute for a state general property tax. *State and Local Taxation: Annual Conference under the Auspices of the National Tax Association, 5*, 253–262.

Foulke, R. A. (1961). *Practical financial statement analysis*. McGraw-Hill.

Gabrini, C. J. (2010). Do institutions matter? The influence of institutions of direct democracy on local government spending. *State and Local Government Review, 42*(3), 210–225.

Gerber, E. R., & Hopkins, D. J. (2011). When mayors matter: Estimating the impact of mayoral partisanship on city policy. *American Journal of Political Science, 55*(2), 326–339.

Gilman, H., & Wampler, B. (2019). The difference in design: Participatory budgeting in Brazil and the United States. *Journal of Public Deliberation, 15*(1), 1–30.

Gilmore, S. (2017). Virginia to begin monitoring local fiscal stress. *National Conference of State Legislatures*. www.ncsl.org/blog/2017/04/21/virginia-to-begin-monitoring-local-fiscal-distress.aspx

Goldberg, J. M., & Neiman, M. (2014). *Managing budgets during fiscal stress: Lessons for local government officials*. IBM Center for the Business of Government. https://repository.usfca.edu/cgi/viewcontent.cgi?referer=&httpsredir=1&article=1003&context=mccarthy_stu

Goodman, C. B., Hatch, M. E., & McDonald, B. D. (2021). State preemption of local laws: Origins and modern trends. *Perspectives on Public Management and Governance*, *4*(2), 146–158.

Gordon, T., Auxier, R. C., & Iselin, J. (2016). *Assessing fiscal capacities of states: A representative revenue system–representative expenditure system approach, fiscal year 2012*. Urban Institute. www.urban.org/research/publication/assessing-fiscal-capacities-states-representative-revenue-system-representative-expenditure-system-approach-fiscal-year-2012/view/full_report

Gorina, E., Maher, C., & Joffe, M. (2018). Local fiscal distress: Measurement and prediction. *Public Budgeting & Finance*, *38*(1), 72–94.

Gorina, E., Maher, C., & Park, S. (2019). Toward a theory of fiscal slack. *Public Budgeting & Finance*, *39*(4), 48–74.

Gouveia, M., & Masia, N. A. (1998). Does the median voter model explain the size of government? Evidence from the states. *Public Choice*, *97*(1), 159–177.

Government Finance Officers Association. (2011). *Working capital targets for enterprise funds*. www.gfoa.org/materials/working-capital-targets-for-enterprise-funds

Government Finance Officers Association. (2015). *Fund balance guidelines for the general fund*. www.gfoa.org/materials/fund-balance-guidelines-for-the-general-fund

Government Finance Officers Association. (2020). *Debt management policy*. www.gfoa.org/materials/debt-management-policy

Government Finance Officers Association. (2021). *GFOA best practices*. www.gfoa.org/best-practices

Governmental Accounting Standards Board. (2022). *Fund balance reporting*. www.gasb.org/cs/ContentServer?c=GASBContent_C&cid=1176156650327&d=&pagename=GASB%2FGASBContent_C%2FProjectPage

Gramlich, E. M. (1976). New York City fiscal crisis: What happened and what is to be done? *American Economic Review*, *66*(2), 415–429.

Greene, J. D. (1996). Cities and privatization: Examining the effect of fiscal stress, location, and wealth in medium-sized cities. *Policy Studies Journal*, *24*(1), 135–144.

Groves, S. M., Groves, S. M., Godsey, W. M, & Shulman, M. A. (1981). Financial indicators for local governments. *Public Budgeting and Finance*, *1*(2), 5–19.

Hajnal, Z. L., & Clark, T. N. (1998). The local interest-group system: Who governs and why? *Social Science Quarterly*, *79*(1), 227–241.

Hajnal, Z. L., & Trounstine, J. (2010). Who or what governs? The effects of economics, politics, institutions, and needs on local spending. *American Politics Research*, *38*(6), 1130–1163.

Hanna, H. S. (1907). *A financial history of Maryland (1789–1848)*. Johns Hopkins University Press.

Hastie, L. K. (1972). Determinants of municipal bond yields. *Journal of Financial and Quantitative Analysis*, *7*(3), 1729–1748.

Hatcher, W., McDonald, B. D., & Abbott, M. (2021). History of public administration education in the United States. In K. A. Bottom, P. Dunning, I. Elliot, & J. Diamond (Eds.), *Handbook on the teaching of public administration* (pp. 57–64). Edward Elgar.

Heller, P. S. (2005). *Understanding fiscal space*. International Monetary Fund.

Hempel, G. H. (1973). An evaluation of municipal "bankruptcy" laws and procedures. *The Journal of Finance, 28*(5), 1339–1351.

Hendrick, R. M. (2002). Revenue diversification: Fiscal illusion or flexible financial management. *Public Budgeting & Finance, 22*(4), 52–72.

Hendrick, R. M. (2004). Assessing and measuring the fiscal health of local governments: Focus on Chicago suburban municipalities. *Urban Affairs Review, 40*(1), 78–114.

Hendrick, R. M. (2011). *Managing the fiscal metropolis: The financial policies, practices, and health of suburban municipalities*. Georgetown University Press.

Hendrick, R. M., & Crawford, J. (2014). Municipal fiscal policy space and fiscal structure: Tools for managing spending volatility. *Public Budgeting and Finance, 34*(3), 24–50.

Henry, M. S., Barkley, D. L., & Bao, S. (1997). The hinterland's stake in metropolitan growth: Evidence from selected southern regions. *Journal of Regional Science, 37*(3), 479–501.

Hildreth, W. B. A. (2009). The financial logistics of disaster: The case of hurricane Katrina. *Public Performance & Management Review, 32*(3), 400–436.

Hildreth, W. B. A., & Zorn, C. K. (2005). The evolution of the state and local government municipal debt market over the past quarter century. *Public Budgeting & Finance, 25*(4s), 127–153.

Hill, E., Sattler, M., Duritsky, J., O'Brien, K., & Robey, C. (2006). *A review of tax expenditure limitations and their impact on state and local government in Ohio*. Urban Publications, Paper 530. http://engagedscholarship.csuohio.edu/cgi

Hinckley, S. M. (2015). *Governing the broken city: Fiscal crisis and the remaking of urban governance* (Doctoral dissertation). University of California.

Holcombe, R. G. (1980). An empirical test of the median voter model. *Economic Inquiry, 18*(2), 260–274.

Holcombe, R. G. (1989). The median voter model in public choice theory. *Public Choice, 61*(2), 115–125.

Holcombe, R. G. (2005). Government growth in the twenty-first century. *Public Choice, 124*(1–2), 95–114.

Holcombe, R. G., & Williams, D. W. (2008). The impact of population density on municipal government expenditures. *Public Finance Review, 36*(3), 359–373.

Holcombe, R. G., & Williams, D. W. (2009). Are there economies of scale in municipal government expenditures? *Public Finance and Management, 9*(3), 416–438.

Honadle, B. W., Costa, J. M., & Cigler, B. A. (2004). *Fiscal health for local governments: An introduction to concepts, practical analysis, and strategies*. Elsevier.

Honadle, B. W., & Lloyd-Jones, M. (1998). Analyzing rural local governments' financial condition: An exploratory application of three tools. *Public Budgeting & Finance, 18*(2), 69–86.

Hood, C., & Piotrowska, B. M. (2021). Who loves input controls? What happened to "outputs not inputs" in U.K. public financial management, and why? *Public Administration*. Published online first. https://doi.org/10.1111/padm.12741

Horrigan, J. O. (1968). A short history of financial ratio analysis. *The Accounting Review, 43*(2), 284–294.

Hsieh, H. F., & Shannon, S. E. (2005). Three approaches to qualitative content analysis. *Qualitative Health Research, 15*(9), 1277–1288.

Huh, K., Murphy, M., Fehr, S., & Lu, A. (2015). *After municipal bankruptcy: Lessons from Detroit and other local governments.* The Pew Charitable Trusts.

Inman, R. P. (1982). Public employee pensions and the local labor budget. *Journal of Public Economics, 19*(1), 49–71.

International City/County Management Association (ICMA). (2001, 2006, 2011, 2018). *ICMA municipal form of government survey results.* https://icma.org/topics/form-government

International City/County Management Association (ICMA). (2007). *Profile of local government service delivery choices, 2007.* https://icma.org/sites/default/files/101785_asd2007_2008web.pdf

International City/County Management Association (ICMA). (2009). *2009 state of the profession survey.* https://icma.org/documents/icma-survey-research-2009-state-profession-survey

International City/County Management Association (ICMA). (2012, 2019). *ICMA survey research: Alternative service delivery survey report.* https://icma.org/research-reports-and-publications

International City/County Management Association (ICMA). (2015). *Local government sustainability practices summary report.* https://icma.org/sites/default/files/308135_2015%20Sustainability%20Survey%20Report%20Final.pdf

International City/County Management Association (ICMA). (2016). *Four factors influencing local government financial decisions.* https://icma.org/blog-posts/4-factors-influencing-local-government-financial-decisions

International City/County Management Association (ICMA). (2021). *Who's who.* https://members.icma.org/eWeb/DynamicPage.aspx?webcode=BneIcmaWhosWhoSearch&Site=icmares

Ivanov, I., & Zimmermann, T. (2018). *The "privatization" of municipal debt.* Hutchins Center Working Paper 45. www.brookings.edu/wp-content/uploads/2018/08/WP45.pdf

Jacob, B., & Hendrick, R. (2013). Assessing the financial condition of local governments: What is financial condition and how is it measured? In H. Levine, J. B. Justice, & E. A. Scorsone (Eds.), *Handbook of local government fiscal health* (pp. 11–41). Jones and Bartlett Learning.

Jacobson, P. D., Boufides, C. H., Chrysler, D., Bernstein, J., & Citrin, T. (2020). The role of the legal system in the Flint water crisis. *The Milbank Quarterly, 98*(2), 554–580.

Jang, S. (2012). *Three essays on tax collection: A historical review, a formal model, and an empirical test of the government's contractual choice of tax collection between tax farming and tax bureaucracy* (Doctoral dissertation). Florida State University.

Jimenez, B. S. (2014). Raise taxes, cut services, or lay off staff: Citizens in the fiscal retrenchment process. *Journal of Public Administration Research and Theory, 24*(4), 923–953.

Jin, M. H. (2020). Models of academic governance. In B. D. McDonald & W. Hatcher (Eds.), *The public affairs faculty manual: A guide to the effective management of public affairs programs* (pp. 33–47). Routledge.

Jordan, M. M. (2003). Punctuations and agendas: A new look at local government budget expenditures. *Journal of Policy Analysis and Management, 22*(3), 345–360.

Jung, C. (2006). Forms of government and spending on common municipal functions: A longitudinal approach. *International Review of Administrative Sciences, 72*(3), 363–376.

Justice, J. B., Fudge, M., Levine, H., Bird, D. D., & Iftikhar, M. N. (2019). Using fiscal indicators systems to predict municipal bankruptcies. In D. Williams & T. Calabrese (Eds.), *The Palgrave handbook of government budget forecasting* (pp. 275–302). Palgrave Macmillan.

Justice, J. B., & Scorsone, E. A. (2013). Measuring and predicting local government fiscal stress. In H. Levine, J. B. Justice, & E. A. Scorsone (Eds.), *Handbook of local government fiscal health* (pp. 43–74). Jones and Bartlett Learning.

Kelly, J. M., & Massey, S. J. (1996). Debt limits and borrowing patterns in twelve southeastern states: Where there's a will. *Southeastern Political Review, 24*(2), 338–360.

Kiewiet, D., & Szakaty, K. (1996). Constitutional limitations on borrowing: An analysis of state bonded indebtedness. *Journal of Law, Economics, and Organization, 12*(1), 62–97.

Kim, J., Maher, C. S., & Lee, J. (2018). Performance information use and severe cutback decisions during a period of fiscal crisis. *Public Money & Management, 38*(4), 289–296.

Kim, J., McDonald, B. D., & Lee, J. (2018). The nexus of state and local capacity in vertical policy diffusion. *American Review of Public Administration, 48*(2), 188–200.

Kioko, S. N., & Marlowe, J. (2016). *Financial strategy for public managers*. Rebus Community.

Kioko, S. N., & Martell, C. R. (2012). Impact of state-level tax and expenditure limits (TELs) on government revenues and aid to local governments. *Public Finance Review, 40*(6), 736–766.

Kioko, S. N., & Zhang, P. (2019). Impact of tax and expenditure limits on local government use of tax-supported debt. *Public Finance Review, 47*(2), 409–432.

Kleine, R., Kloha, P., & Weissert, C. S. (2003). Monitoring local government fiscal health: Michigan's new 10-point scale of fiscal distress. *Government Finance Review, 19*(3), 18–23.

Kloha, P., Weissert, C. S., & Kleine, R. (2005). Developing and testing a composite model to predict local fiscal distress. *Public Administration Review, 65*(3), 313–323.

Krane, D., Ebdon, C., & Bartle, J. (2004). Devolution, fiscal federalism, and changing patterns of municipal revenues: The mismatch between theory and reality. *Journal of Public Administration Research and Theory, 14*(4), 513–533.

Ladd, H. F., & Bradbury, K. L. (1988). City taxes and property tax bases. *National Tax Journal, 41*(4), 503–523.

Ladd, H. F., & Yinger, J. (1989). *America's ailing cities: Fiscal health and the design of urban policy*. Johns Hopkins University Press.

Latouche, R. (1961). *The birth of the Western economy: Economic aspects of the Dark Ages*. Routledge.

Lee, S., Lee, D., & Borcherding, T. E. (2016). Ethnic diversity and public goods provision: Evidence from U.S. municipalities and school districts. *Urban Affairs Review, 52*(5), 685–713.

Levine, C. H. (1978). Organizational decline and cutback management. *Public Administration Review, 38*(4), 316–325.

Levine, C. H. (1979). More on cutback management: Hard questions for hard times. *Public Administration Review, 39*(2), 179–183.

Levine, C. H. (1980). *Managing fiscal stress: The crisis in the public sector.* Chatham House.

Levine, C. H. (1984). Retrenchment, human resource erosion, and the role of the personnel manager. *Public Personnel Management, 13*(3), 249–263.

Levine, C. H. (1985). Public management in the 1980s: From decrementalism to strategic thinking. *Public Administration Review, 45*(Special Issue), 691–700.

Levine, C. H., Rubin, I. S., & Wolohojian, G. G. (1981). *The politics of retrenchment: How local governments manage fiscal stress.* Sage.

Levine, H., Justice, J. B., & Scorsone, E. A. (Eds.). (2013). *Handbook of local government fiscal health.* Jones & Bartlett Publishers.

Levy, F. (2010, June 7). America's best places to raise a family. *Forbes.* www.forbes.com/2010/06/04/best-places-family-lifestyle-real-estate-cities-kids.html?sh=42ac16bb5869

Levy, M. (1988). *Of rule and revenue.* University of California Press.

Lewis, C. W. (1994). Budgetary balance: The norm, concept, and practice in large U.S. cities. *Public Administration Review, 54*(6), 515–524.

Lincoln Institute of Land Policy. (2020). *Significant features of the property tax: Florida.* www.lincolninst.edu/sites/default/files/fl_july_2020_final.pdf

Lindblom, C. E. (1959). The science of "muddling through." *Public Administration Review, 19*(2), 79–88.

Liu, X., Lindquist, E., Vedlitz, A., & Vincent, K. (2010). Understanding local policymaking: Policy elites' perceptions of local agenda setting and alternative policy selection. *Policy Studies Journal, 38*(1), 69–91.

Lofton, M. L., & Kioko, S. N. (2021). The use of short-term debt by general-purpose governments. *Public Budgeting & Finance, 41*(4), 71–93.

Lucy Burns Institute. (2012). *Types and numbers of local government by state.* https://docs.google.com/spreadsheets/d/1t2tudHBq3q5IWhAH_ygQztZsgsdWfcUSC3zXOb9-Wyo/edit#gid=0

Maciag, M. (2012, March 23). Bankrupt cities, municipalities list and map. *Governing.* www.governing.com/archive/municipal-cities-counties-bankruptcies-and-defaults.html

Maciag, M. (2014, November 7). Bankrupt cities, municipalities list and map. *Governing.* www.governing.com/gov-data/municipal-cities-counties-bankruptcies-and-defaults.html

Madani, D., & Einhorn, E. (2021). Former Michigan Gov. Rick Snyder charged in Flint water crisis. *NBC News.* www.nbcnews.com/news/us-news/former-michigan-gov-rick-snyder-charged-flint-water-crisis-n1253966

Maher, C. S. (2013). Measuring financial condition: An essential element of management during periods of fiscal stress. *Journal of Government Financial Management, 62*(1), 20–25.

Maher, C. S. (2022). Financial condition analysis using annual comprehensive financial reports. In B. D. McDonald & M. M. Jordan (Eds.), *Teaching public budgeting and finance: A practical guide* (pp. 171–200). Routledge.

Maher, C. S., & Deller, S. C. (2007). Municipal responses to fiscal stress. *International Journal of Public Administration, 30*(12–14), 1549–1572.

Maher, C. S., & Deller, S. C. (2011). Measuring municipal fiscal condition: Do objective measures of fiscal health relate to subjective measures? *Journal of Public Budgeting, Accounting & Financial Management, 23*(3), 427–450.

Maher, C. S., & Deller, S. C. (2013a). Assessing the relationship between objective and subjective measures of fiscal condition using government-wide statements. *Public Budgeting & Finance, 33*(3), 115–136.

Maher, C. S., & Deller, S. C. (2013b). Measuring the impacts of TELs on municipal financial condition. In H. Levine, J. B. Justice, & E. A. Scorsone (Eds.), *Handbook of local government fiscal health*. Jones and Bartlett Learning.

Maher, C. S., Deller, S. C., & Amiel, L. (2011). Property tax limits and fiscal burdens: The role of organizational structure. *Public Administration Quarterly, 36*(2), 205–240.

Maher, C. S., Deller, S. C., Stallmann, J. I., & Park, S. (2016). The impact of tax and expenditure limits on municipal credit ratings. *American Review of Public Administration, 46*(5), 592–613.

Maher, C. S., Ebdon, C., & Bartle, J. R. (2020). Financial condition analysis: A key tool in the MPA curriculum. *Journal of Public Affairs Education, 26*(1), 4–10.

Maher, C. S., Hoang, T., & Hindery, A. (2020). Fiscal responses to COVID-19: Evidence from local governments and nonprofits. *Public Administration Review, 80*(4), 644–650.

Maher, C. S., & Nollenberger, K. (2009). Revisiting Kenneth Brown's "10-point test." *Government Finance Review, 25*(5), 61–66.

Maher, C. S., Oh, J. W., & Liao, W. J. (2020). Assessing fiscal distress in small county governments. *Journal of Public Budgeting, Accounting & Financial Management, 32*(4), 691–711.

Maher, C. S., Park, J. H., & An, B. (2018). PILOTs: What are they and are they affected by institutional and/or economic constraints? The case of Wisconsin municipalities. *Journal of Public and Nonprofit Affairs, 4*(3), 265–283.

Maher, C. S., Park, S., & Harrold, J. (2016). The effects of tax and expenditure limits on municipal pension and OPEB funding during the Great Recession. *Public Finance & Management, 16*(2), 121–146.

Mallach, A., & Scorsone, E. (2011). *Long-term stress and systematic failure: Taking seriously the fiscal crisis of America's older cities*. Center for Community Progress.

Man, J. Y., & Rosentraub, M. S. (1998). Tax increment financing: Municipal adoption and effects on property value growth. *Public Finance Review, 26*(6), 523–547.

Marlowe, J. (2005). Fiscal slack and counter-cyclical expenditure stabilization: A first look at the local level. *Public Budgeting & Finance, 25*(3), 48–72.

Maser, S. M. (1985). Demographic factors affecting constitutional decisions: The case of municipal charters. *Public Choice, 47*(1), 121–162.

Maser, S. M. (1998). Constitutions as relational contracts: Explaining procedural safeguards in municipal charters. *Journal of Public Administration Research and Theory, 8*(4), 527–564.

Massachusetts Division of Local Services. (2020). *Municipal finance trend dashboard: Key municipal fiscal health indicators*. https://www.mass.gov/service-details/municipal-finance-trend-dashboard

Matsusaka, J. G. (2014). Disentangling the direct and indirect effects of the initiative process. *Public Choice, 160*(3–4), 345–366.

Mazerov, M. (2018). *Kansas provides compelling evidence of failure of "supply-side" tax cuts*. Center on Budget and Policy Priorities. www.cbpp.org/research/state-budget-and-tax/kansas-provides-compelling-evidence-of-failure-of-supply-side-tax

McCabe, B. C., Reddick, C. G., & Demir, T. (2017). Municipal professionalism: More than just a job in government? *American Review of Public Administration, 47*(8), 867–880.

McDonald, B. D. (2010). The Bureau of municipal research and the development of a professional public service. *Administration and Society, 42*(7), 815–835.

McDonald, B. D. (2015). Does the Carter form improve the fiscal health of counties? *Public Administration Review, 75*(4), 609–618.

McDonald, B. D. (2017). *Measuring the fiscal health of municipalities* (Working Paper No. WP17BM1). Lincoln Institute of Land Policy.

McDonald, B. D. (2018). Local governance and the issue of fiscal health. *State and Local Government Review, 50*(1), 46–55.

McDonald, B. D. (2019). The challenges and implications of fiscal health. *South Carolina Journal of International Law and Business, 15*(2), 78–99.

McDonald, B. D., Decker, J. W., & Johnson, B. A. (2021). You don't always get what you want: The effect of financial incentives on state fiscal health. *Public Administration Review, 81*(3), 365–374.

McDonald, B. D., & Gabrini, C. J. (2014). Determinants of charter county decisions: An event history analysis of Florida counties. *Journal of Public Administration Research and Theory, 24*(4), 721–739.

McDonald, B. D., Goodman, C. B., & Hatch, M. E. (2020). Tensions in state-local intergovernmental response to emergencies: The case of COVID-19. *State and Local Government Review, 52*(3), 186–194.

McDonald, B. D., & Jordan, M. M. (Eds.). (2021). *Teaching public budgeting and finance: A practical guide*. Routledge.

McDonald, B. D., & Larson, S. (2020). Implications of the coronavirus on sales tax revenue and local government fiscal health. *Journal of Public and Nonprofit Affairs, 6*(3), 377–400.

McDonald, B. D., & Maher, C. S. (2020). Do we really need another municipal fiscal health analysis? Assessing the effectiveness of fiscal health systems. *Public Finance and Management, 19*(4), 270–296.

McFarland, C., & Pagano, M. A. (2015). *City fiscal conditions 2015*. National League of Cities. www.nlc.org/wp-content/uploads/2016/12/CSAR-City-Fiscal-Conditions-2015-FINAL.pdf

Mead, D. M. (2006). A manageable system of economic condition analysis for governments. In H. Frank (Ed.), *Public financial management* (pp. 383–419). Taylor & Francis.

Mead, D. M. (2013). The development of external financial reporting and its relationship to the assessment of fiscal health and stress. In H. Levine, J. B. Justice, & E. A. Scorsone (Eds.), *Handbook of local government fiscal health* (pp. 77–124). Jones and Bartlett Learning.

Meier, K. J., & Bohte, J. (2007). *Politics and the bureaucracy: Policymaking in the fourth branch of government* (5th ed.). Thompson Wadsworth.

Meyer-Sahling, J., Mikkelsen, K. S., & Schuster, C. (2021). Merit recruitment, tenure protections and public service motivation: Evidence from a conjoint experiment with 7,300 public servants in Latin America, Africa and Eastern Europe. *Public Administration, 99*(4), 740–757.

Michel, A. J. (1977). Municipal bond ratings: A discriminant analysis approach. *Journal of Financial and Quantitative Analysis, 12*(4), 587–598.

Mikesell, J. L. (2002). *Subnational government bankruptcy, default, and fiscal crisis in the United States (Paper 0221)*. International Center for Public Policy, Andrew Young School of Policy Studies, Georgia State University.

Mikesell, J. L. (2016). *Fiscal administration* (10th ed.). Cengage Learning.

Mikesell, J. L., & Liu, C. (2013). Property tax stability: A tax system model of base and revenue dynamics through the great recession and beyond. *Public Finance and Management, 13*(4), 310–334.

Miller, G. J., & Svara, J. H. (2009). *Navigating the fiscal crisis: Tested strategies for local leaders*. International City/County Management Association. https://icma.org/sites/default/files/302108_alliance_icma_crisis.pdf

Miller, G. R. (1983). Taking stock of a discipline. *Journal of Communication, 33*(3), 31–41.

Moody's. (2009). *Rating methodology: Moody's U.S. public finance—general obligation bonds issued by U.S. local governments*. www.moodys.com/researchandratings/methodology/003006001/rating-methodologies/methodology/003006001/003006001/-/0/0/-/0/-/-/en/global/rr

Moody's. (2020). *Rating action: Moody's downgrades Wichita's (KS) to Aa2 and sales tax special obligation bonds to A1*. www.moodys.com/research/Moodys-downgrades-Wichitas-KS-GOULT-to-Aa2-and-Sales-Tax-PR_906656761

Morgan, D. R., & Pammer, W. J. (1988). Coping with fiscal stress: Predicting the use of financial management practices among U.S. cities. *Urban Affairs Quarterly, 24*(1), 69–86.

Moringiello, J. M. (2014). Goals and governance in municipal bankruptcy. *Washington & Lee Law Review, 71*, 403–485.

Mostafavi, B. (2011, November 10). What happened last time? A look back at Flint's 2002 state takeover. *Flint Journal*. www.mlive.com/news/flint/2011/11/what_happened_last_time_a_look.html

Moynihan, D. P. (2008). *The dynamics of performance management: Constructing information and reform*. Georgetown University Press.

Mullins, D. R., & Wallin, B. A. (2004). Tax and expenditure limitations: Introduction and overview. *Public Budgeting & Finance, 24*(4), 2–15.

Municipal Finance Officers Association. (1978). *Is your city heading for financial difficulty? A guidebook for small cities and other governmental units*. Author.

Nakhmurina, A. (2020). *Does fiscal monitoring make better governments? Evidence from U.S. municipalities*. https://static1.squarespace.com/static/5b7b756112b13fa119645013/t/5ea31a4e9b39e36b9f3e57be/1587747408284/fmp_nakhmurina.pdf

Nalbandian, J. (1990). Tenets of contemporary professionalism in local government. *Public Administration Review, 50*(6), 654–662.

National Bureau of Economic Research. (2021). *US business cycle expansions and contractions*. www.nber.org/research/data/us-business-cycle-expansions-and-contractions

National Hurricane Center. (2022). *NHC data archive*. www.nhc.noaa.gov/data/

National League of Cities. (2019). *City fiscal conditions 2019*. www.nlc.org/wp-content/uploads/2019/10/CS_Fiscal-Conditions-2019Web-final.pdf

National League of Cities. (2022). *Cities 101—forms of municipal government*. www.nlc.org/resource/forms-of-municipal-government/

Nelson, A. A., & Balu, R. (2014). Local government responses to fiscal stress: Evidence from the public education sector. *Public Administration Review, 74*(5), 601–614.

Nelson, K. L. (2012). Municipal choices during a recession: Bounded rationality and innovation. *State and Local Government Review, 44*(S1), 44–63.

Nelson, K. L., & Svara, J. H. (2012). Form of government still matters: Fostering innovation in U.S. municipal governments. *American Review of Public Administration, 42*(3), 257–281.

Niskanen, W. A. (1971). *Bureaucracy and representative government*. Aldine Atherton.

Niskanen, W. A. (1975). Bureaucrats and politicians. *Journal of Law and Economics, 18*, 617–644.

Niskanen, W. A. (1991). A reflection on bureaucracy and representative governments. In A. Blais & S. Dion (Eds.), *The budget-maximizing bureaucrat: Appraisals and evidence* (pp. 13–32). University of Pittsburgh Press.

Nollenberger, K., Groves, S. M., & Valente, M. G. (2003). *Evaluating financial condition: A handbook for local government*. International City/County Management Association.

North, D. (1990). *Institutions, institutional change and economic performance*. Cambridge University Press.

Nownes, A. J. (2014). Local and state interest group organizations. In D. P. Haider-Markel (Ed.), *The Oxford handbook of state and local government*. Oxford University Press.

Oates, W. (1991). On the nature and measurement of fiscal illusion: A survey. In W. Oates (Ed.), *Studies in fiscal federalism* (pp. 431–448). Edward Elgar.

Office of the New York State Comptroller. (2017). *Fiscal stress monitoring system manual*. www.osc.state.ny.us/files/local-government/fiscal-monitoring/pdf/system-manual.pdf

Office of the New York State Comptroller. (2021). *Fiscal stress monitoring system*. www.osc.state.ny.us/local-government/fiscal-monitoring

Oi, J. C. (1995). The role of the local state in China's transitional economy. *The China Quarterly, 144*, 1132–1149.

Omstedt, M. (2020). Reading risk: The practices, limits and politics of municipal bond rating. *Environment and Planning A: Economy and Space, 52*(3), 611–631.

Ott, M. (1980). Bureaucracy, monopoly, and the demand for municipal services. *Journal of Urban Economics, 8*(3), 362–382.

Overmans, T., & Timm-Arnold, K. P. (2016). Managing austerity: Comparing municipal austerity plans in the Netherlands and North Rhine-Westphalia. *Public Management Review, 18*(7), 1043–1062.

Palumbo, G., & Zaporowski, M. P. (2012). Determinants of municipal bond ratings for general-purpose governments: An empirical analysis. *Public Budgeting & Finance, 32*(2), 86–102.

Pammer, W. J. (1990). *Managing fiscal strain in major American cities: Understanding retrenchment in the public sector*. Greenwood Publishing Group.

Pandey, S. K. (2010). Cutback management and the paradox of publicness. *Public Administration Review, 70*(4), 564–571.

Park, J. H., Lee, H., Butler, J. S., & Denison, D. (2021). The effects of high-quality financial reporting on municipal bond ratings: Evidence from U.S. local governments. *Local Government Studies, 47*(5), 836–858.

Park, J. H., & Park, S. (2018). The effect of revenue diversification and form of government on public spending. *Journal of Public Budgeting, Accounting & Financial Management, 30*(2), 211–229.

Park, J. H., Park, S., & Maher, C. S. (2018). The effects of tax and expenditure limitations (TELs) on municipal fiscal outcomes during a period of fiscal distress. *Public Finance and Management, 18*(1), 84–110.

Park, S. (2018a). *Game-theoretic thinking of state-imposed tax and expenditure limitations: Rule design, institutional diversity, and municipal fiscal outcomes* (Doctoral dissertation). University of Nebraska at Omaha.

Park, S. (2018b). The impact of state-imposed fiscal rules on municipal government fiscal outcomes: Does institutional configuration matter? *State and Local Government Review, 50*(4), 230–243.

Park, S., Kim, Y., Ebdon, C., & Maher, C. (2021). Fiscal effects of interlocal collaboration: Evidence from Nebraska counties. *Local Government Studies*. Published online first. https://doi.org/10.1080/03003930.2021.1916477

The Patriot-News. (2010, August 30). *Harrisburg area ranked among top 10 recession-proof cities*. www.pennlive.com/midstate/2010/08/harrisburg_area_ranked_among_t.html

Patton, Z. (2011, January 24). Mayors fight to save block grant funding. *Governing*. www.census.gov/programs-surveys/gov-finances/about/glossary.html#par_text image_1669110194

Pennsylvania Department of Community and Economic Development. (2011). *Financial monitoring workbook*. https://dced.pa.gov/download/Financial%20Monitoring%20 Workbook%202011%20Pdf/?wpdmdl=59422

Pew Charitable Trusts. (2010). *Not out of the woods: The recession's continuing impact on big city taxes, services and pensions*. www.pewtrusts.org/en/research-and-analysis/reports/2010/05/26/not-out-of-the-woods-the-recessions-continuing-impact-on-big-city-taxes-services-and-pensions

Pew Charitable Trusts. (2013). *The state role in local government financial distress*. https://www.pewtrusts.org/~/media/assets/2016/04/pew_state_role_in_local_govern ment_financial_distress.pdf

Pew Charitable Trusts. (2015). *After municipal bankruptcy: Lessons learned from Detroit and other local governments*. www.pewtrusts.org/en/research-and-analysis/reports/2015/08/after-municipal-bankruptcy

Pew Charitable Trusts. (2016a). *Fiscal health of large U.S. cities varied long after great recession's end*. www.pewtrusts.org/-/media/assets/2016/04/fiscalhealthoflargeuscitiesva riedlongaftergreatrecessionsend.pdf

Pew Charitable Trusts. (2016b). *State strategies to detect local fiscal distress*. www.pewtrusts.org/en/research-and-analysis/reports/2016/09/state-strategies-to-detect-local-fiscal-distress

Plerhoples, T., & Scorsone, E. (2010). *An assessment of Michigan's local government fiscal indicator system*. Senate Fiscal Agency. www.senate.michigan.gov/sfa/publications% 5Cissues%5Clocalgovfiscalindicatorsystem%5Clocalgovfiscalindicatorsystem.pdf

Poister, T. H., & Streib, G. (1999). Performance measurement in municipal government: Assessing the state of the practice. *Public Administration Review, 59*(4), 325–335.

Porter, E. (2017, October 10). Why big cities thrive, and smaller ones are being left behind. *New York Times*. www.nytimes.com/2017/10/10/business/economy/big-cities.html

Prager Company. (2002). *Analysis of Albuquerque's industrial revenue bond program*. www.cabq.gov/council/documents/completed-reports-studies/irbrpt.pdf

Randall, M., Gault, S., & Gordon, T. (2016). *Federal aid to local governments*. Urban Institute. www.urban.org/sites/default/files/2016/09/07/2016.09.07_state_of_cities_fact_sheet.pdf

Reschovsky, A. (2004). The impact of state government fiscal crises on local governments and schools. *State and Local Government Review*, *36*(2), 86–102.

Ripley, R. B., & Franklin, G. A. (Eds.). (1975). *Policy-making in the federal executive branch*. Free Press.

Rivenbark, W. C., & Kelly, J. M. (2006). Performance budgeting in municipal government. *Public Performance & Management Review*, *30*(1), 35–46.

Rivenbark, W. C., & Roenigk, D. J. (2011). Implementation of financial condition analysis in local government. *Public Administration Quarterly*, *35*(2), 241–267.

Rothenberg, J., & Smoke, P. (1982). Early impacts of proposition 21/2 on the Massachusetts state-local public sector. *Public Budgeting & Finance*, *2*(4), 90–110.

Roybank, H. M., Coffman, E. N., & Previts, G. J. (2012). The first quarter century of the GASB (1984–2009): A perspective of standard setting (Part 1). *Abacus*, *48*(1), 1–30.

Rubin, I. S. (1982). *Running in the red: The political dynamics of urban fiscal stress*. State University of New York Press.

Rubin, I. S. (1990). Budget theory and budget practice: How good the fit? *Public Administration Review*, *50*(2), 179–189.

Rubin, I. S. (1992). Budget reform and political reform: Conclusions from six cities. *Public Administration Review*, *52*(5), 454–466.

Rubin, I. S. (2019). *The politics of public budgeting: Getting and spending, borrowing and balancing*. Sage.

Schick, A. (1983). Incremental budgeting in a decremental age. *Policy Sciences*, *16*(1), 1–25.

Scorsone, E., & Pruettt, N. (2020). *Assessing existing local government fiscal early warning system through four state case studies: Colorado, Louisiana, Ohio and Pennsylvania*. Michigan Center for Local Government Finance and Policy. www.canr.msu.edu/center_for_local_government_finance_and_policy/uploads/files/FiscalWarning-Sytems%20white%20paperWEB.pdf

Selden, S. C. (1997). *The promise of representative bureaucracy: Diversity and responsiveness in a government agency*. M. E. Sharpe.

Shadbegian, R. J. (1998). Do tax and expenditure limitations affect local government budgets? Evidence from panel data. *Public Finance Review*, *26*(2), 118–136.

Shaffer, R., Deller, S. C., & Marcouiller, D. W. (2004). *Community economics: Linking theory and practice*. Blackwell Publishing.

Shaffer, R., Deller, S. C., & Marcouiller, D. W. (2006). Rethinking community economic development. *Economic Development Quarterly*, *20*(1), 59–74.

Shafritz, J. M., Russell, E. W., & Borick, C. (2015). *Introducing public administration*. Routledge.

Sharp, E. B. (1986). The politics and economics of the new city debt. *American Political Science Review*, *80*(4), 1271–1288.

Sharp, E. B., & Elkins, D. (1987). The impact of fiscal limitation: A tale of seven cities. *Public Administration Review*, *47*(5), 385–392.

Shi, Y., Aydemir, N. Y., & Wu, Y. (2018). What factors drive municipal fiscal policy adoption? An empirical investigation of major cities in the United States. *State and Local Government Review, 50*(3), 177–188.

Shi, Y., & Tao, J. (2018). "Faulty" fiscal illusion: Examining the relationship between revenue diversification and tax burden in major U.S. cities across the economic cycle. *Local Government Studies, 44*(3), 416–435.

Shon, J., & Kim, J. (2019). The impact of revenue diversification on municipal debts: Comparing short-term and long-term debt levels. *Local Government Studies, 45*(2), 241–261.

Sigelman, L., Lowery, D., & Smith, R. (1983). The tax revolt: A comparative state analysis. *Western Political Quarterly, 36*(1), 30–51.

Skidmore, M., & Scorsone, E. (2011). Causes and consequences of fiscal stress in Michigan municipal governments. *Regional Science and Urban Economics, 41*(4), 360–371.

Smith, J. S. (2014). *A concise history of the New Deal.* Cambridge University Press.

Snow, D., Gianakis, G. A., & Haughton, J. (2015). The politics of local government stabilization funds. *Public Administration Review, 75*(2), 304–314.

Southwick Jr., L. (1997). Local government spending and at-large versus district representation: Do wards result in more "pork"? *Economics & Politics, 9*(2), 173–203.

Spiotto, J. E., Acker, A. E., & Appleby, L. E. (2016). *Municipalities in distress? How states and investors deal with local government financial emergencies.* Chapman and Cutler LLP.

Spreen, T. L., Afonso, W., & Gerrish, E. (2020). Can employee training influence local fiscal outcomes? *The American Review of Public Administration, 50*(4–5), 401–414.

Spreen, T. L., & Cheek, C. M. (2016). Does monitoring local government fiscal conditions affect outcomes? Evidence from Michigan. *Public Finance Review, 44*(6), 722–745.

Springer, J. D., Lusby, A. K., Leatherman, J. C., & Featherstone, A. M. (2009). An evaluation of alternative tax and expenditure limitation policies on Kansas local governments. *Public Budgeting & Finance, 29*(2), 48–70.

Stallmann, J. I., Maher, C. S., Deller, S. C., & Park, S. (2017). Surveying the effects of limitations on taxes and expenditures: What do/don't we know? *Journal of Public and Nonprofit Affairs, 3*(2), 197–222.

Stanton, T. A. (2016). *Emergency financial manager/emergency manager appointment history.* www.michigan.gov/documents/treasury/EM-EFM_Appointment_History_2-12-16_514604_7.pdf

Stazyk, E. C., & Goerdel, H. T. (2011). The benefits of bureaucracy: Public managers' perceptions of political support, goal ambiguity, and organizational effectiveness. *Journal of Public Administration Research & Theory, 21*(4), 645–672.

Stiglitz, K. (2018, January 22). 1,000 furloughed due to shutdown across MCI East. *Sun Journal.* www.newbernsj.com/story/news/politics/government/2018/01/22/1000-furloughed-due-to-shutdown-across-mci-east/16029388007/

Stoker, G. (1991). *The politics of local government.* Macmillan International Higher Education.

Stone, S. B., Singla, A., Comeaux, J., & Kirschner, C. (2015). A comparison of financial indicators: The case of Detroit. *Public Budgeting and Finance, 35*(4), 90–111.

Stonecash, J., & McAfee, P. (1981). The ambiguities and limits of fiscal stress indicators. *Policy Studies Journal, 10*(2), 379–395.

Su, M. (2019). Understanding the accumulation of local government savings: A dynamic analysis. *International Journal of Public Administration*, *42*(11), 893–903.

Subik, J. (2019, September 27). Amsterdam ranked most fiscally stressed local government in state. *Daily Gazette*. https://dailygazette.com/2019/09/27/amsterdam-ranked-most-fiscally-stressed-local-government-in-state/

Sun, R. (2014). Reevaluating the effect of tax and expenditure limitations: An instrumental variable approach. *Public Finance Review*, *42*(1), 92–116.

Svara, J. H. (2003). *Two decades of continuity and change in American city councils*. National League of Cities.

Tang, S. Y., Callahan, R. F., & Pisano, M. (2014). Using common-pool resource principles to design local government fiscal sustainability. *Public Administration Review*, *74*(6), 791–803.

Tausanovitch, C., & Warshaw, C. (2014). Representation in municipal government. *American Political Science Review*, *108*(3), 605–641.

Tax Policy Center. (2021). *Briefing book: A citizen's guide to the fascinating (though often complex) elements of the U.S. tax system*. www.taxpolicycenter.org/briefing-book

Temple, J. A. (1996). Community composition and voter support for tax limitations: Evidence from home-rule elections. *Southern Economic Journal*, *62*(4), 1002–1016.

Toma, M., & Toma, E. F. (1980). Bureaucratic responses to tax limitation amendments. *Public Choice*, *35*(3), 333–348.

Town of Carrboro, North Carolina. (2013). *Financial trends: Past, present and future*. https://townofcarrboro.org/DocmentCenter/View/373/Section-14—Financial-Trends-Past-Present-and-Future-PDF

Town of Northborough, Massachusetts. (2015). *Financial trend monitoring report*. www.town.northborough.ma.us/sites/g/files/vyhlif3571/f/uploads/appendix_c_-_financial_trend_monitoring_report.pdf

Truth in Accounting. (2021). *Financial state of the cities 2021*. www.truthinaccounting.org/news/detail/financial-state-of-the-cities-2021

Turley, G., Robbins, G., & McNena, S. (2015). A framework to measure the financial performance of local governments. *Local Government Studies*, *41*(3), 401–420.

Turnbull, G. K., & Djoundourian, S. S. (1994). The median voter hypothesis: Evidence from general purpose local governments. *Public Choice*, *81*(3), 223–240.

Turnbull, G. K., & Mitias, P. M. (1999). The median voter model across levels of government. *Public Choice*, *99*(1), 119–138.

U.S. Census Bureau. (1972–2012). *The census survey of state and local government finances*. www.census.gov/programs-surveys/gov-finances/data.html

U.S. Census Bureau. (1972–2017). *Population and housing unit estimates*. www.census.gov/programs-surveys/popest/data/data-sets.html

U.S. Census Bureau. (1987, 1992, 2017). *Census of government*. www.census.gov/programs-surveys/cog.html

U.S. Census Bureau. (2006). *Government finance and employment classification manual*. https://www2.census.gov/govs/class/classfull.pdf

U.S. Census Bureau. (2020). *Annual survey of state and local government finances glossary*. www.census.gov/programs-surveys/gov-finances/about/glossary.html?cq_ck=1517854683624

U.S. Census Bureau. (2021). *Quick facts*. www.census.gov/programs-surveys/sis/resources/data-tools/quickfacts.html

U.S. Department of the Treasury. (1978). *Report on the fiscal impact of the economic stimulus package on 48 large urban governments.* U.S. Government Printing Office.

U.S. Government Accountability Office. (2019). *State and local governments' fiscal outlook.* www.gao.gov/products/GAO-20-269SP

Upson, L. D. (1935). Local government finance in the Depression. *National Municipal Review, 24*, 503–511.

Virginia Auditor of Public Accounts. (2020). *Monitoring for local government fiscal distress: 2019 report.* www.apa.virginia.gov/reports/MonitoringforLocalGovernmentFiscalDistress2019.pdf

Von Hagen, J. (2002). Fiscal rules, fiscal institutions, and fiscal performance. *Economic and Social Review, 33*(3), 263–284.

Wagner, R. E. (1976, Spring). Revenue structure, fiscal illusion, and budgetary choice. *Public Choice, 25*, 45–61.

Wagner, S. (2019). *How Lincoln, Nebraska weathered the great recession.* National League of Cities. www.nlc.org/article/2019/10/25/how-lincoln-nebraska-weathered-the-great-recession/

Wall, A. (1919). Study of credit barometrics. *Federal Reserve Bulletin*, 5.

Wang, X., Dennis, L., & Tu, Y. S. (2007). Measuring financial condition: A study of U.S. states. *Public Budgeting and Finance, 27*(2), 1–21.

Wang, X., Hawkins, C. V., Lebredo, N., & Berman, E. M. (2012). Capacity to sustain sustainability: A study of U.S. cities. *Public Administration Review, 72*(6), 841–853.

Warner, M., & Hebdon, R. (2001). Local government restructuring: Privatization and its alternatives. *Journal of Policy Analysis and Management, 20*(2), 315–336.

Watson, D. J., Handley, D. M., & Hassett, W. L. (2005). Financial distress and municipal bankruptcy: The case of Prichard, Alabama. *Journal of Public Budgeting, Accounting & Financial Management, 17*(2), 129–150.

Webber, C., & Wildavsky, A. (1986). *A history of taxation and expenditure in the Western world.* Simon & Schuster.

Wildavsky, A. (1966). The political economy of efficiency: Cost-benefit analysis, systems analysis, and program budgeting. *Public Administration Review, 26*(4), 292–310.

Wildavsky, A. (1974). *The politics of the budgetary process.* Little, Brown and Company.

Wildavsky, A. (1979). *The politics of the budgetary process* (3rd ed.). Little, Brown and Company.

Wildavsky, A. (1986). *Budgeting: A comparative theory of the budgeting process.* Transaction Publishers.

Wolman, H., & Davis, B. (1979). Local government strategies to cope with fiscal pressure. In C. H. Levine & I. Rubin (Eds.), *Fiscal stress and public policy* (pp. 231–248). Sage.

Wong, J. D. (2004). The fiscal impact of economic growth and development on local government revenue capacity. *Journal of Public Budgeting, Accounting & Financial Management, 16*(3), 413–423.

Wyoming Economic Analysis Division. (2021). *Economic data.* http://eadiv.state.wy.us/wef/Economic.html

Yadavalli, A. (2018). *City fiscal conditions: A five-year review.* National League of Cities. www.nlc.org/article/2018/09/10/city-fiscal-conditions-a-five-year-review/

Yanes, D. (2021, April 8). State comptroller: Long Beach under significant fiscal stress. *Long Island Herald.* www.liherald.com/stories/state-comptroller-long-beach-under-significant-fiscal-stress,131566?

Yang, L. (2019). Negative externality of fiscal problems: Dissecting the contagion effect of municipal bankruptcy. *Public Administration Review, 79*(2), 156–167.

Yusuf, J., Fowles, J., & Grizzle, C. (2013). State fiscal constraints on local government borrowing-Effects on scale and cost. In H. Levine, E. A. Scorsone, & J. B. Justice (Eds.), *Handbook of local government fiscal health* (pp. 475–504). Jones and Bartlett Learning.

Zhao, J., Ren, L., & Lovrich, N. P. (2010). Budgetary support for police services in U.S. municipalities: Comparing political culture, socioeconomic characteristics and incrementalism as rival explanations for budget share allocation to police. *Journal of Criminal Justice, 38*(3), 266–275.

Index

Note: Page numbers in *italics* indicate figures and those in **bold** indicate tables.

Made in United States
Cleveland, OH
09 September 2026

44052174R00195